ENTHUSIASMS AND LOYALTIES

MCGILL-QUEEN'S STUDIES IN EARLY CANADA / AVANT LE CANADA

SERIES EDITORS / DIRECTEURS DE LA COLLECTION : ALLAN GREER
AND CAROLYN PODRUCHNY

This series features studies of the history of the northern half of North America –
a vast expanse that would eventually be known as Canada – in the era before
extensive European settlement and extending into the nineteenth century. Long
neglected, Canada-before-Canada is a fascinating area of study experiencing an
intellectual renaissance as researchers in a range of disciplines, including history,
geography, archeology, anthropology, literary studies, and law, contribute to a new
and enriched understanding of the distant past. The editors welcome manuscripts
in English or French on all aspects of the period, including work on Indigenous
history, the Atlantic fisheries, the fur trade, exploration, French or British imperial
expansion, colonial life, culture, language, law, science, religion, and
the environment.

Cette série de monographies est consacrée à l'histoire de la partie septentrionale
du continent de l'Amérique du nord, autrement dit le grand espace qui deviendra
le Canada, dans les siècles qui s'étendent jusqu'au début du 19ᵉ. Longtemps négligé
par les chercheurs, ce Canada-avant-le-Canada suscite beaucoup d'intérêt de la
part de spécialistes dans plusieurs disciplines, entre autres, l'histoire, la géographie,
l'archéologie, l'anthropologie, les études littéraires et le droit. Nous assistons à une
renaissance intellectuelle dans ce champ d'étude axé sur l'interaction de premières
nations, d'empires européens et de colonies. Les directeurs de cette série sollicitent
des manuscrits, en français ou en anglais, qui portent sur tout aspect de cette
période, y compris l'histoire des autochtones, celle des pêcheries de l'atlantique,
de la traite des fourrures, de l'exploration, de l'expansion de l'empire français ·
ou britannique, de la vie coloniale (Nouvelle-France, l'Acadie, Terre-Neuve, les
provinces maritimes, etc.), de la culture, la langue, le droit, les sciences, la religion
ou l'environnement.

1 A Touch of Fire
Marie-André Duplessis, the Hôtel-
Dieu of Quebec, and the Writing of
New France
Thomas M. Carr, Jr

2 Entangling the Quebec Act
Transnational Contexts, Meanings,
and Legacies in North America and
the British Empire
Edited by Ollivier Hubert
and François Furstenberg

3 Listening to the Fur Trade
Soundways and Music in the
British North American Fur Trade,
1760–1840
Daniel Robert Laxer

4 Heirs of an Ambivalent Empire
French-Indigenous Relations and the
Rise of the Métis in the Hudson Bay
Watershed
Scott Berthelette

5 The Possession of Barbe Hallay
Diabolical Arts and Daily Life in
Early Canada
Mairi Cowan

6 Enthusiasms and Loyalties
The Public History of Private
Feelings in the Enlightenment
Atlantic
Keith Shepherd Grant

ENTHUSIASMS
and
LOYALTIES

The Public History of Private Feelings

in the Enlightenment Atlantic

KEITH SHEPHERD GRANT

McGill-Queen's University Press

Montreal & Kingston • London • Chicago

© McGill-Queen's University Press 2022

ISBN 978-0-2280-1421-8 (cloth)
ISBN 978-0-2280-1422-5 (paper)
ISBN 978-0-2280-1520-8 (ePDF)
ISBN 978-0-2280-1521-5 (ePUB)

Legal deposit fourth quarter 2022
Bibliothèque nationale du Québec

Printed in Canada on acid-free paper that is 100% ancient forest free
(100% post-consumer recycled), processed chlorine free

This book has been published with the help of a grant from the Canadian Federation
for the Humanities and Social Sciences, through the Awards to Scholarly Publications
Program, using funds provided by the Social Sciences and Humanities Research
Council of Canada.

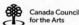

Funded by the Government of Canada   Financé par le gouvernement du Canada   Canadä   Canada Council for the Arts   Conseil des arts du Canada

We acknowledge the support of the Canada Council for the Arts.
Nous remercions le Conseil des arts du Canada de son soutien.

Library and Archives Canada Cataloguing in Publication

Title: Enthusiasms and loyalties : the public history of private feelings in the
 enlightenment Atlantic / Keith Shepherd Grant.
Names: Grant, Keith S., author.
Series: McGill-Queen's studies in early Canada ; 6.
Description: Series statement: McGill-Queen's studies in early Canada / Avant le
 Canada ; 6 | Includes bibliographical references and index.
Identifiers: Canadiana (print) 20220390924 | Canadiana (ebook) 20220391149
 | ISBN 9780228014218 (cloth) | ISBN 9780228014225 (paper) | ISBN
 9780228015208 (ePDF) | ISBN 9780228015215 (ePUB)
Subjects: LCSH: Emotions—Political aspects—Nova Scotia—History—
 18th century. | LCSH: Emotions—Religious aspects—History—18th century. |
 LCSH: Emotions—Social aspects—Nova Scotia—History—18th century. | LCSH:
 Nova Scotia—History—1775-1783. | LCSH: United States—History—Revolution,
 1775-1783—Influence.
Classification: LCC FC2321.3.G73 2022 | DDC 971.6/01—dc23

This book was typeset in 10.5/13 Sabon.

Dedicated to the memory of Shepherd F. Grant (1938–2016)

Contents

Figures ix

Acknowledgments xi

Introduction: Social Affections 3

1 Commonplace Loyalty: Handley Chipman's British Affections and American Sympathies 23

2 Textual Affections: Handley Chipman and the Emotions of Transatlantic Protestantism 49

3 "Enthusiasm in politicks, as well as religion": Jacob Bailey's Emotional History of the American Revolution 77

4 "Not from any remainders of affection": The Disaffection of Jacob Bailey's Loyalty 103

5 "A good Degree of Affection in Things of Religion becomes us": Henry Alline, Jonathan Scott, and the Long Argument 130

6 Unfeeling Enthusiasts: Nova Scotia New Lights as an Emotional Community 150

7 From Enthusiasm to Sympathy: Edward Manning, Heart Religion, and Society 176

Conclusion 206

Notes 213

Bibliography 267

Index 317

Figures

0.1   Charles Morris, *A chart of the peninsula of Nova Scotia* (detail), [1761]. Library of Congress. Inset map of Nova Scotia by Vectorstock. | 2

0.2   William Hogarth, *Credulity, Superstition, and Fanaticism*, 1762. | 14

0.3   John Elliott Woolford, "View near Cornwallis," 1817. Watercolour Painting. Courtesy of Nova Scotia Museum, 78.45.55. | 16

1.1   Handley Chipman, "Remarkable Events of Providence," Commonplace Book, 1776. Nova Scotia Archives, MG 1 Vol. 218, page 5 detail. | 24

2.1   Some of Handley Chipman's manuscript books, 1793 and 1797. Esther Clark Wright Archives, Acadia University, 2007.004–CHI/1 and 1931.005– CHI/3. | 55

2.2   Handley Chipman, Essays, 1793. Esther Clark Wright Archives, Acadia University, 2007.004–/1. | 69

3.1   Portrait of Jacob Bailey (photographic reproduction), undated. Annapolis Heritage Society, Jacob Bailey Fonds, 2001–1139 F. | 81

5.1   Jonathan Scott, *A Brief View of the Religious Tenets and Sentiments lately published and spread in the province of Nova-Scotia* ... (Halifax, NS: John Howe, 1784), title page. | 143

6.1   *The Life and Journal of the Rev. Mr. Henry Alline* (Boston: Gilbert & Dean, 1806), title page. | 153

6.2   Elizabeth Blair to Betsy Lusby, Letter, 17 August 1790, in Thomas Bennett, "New Light letters and spiritual songs," [179?], Esther Clark Wright Archives, Acadia University, 1900.471–BEN/1. | 171

7.1   Engraving of Edward Manning, [18-?], Esther Clark Wright Archives, Acadia University, D1846.001/8. |180

Acknowledgments

It is a pleasure to acknowledge the personal and intellectual connections that made this project possible. The unusually rich archival sources for Cornwallis Township are found in several repositories, but I owe particular debts to Christine Jack and Leah Grandy in the University of New Brunswick Libraries' Loyalist Collection, and to Patricia Townsend, Wendy Robicheau, and Catherine Fancy at the Esther Clark Wright Archives at Acadia University, all of whom nurture scholarly environments that are welcoming and collaborative. Thanks are also extended to archivists and curators at the Nova Scotia Archives, the Annapolis Heritage Society, the United Church Maritime Conference Archives, and the John Rylands Library in Manchester, UK. Long-distance research assistance was provided by the American Antiquarian Society (Worcester, MA) and the Newport Historical Society (RI). The project could not have been completed without the resourcefulness of the University of New Brunswick Document Delivery team and the George A. Rawlyk Library at Crandall University.

Funding from several sources supported the research for this study, and I acknowledge with gratitude the support of the Social Science and Humanities Research Council (SSHRC) for a Joseph Bombardier Canada Graduate Scholarship, the University of New Brunswick School of Graduate Studies, the New Brunswick Innovation Fund, the Institute for Religion and Culture (British Columbia), the Acadia Centre for Baptist and Anabaptist Studies, and the Omohundro Institute for Early American Culture and History. The book manuscript was completed while on a research leave made possible by a Stephen S. Steeves faculty research scholarship at Crandall University.

I presented portions of this material at various conferences, seminars, and lectures, including the American Historical Association (Atlanta), the American Society of Church History (Washington, DC), the Atlantic Canada Studies Conference (Fredericton and Sackville), the Atlantic Medieval and Early Modern Conference (Fredericton), the Bibliographical Society of Canada (Calgary and Vancouver), the Canadian Historical Association (Ottawa, Calgary, and Vancouver), the Canadian Society for Church History (Calgary), the International Conference on Baptist Studies (Manchester, UK), and the University of Maine/University of New Brunswick Graduate History Conference (Orono). Questions, comments, and generous conversations at those venues and elsewhere helped to sharpen the project's focus, with particular thanks to: Cindy Aalders, Jerry Bannister, Stuart Barnard, David Bell, Catherine Brekus, Sylvia Brown, Kate Carté, Dan Goodwin, Julian Gwyn, Maxine and Cam Hancock, Michael Hattem, Gordon Heath, Bruce Hindmarsh, Leslie Howsam, Christopher C. Jones, Hannah Lane, Denis McKim, Scott McLaren, Barry Moody, Jessica Parr, Stephanie Pettigrew, Marshall Rand, Liam Riordan, Elissa Rodkey, Daniel Samson, Sharon Jebb Smith, Jennifer Snead, John Stackhouse, and Jonathan Yeager.

Supervisor and mentor Elizabeth Mancke taught me to think about local places in wide, transnational frameworks and has, by her own habit of thinking aloud and her capacious interests, encouraged me to contribute to broader historical and public conversations than those with which I started. I am thankful, as well, for the insightful reading and suggestions made by doctoral committee members Bonnie Huskins, Gary Waite, and Gwendolyn Davies. External dissertation examiner Jane Errington sharpened the argument of the book with her probing questions, generous suggestions, and intellectual hospitality. The anonymous readers at McGill-Queen's University Press helped me to think more carefully about the contributions the book might make to several scholarly conversations. Senior editor Kyla Madden took an encouraging early interest in the project, and conversations with her helped to shape the book's analysis and narrative. The editorial team at McGill-Queen's University Press could not have been more supportive and professional.

Enthusiasms and Loyalties was completed after joining the faculty at Crandall University, where I have found a rich, supportive, and interdisciplinary academic community. The arrival of Mark Lee in the history department has been a breath of fresh air for many reasons, not the least of which is our shared interest in the history of emotions. He generously read the entire manuscript, making it much better by his trenchant comments and suggestions. For the duration of this project, I have been – with Denis McKim and Laura Smith – editing *Borealia*, a collaborative academic blog on early Canadian history. The diverse community of fellow editors, contributors, and readers has stimulated my own research in direct and indirect ways and has energized me to think about British North America in transnational frameworks.

Undertaking this study entailed significant change for our family, and we are so thankful for the amazing communities of friends and neighbours that embraced us first in New Maryland and now in Riverview, for the sustaining support of our parents and siblings, and for longtime friends Cindy Aalders, Gordon Dickinson, and Rob Nylen.

Joy and our daughters, Abigail, Lily, and Hannah, made this project possible by their love and support, and by their interested (or at least patient) table conversation about the lives of early Nova Scotians.

My parents, Shepherd and Doris Grant warmly supported and encouraged my scholarly aspirations. *Enthusiasms and Loyalties* is dedicated to the memory of my father, Shepherd F. Grant (1938–2016), with love and appreciation for his legacy of loyalty, faith, and affection.

ENTHUSIASMS AND LOYALTIES

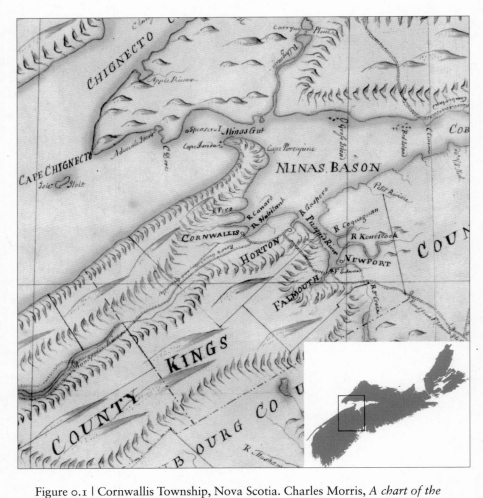

Figure 0.1 | Cornwallis Township, Nova Scotia. Charles Morris, *A chart of the peninsula of Nova Scotia* (detail), [1761].

INTRODUCTION

Social Affections

This was Charles Inglis's second revolution. Standing in his Halifax,
Nova Scotia, pulpit in 1793, he urged his hearers to maintain "Steadfastness in Religion and Loyalty" – but he feared that both would
be overturned once again by unbridled passions and a revolutionary ferment of feelings.[1] Years earlier, on the eve of the American
War of Independence, when he was then an Anglican rector in New
York, Inglis took up his pen to criticize Thomas Paine's *Common
Sense*, a pamphlet that he said was "addressed to the passions of the
populace, at a time when their passions are much inflamed." Inglis
claimed that despite its title, the work did not promote reasoned
sense, but "uncommon phrenzy," that Paine's appeal to the passions
of the colonists was nothing less than an "insidious attempt to ...
seduce them from their loyalty and truest interest." When the passions of Americans subsided, Inglis was sure, then their former affections for the king and constitution would return.[2] Yet as a Loyalist
refugee, Inglis had become keenly aware that those passions did *not*
always subside.

As Inglis preached, France was in revolution, its king executed
only weeks earlier. Now the Anglican bishop of Nova Scotia, Inglis
stood with a sense of déjà vu to address the province's legislature.
Inflamed passions were once again at the root of revolution. He
charged that a *"spirit of enthusiasm"* led the French revolutionaries to "overturn the Religion and Civil Constitution of their
country ... subverting all order and government," to the horrify-
ing extreme that they "embrued their hands in the blood of their
lawful Sovereign." Unrestrained emotion destroyed any trace of
civil society or social conscience: "They are unchaining the unruly

appetites and affections of men to prey upon one another." Like other commentators in the Revolutionary Atlantic, Inglis employed the term "enthusiasm" as a smear word to describe the spectre of unrestrained feelings and radical individualism – tendencies that were "malignant to government, and subversive of the peace and welfare of society."[3] Sharing the fears of many observers, he asked his Halifax listeners, "Can a more frightful picture of human depravity, let loose by infidel principles, be imagined, than is at this day exhibited by France?"[4]

So it was unthinkable to Inglis that the French Revolution had its British North American sympathizers, those who reveled in its passions and echoed its sentiments in their criticism of Britain's constitutional monarchy. Are there not, the horrified preacher asked, those who "wish the same scenes may be acted on the theatre of the British empire? Can we therefore be too much on our guard?" That fear of spreading revolutionary enthusiasm would have had even more resonance to those who read Inglis's sermon in print. Remarkably, it was printed in the same week that news reached Halifax that Britain and France were again at war. Having lived through the turmoil of the American Revolution, would Loyalists like Inglis – would British North Americans – be engulfed again in revolutionary commotion?[5]

Inglis linked the unrestrained passions of the French Revolution – somewhat surprisingly – with religious "fanaticism" and populism closer to home. Inglis was alarmed by the apparent spread of enthusiasm in Nova Scotia and New Brunswick by New Lights and Methodists. Having sketched the effects of enthusiasm in French society, he explained its consequences in the religious sphere:

> A mighty zeal for truth, for great purity, and other good purposes, is displayed; and it is observable, that this zeal generally rises in proportion as the peculiar tenets of the innovators, deviate from scripture and common sense; zeal being the substitute to make up the deficiency. Claims are often made to extraordinary revelations, to higher degrees of grace, and divine illumination; and this at the very time that the regular institutions of Christianity, are disregarded – perhaps trampled on. Bitter invectives are thrown out against others – against their persons, their principles, and mode of worship; as if all who did not think with the innovating leaders, were in the direct way to

perdition. A rigid, external sanctity is assumed, and a glowing ardour to make proselytes is exerted; so that sea and land will be compassed for the purpose.[6]

The emotional fervour and antiauthoritarianism that characterized such religious movements had their effects on individuals. Inglis reported that in recent meetings in Halifax, "*three persons* have been driven to actual madness, to the most deplorable state of insanity, and become maniac," and he hinted at even more shocking transactions in New Brunswick. But it was the *social* consequences that most concerned Inglis, consequences that tied religious populists to revolutionary atheists: their common "turbulence" produced the same disorder in society.[7]

Rather than jettisoning the language of feeling altogether, however, Inglis sought to draw upon a different – more sociable – discourse about emotions. He wrote, "Whoever reflects on the *social affections and instincts* that are implanted in our nature will be inclined to think that man was designed by his Creator for a state of society." Look to fellow feeling and the universal need for belonging, said Inglis, and it is evident that "happiness ... can only be attained in a state of society." He rejected the philosophical idea of a "state of nature," in which humanity was theorized to have lived "separate, independent, and without any social connection between individuals." "Such a state," he asserted, "is wholly fabulous; it never had an existence." Individuals cannot willy-nilly enter or leave society – humanity is necessarily social.[8]

Inglis sought to cultivate those "social affections" that held people together, rather than the unrestrained passions and unruly appetites that atomized society. *Religion* and *loyalty* together provided the antidote for revolutionary disorder and unsocial passions. They are, he argued, "the pillars, as it were, on which society rests, and by which it is upheld."[9] The kind of religion that supported society, instead of undermining it, was "the pure, peaceable and rational Religion of Jesus Christ, which requires holiness and benevolence in its professors, and strongly inculcates order and subordination." Christianity, he said, had eternal and interior purposes apart from this public influence, but it also cultivated social virtues so necessary for civic life.[10] Inglis also suggested that loyalty to the British king and constitution was grounded in affections as well as reason. He wrote about George III's desire to "promote the happiness and

prosperity of his subjects" and "the eminent virtues that adorn him."
He asserted that the British constitution "is the best calculated to
procure political happiness, of any that was ever framed by human
wisdom." In other words, he made a particularly affectionate case
for British loyalism, and not simply for social peace in general.[11]

Social affections competed with more turbulent passions, even
within an individual heart. While he contended that happiness is to
be found in the "social state," Inglis admitted that "some persons
are naturally of a more restless and turbulent cast than others. They
are fond of innovation and change, for the sake of innovation. The
calm shade of peace and quiet pleases them not; their delight is in a
storm." The destructive turmoil of revolution originated in a "turbulent temper" and had emotional rather than political origins: "For
if any are discontented under [the British Constitution], if they are
restless and given to change, the cause must be sought in their own
bosom, and not in the Constitution." Reasoned loyalty and religion,
then, provided a check on such turbulent, enthusiastic passions and
fostered more social affections.[12]

The way that Inglis linked the most consequential public events of
the eighteenth century – the American and French revolutions – with
the interior movements of the heart raises a number of intriguing
questions. Why did people in the Enlightenment Atlantic ascribe
such power to emotions? How did they think feelings were related
to other kinds of causation, such as diplomacy, ideas, economics,
or polities? What could passions *do*? If feelings were potentially so
disruptive to social order, why did people appeal to emotions when
attempting to construct coherent communities? How did religious
and political emotions converge or conflict? The ways that Inglis
used "passions," "affections," and "enthusiasm" suggest that these
were not synonyms and begs the question of how their meanings
at that time differed from their current connotations. And Inglis's
own experience as a Loyalist refugee invites exploration of how his
feelings contrasted with the political affections of Americans who
supported the revolution, or Britons across the Atlantic, or loyal
Nova Scotians who settled in the province prior to the imperial crisis.

The chapters that follow take up some of these questions, examining political and religious emotions in the Enlightenment Atlantic
world from a vantage point in British North America. They attend
to the ferment of feeling in the community of Cornwallis Township,
Nova Scotia, from about 1770 to 1850. This study argues that Nova

Scotians vigorously participated in transatlantic debates about emotions and sentiments, and that they used those emotional discourses and the fashioning of their own feelings to navigate changing political and religious communities.

The Revolutionary Atlantic was awash in deep feelings. People expressed the ardour of patriots, the homesickness of migrants, the fear of slave revolts, the ecstasy of revivals, the anger of mobs, the grief of wartime, the disorientation of refugees, the joys of victory. Not only did the events of the period *evoke* a variety of powerful emotions but also both women and men regarded the *cultivation* of appropriate feelings as a marker of morality, taste, and sociability. The importance of feelings was clearly expressed in the titles of some of the era's popular novels: *A Sentimental Journey* (1768), *The Man of Feeling* (1771), *The Power of Sympathy* (1789), and, of course, *Sense and Sensibility* (1811).[13]

Emotions were also a special preoccupation in the culture of the Enlightenment, belying its characterization as primarily an "age of reason." An emphasis on sense perceptions encouraged people to examine their feelings as tangible evidence, rather than impulsive distractions. Philosophers such as Francis Hutcheson (1694–1746) went further, arguing that affections could offer reliable moral guidance.[14] David Hume (1711–1776) suggested that emotion, rather than reason, motivated human action, asserting that "Reason is, and ought only to be, the slave of the passions."[15] Adam Smith (1723–1790), perhaps more famous for advocating economic self-interest, also wrote *The Theory of Moral Sentiments*, the century's most influential articulation of how *sympathy* could be the basis of sociability in an increasingly commercialized society.[16] Jonathan Edwards (1703–1758), the theologian of the Great Awakening, engaged with many of these themes, declaring, "True religion, in great part, consists in holy affections."[17] The eighteenth century was not so dispassionate or disenchanted after all.

As these brief glimpses suggest, several terms were prominent in the emotional lexicon of the Anglo-Atlantic world. Until the end of the eighteenth century, it was less common to use "emotion" than one of the other words that had distinct, if often overlapping, connotations.[18] Since debate about the meaning of these terms (and experiences) features prominently in this study, a brief working definition of some of them may be helpful. *Passions* were strong feelings that, if left unchecked, threatened to overwhelm the will.

Affections were the habituated inclinations or dispositions of the heart toward another person or an idea. *Feelings* were the sensory experience of particular emotions. *Sensibility* was the capacity to perceive another's feelings, or to respond morally and feelingly to a situation. *Sentiments* were reasoned feelings or deeply felt opinions. *Sympathy* was the imaginative identification with the feelings, ideas, or circumstances of another person. Then, as now, such terms were often used interchangeably or with less precision; this study will identify those moments when a particular meaning was intended or being debated.[19]

Feelings were not only central *to* history; feelings themselves *have* a history. The expression and meaning of particular emotions have changed in different times and places. Historical context is what made tears, for example, sometimes essential to masculinity, and at other times its antithesis. While some historical emotional expressions may seem recognizable to moderns, there are also jarring differences. The meanings of anger, boredom, and happiness have varied widely by culture or century. Tracing the continuities and changes of feelings has made the history of emotions a burgeoning field of inquiry.[20]

Scholarship on emotions in the Age of Revolutions has helped to uncover the role of feelings in public and political realms, and not only in interior or domestic spaces. Sympathetic bonds helped citizens create coherent national communities, just as tumultuous passions were channelled into revolutionary disruptions. Affections now find a place – alongside ideology, polity, economics, and print – in discussions of historical causation, as well as in the examinations of the "lived experience" of revolutions.[21] This study attends to the way that individuals in British North America debated the role of emotions in the great changes of their lifetimes, and how they understood their emotional experience of those events. A particular focus of this study is how political and religious passions were intertwined.

Historians now see affect as an important element in the construction of early modern national identities and in the fashioning of individual political identities. Benedict Anderson influentially includes this emotional aspect of nationalism in his account of nations as "imagined communities."[22] He asserts that political ideologies or bureaucratic structures do not, in themselves, make nations "emotionally plausible."[23] Historians must also consider the "*attachment* that peoples feel for the inventions of their imaginations" to better explain why citizens will make sacrifices, or even die, for their nation.[24] "Political love," Anderson says, is an important dimension of national belonging.[25] Historians of Britain and America have developed these themes, describing how national or imperial officials intentionally cultivated this affective facet of political identity through public ceremonies and holidays, the language of petitions and bureaucracy, and the cultivation of historical culture.[26] From the perspective of the individual, there is a rich literature on how individuals appropriated these elements, alongside burgeoning print culture, in the self-fashioning of their political identities.

Recent studies have both proposed the centrality of passion in the American Revolution, and conversely, suggested that the Revolution marked a juncture in the transatlantic history of emotions. John Adams famously wrote that "The Revolution was in the minds and hearts of the people ... this radical change in the principles, opinions, sentiments, and affections of the people, was the real American Revolution."[27] Nicole Eustace, for one, argues for the development of an "American emotional vernacular in the decade before the Declaration of Independence."[28] She holds that even though British North Americans participated in a transatlantic culture of sensibility, the unique conditions of the colonial setting – particularly encounters with Indigenous and African peoples – undermined the distinction between elite sentiments and popular passions. When the simmering tensions between Britain and the colonies further weakened the affectionate bonds of empire, American Patriots came to embrace more vehement emotions to fuel their resistance. Eustace describes the American *spirit* as a unique amalgam of patriotic passion and social feeling – a combination that she acknowledges was potentially unstable.[29] Scholarship focused on American literary history has tended to emphasize the instrumentality of emotions in the creation of an "imagined" American national identity. The leaders of the early republic attempted to strengthen ties of affection and sensibility in order to give the new nation the emotional cohesiveness it lacked, even as they attempted to mitigate more divisive passions and interests.[30]

Yet it would be a mistake to assume that emotions served only *national* interests. The history of sentiment is a transatlantic story. In the colonial period, sensibility contributed to a common, cosmopolitan, polite culture.[31] Alongside her assertion that "The history of the

American Revolution is in part a history of sensibility," Sarah Knott
can also observe, "The transatlantic circulation of sensibility allowed
colonists to see themselves as part of British culture, and also apart
from it."[32] Americans and Britons alike learned to be "spectators"
to their feelings, wept over the same novels, and sought to cultivate
social affections. Letters and texts also helped individuals imagine
their places in transatlantic "webs of affection," communities shaped
by familial, religious, or political identities.[33] Across the Atlantic
world, a range of actors "harnessed popular languages of feeling –
whether passions or sensibility – to serve their own political ends."[34]

One way to recover a broader range of political feelings in North
America would be to put *Loyalists* back into the story, as Sarah
Pearsall has argued in an incisive review.[35] Historians of loyalism, at
least, have not entirely neglected emotions in ideology or experience.
Robert M. Calhoon's series of case studies remains the most sophis-
ticated depiction to date of how Loyalists attempted to "explain
and organize their experiences and sensations" as they reflected on
their disaffection from the Revolution.[36] Janice Potter has offered
a persuasive account of Loyalist ideas about reason and passion,
emphasizing their views that passion was "aesthetically abhorrent"
and "undermined both freedom and morality."[37] She also suggests that Loyalists and Patriots exhibited very different emotional
styles: "Whereas Patriots tended to admire zeal, audacity, and commitment, Loyalists preferred moderation, propriety, and prudent
detachment."[38] And yet, it was not that Patriots *did* and Loyalists
did not employ political emotions, but rather that they attempted to
mark out different kinds of emotional communities. Many Loyalists
argued that participating in the transatlantic, cosmopolitan culture
of sensibility was not irreconcilable with their American identity.
They worried that the violent passions that their Patriot neighbours
had embraced would only serve to desensitize them to those sympathies that knit diverse people together.

This study's focus on the emotions of loyal British North
Americans also positions it in scholarly conversations about the
definition of loyal*ism*, as distinct from Loyal*ists*. The conflict over
American independence did not create loyalism – reaching back, as
it did, at least to the seventeenth century – nor were the American
refugees the first to fashion or dispute their loyalty. Attending to the
political emotions expressed by the Nova Scotians here in view contributes to the effort urged by Jerry Bannister and Liam Riordan in

their important essay on reframing the long history of loyalism: "to conceptualize loyalism as an affective sensibility as well as a specific program."[39] Mapping the complex emotional terrain of loyalism before, during, and after the American Revolution makes it possible to reconceptualize the period; this study argues for the decentring (though certainly not the erasure) of the Revolution in the histories of emotion and loyalism. Focusing on individuals in British North America recovers some sense of the broad spectrum of political affections and overlapping loyalties that were available – *feel-able* – in the Enlightenment Atlantic.[40]

As Charles Inglis's invocation of "enthusiasm" suggests, *religious* feelings were a special preoccupation in the "long" eighteenth century: from the transatlantic awakenings of evangelical Protestantism to the stoking of anti-Catholic fears, from the sensational claims of the "French Prophets" to the exuberance of revivals among enslaved Africans, from the ecstasies of Methodist camp meetings to the sympathies that motivated the abolitionist movement. "Heart religion" flourished in the Age of Enlightenment. Yet until recently, religious emotions have fit uncomfortably in the histories of the Enlightenment and the culture of sensibility. Seen as a reactionary response to Enlightenment rationality, evangelical piety has largely been absent from the story of the more refined culture of sensibility. As historians of religion have engaged with the history of emotions, new scholarship has gone some distance to reintegrate evangelical feelings into those histories.[41]

There is now a growing literature about the prominence and diversity of emotions in Puritan life and thought, making it difficult to sustain the stereotype of the Puritans as dour killjoys or despairing predestinarians. There are studies of Puritan happiness, affection, friendship, and delight, alongside the more familiar themes of assurance and anxiety.[42] And while the history of sentimentalism has often been framed as a secular development, Abram Van Engen has recently demonstrated the importance of sympathetic fellow-feeling in key Puritan texts, arguing that religious impulses dovetailed with other sources in the emergence of eighteenth-century sentimental culture.[43] The resulting picture is that Protestantism did not inhibit early modern people from participating in wider debates about emotions or the literary culture of sentiment.

It is perhaps no surprise that historians have given considerable attention to the intense emotionalism of the evangelical Protestantism emerging from the Great Awakening of the 1740s.[44] In *Fits, Trances, and Visions*, Ann Taves explores the range of spiritual and natural explanations offered by intellectuals as they debated the meaning of heart-warming conversions, bodily ecstasies, and raucous camp meetings. Sarah Rivett traces the entwining of scientific empiricism and religious "experience" in Puritan and evangelical thought. Like Isabel Rivers, Norman Fiering, and Michael Crawford in their important earlier studies on dissenting and evangelical engagement with British sentimentalist philosophy, Taves and Rivett portray religious emotions as having been at the heart of a complex relationship – as opposed to a simple opposition – between evangelicalism and Enlightenment.[45]

But ordinary evangelicals, and not only the movement's leading thinkers, also reflected deeply upon their emotional experiences and aspirations. This is one of the signal contributions of Phyllis Mack's *Heart Religion in the British Enlightenment*.[46] She counters previous characterizations of evangelicals as irrationally "emotional," and argues that in their life-writing, British Methodists were attempting to understand, discipline, and cultivate their emotions, and so, were engaged in that quintessentially Enlightenment endeavour of self-fashioning. Mack helps to uncover the emotional experience of Methodists in their daily lives, and not only at the heights of revival meetings. In another study on emotions and the agency of ordinary evangelicals, Calvin Hollett argues that lay people in eighteenth- and nineteenth-century Newfoundland embraced individual and communal religious rapture to shape their own religious culture, rather than relying on clerical leadership.[47]

Just as emotions helped early modern people "imagine" their participation in emerging national communities, so too did feelings structure the experience of far-flung religious communities. With a burgeoning evangelical print culture, readers formed emotional attachments beyond their own locales and used newly abundant texts to help fashion their religious affections.[48] Emotions were also central in the experience of missionary expansion, as, on the one hand, missionaries attempted to shape the emotional lives of Indigenous converts, and at the same time, as sympathy helped Anglo-American evangelicals identify with both missionaries and the inhabitants of imperial spaces.[49]

Worries about "enthusiasm" linked the religious and political histories of emotion in the late Enlightenment Atlantic, where private emotions and experiences could dangerously reverberate through society. As the title of this book suggests, the pages that follow explore the relationship between varieties of "enthusiastic" religion and a spectrum of political loyalties. Lingering over the powerful resonances of "enthusiasm" in the early modern period clarifies what British North Americans thought was at stake. Enthusiasm was a term that no group adopted as its own, but was a smear word used to cordon off any number of religious practices from polite Enlightenment culture. Though the word has the basic sense of either inspiration (god in the person) or ecstasy (the person in god), in the early modern period it acquired the negative connotation of a *false revelation*.[50] Samuel Johnson's 1755 dictionary defined enthusiasm as "a vain belief of private revelation; a vain confidence of divine favour or communication."[51] William Hogarth vividly portrayed this usage in a satirical print published in March 1762, contemporary with most of the figures in this study. Labelled "Credulity, Superstition, and Fanaticism: A Medley," it was based on Hogarth's unpublished drawing called "Enthusiasm Delineated."[52]

The complex image depicts an animated evangelical preacher (probably George Whitefield) addressing an overwrought and unruly congregation from a high pulpit. The emotional depths and heights to which the preacher provokes the hearers is measured, in the print, by a brain-shaped thermometer, ranging from "settled grief," "despair," or "madness," to "love heat," "extacy," "convulsion fits," and "raving." The many kinds of fanaticism and the overall disorder of the scene powerfully convey what one historian calls the "anarchy of religious individualism" implied in the charge of enthusiasm.[53] These religious passions were not, however, seen as merely private – they invoked the spectre of the seventeenth-century wars of religion and the English Civil War. Britons remembered all too well the horrors of levelling sects, the death of the king, and the "world upside down."[54] Enthusiastic emotions could corrode social and religious order.[55] Over against the culture of politeness, so-called enthusiasts insisted on thrusting religious zeal, candour, and controversy back into the public sphere, causing one historian to describe enthusiasm as "the monstrous alter ego of eighteenth-century civility."[56]

This is a story about how people in one community participated in the transatlantic swirl of debates over emotions, and how they adapted emotional practices and discourses to their own communities. The focus is on the emotional communities that overlapped in Cornwallis Township, Nova Scotia, from about 1770 to 1850. At its

CREDULITY, SUPERSTITION, and FANATICISM.
A MEDLEY.

Believe not every Spirit but Try the Spirits whether they are of God: because many false Prophets are gone out into the World.
1.John, Ch.4.V.1.

Design'd and Engrav'd by W.m Hogarth.

Publish'd as the Act directs March y.e 15.th 1762.

Figure 0.2 | William Hogarth, *Credulity, Superstition, and Fanaticism*, 1762.

heart are four case studies of individuals whose lives intersected in the township, and the very different transatlantic emotional communities to which they belonged: Handley Chipman and the Whiggish New England migrants that persisted in their British loyalties, Jacob Bailey and the Loyalist refugees disaffected from both their American *and* British sense of belonging, Henry Alline and the community of New Light women whose evangelical otherworldliness depended upon Britain's loosely-defined Protestant establishment, and Edward Manning and his cross-border and imperial community of sympathy. They have been chosen because of the richness of those of their personal writings that are available, and because they illuminate the emotional, religious, and political communities in which they participated. Cornwallis Township provides a unique vantage point for engaging with the period's long-running debates about the meaning and social consequences of emotions. For good reasons, historians often turn to the likes of Adam Smith or Jonathan Edwards to frame the terms of that conversation. Yet, this study assumes that the circle of conversation and debate included many other, less recognizable voices. To borrow the words of historian Emma Rothschild, this study, too, "is about large and abstract ideas in the lives of individuals who were not themselves philosophers or theorists of enlightenment," or, for that matter, theologians of religious experience.[57] Through a pastiche of commonplace selections, a volley of regional polemics, an exchange of letters, the circulation of manuscript essays, or the singing of locally composed hymns, Nova Scotians participated in that transatlantic conversation. This study does not claim that Chipman, Bailey, Alline, or Manning deserve wider recognition as major thinkers; rather, it argues that ordinary people, middling writers, and local leaders also engaged in the conversation about the meaning and consequences of religious and political emotions.[58] As Ann Taves demonstrates, "claims about religious [and emotional] experience were consistently contested at a grassroots level and significant theoretical explanations of experience were generated by the self-educated as well as by intellectual elites."[59] In addition to their individual and distinctive ways of making sense of emotional experience, Nova Scotians also drew on discourses available throughout the Atlantic world, such as passion, affection, and sentiment.

Some background may give a sense of the history that shaped the emotional discourses of Cornwallis Township. Cornwallis was

Figure 0.3 | John Elliott Woolford, "View near Cornwallis," 1817.

reconstituted as a British and Protestant settlement in the 1760s, following the *grand dérangement* of *l'Acadie* in 1755–56 and the ongoing displacement of the region's Mi'kmaq. In proclamations of October 1758 and January 1759, Governor Charles Lawrence offered generous grants of that fertile land to New England settlers ("Planters"), along with free passage and promises of religious liberty (for Protestants) and a representative assembly. Cornwallis Township was thirty miles long, stretching from the Minas Basin in the east to Berwick in the west, and twelve miles from the Bay of Fundy in the north to the Cornwallis River. In the words of Jacob Bailey, it was "the most fertile and delightful apartment of Nova Scotia, an extensive plain bounded by Mountains."[60] The population of the township in 1763 was 656, and by 1827 had grown to 4,400.[61] Like the rest of Nova Scotia, Cornwallis Township was shaped by successive waves of immigration and Revolutionary-era mobility. Resettled first by New Englanders from Connecticut,

Rhode Island, and Massachusetts, it was part of the larger story of northeastern expansion into territories that became Maine, New Hampshire, and Vermont. Just as importantly, Nova Scotia was a site of expanding British imperial power from as early as 1749, and of the reconstitution of the empire after 1783. After the American War of Independence, free and enslaved Loyalist refugees swelled the population of the province. And although Cornwallis Township was more homogeneous than other regions of the province, immigration into Nova Scotia during the late eighteenth century mirrored the cultural diversity of the British Empire, as Jamaican Maroon, English, Scottish, Irish, and Welsh settlers joined the region's New England settlers. Bailey, once again, memorably described the Annapolis Valley's population as "a collection of all nations, kindreds, complexions and tongues assembled from every quarter of the Globe, and till lately strangers to me and each other."[62] It is just this diversity and mobility that makes Cornwallis Township an ideal place to stand, looking outward, to explore the debates and emotional experiences of the Revolutionary Atlantic world.[63]

It is not surprising, then, that Nova Scotians did not exhibit a unitary political or emotional response to the events of the American Revolution. Some lobbied the nascent Continental Congress to invade the province or even participated in "Eddy's Rebellion" of 1776, laying siege to British Fort Cumberland. Others joined militias and circulated reaffirmations of their British loyalty. Still others feared the incursions of privateers, agonized over wartime rifts in families, were preoccupied with religious concerns, or expressed complex political opinions that would have been unthinkable in the thirteen colonies further down the Atlantic coast.[64] At the seaboard intersection of two political entities under transformation – the United States and the British Empire – and recent migrants themselves, Nova Scotians in the Revolutionary era self-consciously wrestled with feelings of identity and belonging.[65]

Just as religion and loyalty were twinned commitments for Charles Inglis, so were political and religious emotions intimately linked in the experience of his Cornwallis Township contemporaries. They do not tell a unitary story, however. Bailey, Alline, Chipman, and Manning – and the emotional communities in which they participated – exhibited a spectrum of feelings and employed multiple discourses about emotions. While Anglicans Inglis and Bailey found enthusiasm and loyalty irreconcilable, Alline, Chipman,

and Manning were each committed to some version of evangelical
Protestantism and attempted to square their religious convictions
with varied conceptions of British loyalty and social order.

Handley Chipman (1717–1799) migrated from New England to
Nova Scotia in 1761, and his writings attest to how he remained
emotionally connected to a wider Anglo-American world. On the
eve of the American Revolution, Chipman compiled a commonplace
book – a digest of his reading in British and American publications.
The document reveals that although Chipman sympathized with
the complaints of his former New England neighbours, he continued to express surprisingly strong British affections. His writings
recover an emotional experience of British American loyalism that
was obscured elsewhere by the polarization of war. In still other
manuscripts, Chipman wrote at length about the role of emotions in
religious life, attempting to balance the experiential piety of evangelicalism with a concern for social order. In New England, Chipman
knew evangelical leaders George Whitefield and Sarah Osborn,
and in Nova Scotia, he was a warm supporter of itinerant preacher
Henry Alline, even transcribing and circulating the latter's diary. Yet
Chipman also wrote with concern about what he perceived as emotional excesses in the New Light community that Alline founded. He
demonstrates how people in British North American communities,
along with better-known philosophers and theologians, grappled
with the cultivation of affections and the meaning of feelings.

Jacob Bailey (1731–1808) arrived in Cornwallis Township
as a Loyalist refugee from the American Revolution. Born in
Massachusetts, educated at Harvard College, and a convert to
the Church of England, Bailey had been an Anglican missionary
for the Society for the Propagation of the Gospel (SPG) in eastern
Maine (then Massachusetts). Bailey's experience of the Revolution
was emotionally fraught. His letters and diaries express the fear and
anger of his Loyalist ordeal with the Pownalborough Committee of
Safety, which accused him of being "disaffected" with the cause of
liberty. Bailey did not see this ordeal as an isolated event, however. In
a manuscript prepared for the press (though never published), Bailey
traced the themes of enthusiasm and disloyalty through the history
of New England. Despite these bitter reflections, he cultivated a
deep affection for his American birthplace within a cosmopolitan
and imperial framework. Forced to seek refuge in Nova Scotia in
1779, Bailey documented the complex feelings of dislocated British

American Loyalists. Disillusioned by British overtures of peace, angered by what he perceived as neglect of Loyalist refugees, and living among former New Englanders with republican sympathies, Bailey became profoundly disaffected with Britain. Yet he did not abandon his loyalty; rather, he had to find a way to be loyal without affection. He lost confidence that a culture of sentiment could overcome differences in the Anglo-American public, and in his writing turned to acerbic satirical poetry to express his sense of a world overturned. His is an account of the passions and disaffections that shaped the revolutionary Atlantic.

New Light itinerant preacher Henry Alline (1748–1784) was instrumental in kindling a period of religious revival in the British Maritime provinces that coincided with the American War of Independence. Critics at the time worried that his message of spiritual liberty was a Trojan horse for republican politics and passions. Some historians have suggested, to the contrary, that Alline's message was a psychological antidote to the turmoil of the period, helping to shape a distinctly Nova Scotian identity. This study suggests that while Alline's evangelical Protestantism was, in fact, compatible with – even dependent upon – British loyalty, it is time to examine the (non-political) emotional community he attempted to foster. Opponents considered Alline a quintessential "enthusiast" and, to be sure, his message emphasized personal conversion, emotional experiences of religious ecstasy, and the right of lay people to criticize traditional clerical authority. Yet there was more to the emotional experience of Alline's New Light community than rapture. The letters and hymns of a community of primarily female Nova Scotian correspondents demonstrate that while these New Lights did indeed aspire to moments of selfless ecstasy, they also cultivated a wide range of religious affections over the course of their lives.

As a coda to the book, Edward Manning's (1766–1851) story of dramatic emotional transformation carries its themes into the next generation. Born to Irish Catholic immigrants to Nova Scotia's Planter community, Manning was converted to Alline's New Light faith. As a young man, he became an itinerant preacher with a network extending throughout the Maritime provinces and Maine. Along with a cadre of other preachers, Manning embraced radical evangelical beliefs, spurned the necessity of education, and adopted an emotive style of preaching. Yet over the following decade, he rejected his own "enthusiasm" and became the leading advocate of a more moderate evangelicalism. He became a Calvinist, a Baptist, a supporter of theological education, and an extensive reader. His daily diary reveals an intensely emotional reader – using newly abundant religious print to help shape his religious affections. Emotions remained crucial to Manning's faith, but in a different way. He continued to forge affectionate ties throughout the region and across the border, even during the heightened nationalism of the War of 1812. And during crucial years of imperial and missionary expansion, Manning used sympathy to identify with missionaries and Indigenous inhabitants in locales far removed from his Cornwallis home. Manning assumed British loyalism in a way that Chipman, Bailey, and Alline could not, and was anxious to avoid any suggestion that his evangelical faith was inimical to an orderly society. To the contrary, he marshalled religious affections in the service of an ambitious, optimistic program of voluntary social reform.

The kind of history of emotions ventured here is not enabled by unusually revealing historical documentation of the psychological states of the residents of Cornwallis Township; nor is it a variation on psychohistory. Rather, this microhistory of emotions is possible because Nova Scotians, like other early modern people, wrote reflectively about the meaning of their emotions, their aspirations to cultivate certain affections and sentiments, and their worries about the role of passions in the momentous events of public life. The figures whose lives and feelings are traced here all exhibited what Phyllis Mack calls "reflexive emotionalism ... [the] desire both to feel and to analyze feelings."[66]

William Reddy, one of the foremost theorists of the historical study of emotions, has argued that our knowledge of emotions is *always* mediated. There is necessarily "a gap between experience and expression ... between feeling and language."[67] Reddy supplies the term "emotives" to describe the words, phrases, and gestures by which we interpret or translate feeling sensations into emotional expressions. It is these written emotives, whether "spontaneous" or "conventional," that provide one general kind of evidence for historical inquiry. As Barbara Rosenwein contends, how we interpret and express feelings is constrained by "our emotional vocabulary and gestures, ... our conventions, values, and even implicit 'theories' of emotion."[68] Those "implicit" assumptions about emotions were brought nearer to the surface by the tumult and debates of the Enlightenment era.

This study also explores emotion as a "domain of effort."[69] The Cornwallis individuals wrote as often about the feelings *to which they aspired* as they did about those they actually experienced. Alline's desire for ecstatic communion with God, and Bailey's polite Christian sentimentalism, as very different as they were as emotional styles, shared the view of emotions as a domain of effort, as they each sought to cultivate particular affections. This, too, brought emotions to the surface in their writings and compelled them to draw upon a variety of philosophical and theological discourses about passions and sentiments.

A particular concern of this study is the role of emotions in creating, maintaining, and reconfiguring *communities*. While feelings are, in one sense, the most private of experiences, it is often in their public expression and shared description that emotions acquire their meaning. Early modern people had a profound sense of the social dimension of emotions. To emphasize this corporate and cultural context for feelings, historian Barbara Rosenwein has coined the term "emotional communities." It is not that such groups are particularly "emotional"; rather, emotional communities "share important norms concerning the emotions that they value and deplore and the modes of expressing them."[70] As they did in Cornwallis Township, several emotional communities can overlap in a given society at one time, and debates between them helped to define the emotional styles of those communities.[71] By attending to the several emotional communities – political and religious – that overlapped or competed in this one township, this study is a micro-history that looks outward. Of course, there remains the question of the representativeness of Cornwallis or any of the individual case studies. To be sure, there are unique elements and idiosyncrasies in these stories; but by embedding their accounts in the contexts of both local and transatlantic emotional communities, and by using the writings of these Nova Scotians to illuminate the widely accessible and debated discourses about emotions, the study speaks to some of the fraught emotional experiences and pressing intellectual questions of the Enlightenment Atlantic.[72]

This study contends that colonial Nova Scotians drew upon several kinds of resources to help them make meaning of their emotions and to navigate the revolutionary changes in political and religious communities. In addition to articulating the meanings of feeling and experience in their own, idiosyncratic ways, they also appropriated the discourses about affections and sentiments that were debated throughout the Atlantic world. There was not a hard line between learned culture and common experience. When revolutionary committees or Loyalist militias policed the attachments and affections of citizens, when church members met to help one another feel more deeply or more properly, and when both religious and political leaders raised their voices against "enthusiasm," it is unsurprising that British North Americans became adroit participants in transatlantic debates about emotions, if not always the masters of their own feeling.

Commonplace Loyalty:
Handley Chipman's British Affections and
American Sympathies

Under the heading, "Remarkable Events of Providence," Handley Chipman, Esq., began the body of his commonplace book with this timeline:

> About the year 1388 much Popish hipocrisy was discover'd
> to Amazment
> About the year 1488, The reformation from Popery was at
> a great height in Germany, &c.
> And in the Year 1588, The Spanish Armada was destroyed
> that was Sent against England in Queen Elizabeth's day, &c.
> And in the Year 1688, Our Nation was deliverd from Popery
> by King Wm the 3d and Queen Mary coming on the Throne
> of England, &c.[1]

Working from the precise dates of 1588 and 1688, and by massaging the earlier dates, Chipman tightly plotted the move from "Popery" to Protestantism, with English liberty providentially established by naval prowess and the Glorious Revolution. It is a selective outline of Protestant and English history – and an expression of passionate British identity – that could have been written anytime during the eighteenth century. What makes Chipman's document remarkable, however, is that it was written by a former New Englander living in Nova Scotia during the early months of 1776. At that time and in that place, mere months after the outbreak of revolutionary hostilities, and with the participation of Nova Scotia still unclear, it was not at all certain how the chronology would be concluded. He could

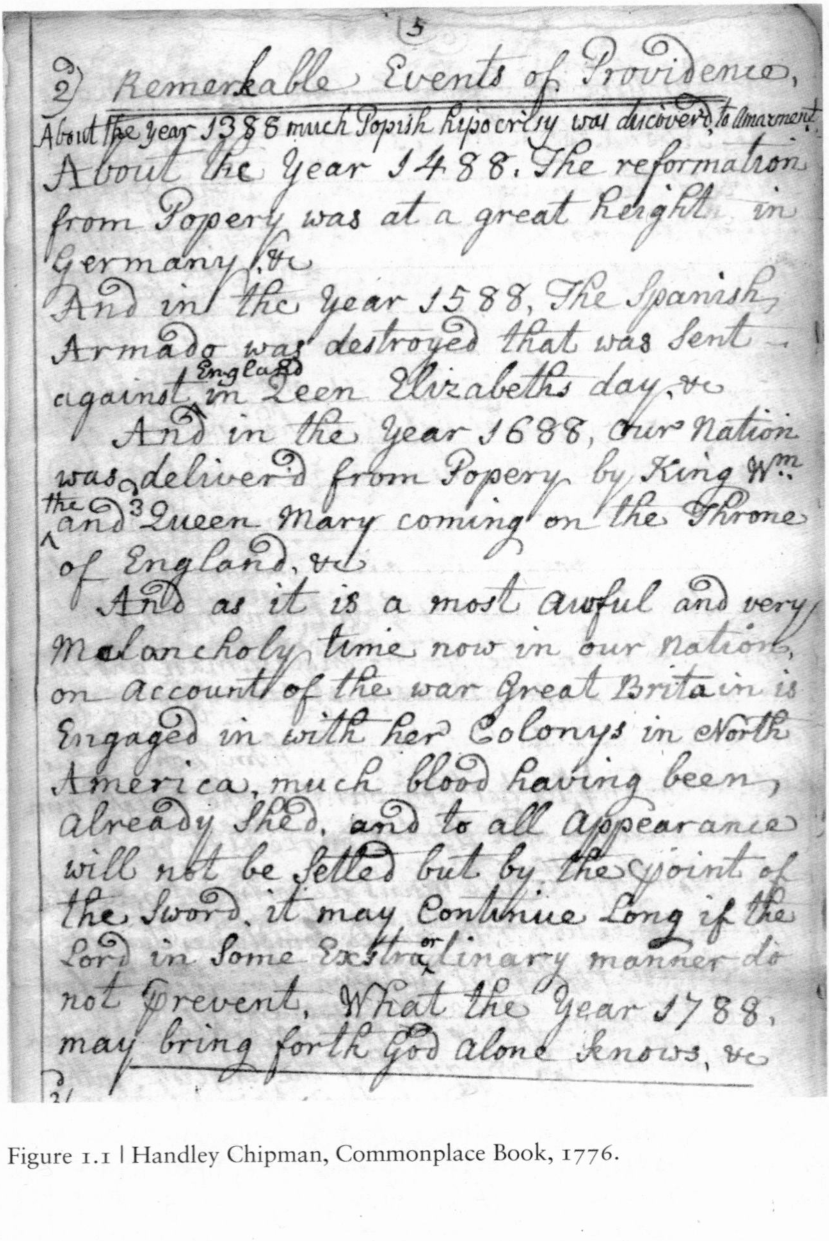

5

2) Remerkable Events of Providence,

About the year 1388 much Popish hipocrisy was discover'd to Amazment

About the year 1488. The reformation from Popery was at a great height in Germany, &c

And in the year 1588, The Spanish Armado was destroyed that was Sent against in England Queen Elizabeths day, &c

And in the year 1688, our nation was deliver'd from Popery by King W.m the and 3.d Queen Mary coming on the Throne of England, &c

And as it is a most awful and very Melancholy time now in our nation, on account of the war Great Britain is Engaged in with her Colonys in North America, much blood having been already Shed, and to all appearance will not be Setled but by the joint of the Sword, it may Continue Long if the Lord in Some Extra ordinary manner do not Prevent, What the year 1788, may bring forth God alone knows, &c

Figure 1.1 | Handley Chipman, Commonplace Book, 1776.

only write, "It is a most awful and very Melancholy time now in our Nation, on account of the war Great Britain is Engaged in with her Colonys in North America ... What the Year 1788 may bring forth, God alone knows."

Handley Chipman expressed political passions that have become difficult for us to imagine. He was, without contradiction, a proud New Englander *and* an ardent British subject. He had a Whig's passion to safeguard liberty *and* a monarchist's deep affection for the king. Chipman was, in short, a loyalist before the Loyalists. This emotional and political juxtaposition was not unique among British Americans, and indeed, this kind of loyalism may have been their default disposition for most of the eighteenth century.[2] It is challenging to recover the emotions of loyalism before the Revolution, however, obscured as they were by the increasing polarization of North American politics in the months leading up to 1776, and because historians have been more interested in the emergence of Patriot feelings.[3] An examination of Chipman's writings contributes to such a recovery and also highlights the emotional dimensions of early modern political identity. Chipman's expressions of strong, loyal British affections illustrate the persistence of such an emotional and political possibility up to the eve of the American Revolution – and even beyond. The coming of the Revolution did not diminish Chipman's feeling of Britishness; nevertheless, as a former New Englander with sympathy for colonial complaints, the ruptures of those years were profoundly unsettling, mixing his loyalism with sadness.

Before moving to Nova Scotia in 1761 as part of the "Planter" migration of New England settlers into the province, Handley Chipman (1717–1799) had lived on Cape Cod, Martha's Vineyard, and in Newport, Rhode Island.[4] When later narrating his family story, he began by emphasizing the close link between "Old England" and New England, and the Atlantic migrations of his grandfathers.[5] Trained in Newport as a cabinetmaker, Chipman capitalized on the Atlantic networks of the city, owning a rum distillery and soap-boiling business, and expanding his holdings with cooper and joiner shops, a warehouse, and a stable. The same dependence on the Atlantic networks that had allowed him to profit also proved to make his business vulnerable during the wars of the middle decades of the eighteenth century. Wartime privateering disrupted shipping to and from the British Caribbean and therefore the rum trade. Going to sea himself with a cargo that he hoped would clear his debts, Chipman "lost all he had with him, which was pretty considerable" when his ship was "taken by the enemy."[6] Though hardly left destitute, Chipman was forced to petition the Rhode Island Assembly for a licence to hold a lottery as a means of repaying his creditors. The offer to New England settlers of land grants in Nova Scotia was thus a timely opportunity for Chipman to rebuild his fortune as a farmer and property owner and to maintain – perhaps to better – his social status. Like his father, Chipman was a public office holder for much of his adulthood.[7] In Rhode Island, he was a justice of the peace and a deputy to the colony's general assembly, and upon removing to Nova Scotia, was a justice of the peace and judge of the probate court. Chipman's business ledger and a large archival collection of legal documents attest to how extensive was the influence of Handley Chipman, Esquire, and his family in the social life of Cornwallis Township.

Chipman was a British subject with a New England accent, literally as well as metaphorically. Occasional lapses in spelling – *au*thodox instead of orthodox, *Doset*shire rather than Dorsetshire – allow us to hear his non-rhotic "Yankee" dialect.[8] But if he sounded like a New Englander, he also cultivated his persona as a British gentleman, including in the way he avidly read and copied British gentlemen's magazines. Chipman's writings provide an individual perspective on the emotions and practices of anglicization – that cultural process by which eighteenth-century Americans became *more*, not less, British in the decades before the American Revolution.[9] Instead of the cultural drift that might be expected a century after settlement, colonists became more integrated into the British Atlantic world due to a combination of factors including imperial centralization, transatlantic religious awakenings, a common print culture, and a shared culture of consumption. Provincials like Chipman self-consciously constructed a loyal British identity by the offices they held, the Protestant beliefs they professed, the tea they consumed, and the metropolitan magazines they read.[10] They happily envisioned a steadfastly British future for the American colonies.

Emotions were an important aspect of this anglicizing convergence. British subjects experienced a felt sense of belonging to the empire in several ways: they embraced the "Protestant interest," in part because of fearful anti-Catholicism; pride and confidence swelled with Britain's military victories and territorial gains; and British subjects nurtured a warm affection for the king, a monarchist sentiment that was particularly passionate in the American colonies. Passion, writes one historian, "gave the first British empire coherence."[11]

Chipman articulated his political feelings in his manuscript notebooks, which included a commonplace book created in the unsettling early months of 1776, and a personal and spiritual diary kept from 1794 to 1796, in which he reflected on his emotional experience of the Age of Revolutions. While he did not publish them, Chipman intended that family and neighbours in the township would read his manuscripts ("for me and mine therein to look"), circulating them locally.[12] His handwritten compositions are an important counterweight to the printed sources most often consulted to reconstruct national feeling.[13] Historian Michael Eamon, for example, has recently argued that the eighteenth-century newspapers of Halifax and Quebec helped to "imprint" an idealized sense of Britishness on colonial readers.[14] Yet political identity was not passively received; individuals engaged in an active process of fashioning their own political emotions. Reading and structured note-taking were, collectively, one means of shaping "how individuals understood their own membership of communities," as they decided which events had heightened significance for them.[15] British subjects like Chipman actively and feelingly negotiated a way forward through their reading and experiences, sometimes literally writing their own version of Britishness.

Matter-of-factly entitled "History of Matter Remarkable and Common," Chipman's 1776 commonplace book compellingly depicts that subjective construction of political identity and his cultivation of particular political affections.[16] The tall, slender volume of 244 pages is a self-made anthology of selections that Chipman compiled from his reading in a number of genres: contemporary news, clever bon mots, moralizing poetry, interesting facts, reports of unusual events, and historical chronologies. While the creators of some early modern commonplace books followed John Locke's model of highly structured collections of quotations arranged by topic, Chipman's was a miscellany, in which he transcribed extracts from his reading page by page. His verse preface asserted his dual purpose for commonplacing:

And Thus pains I have taken to amuse my mind.
O that God herein may to me be really kind.
And help me and mine to Improve them Aright
And Serve him, my God, with all my heart & Might.[17]

Chipman's pairing of *amusement* with *improvement* suggests that his reading experience combined pleasure with self-fashioning.

The materials Chipman chose for constructing his political affections were especially drawn from metropolitan magazines and colonial almanacs. Creating his commonplace book in 1776, he extracted items from back issues – from the 1750s and 60s – of periodicals such as the *Gentleman's Magazine* and the *London Magazine*.[18] The selections from these London periodicals reveal how one British American imagined his place in a transatlantic British emotional community. Chipman also transcribed material from colonial almanacs from the 1760s and 1770s. These ubiquitous publications were "the empire's basic historical-political literature," helping to shape the British affections of American colonists.[19] Chipman's commonplace book makes his engagement with all of these texts visible, a practice that, as historian David Allan has observed, was a means of "expressing and thus reinforcing one's own patriotism through selective textual appropriation."[20] Chipman's selections, then, provide some insight into the complex political emotions that he chose to express and reinforce at a moment of uncertainty in British America.

INTERNALIZING A HISTORICAL NARRATIVE

Chipman wrote and copied historical chronologies into his commonplace book, creating and internalizing a particular narrative of British history. It may be hard to imagine lists of names and dates as gripping reading material, but chronologies have a long history and remained a popular genre of historical writing during the eighteenth century.[21] Chipman composed or transcribed seven such timelines in the space of only a few months, demonstrating how historical culture helped to shape his emotional connections to Britain.[22]

Headed with titles such as "Memorable Events of Providence" or "Remarkable Events," the commonplace timelines were drawn from several kinds of print sources. Best known are the chronologies found in almanacs, presenting a "highly selective and imaginative resumé of world history."²³ Some of Chipman's chronologies drew upon the annual reviews published in the London gentlemen's magazines (one of which even had the subtitle, the "Monthly Chronologer"). Chipman compiled the longest of his commonplace chronicles, with 250 entries over seven pages, from the three-volume *British Chronologist.*²⁴ Another book-length source was *The Chronological Remembrancer*, the title suggesting that readers turned to these works as aids to memorization.²⁵ The chronologist complements the historian, claimed one volume's preface, by giving "system to description and regularity to facts." They did this by "erecting *landing places* ... for the Reader's recollection."²⁶ Another publication less loftily but more forthrightly declared itself to be "Designed for the Pocket, in order to set People right in Conversation."²⁷

Despite their claims to objectivity, however, chronologies were necessarily selective histories, conveying a particular narrative and evoking certain emotions. The chronologies that Chipman read and created can be understood in the broader context of a historical culture fostered in the decades after the Glorious Revolution of 1688 – what one historian describes as the "royalization of public life and political time."²⁸ "Britishness" came to be identified with Protestantism (and anti-Catholicism), constitutional liberties, territorial expansion, naval prowess, and devotion to the Hanoverian monarchy. In the early eighteenth century, imperial officials began to transform the calendar, promoting the popular celebration of royal birthdays, military victories, and milestones in English Protestantism. While ceremonial culture helped British subjects to "perform" those events, chronologies marked out that historical narrative in print so that it could be internalized.²⁹ That Chipman not only read and copied such timelines, but actually composed his own, suggests the extent to which he emotionally identified with that narrative of Britishness.

Eighteenth-century British chronologies put the events since the Glorious Revolution in the longest possible context, connecting them to ancient history. One of Chipman's timelines reaches back to the world's creation.³⁰ Another begins with the birth of Jesus Christ, and takes in such other momentous events as "Rome burnt by Command of Nero" and "the Art of Printing found out," before eventually concluding with the capture of Louisbourg.³¹

The early history of England was well represented in the commonplace timelines. Chipman noted that the word "parliament" was first used in 1205, that "the common people in England [were]

Still in Slavery" in 1375, and that cherry trees were first planted
in England in 1540. One chronology focused almost exclusively on
English exploration and colonization, and another on the emergence
of England as a trading nation.³²

A contest between "popery" and Protestantism ran through the
chronologies. A few key moments in the European and English ref-
ormations were noted, as were translations of the Bible into English.
Anti-Catholic anxieties were expressed in the numerous entries about
the Gunpowder Plot, including its discovery in 1605, the conviction
of the conspirators in 1606, and, in that same year, Parliament's Act
for a "Yearly thanksgiving for Discovery of the powder Plot." The
central event in the narration of England's history as a Protestant
nation in this telling was unquestionably the Glorious Revolution
of 1688, about which Chipman wrote, "Our Nation was deliver'd
from Popery by King Wm and Queen Mary coming on the Throne
of England." Another chronology exclusively recorded "Memorable
Events of Providence Since the Revolution in 1688," highlighting the
date as a turning point in this narrative.³³ The coronations, victories,
proclamations, and deaths of England's royalty feature prominently
in the chronologies: Henry VIII, Elizabeth, Charles I, James I, Charles
II, James II, Anne, and the Hanoverian kings are all noted. A separate entry from 1760 listed the current royal family, including their
births and marriages.

Many entries reflected Chipman's identity as a British subject in North America. While he exhibited a general interest in
Britain's martial victories, his numerous entries on the 1745 attack
on Louisbourg detailed the specific dates of New England troop
movements and the number of guns on Warren's ships. And while
the milestones of what we might call generic Protestantism were
certainly included, so too were moments in George Whitefield's
itinerancy in New England. Chipman folded these American events
into a larger British narrative.

Chipman's transcription and creation of historical timelines
demonstrates the importance of historical culture in the construction of British identity, and how internalizing a particular historical
narrative helped to shape common imperial passions. Crafting these
chronologies during the unsettling events of 1776 was a way for
Chipman to rehearse and reaffirm this narrative, and to make some
emotional sense of British American anxieties. It is also notable
that Chipman continued to locate his British *American* identity in

England's long history – ancient constitutions, royal lineages, imperial exploration. The Declaration of Independence, drafted only
months after Chipman's chronologies, reflected the conscious choice
not to ground the new American nation in that same historical culture. As Benedict Anderson observed, there was a "profound feeling
that a radical break with the past was occurring," notwithstanding the many historical continuities that such a declaration glossed
over.[34] Despite his anxieties, Chipman remained committed to
plotting his North American identity in that long British timeline.
More generally, Chipman's resolutely historical text speaks to the
importance of "humility in the face of the past" to his expression of
loyalism and political moderation.[35]

COMMONPLACE LOYALTY

Affection for the king was at the centre of Chipman's political feelings, and in this he was a typical eighteenth-century British American.
He copied into his notebook some effusive poetic lines from a 1762
almanac on the transfer of the crown from George II to George III:

> The best of Kings has Laid his Scepter down,
> And George the Third adorns the British Crown
> New Conquered Realms join to his boundless Sway
> And Savage Chiefs their willing Homage pay
> He Reigns o'er Realms to former Kings unknown
> Whose Vanquish'd Monarks due Subjection own.[36]

The verse lauded the superiority of Britain's monarch above all con-
tenders, as well as the global reach of the empire. The encomium,
"best of Kings," here applied to George II (d. 1760), was in turn used
to laud George III. Boston engraver Nathaniel Hurd, for example,
produced a 1762 print entitled, "Britons Behold the Best of Kings,"
featuring George III flanked by William Pitt and James Wolfe. The
inscription reads, "Beloved by the Bravest of People. Justly Admired
by all. By his Enemies Dreaded. May he live long and happy. No
Evil and Corrupt Ministers are to Approach his Sacred presence.
Let none but such as Imitate his Virtues, have any Power. Then shall
Britannia be Blest for Ever."[37] The "best of kings," then, was not only
an abstract statement about British monarchical polity, but also a
personal attachment to a particular king's virtues.

No less exuberant was the "remarkable address" to the king from the formerly French subjects of Grenada, written in 1765.[38] As Aaron Willis has argued, French Catholic Grenada was part of an ongoing debate, following the Treaty of Paris of 1763, about how the British state would cultivate loyalty among non-Protestant colonial populations.[39] Aware of this debate, Grenadians employed affective language to demonstrate their loyalty and thereby lay claim to the benefits of imperial citizenship. They declared their new British king to be "the Sovereign of the Seas, the Conqueror of the age, the pacifier of Europe, and the illustrious object of the Love of the most flourishing of all Nations." They praised "the Splendor and glory, which your Majesty gives to Great Britain and to the name of British Subjects." Informed by their own experience of being ceded to Britain following the Seven Years' War, they remarked on his military victories (a "rapidity of conquest, of which the astonished universe Scarcely finds any Example in History") and his treatment of former enemies ("your benevolence for all mankind, the greatness of your Soul, and the profound wisdom of your Councils"). Is it any wonder, they asked, that the King rules over "happy Britons" – happiness not referring merely to a general sense of contentment, but, as Michael Hattem describes the term's eighteenth-century political meaning, "the enjoyment of civic equality by white males, which provided the basis and opportunity for those individuals to pursue their own interests and pleasure in a manner congruent with the public good."[40] Unpacking the eighteenth-century meanings of this emotional vocabulary helps us appreciate the concrete imperial aspirations of the Grenadians and the values of ideal imperial citizenship.

The Grenadian address also demonstrates how feelings did real political work. The petitioners were no doubt aware that the affections of a conquered people were not incidental to the peaceful functioning of an empire attempting to extend its authority into new regions. Moreover, the affectionate ties between king and subjects also provided the basis for petitioning. Their address requested the king to grant them, "without distinction, every Advantage of a British Subject," which would render him "the object of the Admiration, the Confidence, and Affection of the Conquered people, and that in a Manner as honourable to himself as advantageous to his Country." They continued: "We beseech your Majesty to permit us to assure you, that your Majesty has no subjects more faithful and thankful, more jealouse of the Support and increase of your glory, none in whose hearts you reign more Sovereignly and who are more warmly disposed to Serve their New Country, with their Lives and fortunes, than your Subjects of Grenada." The monarchy was conceived as a relationship between a benevolent Parent and loving dependents, giving both parties reciprocal (if uneven) responsibilities.[41] By lauding the benevolence of the king in his treatment of enemies, the new subjects were employing that benevolence as a standard by which the king's future conduct might be measured. They offered their loyal passions as evidence that they were ready to contribute as subjects. The emotional language of this address, then, was not merely a manipulative sop, but was actually a performative appeal to the nature of monarchical governance. By copying the text into his commonplace book, Chipman rendered it a "remarkable" example of how loyal subjects should feelingly address their sovereign, and how the empire was expanded and structured by emotional ties, alongside conquest and bureaucracy. If the king's conquered subjects could express such a fulsome declaration of their devotion, how much more should those born with the privileges of English liberty express their warm, loyal affections?

Chipman chose to reaffirm his affection for the king by including these selections at about the same time that Thomas Paine's *Common Sense*, published in January 1776, was proposing to overturn Americans' passionate cult of monarchy, declaring, "There is something exceedingly ridiculous in the composition of monarchy" and that the "monarchy in every instance is the Popery of government."[42] Chipman's fervently royalist excerpts were far more representative, right up to (and perhaps beyond) the eve of the War of Independence, and a reminder of just how revolutionary Paine's anti-monarchical passion was.

Chipman thrilled at the extent of Britain's military victory and acquisition of territory at the conclusion of the Seven Years' War. He recorded a French author's reflections on the North American colonies, made *before* British conquests in St Augustine and Quebec. The observer noted that though England had a "Chain of Colonies ... reaching to Spanish Florida," the French possessions stretched "without bounds up the Country," enclosing the English and Spanish colonies.[43] French colonies, the author boasted, "may be Said to form a kind of bow, of which those of the other Nations are the String." With great relish, Chipman observed how the map had been redrawn

after Britain's victory in the Seven Years' War: "But now thanks to
divine providence we are in possession not only of the String but
bow also, and doubtless with a Common blessing may Still keep it
in Spite of any Earthly power whatever." Contemporaries and historians alike have noted "the sheer enjoyment the British public seems
to have felt amidst the cascade of imperial triumphs" – the victories
supplying much-needed relief after the uncertainties and national
self-doubts of the war years.[44] Any doubts that had arisen due to the
century's back-and-forth conflicts with France were set aside, and
the narrative of an ascendant Protestant empire was confirmed.

Yet even stories of British military *defeat* could elicit patriotic
feelings. In March 1776, Chipman copied Nathaniel Ames's poem
on Braddock's Defeat, more than two decades after one of Britain's
most ignominious military losses.[45] At the start of the French and
Indian War, in 1755, Major General Edward Braddock was to lead
British regular troops to capture the French Fort Duquesne in the
Ohio Valley, but they were overwhelmed and outmanoeuvred by
a combined French and Indigenous force at what became known
as the Battle of the Monongahela. Ames's poem articulated several
emotions. It invited the reader to enter into a sympathetic *pathos*
with the "Noble Heroes, most Ignobly Slain," a meditation on
"Britain's bleeding Glory." But loss would not be the last word. With
confidence in Britain's martial prowess, the poem boasted, "This
foul Defeat Shall full revenged be." Written several months after
the events it describes, the poem mentioned hopeful rumours that
the tide of the war was turning, and that Britain's perpetual enemy
would be defeated: "The Proud Gallic Powers / Prostrate themselves
before the Leaden Show'rs ... / How Like the Leaves the dying
Frenchmen fall."

Chipman, copying the poem years afterward, would have felt the
satisfaction of knowing just how extensive was Britain's victory in
the wider conflict. The poet asserted that the moral character of the
British army was worthy of regard. He declared, "Your Soldiers
are Like their great Leaders – true." He also drew a sharp contrast
between the "skulking" battlefield behaviour of the French and
Indigenous "others" and the nobility of the British: "Behold our
Camp from fear, from Vice refin'd / Not of the filth, But flower of
human kind." The putative morality of their military was yet another
reason for British subjects like Chipman to feel pride in imperial
expansion. The prominence of martial themes among Chipman's

handwritten selections from the *Gentleman's Magazine* and other sources speaks to the gendered nature of the British gentility to which he aspired. As Julia Bannister has argued, the culture of sensibility was not incompatible with the theme of military masculinity so central to eighteenth-century Britishness.[46]

Chipman shared in the veneration of popular figures in Britain's public life. Among those represented in the commonplace book was William Pitt the Elder, Whig champion and architect of Britain's victory in the Seven Years' War. Pitt's popularity was perhaps even greater in America, reflecting his steady support of colonial causes. Chipman copied in its entirety the paean to Pitt that appeared, with his image, on the cover of *Bickerstaff's Boston Almanack* for 1772:

> Hail first of Patriots whose Extensive mind
> Revolves the vast concernments of mankind,
> Contending Realms accept control from thee,
> And Britain's Glory hangs on thy decree.
> *War* deals destruction, *Peace* her olive brings,
> As thy supreme direction governs Kings.
> Whene'er thou bid'st, the wreaths of conquest fall,
> The guide, the friend, the guardian of us all.[47]

Chipman did admit, at the bottom of the page, that the verse "Exalts too high," but still chose to include its expressive celebration of a Briton who elicited such strong feelings throughout the empire.

Few themes could rouse the passions as did liberty. British subjects traced their history as a narrative of freedoms secured from the tyranny of kings, popes, and enemies, and took pride in the enshrinement of those liberties in the English constitution. Yet liberty was to be protected as much as celebrated. Like other British Americans in the eighteenth century, Chipman was influenced by the Whig tradition of political writers – a loyal "country" opposition to courtly power – who upheld vigilance against corruption and tyranny.[48] Brendan McConville argues that metropolitan and colonial experiences of this tradition were often different. For most of the eighteenth century, while colonists ascribed a greater role to the king in guarding their liberties by providing a check to ministerial power, metropolitan Whigs were more indifferent to the Hanoverian monarchy.[49] In Chipman's commonplace book, that difference is noticeable in the contrast between the selections on endangered

liberty from metropolitan magazines and the strongly monarchist
items from colonial almanacs. It is more than a little ironic that
Chipman's more Whiggish commonplace selections were drawn
from metropolitan sources, while his more monarchist pieces came
from American almanacs. The dovetailing of loyalism and criticism
suggests how nuanced Chipman's political emotions could be.[50]

The long history of English liberty was often traced to the
thirteenth-century Magna Carta, a discussion of which appears
early in Chipman's volume. Excerpted from a 1768 almanac, the
item described "Magnacharta" as "the great Charter of the Liberties
of England."[51] The short paragraph outlined the document's early
history, in which kings "several times confirmed, and often broke"
their oaths to "faithfully and inviolably ... observe the things therein
contained." Apparently for want of space at the bottom of his page,
Chipman left out the almanac's assertion that "This excellent charter,
so equitable and beneficial to the subject, is the most ancient written
law in the kingdom." He does, however, include his own brief but
poignant parenthetical comment, "O that it was now observ'd" – a
remark that implies a sorry gap between the nation's legacy of constitutional liberties and its contemporary experience.

In a series of entries on liberty and faction, Chipman expressed the
sense that his devotion to British liberty was tinged with anxiety, in
the mid-1770s, as a result of ministerial mismanagement and overreach. Supplying the heading "Of English Liberties," Chipman selected
lines from a 1764 letter to the editor of the *Gentleman's and London
Magazine* complaining of the English excise tax on cider. The tax,
intended to recoup some of the costs of the Seven Years' War, was as
unpopular in England as the Stamp Act was in America, and was similarly interpreted as an overreach of government. The letter continued,
"If there is to be no alteration in the Cyder act, farewell to English liberties, which has Cost this Nation So much blood & treasure." Chipman
paraphrased the letter, and then inserted this pessimistic commentary:
"O what do we ever git again that is once yielded up[?]." He then
noted the author's typically Whig worry about power and tyranny:
"Power, Like Avarice, has a devouring appitite, which increases the
more it is fed, and thus Government becomes Arbitrary."[52]

Chipman was also disquieted by attempts to curtail the freedom
of the press. In an entry on "Faction and Licentiousness," he copied
a letter-writer's contention that "attempts are now made on the

Liberties of the people or the Liberty of the press, that guardian of all our other Liberties."[53] He claimed that acts that restricted the press with the flimsy justification of political "faction" were nothing more than the "artful insinuations of ministerial writers." And in what appears to be his own emotional summation of the magazine's feature on "Laws in England, Subversive of the Rights of Englishmen," Chipman wrote, "It is a Lamentable thing that people are So regardless of Liberty. Liberty can only be guarded in a free State with a jealous eye; indifference opens a door to Lay a foundation for Slavery, which has been the Case in most Nations."[54] Chipman's British loyalism was tinctured with lament. While he took pride in the nation's history of constitutional freedoms, he was angry at ministerial attempts to limit those liberties and grieved that many subjects took them for granted. He prized, in the words of one of his selections, that most political of passions – "zeal in Asserting the Rights and Liberty of the Subject."[55]

It is striking that in early 1776, this former New Englander chose to express *both* his ardent British and royal affections *and* his Whig criticism of ministerial authority, views that he did not regard as contradictory. Indeed, for much of the eighteenth century, Chipman's emotional and political stance was typical for British Americans, rather than extraordinary. With the intensification of the American imperial crisis and the onset of the War of Independence, however, it was increasingly difficult for British Americans to avoid the polarization of their political emotions.

Having established Chipman's full-throated British affections, one might ask, is anything particularly North American about his perspective and feelings? To be sure, on the very first page of the commonplace book, Chipman established his New England bona fides; he began his family notes with the declaration that his grandfather married the daughter of "the first man that Set foot on Plimoth Shore in New England from the first Vessel that came to bring Settlers into those parts."[56] On the other hand, he also stressed his British pedigree; one grandfather was born in "Do[r]setShire in Old England" and the other was "a Londoner."

Chipman's British identity seems to have coincided with his aspirations for North American society.[57] He reproduced Nathaniel Ames's poem, "On America," written in 1762, when the *British* future of the American colonies still seemed secure:

America, kind Heav'ns peculiar care
Vast heaps of Nature's Stores are treasur'd here,
Here the kind Earth produces yearly grain,
· Soften'd by waters and descending rain
In time thy Towers will vie with Europe Pride,
And Scepter'd heads will Gladly here reside.[58]

The poem described the colonial development of the natural bounty of North America, and envisioned that one day, royalty would reside there, and not just in distant Europe. For Chipman, his North American and British loyalties ran side by side, in a way reminiscent of Benjamin Franklin's pre-revolutionary view that "the Foundations of the future Grandeur and Stability of the British Empire lie in America."[59] That sentiment, expressed by Ames and Franklin in the early 1760s, may have seemed less assured in the early months of 1776 when Chipman copied them into his notebook. Yet it was a political vision he consciously preserved.[60]

IMPERIAL AFFECTION AND SUBJECTION

The last fifty pages of Chipman's commonplace book were devoted to his careful note-taking and commentary on Cadwallader Colden's *The History of the Five Indian Nations of Canada* (1747, revised 2nd edition), a decidedly British and settler colonial history of the Haudenosaunee Confederacy. Colden's agenda in writing his *History* was to convince readers that imperial relationships founded in mutual affections and friendship were more secure than those that relied upon heavy-handed coercion. By supplying British officials with a more accurate and sympathetic history, he hoped it would be possible to repair the tenuous alliance between the British and the Haudenosaunee, and to adopt a policy that appealed to their affections, rather than attempting to subject them through force. Chipman proved to be receptive to this argument, and read the book as a study in English, French, and Haudenosaunee political virtue. The relationship between subjection and affection in Britain's North American policy was never timelier than during those tense early months of 1776 when Chipman meditated on Colden's text.[61]

In his notes and comments, Chipman portrayed the loyalty of the Haudenosaunee. Selfless devotion to their own people elicited

Colden's (somewhat condescending) admiration that "None of the Roman heroes have discover'd a greater Love for their Country ... than these Barbarians have done."[62] He qualified his praise by claiming that the Haudenosaunee's "noble Virtues" were "sullied" by indulging in "that Cruel passion, Revenge." In his own words, Chipman likewise commended the Five Nations for their political fidelity: "Possibly it cannot be found that any Christian Nation has kept to their alliance with So much Strictness and truth for so Long a time as the five Nations has with the English, even from 1664 to this year 1776." By carefully note-taking his way through Colden's ethnographic study, he became sympathetic enough to Haudenosaunee history and culture to challenge, at least in part, the discourse that set Indigenous "Others" over against British "civilization." He concluded, "Thus hath these Savage Nations in many respects taught the English Lessons of Morality far Exceeding what many of us have taught them, but it is to be Lamented we have taught many Vices to them formerly altogether unknown."[63]

Chipman also read Colden's *History* as a comparative study of French and English imperial policies, assessing which approach was better suited to win and retain the affections of the Haudenosaunee. In summarizing the breakdown of the French alliance with the Five Nations, he observed a pattern – "The French, behaving roodly to the five Nations Still and Sometimes deceiving them" – and he noted their cruel treatment of Indigenous prisoners of war. He commented that such conduct had the inevitable result that "All the Nations that had Shewn friendship to the French now openly came to the English, Seeking their friendship and Alliance."[64] Violence and duplicity were no foundations for loyalty.

Were the English any more deserving than the French of the affections of the Haudenosaunee? Drawing on his own experience with New England traders, as well as his reading of Colden, Chipman admitted that "doubtless the English has wronged them ofton in Trade [and] ... in the purchase of Lands." But he qualified that admission by suggesting that those wrongs were committed "not as a body, but by individuals." What then of imperial relationships? He wrote that (unlike the French), "the English prosecuted their Measures ... only with the Arts of Peace, Sending their people among them in a very friendly Manner."[65] Chipman concluded his meditation, "Thus we have gone through the Material transactions which the five nations had with the English, in which we find the English pursuing nothing but peaceable and Christian Measures, and the five Nations Living in the Main Like friends." And as he so often did, Chipman also expressed himself in verse:

> Thus is concluded [this] Account of the English
> In which there doth not appear much blemish,
> in their transactions with the five Nations.
> But they Conducted with honesty and Patience.[66]

Chipman's assessment of English relations with the Haudenos-aunee appears to have been (perhaps naively) more positive than Colden's. The *History*, after all, was written in the early decades of the eighteenth century to urge British officials to change their policy, to return to friendship as a form of diplomacy so that the Covenant Chain could be repaired. Yet it may be that Chipman was also reading with a *later* set of imperial tensions in mind, at a moment when American colonists were resisting what they perceived to be the coercive treatment of British subjects. On Chipman's reading of Colden, British imperial policy in North America was vindicated as benevolent, an assessment that confirmed his own loyal affections.[67]

A MELANCHOLY HISTORY
OF BRITAIN'S EIGHTEENTH CENTURY

Did the unfolding events of the American Revolution cause an alteration in Chipman's political passions? His commonplace book was completed only a few months before the Declaration of Independence, and in Nova Scotia political allegiances were in turmoil for the duration of the conflict. Entries made in another manuscript – a primarily spiritual journal – more than a decade after the conclusion of the Revolution, reveal Chipman to have maintained his affectionate loyalty for Britain and the Crown. Nevertheless, he expressed profound sadness at the changes wrought by the Revolution, much of which he felt could be blamed on the pride of his ungrateful nation and the "haughty Zeal" of an "arbitrary ministry." Even as he prayed for the king, he worried about the war underway with France and the abhorrent possibility of a "Government without a King."

In a particularly long entry in his diary for 1794, Chipman used expressive, emotional language to reflect on the wars of his lifetime, and to comment on the role that public affections played in those events. He lamented, "O what Sad Wars and bloodshed has there been almost ever since I have been a free man of age ... and great overturns has been made by the Wars in the time."[68] He traced the "overturns" of four major conflicts in his lifetime, and found much to mourn in the recent history of the nation he continued to love.

King George's War (1744–48), Chipman claimed, "Ended not much to the Credit of our Nation." For American colonists the war started propitiously enough with the capture of Louisbourg in 1745. As Chipman proudly noted, "Cape-Brittain ... was taken mainly by the New England forces with the favour of thy holy Providence." New Englanders interpreted the conflict as a turning point of eschatological significance, a victory securing Protestant colonists from the Catholic threat to the North. Chipman's longest commonplace chronology, discussed earlier, memorialized numerous individual moments in the battle. So it was profoundly disappointing when "we did give [Louisbourg] up to the french" as a condition of the Treaty of Aix-la-Chapelle (1748).

The pattern of victory being swallowed up by the broader consequences of a war was repeated in Chipman's description of the Seven Years' War (1754–63). Like other British subjects, especially in North America, Chipman surged with pride at the expansion of the empire at the war's conclusion: "In the Course of thy alwise providence ... our Nation gained Victory by Sea and Land against the French and Spainard almost every where, taking a Vast many and Some very Valuable places from them, as well as great treasures by Sea." Once again, Chipman interpreted the victory as providential, a triumph for Protestantism as much as the British Empire. Yet despite the extent of Britain's conquest, the war was settled with "an inglorious peace." Chipman was disappointed that, notwithstanding its territorial gains, Britain was forced to concede some "Valuable Islands and other places that we had Captured." Of even more significance, the defeated French and Spanish were not made to pay restitution for the costs Britain incurred in the war – "Expences, great and Enormous Expences."

Besides the territorial and fiscal legacies of the Seven Years' War, Chipman pointed to its moral outcome, which he expressed in emotional terms. He perceived, first, that with the victorious conclusion of the war, "the Nation appeared to be much Lifted up with Pride." After the uncertainty of the long conflict, a spirit of national self-sufficiency and hubris dominated civic life. Not only did "Vital religion" decay, but even a concern with "the form of Religion" or public morality had waned. Victory apparently did Britain little spiritual good. He lamented "that no better thanks should be given nor returns made to God, who had given the Nation so many remarkable and most Uncommonly Glorious Victories and Conquests." Gratitude, rather than pride, he argued, was a more appropriate public feeling for the health of the nation.

Pride may have been a general malaise, but Chipman also blamed many of Britain's subsequent troubles on the arrogance of a few. "The Nation has had, from that time to this ... a very Arbitrary and Imprudent Ministry." Chipman charged that the arbitrary measures taken to deal with war debt led to the American Revolution, "the ruin of our Nation, and a means of dismembering Great Britain ... the Loss and distress of the Nation, which they now feel."

In their "haughty Zeal" and "forceable ways and means," the ministry attempted to impose new taxes on all British subjects, both "Island People" and American colonists. Of the 1765 Stamp Act, levied not long after Chipman settled in Nova Scotia, he observed, "Americans thought it very Oppressive," and then added, leaving no doubt about his own view: "as really it was." He recalled the "great and Unspeakable joy of the American Provinces and Colonies" when the Stamp Act was repealed. The lesson was not learned, however, and the arbitrary parliamentarians shortly thereafter imposed new direct duties on a "Multitude of Articles." Seeing the renewed "bluster and certain opposition" to those measures, all of the acts were again repealed, except for "a duty on Teas." Parliament unwisely "Stood resolutely to it" and backed up their determination by measures that the colonists knew as the Intolerable Acts, including the suspension of colonial charters, appointing judges from England, and other "Arbitrary steps." The unnecessary and tragic result: "Great Britain broke out into a most terrible and bloody War against them, which Ended as it did in the dismembering of thirteen fine prosperous Provinces and Colonies from Great Britain, and obliging Great Britain to acknowledge them free and independent States for Ever, to the grief and Sorrow of thousands."

Chipman's emotional reflection on the American Revolution was complex. On one hand, he entirely sympathized with the colonists' resistance to imperial overreach in the years following the Seven Years' War. His longstanding Whiggish criticism of the "Arbitrary and Imprudent ministry" echoed American reaction. He assigned little blame to the colonists for the conflict. Yet Chipman narrated the birth of the United States as a tragedy for greater Britain, rather than a triumph of liberty. He poignantly concluded, "for while they was together, to the Eye of reason, no Power could Vie with them. But now they are Separate they are both weakened."

Chipman's consideration of the fourth major military conflict of his lifetime, the French Revolutionary Wars (beginning in 1792), further elaborated his political affections. His dominant feelings are unmistakable: "O what Lamentable Slaughter and blood Shed has there been, by means of the present War, from the Sad Confusion in France, and the War with them." Writing in 1796, only months after the stunning early victories of Napoleon Bonaparte, Chipman's prognosis was grim: "Looks very Melancholy." Despite his sympathies for the Americans, Chipman had not become a republican. He was troubled that France had set up a "Goverment without a King." He observed that there was "discontent and disturbance ... in England on Account of the War," including the agitation of many Whigs that the French Revolution heralded the future of liberty. Chipman prayed, "O that Matters may not come to Extremities, Least ... it be the final ruin of our Nation." For him, criticism of arbitrary measures in governance was not incompatible with loyalism, and did not inevitably lead to revolt. Rather, he viewed the republican changes in America and France as extremes that promised ruin, rather than liberty.

Despite his pointed criticisms and melancholic feelings, Chipman still retained a commitment to the monarchy and affection for the king. In his diary, he wrote a prayer for the king and the royal family. He sympathetically recalled "the trouble and great Anxiety thousands were under ... when our King George 3d was for a considerable time not capable of transacting affairs of the kingdom, by reason of his Senses being impared." It was important for his political as well as spiritual feelings, he wrote, to remember "with what thankful hearts the most of the Nation was filled with on his recovery." Chipman offered an assessment of the King's reign: "He has been, I trust, in the main a well-designing King, and what has been amiss has been, it appears, owing to an ill-conducted Ministry, particularly Lord North's." Though hardly effusive praise, it demonstrated how Chipman managed his monarchism with his political criticism. He continued to pray for the king, that God would "preserve his precious Life, Stil a very great blessing to the Nation," and for the Queen ("pious and ... Amiable"), the Prince of Wales, and "every branch of the Royal family." Despite all that had been "overturned" by the wars of his lifetime, and despite his criticism and melancholy, Chipman still considered Britain "our Nation and Land."

PROVIDENCE, COMFORT, AND CRITIQUE

The chronology that began Chipman's commonplace book was headed, "Remarkable events of Providence."[69] It appeared to frame a Whiggish narrative of British history with all the standard eighteenth-century elements: Protestantism, naval prowess, and constitutional liberties. These "remarkable" historical events were memorialized and internalized because British subjects felt they demonstrated divine direction in their nation's history. But the American Revolution unsettled any inevitability to that narrative. "What the Year 1788 may bring forth, God alone knows." In the same vein, at the end of his commonplace book, Chipman poetically linked providence and the uncertainty of the unfolding American Revolution. He began:

> Thus is fill'd this 244 page Book,
> For me and mine therein to Look,
> And to observe God's providence
> In transactions many years Since.

He then referred to the long conflict between the French and English in North America, and humbly demurred, "But God alone, he has done this." He continued, poignantly connecting that earlier conflict with present upheavals:

> And may [God's] name be prais'd herefor
> And the English Nation Sin abhor,
> And Settle Peace and Unity,
> Least by our feuds we pine and die.
> 1776. Amen.[70]

Perhaps providence was not so straightforward. But he did not abandon the idea, and providence was prominent in the diary he kept in the mid-1790s. Chipman's deployment of the idea of providence in the long diary entry for 30 August 1794 – notably, half a dozen years after 1788 – suggests how he was able to make emotional sense of history, religious belief, and national loyalty.[71]

The older Chipman was no less ready to use the language of providence to reflect upon British history. He confidently recalled that the taking of Louisbourg by New Englanders was with "the favour of … holy Providence." The extensive British victory in the Seven Years' War was won "by alwise providence." Yet Chipman did not see his nation's history through rose-coloured glasses. Every "remarkable" moment of providence, in his telling, was paired with a lamentable example of mismanagement or bloodshed.[72]

Having committed several pages of his diary to a troubling account of British history, he paused, as if to explain why he included these historical recollections in his otherwise spiritual diary (about which more will be said in the following chapter). He explained: "I do it to keep these things in Remembrance for [God's] Glory and my Soul's real good." It was, for Chipman, an intentional discipline of faith, as well as citizenship. "All is well," he asserted, "in the proceedings of thy Providence. … This, this thought Comforts my Soul and alays my doubts and fears when things has a gloomy Aspect on my mind."[73] His belief in providence gave Chipman comfort at those times when history seemed to contradict, rather than support, confidence in his nation.[74] Rather than using providence as religious window-dressing for British progress, Chipman seems to have invoked the doctrine because he could not easily narrate such a linear national story: he *trusted* that there was divine purpose in history, though he could not always see it.

Likewise, Chipman drew on the idea of providence to mediate his affection and his dissent. His deployment of that belief was, in the words of historians Tony Claydon and Ian McBride, anxiously *aspirational* rather than triumphantly descriptive.[75] As Chipman said of the euphoria after the conquests of the Seven Years' War, God-given victories were not an invitation to national hubris; instead, they imposed humbling moral obligations for which the nation was accountable. The perceived gap between the divine purpose of Protestant Britain and its sad, bloody history left room for Chipman's expressions of lament and critique. Without exchanging either his affectionate loyalty or his belief in providence, Chipman could – and did – write about the uncertain future (rather than the inevitable progress) of the British nation.

CONCLUSION

In October 1781, the same month that General Charles Cornwallis surrendered at Yorktown, Chipman was cursed as "an Old Rebel dog."[76] The accusation, made by Timothy Newman, a known drunk and disturber of the peace, was nothing more than a timely slur. And yet Newman was not alone, then or since, in his suspicions that former "Yankees" in Nova Scotia shared the passions of American Patriots, no matter how muted by their ostensible loyalty. Indeed, as we will discover, when Jacob Bailey arrived in Cornwallis as a Loyalist refugee in 1779, his own political feelings were so galvanized by his ordeal in more polarized Massachusetts that he was unable to recognize the Britishness and loyalism assiduously cultivated by Chipman or many of his Nova Scotia neighbours, despite a remarkable coincidence of reading habits and basic political affections. However, the sentiments expressed in Chipman's commonplace book should put to rest any lingering uncertainty about his loyalties. In its pages, he articulated his deep affection for British constitutional liberties, his pride in imperial expansion, and his devotion to the king. He offers a portrait of what constituted loyalism *before* the Revolution – not as a reactionary impulse, but as a set of feelings and ideas that were shared by perhaps most British Americans during the eighteenth century. Elizabeth Mancke observes that Nova Scotia remained a space where "loyalism" retained a wider, less polarized meaning: "The ideological polarization in some parts of Anglo-America also created new meanings for loyalism and patriotism, definitions that no longer represented ranges on a spectrum of sentiment but rather quite circumscribed points. In Nova Scotia most people continued to use a definition of loyalty that was defined not in the heat of the Revolution, but by the range of loyal behavior that had been acceptable in more peaceable times."[77] Chipman's writings help to recover this broader range of loyal affections and sentiment.

Chipman's writings also portray how very anglicized the feelings and commitments of one New Englander had become, and offer insights into how British subjects in provincial spaces, far from the metropole, fashioned a sense of attachment to the empire. He used his commonplace book as a space for fashioning his political emotions, for making them his own. It is a document that speaks to his agency as a reader, and to the self-consciousness with which he selected, arranged, and considered the elements that constituted his political affections and identity. The prominence of chronologies, for example, illustrates how important historical culture was in the construction of Britishness. Historians have described how imperial officials used the calendar and festivals to shape such a historical consciousness, but on Chipman's handwritten pages, it is more apparent how active individual subjects were in internalizing and adapting such deeply felt historical narratives. Similarly, it has been well understood that print culture contributed significantly to feelings of national belonging, but it is illuminating to observe how an individual reader interacted with those texts to create a digest of their own feelings and convictions.

That Chipman's commonplace volume was created during the contested early months of 1776 only underlines the significance of his emotional self-fashioning. Rather than allowing himself to get caught up in the passions of that political moment, as many of his former American neighbours did, Chipman disciplined his emotions with history, putting the present in a longer narrative that he had internalized. Likewise, he transcribed selections from his reading to reinforce his loyal affections. He copied the "remarkable address" of the Grenadians to remind himself of the language of warm devotion, and perhaps to shore up his confidence in an expanding empire. He wrote extensive notes on Colden's *History* to reiterate the notion that affectionate friendship and the cultivation of sympathy were essential to the success of the British Empire. Such emotional virtues were not merely sentimental courtesies, superfluous to the hard realities of military might and bureaucratic organization; to the contrary, social affections bridged differences and distance. During a tumultuous period, Chipman reaffirmed his own political sentiments and reflected on the kinds of imperial emotions that he thought would be necessary for America to have a future in the British Empire.

Chipman's diary reflections dating from the 1790s, looking back on the wars Britain had fought during his lifetime, continued to express a complex set of political emotions. His laments about British policy reveal the extent to which he sympathized with the complaints of the American revolutionaries. Taken in isolation, his statements about the Stamp Act or the "arbitrary" measures of the British ministry could conceivably have spurred more fractious, even rebellious, passions. Instead, Chipman reaffirmed his British loyalty, choosing to fold his lament *into* his loyalty, adopting an aspirational hope for his nation's future.

Protestantism was an essential ingredient in Chipman's conception of Britishness, just as reading history and current events providentially was one of his most characteristic habits of mind. And yet his religious convictions were not generically Protestant but, rather, warmly evangelical – shaped by transatlantic movements of devotional piety and religious awakening. Just as his manuscripts reveal the fashioning of his British loyalism, so his writings show him attempting to cultivate religious affections that were warmly personal but not dangerously enthusiastic.

2

Textual Affections:
Handley Chipman and the Emotions of
Transatlantic Protestantism

In the final pages of his ledger, just below an inventory of the tools in the blacksmith's shop and next to a recipe for medicinal "black water," Handley Chipman jotted what could be described as field notes from the intersection of evangelical piety and Enlightenment epistemology:

> Mr. E.T. said that Mr. T. told him his own wife, Son in Law & daughter opposed his praying in the family & asking a blessing at table. Mr. T. told me, but Mr. Lockwood Saith to me the Story is false.

> These people pronounce people converted without knowledge.

> Julia Ann pronounced Mr. D's Daughter Lately Converted without any just grounds at all, as her father told me & So did M.B., I am told. The Girl & her father both told me that Julia Ann told her She might now Sing Yankey duddle as much as She pleased, as She was converted, with many other things to Same purport.[1]

Chipman recorded these notes circa 1792–93, when some members of the Cornwallis New Light Congregational Church (of which he was then a member) began to claim that sudden spiritual impressions gave them certainty about the conversion of various individuals in the community, including Mr D's young daughter. For "these people" – a distinctive emotional community within the New Light church – *feelings* seem to have replaced more traditional forms of spiritual assurance.

The report that Julia Ann told the young "convert" that she might sing "Yankey duddle as much as She pleased" seems, to modern readers, amusing and harmless enough. But this licence to sing such "worldly" songs was apparently in opposition to the strict morality of the church community, and, more importantly for observers like Chipman, the justification ("as much as She pleased, as She was converted") represented a troubling instance of antinomianism – the idea that the "elect" were no longer subject to external rules and order.

At about this time, Chipman filled a notebook with long essays outlining his concerns about relying on feelings and sudden impressions, and about the "Bodily Extasies" that New Light preachers were encouraging, to the detriment of congregational order. As a moderate evangelical who came of age during New England's Great Awakening, Chipman valued the religious affections and zeal in preaching, but as his ledger notes suggest, what constituted appropriate evangelical emotions was a contested question even within the Cornwallis New Light church.

This contretemps in Cornwallis was not merely an internecine local dispute. Nova Scotia New Lights were grappling with questions about emotions that preoccupied philosophers and theologians throughout the eighteenth century. For evidence that British North Americans were aware of these debates, one need only turn back one page in Chipman's ledger to the inventory of a shared local library. The catalogue is headed, "List of Book[s] in Mr. Graham's People and Some others' Library."[2] Listed are the titles and authors of 108 books, organized into sections on "divinity," "history civil & ecclesiastical," and "miscellanie." Among the volumes are several books on affections, passions, or sentiments. From Charles Chauncy's broadside against enthusiasm to Adam Smith's ethic of sympathy, the titles reflect the variety of eighteenth-century discourses about emotions. The library inventory, Chipman's ledger notes, and his other manuscript writings demonstrate that these transatlantic debates about emotions and sentiment were read and appropriated in local settings. Nova Scotians engaged these questions as they made sense of their own or their neighbours' religious affections, and as they contested the boundaries of local and transatlantic emotional communities.

Chipman's approach to these questions was to moderate the religious affections. On the one hand, he emphasized the experiential piety of the Great Awakening, was active in the New Light

community, and participated in an affectionate devotional and textual culture. On the other hand, Chipman emphasized interiority and
the management of the passions, and prioritized the long-term disposition of the heart over the ecstasy of the moment. He attempted
to kindle personal feeling without overwhelming the social affections, and to cultivate evangelical experience without slipping into
enthusiasm. It was an often-tenuous balancing act.

READING EMOTIONS IN A COLONIAL LIBRARY

The books catalogued in the back of Chipman's ledger reflect how
emotions were described, cultivated, feared, regulated, and debated
during the eighteenth century. The provenance of the library is
unfortunately not known with certainty, though it was in some
way associated with the members of the Cornwallis Congregational
Church ("Mr. Graham's people and some others"), and it suggests
there was a vigorous local culture of reading. Shortly after minister
Hugh Graham (1758–1829) arrived in the town in 1785, he admitted with some surprise in a letter to family in Scotland that he found
the congregation more intelligent and "more Enquiring about Points
in Religion" than he expected.[3] In time he would also find that it was
a place where religious ideas and emotions were contested.

The library featured many of the "steady sellers" of transatlantic
English Protestant devotional culture, from its Puritan roots through
the affectionate piety of early eighteenth-century English dissent to
the warm (and controversial) affections of the evangelical revivals.[4]
Puritan "heart religion" was well represented by Richard Baxter's
Saints Everlasting Rest (1650), in which readers were guided through
considerations of heaven (or other biblical themes) designed to affect
both heart and mind.[5] Baxter's address assumed that human happiness was primarily a heavenly goal, rather than an earthly reality.
This view was shared in other library volumes, including Étienne
François de Vernage's *The Happy Life, or The Contented Man*
(1706) and Matthew Henry's *The Pleasantness of a Religious Life*
(1714).[6] Yet these works also reflected changing expectations about
happiness in the era of the Enlightenment; alongside the hope of
heaven, orthodox writers increasingly emphasized the possibility of
this-worldly happiness and religious pleasures. Against stereotypes
of dour, passionless Puritans, Matthew Henry asserted, "They did
not *renounce* Pleasure, when they *embrac'd Religion*."[7]

There were also two influential guidebooks for raising the affec-
tions during the sacrament of the Lord's Supper: Matthew Henry's
The Communicant's Companion (1704) and John Willison's
Sacramental Meditations and Advices (1747).[8] In his diary, Chipman
reported using such guides to raise his own religious affections. In
1794, he wrote, "When reading in my family Mr. Henry on the
Institution of the Sacrement of the Lords Supper, and of dear Jesus'
Sufferings, I was So overwhelmed I could not contain myself as
I would, Strangers being present. O how burdened to my Soul did
Sin appear, and Sweet and Affecting my dear redeemer's undertaking for my redemption."[9] Having prepared himself by reading and
meditating, Chipman said, "In a heavenly frame did I go to meeting," and reported that he "very Sencibly pertook" of the sacrament
"in a Spiritual Manner to my Spiritual Nourishment." Chipman's
use of such devotional texts was not passive; he recorded his "Soul
Satisfying delight" in his diary, "pen[ning] here the Sweet and blessed
remembrance of it," essentially creating a new devotional text for
future recollection.[10]

The library also contained several prose works by English hymn-
writer and practical theologian Isaac Watts (1674–1748), including
*Discourses of the Love of God and the Use and Abuse of the Passions
in Religion ... to which is prefix'd A plain and particular Account
of the Natural Passions, with Rules for the Government of them*
(1729).[11] This influential pair of treatises differentiated between natural passions and religious affections, and provided directions for
the regulation of the emotions. Watts attempted to reconcile affections to reason. He was representative of the eighteenth-century
view (among both devotional and philosophical writers) that the
affections were a form of *knowledge* involving both mind and heart:

The Affections being once engaged, will keep the Soul fixed to
divine Things. The Sense of them is imprest deeper on the Mind,
by the Exercise of devout Passions, and it will abide there much
longer. Even where Reason is bright, and the Judgment clear, yet
it will be ineffectual for any valuable Purposes, if Religion reach
no further than the Head, and proceed not to the Heart:
It will have but little Influence, if there are none of the Affections
engaged. Notions of Religion in the Understanding, without any
Touch upon the Passions, have been compared to the Stars in a
Winter Midnight, bright and shining, but very cold.[12]

If Watts's *Discourses* represented something of a polite Protestant consensus on the passions, other volumes in the Cornwallis library demonstrated the contentious nature of emotional discourses, particularly in the wake of the Great Awakening. The catalogue lists Jonathan Edwards's *History of Redemption* (1739), his *Some Thoughts Concerning the Present Revival of Religion in New-England* (1742), and Charles Chauncy's *Seasonable Thoughts on the State of Religion in New England* (1743).[13] Edwards and Chauncy represented opposing perspectives in the intense debate about emotions during the Great Awakening. Edwards offered a moderate theological defence of the revivals and a philosophical framework for distinguishing "gracious" from merely "natural" affections. He admitted that there were emotional excesses during the Great Awakening, but did not on that account abandon the prominence of affections in the spiritual life: "Though there are false affections in religion, and affections that in some respects are raised high, that are flashy, yet undoubtedly there are also true, holy and solid affections; and the higher these are raised, the better."[14] It was a delicate balance to maintain.[15] Chauncy (1705–1787) opposed the revivals and their emotionalism as irrational "enthusiasm," and in *Seasonable Thoughts* catalogued the Great Awakening's most egregious excesses. Nevertheless, even Chauncy in his own way maintained the importance of well-managed affections rather than ignoring emotions altogether.[16]

Not all of the relevant titles in the Cornwallis library were theological in nature. Most notably, the library contained Adam Smith's *The Theory of Moral Sentiments* (1759), which one historian has described as "perhaps the most thorough work codifying the culture of sensibility."[17] Smith proposed that *sympathy* and other "social passions" could provide the basis for ethical, moral behaviour. (More will be said about Smith's philosophy in later chapters.)

The Nova Scotia readers of the Graham library, then, knew that emotions could be raised or regulated, classified or cultivated, meditated upon or fought over. But emotions could not be ignored. They knew that ideas about emotions changed over time, and that feelings prompted some of the most contentious debates of the eighteenth century. These were themes that had immediate bearing on their own lives in British North America – from the fashioning of their personal piety, to the ways that migration had strained their own affectionate ties, to the furor (in both politics and religion) caused by the power of feelings in the public sphere. And as the manuscript writings of Handley Chipman demonstrate, Nova Scotians were not merely passive readers: they were active participants in these transatlantic conversations, adapting those ideas and debates to local controversies.

TEXTUAL AFFECTIONS

Chipman produced a series of manuscript books, four of which are now extant, that are best described as self-made scripture commentaries. Just as his commonplace book revealed – by his selection, arrangement, and commenting – Chipman's political passions, so his self-made scripture commentaries and theological abridgements reflected his religious affections. Putting his pen to these pages, this Nova Scotian "authored his piety."[18]

As an act of devotional reading and study, Chipman transcribed, abridged, paraphrased, and commented upon several large works of theology. In one volume Chipman abridged printed commentary on the biblical books of Job and the Psalms, mostly by English Puritan Matthew Henry (1662–1714). Two other volumes summarized the "Contents of the Chapters of the Old Testament & Short Comments thereon," each page discussing a single chapter of the Bible (1 Samuel to Hosea, in the surviving volumes). Those books drew upon commentaries by several seventeenth- and eighteenth-century authors. A fourth book contains "Some Short Sketches of Metaphors, Parallels, &c, on Scriptural, Spiritual Matters," selecting material from books by Benjamin Keach (1640–1704) and John Brown (1722–1787). Chipman drew on lengthy scholarly discussions and multiple sources to write disciplined (if idiosyncratic) summaries that fitted onto one or two pages in a consistent, readable format. These were ambitious undertakings. The existing manuscripts, originally part of multi-volume series, together contain over one thousand pages and reflect a habit of extensive reading and study.[19]

The books were not the product of a passive copyist. Chipman created them as a devotional discipline for the purpose of cultivating religious affections. Just as his commonplace book reflected an engaged reader's agency in selecting, arranging, and commenting to shape his political emotions, so his theological volumes portray Chipman sifting and evaluating his sources, turning study into a heartfelt spiritual experience. The significant effort, and also the spiritual

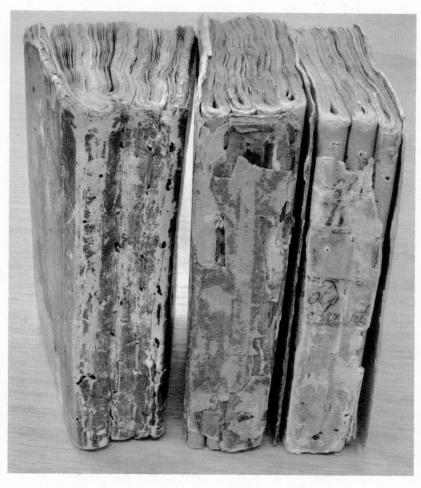

Figure 2.1 | Some of Handley Chipman's manuscript books, 1793 and 1797.

purpose, for these literary creations is evident in an editorial comment made in one of his volumes: "Thus I have got thro' with a great number of Metaphors respecting Saints and Parellels, &c ... short Sketches from Sound Divin[e]s of Several Denominations, as I first proposed, which, thanks to God, has, I trust, been a means of Some Spiritual Consolation to my Soul, which made the task, to me, instead of being a Burthen, very delightful and pleasant, altho' I have followed it

almost Steadily, every day and Evening, for above a week past."[20] The
devotional discipline of daily reading and writing afforded Chipman
"Spiritual Consolation." As one scholar of Puritanism notes, "The
reading and study of religious texts, though an intellectual activity, did
not primarily or finally have an intellectual end. The exercise of the
rational faculty opened the way to a changed heart."[21] For Chipman,
such rigorous study nourished the mind, but his purpose was also to
know scripture with the heart, to find it "delightful and pleasant."

Chipman's religious reading is best understood in the context of early modern transatlantic Protestant devotional culture.[22]
Protestantism encouraged individual believers to read the Bible
for themselves, and had a vigorous print culture to promote devotional reading and theological study. This devotional culture was
nicely expressed on the title page of one of the commentaries from
which Chipman copied, declaring that its reading was "of singular
Advantage to Persons of every Religion and Capacity; and design'd
to promote the Knowledge of the *Scriptures*, and the Practice of
sincere Piety and Virtue."[23] Chipman had one of the largest libraries
in the Planter townships, and had access to many of the most influential texts of Protestant piety, including works by Richard Baxter,
John Flavel, Isaac Watts, Philip Doddridge, and Matthew Henry.
Chipman also exhibited the *habits* of this devotional culture, particularly his focus on personal spiritual experience.

Transcribing texts, as Chipman did, was an intensive kind of reading practice.[24] For someone whose handwriting was as neat and
consistent as Chipman's, copying was a slow, deliberative process –
line by line, word by word, letter by letter. It was a practice uniquely
adaptable to spiritual meditation, ruminating on the sentiments of
the text. The *intensity* of reading – close, attentive, repeated reading
of a text – was one aspect of what historians have described as a
"traditional" reading strategy. Early modern readers employed this
kind of reading with devotional texts to internalize their message
and affect the heart.[25]

Chipman intended his studious transcriptions to lead beyond
the page; they were, as he described them, "Meditations and Soul
Contemplations."[26] He was heir to a long tradition of spiritual
reading, which remained an integral aspect of Puritan spirituality.[27] Reading a text was followed by meditation (ruminating on its
message) and then contemplation (prayerful communion with God).
Such reading was a form of "affective appropriation" – drawing the

meaning of a text into one's heart.[28] The books that Chipman transcribed often included instructions for this meditative practice. In his
exposition of the Psalms, for example, Matthew Henry often made
use of the phrase "In Singing this, and praying it over" as a way of
modelling how to meditatively internalize the scriptures. Chipman
included many of these moments of instruction in his notebooks.
Several of these direct how one's religious affections should be influenced by a particular passage of scripture:

> In Singing this, & praying it over we Should not only have our
> hearts filled with an holy awe of God, but borne up with a
> Chearful Confidence in Christ, in whose mediation we may
> comfort & Encourage our Selves, and one another.

> In Singing this, we Should git our hearts much affected with the
> Excellency of the word of God, & much affected with the Evil
> of Sin, the danger we are in of it, & by it, & fetch in help from
> Heaven against it.

> In Singing this we Should Meditate on the Sufferings &
> Resurrection of Christ, till we Experience on our own Souls the
> power of his resurrection & the fellowship of his Sufferings.[29]

Devotional guides such as Henry's often suggested that readers imag-
inatively identify with the circumstances of the biblical narrative.
Or they might urge readers to reflect on a particular aspect of the
salvation story, especially the suffering and resurrection of Christ, to
better apply those doctrines to their own experience: "meditate …
till we Experience on our own Souls," till "our hearts [are] filled"
and "our hearts [are] much affected."

Chipman adopted another striking form of heart-felt meditation
in his manuscript books on the Old Testament. At the bottom of
each page is a two-line prayer of Chipman's composition, beginning with the words, "O my Soul."[30] Consider for a moment the
sheer number of these homespun invocations: several hundred of
them in just two of a longer series of such books. The phrase "O
my Soul" signals the application of the text to the most personal,
interior aspect of his being. The daily repetition of that phrase indicates the cultivation of a habit, developing a reflexive pattern of
thinking and meditation.

Some of the "O my Soul" prayers directly addressed reading and meditation as a spiritual practice. Chipman emphasized the application or "improvement" of scripture, as well as intellectual knowledge: "O my Soul, may every observation of Scripture truth be Suitably improved by us for our real Benifit."[31] Reading and meditation could also remedy the problem of the *unfeeling* heart, and rouse one's religious affections: "O my Soul, how often, to our Sorrow, do we find our Heart dull & Lifeless. When we read these holy transports, O quicken, quicken us, by thy Spirit, O our God."[32] Of course even the most devout reader could encounter scriptural passages or commentary that seemed to lack spiritual relevance. After encountering such a dry discussion, Chipman prayed matter-of-factly, "O my Soul, blessed be God, this is not very material. O that we may Love God."[33] Even this humorous moment of candour suggests that he was constantly seeking in his reading those themes that were most "material" to heartfelt piety.

Chipman's prayers were often meditations on specific religious emotions. He prayed for a greater capacity for love and gratitude toward God: "O my Soul, may we be always Suitably Affected with God's Goodness & wonderful Providences to his Church & People, and Seek to Love him more & better."[34] He also drew on the language of habitual disposition to emphasize the long-term cultivation of particular emotional responses, rather than only the ecstasy of the moment: "O my Soul, may I always be of a Merciful disposition, and always make it as our Steady rule, to do as we would be done unto, Amen."[35] But not just any emotions would do, so he prayed to know the difference between authentic and affected religious emotions: "O my Soul, Let us not be deceived by specious pretences and Shews in Religion. But may we Enjoy true Vital Religion in our Heart. Amen."[36] Chipman's rigorously disciplined habit was to abridge and paraphrase long scholarly discussions into the space of a single page, attentive to how the text in question addressed experiential piety, and then to write a prayer that meditatively applied that reading to his own heart and soul.

Textual meditations occasionally led to "Soul Contemplations" – to a spiritual experience *beyond* the page. On one occasion, while meditating on his heavenly hope, he breathlessly recorded in his diary, "my Soul Exult[s] in Some measure while I am thus praying and writing."[37] At another time, while describing how God sometimes granted believers a sense of assurance of their salvation, he wrote that God was "*at this very time* So doing to my Soul."[38] He continued in a direct, stream-of-consciousness address to God, writing, "[I] have now at this very time Sweet Communion with thee." And again, "O dear father, I bless thee that thou art indulging me with free communion with thee, and for what I have and do enjoy at this Sweet Moment." Some hours later, when he resumed his writing, he reflected on the spiritual pleasure he enjoyed when meditative writing became contemplation: "O I thank thee, I thank thee holy father for that Glow of Sweet Comfort and Communion I have had this forenoon with thee, which has taken me off from the historical Course of my writing, to close Communion and prayer to and with thee."[39]

Chipman's self-made scripture commentaries demonstrate the centrality of the heart in the devotional culture of transatlantic Protestantism. Readers in Dissenting England, Puritan New England, or in Chipman's Nova Scotia read many of the same devotional texts and adopted many of the same reading habits. In some ways, Chipman was a mediating figure in this culture: not himself a biblical scholar, but instead a student and popularizer of that literature, creating a new devotional text for others. As he demonstrated in his own meditative, contemplative practice, such reading was meant to enable the enjoyment of "true Vital Religion in our Heart."[40]

"CLOSE AND VERY SOUL SEARCHING": EARLY EVANGELICALS AND THE HEART

Chipman's moderate, affectionate evangelical piety was also shaped through personal connections. In his family memoir, he traced a "genealogy of piety," highlighting family associations with religious leaders of Puritan New England and in the emerging evangelical movement.[41] In his family memoir, he traced arms-length connections to prominent Puritan leaders such as Increase and Cotton Mather.[42] He mentioned his father's tenure as an agent of the Society for the Propagation of the Gospel (SPG) and his mother's membership at the Boston church of Benjamin Colman (1673–1747). And he wrote about his wife's grandfather, the Congregational minister and author William Homes.[43]

During his years in Newport, Rhode Island, before moving to Nova Scotia, Chipman knew George Whitefield and Sarah Osborn, significant figures in the story of Anglo-American evangelicalism.

Only a few details of these Newport acquaintances are now documented, but Chipman clearly expressed his affinity for the approach
to the affections that Whitefield and Osborn promoted, and did so
at a time when these were contested ideas. Chipman's Newport connections, like his reading in Protestant devotional culture, helped to
frame his experience of Henry Alline's revivalism and the controversies in the Nova Scotia New Light community.[44]

Chipman attempted to combine Puritan orthodoxy with experiential piety that spoke to the heart. This theme emerged as he discussed
the preaching of William Homes (1663–1746), a Congregational
minister and author in his family tree. Homes, he wrote, had a
reputation as being "very Sound in principles and Authodox," and
"Remarcably Grave in his publick devotion."[45] His sermons, which
Chipman suggested were probably somewhat plodding, were, however, not without some evidence of "heart religion."[46] In one of his
printed addresses, Homes said that "It is the Heart that God chiefly
regards in our religious Performances," and that in duties such as
family prayer, what matters most is that "our Hearts be rightly
affected towards [God]." Elsewhere he suggested that spiritual reading was meant not only to prepare people for heaven but also "for
the Immediate Enjoyment of God."[47]

Yet Chipman felt that the traditional Puritan sermon style damp-
ened rather than kindled the affections of hearers. Homes's practice
in preaching was "first, to speak something Large on the purport of
his Text, then to raise a Number of Docterrinul heads, ... then, dev-
ide them also into many parts or heads, So that the greater part of
the time by far was taken up in Explanation of Said Doctrinal heads.
then the application or improvement of the Sermon ... would ... be
very Short." Chipman, on the other hand, preferred a different style
of preaching: "Short and Comprehensive discourses ... Large on the
application or Improvement." Emphasizing the religious affections,
he argued that "Such Comprehensive preaching is most Eddifying
and profitable to the Soul, Especially when the Application is Close
and very Soul Searching."[48] Chipman did not have any quarrel with
Homes's Puritan doctrine, but he did advocate a more direct and
confident address to the heart.[49]

Chipman found such a direct address to the heart in the preach-
ing of the Great Awakening's "Grand Itinerant," George Whitefield:
"I much admire the Close Soul Searching Comprehensive way and
Method of Preaching that much famed, pious Minister of the blessed

Gospel of Jesus Christ, the Rev'd Mr. George Whitefield had, whom I was well acquainted with."⁵⁰ The full extent of Chipman's acquaintance with Whitefield is unknown, though it is likely that he first heard Whitefield during his September 1740 visit to Newport.⁵¹ Whitefield preached several times to large audiences, and he recorded in his journal that he was "enabled to ... preach with much Flame, Clearness and Power."⁵² Whitefield was warmly received by the minister and hearers at First Congregational Church, where the Chipmans were members.⁵³ On one day, Whitefield "went to venerable Mr. [Nathaniel] Clap's, and exhorted and prayed with a great Multitude, who not only crowded into the House, but thronged every Way about it."⁵⁴ Chipman perhaps met the evangelist for the first time at this gathering at his minister's house.

One historian has suggested that the marked difference between Puritan preaching, which, to be sure, did make intentional addresses to the affections, and the preaching of Whitefield was that he "spoke simply and overwhelmingly to the passions of the heart." Informed by his early love of the stage, Whitefield's sermons fused "Tears, passions, and consolation ... to produce a new and powerful form of preaching."⁵⁵ Whitefield used his actor's sensibility to speak *with* passion and *to* the heart-felt imagination of his hearers. In the weeks after Whitefield left Newport, he visited the Connecticut River Valley, where Sarah Edwards (wife of Jonathan Edwards) heard him preach. Her assessment captures the features that seemed to draw Chipman to him:

> He makes less of the doctrines than our American preachers generally do, and aims more at affecting the heart. He is a born orator ... It is wonderful to see what a spell he casts over an audience by proclaiming the simplest truths of the Bible. I have seen upwards of a thousand people hang on his words with breathless silence, broken only occasionally by a half-suppressed sob ... A prejudiced person, I know, might say that this is all theatrical artifice and display; but not so will any one who has seen and known him ... He speaks from a heart all aglow with love, and pours out a torrent of eloquence which is almost irresistible.⁵⁶

It might be said that Whitefield used the *passions* (feeling responses of the moment) as a way of shaping the *affections* (the longer-term disposition of the heart). For Chipman, the New England encounters with Whitefield's "Close Soul Searching Comprehensive way and Method of Preaching" would shape, in part, his own evangelical piety as well as the way in which he interpreted the message of Henry Alline and Nova Scotia New Lights.

Handley and Jane Chipman were also drawn into the orbit of evangelical teacher and author Sarah Osborn (1714–1796). Osborn, who operated a boarding school in Newport, Rhode Island, attended the same Congregational church as the Chipmans. She experienced an evangelical conversion through the Newport visits of Whitefield and fellow itinerant Gilbert Tennent (1703–1764) and became a regular correspondent of many of the leading Protestant ministers of her generation. A recent biography of Osborn has recovered an awareness of how prominent she and other women were in the evangelical movement and in the American Enlightenment.[57] Fittingly, Jane Chipman was a member of the women's religious society that met in Osborn's home at least once each week to read scripture and other devotional books, and for religious conversation and prayer.[58]

During the time that Jane Chipman was a part of this religious society, Osborn published *The Nature, Certainty and Evidence of True Christianity* (1755).[59] Framed as a letter, the book was written in response to a friend's doubts about spiritual assurance: How could a person have confidence in their salvation? How could one *know* and not doubt? Osborn answered, "By the *Evidences* of a *Work of Grace* wrought in [the] Soul."[60] Though a deeply existential question for individuals, this was also an important epistemological problem in the Enlightenment.

Osborn's emphasis on "certainty" and "evidence" bridged religious experience and Lockean empiricism; her stress on the *affections* resonated with Enlightenment moral philosophy.[61] As eighteenth-century observers, under the influence of Enlightenment rationalism, became more confident in a rational, ordered universe, they looked to *experience* and information from the senses (not authorities or tradition) as the bases of knowledge about that universe. Religious experience, including one's own feelings, was a form of evidence, just like other natural phenomena. As historian Sarah Rivett explains, "The status of the soul became increasingly intelligible through the display of human affections, as emergent currents of moral philosophy transformed understanding of the human faculties."[62] Passions provided empirical information about the soul.

To be sure, Enlightenment philosophy was not the only source for such experiential, feeling language. Evangelicals also drew from a rich vein of Puritan affective piety. Yet the dovetailing of Enlightenment empiricism and religious experience gave evangelicals a greater sense of certainty, of assurance.[63] So in answer to the question, "How do I *know* this God is mine, and that I am not deceived?" Osborn turned to her own religious experience for such assurance: "I'll tell you truly what God has done for my Soul, and what I call *Evidence of a Work of Grace.*"[64]

The evidence that Osborn sought in her soul? Affections. Osborn explained that she had once been indifferent or even hostile to many evangelical doctrines – the existence of God, the mediation of Christ, the hope of heaven. Now, however, she *felt* differently, and those new feelings witnessed to an inner, spiritual change. She described her religious affections in the language of desire: "Yea, God caus'd my Heart to go out after Him in strong and vehement Desires ... He appear'd to me to be in Himself the most lovely and desirable Object." She pointed to the "ardent Longings, and Pantings, which [God] at sometimes excites in my Soul."[65] Note that Osborn credited God with causing and exciting these new sentiments. Like Jonathan Edwards (and unlike the optimism of Enlightenment philosophers), she believed that God furnished a new "sense of the heart," supplying by grace what nature could not.[66]

Osborn suggested that the most reliable emotional evidence was observable over the long term, and not only in moments of ecstasy: "And tho' Grace is not always alike in Exercise; (no I am sometimes dull and lifeless as to Exercise) yet blessed be God it has been the habitual and settled Bent of my Soul for many Years, to choose God, his Christ, and *Grace* for my Portion in all Conditions, both adverse and prosperous."[67] For Osborn, the religious affections that mattered most were not those that impulsively flashed and just as quickly burned out. Instead, she (and most moderate evangelicals, like Chipman) valued those that had been internalized enough to be, in the language of theorist Pierre Bourdieu, a *habitus* even in changing circumstances – or, in Osborn's own words, "the habitual and settled Bent of my Soul."[68] Alongside this basic disposition of the heart, Osborn also spelled out a number of specific affections or habituated emotions that she considered "evidences of Grace": "That you do hate *Sin* as Sin; that you do love *Holiness* for its own sake, and God because an holy God; that you love his Law, and long perfectly to obey; that you do prize Christ as a King, as well as *Saviour*; that you do love *his Image* in *his Children*; that you do love *your Enemies*; and are wean'd from *this World*, and all its trifling Enjoyments; that you are reaching after *greater Degrees of sanctifying Grace*."[69] It was an ambitious plan of emotional formation. Osborn, however, expected a *gradual* change of feelings; sincere *aspiration* ("that you ... *long* perfectly to obey"), and not only the achievement of emotional maturity, could provide assurance of an inward change.

Feelings, of course, were a subjective measure. But Osborn attempted to ground her assurance in the empirical observation of specific experiences and particular emotional responses. She contrasted this method with "enthusiasm," which based certainty on special revelations and sudden impulses. She explained, "*These*, my dear Friend, are what I call *Evidences of a Work of Grace*: and for my part I had rather be able to read them, than to hear a Voice from Heaven telling me, *I am a Child of God*."[70] Despite the alluring certainty that such a mystical experience might promise, Osborn preferred to "read" the more observable evidence of new and changed affections. Like Chipman, Osborn and other moderate evangelicals drew upon Enlightenment modes of thinking rather than "enthusiastic" impulses as they shaped an affectionate and experiential evangelical piety.

"PIOUS AND GODLY MR. HENRY ALLIN"

Among Chipman's "wrote books," in his distinctive handwriting, is a transcription of the journal of Nova Scotia evangelist Henry Alline (1748–1784). The New Light itinerant, about whom much more will be said in subsequent chapters, sparked religious awakenings throughout the colony's young settlements during the period of the American Revolution. Critics of the charismatic Alline and his followers charged them with enthusiasm and unthinking emotionalism, with heterodox theological views, and with sowing separatism among the region's tentatively transplanted Congregational churches. Yet to Chipman, he was "Pious and Godly Mr. Henry Allin[e]."[71] Chipman transcribed and apparently circulated Alline's journal, which had originally been written in shorthand, helping to shape Nova Scotia New Lights into a coherent emotional community in the two decades before the journal was eventually published in Boston.[72] Given Chipman's personal religious history and his textual participation in the culture of transatlantic evangelicalism, his warm support of Alline helps to locate the itinerant in wider contexts. Some contemporaries (and historians following them) described Alline as the "Whitefield of Nova Scotia."[73] For Chipman, this was more than an honorific, he having known both itinerants, and at least once in his journal he cited the words of Whitefield and Alline together as twinned examples of assured evangelical piety.[74]

In 1777, Chipman wrote a letter to two Nova Scotia ministers to defend Alline's ministry and to explain some of the turmoil in the Cornwallis Congregational Church. Though much of the letter expressed Chipman's concern for order in church government, he was unequivocal in his support of Alline: "I have heard him, and am acquainted with him, [and] I must acknowledge I like him much ... and this I am sure I never saw so many sin sick souls since I liv'd here as there now is, and some near and dear to me, and that caus'd, I certainly see, by God's blessing on Mr. Allen's preaching."[75] The reference to "sin sick souls" pointed to the "awakening" effect of Alline's ministry on the town – that many previously indifferent individuals had become spiritually concerned and were starting to seek conversion. Chipman had no difficulty whatsoever communicating disapproval of individuals with whom he differed, but of Alline he wrote, "I like him much." Chipman's continued commitment to orthodox Puritan theology and Congregational order suggests that he heard Alline's preaching as consonant with that tradition, though certainly in its more affective stream.

Chipman's opinion of Alline seems to have been shared by his Nova Scotia contemporary, Liverpool merchant and diarist Simeon Perkins (1735–1812). Like Chipman, Perkins was a moderately evangelical Congregationalist. A significant leader in the Liverpool Congregational Church, he later embraced Methodism. Perkins heard Alline preach on many occasions during his Liverpool itinerancy, from 1781 to 1783, and declared that he was "much pleased with his performances."[76] In February 1783, Perkins recorded in his diary, "Mr. Alline Preached both parts of the day & Evening. A Number of People made a Relation of their Experiences after the Meeting was concluded & Expressed Great Joy & Comfort in what god had done for them. Mr. Alline made a long Speech, Very Sensible, Advising all Sorts of People to a Religious Life, & gave many directions for their outward walk. This is a wonderfull day & Evening. Never did I behold Such an Appearance of the Spirit of God moving upon the people Since the time of the Great Religious Stir in New England many years ago."[77] Perkins's comments mention the "Very Sensible" nature of Alline's preaching, and the effect of that preaching in encouraging people to give "a Relation of their Experience" to the church. By drawing a comparison between Alline's ministry and the "Great Religious Stir in New England" – surely the Great Awakening of the 1740s – he, like Chipman, located Alline within the evangelical tradition.[78] It is, of course, possible that Chipman and Perkins overlooked or were unaware of aspects of Alline's written or preached message that may have changed their views, but the approbation of these two well-read laypeople suggests that his New Light message fell within an acceptable range of evangelical Protestant teaching.

Chipman's warm devotion to Alline is all the more intriguing given the stridency of his opposition to the enthusiasm that emerged in the New Light movement in the early 1790s. If Chipman thought that Alline's experiential piety managed to avoid the extremes of enthusiasm and formalism, events in the Cornwallis New Light church over the next decade proved how tenuous such a balance could be.

AFFECTIONS AND "EXTASIES": DEBATING EMOTIONS IN NOVA SCOTIA

When it came to the regulation of the passions, or the pursuit of happiness, or the experience of religious ecstasies, Nova Scotians, like others in the early modern world, had to define the style and boundaries of their own emotional communities. Certainly, they drew upon the discourses and ideas that they read in volumes such as those found in the Graham library, and adapted them to their local circumstances. They also made their own contributions. In January 1793, Chipman wrote and circulated three long essays (bound together in a volume comprising 460 handwritten pages), two of which were intended to try to bring the New Lights back from the brink of enthusiasm. Those essays show that there were deep divisions in the community about the embodiment and sociality of religious emotions, and about affections and assurance.[79] Chipman's handwritten essays not only reveal the specifics of a local religious controversy; they also demonstrate how Nova Scotians grappled with some of the most vexing questions about emotions being discussed throughout the Enlightenment and evangelical Atlantic world.

The division in Chipman's Cornwallis-Horton New Light community became apparent in May 1790, when Lydia Randall rose
in a church meeting to declare herself "against all the orders of
the Church, and that they were but outward forms and Contrary
to the Spirit of God."[80] When minister John Payzant (1749–1834)
talked with Randall after the meeting, she told him that "she had
seen by the Spirit of God, that Baptism and the Lord Supper, with
all the Discipl[in]es, of the Church, was contrary to the Spirit of
God and his Gospel, and that Marriage was from the Divel." These
views spread locally, and in August 1791, several members and
adherents of the New Light church also expressed their opposition
to sacraments and church government, "Declaring them to [be] of
no use to them in these Days."[81] Such exterior forms, they said, were
"none-assenual [non-essential]" since true religion was an exchange
between the Spirit of God and the soul.[82]

The group believed that they had received a "new dispensation"
of divine teaching by the Spirit of God, that they "had great discoveries beyond what ever was known before." In short, Payzant
wrote, "They were very Zealous in it."[83] On the one hand, the "new
dispensationers" could be seen as an expression of evangelical individualism. On the other hand, however, more moderate evangelicals
(like Chipman and Payzant) pointed to the group's claims to new
revelations and discoveries as typical of enthusiasm. Hugh Graham,
minister of the Congregational church, similarly described the
enthusiastic disorder among the New Lights: "Without prejudice it
may be said ... that being unenlightened by knowledge, and united
by delusion, animated by party spirit and carried away by religious
zeal, they seem to vie with each other in the wildness and absurdity
of their opinions and practices and they seem to breathe fire and
vengeance against each other and against everybody else."[84]

The differing emotional communities in the church literally lined
up on opposite sides of the meetinghouse during a June 1792 conference. Another debate on that occasion dissolved into "confusion and
clamour," the members physically sorting themselves according to
their opposing views: "those who were resolved to walk together in
the Ordinances of the Gospel as usual declared their minds by divid-
ing to a particular part of the house."[85] For several more months,
the "new dispensation" preoccupied the congregation before many
of the participants turned from its excesses. Chipman subsequently
worked out his reactions and understanding of these debates and

divisions in his essays. In them, he addressed specific emotional aspects of this rift, exploring the physical and social implications of particular religious affections.

"Bodily Extasies"

In his first essay, "Some observations on the Sad Practice of Some of our New Light Preachers and Exhorters," Chipman focused on the "Distortions of [the] bodies" of New Light preachers in the pulpit, and on the "Distorted Conduct" of many members of the New Light community.[86] The disordered emotions these itinerant preachers bodily expressed, Chipman worried, threatened to sow disorder in the church, the "body of Christ." And yet Chipman was not advocating unfelt preaching or an unaffected congregation. Though certainly written as an intervention in this very local dispute, the essay drew upon wider debates about the corporeal and corporate dimensions of religious emotions.

Divided into two parts, Chipman's essay began with "Some observations on the Sad Practice of Some of our New Light Preachers and Exhorters, in their Distortions of their bodies while they are Praying, Preaching, Exhorting, &c, by their wringing and twisting their Bodies to a Strange Degree."[87] Although John Payzant was the ordained minister of the Horton-Cornwallis New Light Church, several young men served as itinerant preachers or lay exhorters throughout the region. It was what Chipman perceived as the "Distortions, Adgitations, and Gestures of Body" among these preachers that occasioned his polemic, singling out the actions of several preachers as particularly egregious.[88] "Mr. Joseph Dimock, who I have Seen So wring and twist his Body in Preaching, &c, that when Meeting was done, he has wiped the Sweat off of his face, and then wrung his handkerchief, which has run in a Manner in a Stream, and I verily believed he had not a dry thread in his Shirt." Brothers Edward and James Manning, Chipman reported, had "odd Postures of Body" and Edward Manning "used frequently to make such a Noise [in his throat] in his Preaching and Praying that perhaps not half his Sentences could be understood, but he Seemes to be got over it in Some Measure."[89]

Chipman marshalled several overlapping arguments against these energetic gestures during preaching. He thought that this kind of animated preaching posed a danger to physical health, claiming that

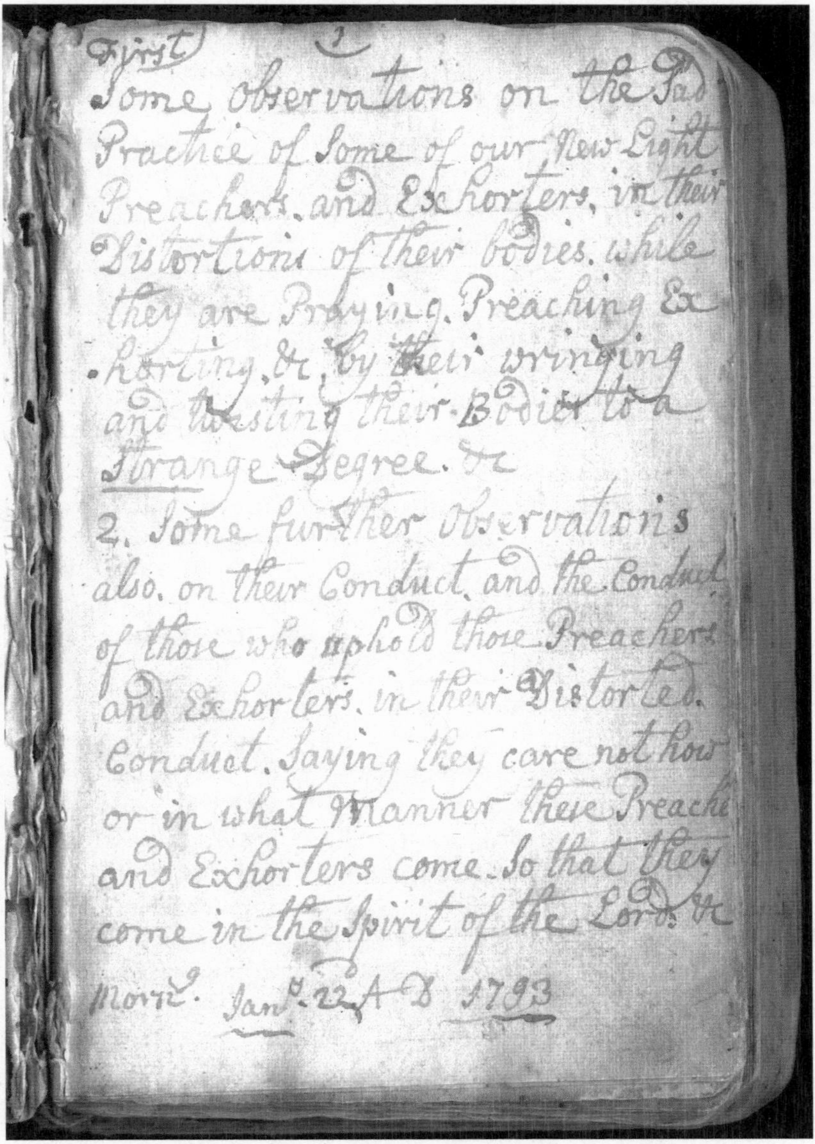

First

Some observations on the Sad Practice of Some of our New Light Preachers. and Exhorters. in their Distortions of their bodies. while they are Praying. Preaching & horting. &c by their wringing and twisting their Bodies to a Strange Degree. &c

2. Some further observations also. on their Conduct. and the Conduct of those who uphold those Preachers and Exhorters. in their Distorted. Conduct. Saying they care not how or in what manner these Preachers and Exhorters come. So that they come in the Spirit of the Lord. &c

Morris. Jan'ry 22 A D 1793

Figure 2.2 | Handley Chipman, Essays, 1793.

"Such Distortions of Body is Exceeding Spending to Nature, weakening and destroying the Constitution fast."[90] He cited examples of sweaty preachers going into the cold air and developing a fever, and he mentioned instances of overstraining the voice and lungs.[91] At worst, a preacher of this sort might "endanger his Life."[92] Chipman also suggested that there was a link between unwise physical exertion and unstable mental health, that these excesses could render a preacher a "weakley, Crazey Person."[93] The association between religious enthusiasm and madness was a familiar one in the early modern era. Charles Inglis described enthusiasm, for instance, as "the reveries of a disordered head, or heated imagination" and cited the example of Halifax Methodists slipping into "insanity" and becoming "maniac." Defining enthusiasm as a symptom of overheated passions provided a physical, rather than authentically spiritual, explanation.[94]

Ecstatic preaching drew a range of responses from New Light hearers. Some could not take their eyes from a style of preaching that differed from so many staid pulpit oratories; they were simply "revitted" by the spectacle.[95] Others were distracted and unsettled by this mode of preaching: "They have been forced to turn their Eyes from the Preacher or Exhorter, that they might hear the Person but not See his Bodily Extasies, which so discomposed them."[96] Like Chipman, this class of hearer was in the "discomposing" situation of being sympathetic to the *matter* of New Light preaching, but finding its *manner* painfully off-putting.

If not "Bodily Extasies," then what? What, according to Chipman, was the proper place of the affections in preaching? Despite his reservations about some bodily manifestations of intense religious feeling, Chipman agreed that "the work of the Lord ought to be done with great Vigour."[97] Deep feeling was absolutely necessary. He insisted, "I would by No Means be thought that I would uphold and approve of ... Ministers or Exhorters having no Life nor Activity of Body in his Preaching. No by no means."[98] Referring likewise to a minister's leadership of the "Publick Exercises" of worship, he declared, "I Love to See a Man or Minister Earnest and very Zealous in the Publick Divine Service."[99] Not just any zealous display would do, however. It should be "an Earnestness and Zeal *according to knowledge*."[100] While some preaching styles distracted from – or even supplanted – the content of the message, Chipman valued affections that arose out of particular gospel doctrines: "But

Especially I delight and Joy to See the Speaker inwardly Affected with the pious Matter of Divine truth or Truths he is Delivering, that So it may be discoverable what is delivered comes from the Heart. Such-like Preaching and Exhorting appears to me Most Likely to go to the Heart." In contrast to the New Light preachers whose words could not be understood, and whose gestures distracted from their message, Chipman emphasized the connection between the mind's understanding of religious knowledge and the heart's affective inclination toward that teaching. Chipman asserted, "O it is very Evident that Scripture Truths plainly, fully, and intelligibly taught, yea Taught, has a wonderful aptness or influence for to Awaken and rouse the Conscience and Enter the heart." [101]

While the New Light preachers exhibited their religious emotions through dramatic physical displays, Chipman emphasized *interiority*: "inwardly Affected," and coming from "the Heart." Chipman emphasized the depth, authenticity, and reasonableness of feelings more than their bodily expression. In the words of one of his favourite authors, Matthew Henry, the pleasure of religion "may *at second hand* affect the Body ... but its Residence is in the hidden Man of the Heart." [102] Yet, Chipman's language of interiority obscured the reality that emotions are embodied. As Monique Scheer observes, "attending to 'inner' experience is a practice, it is also always embodied, dependent on brain cells, bodily postures, and the disciplining or habituating of these." [103] The exuberant preachers actively demonstrated their feelings while Chipman actively restrained his. *Both* approaches were embodied (though in different ways), and both emotional styles were a "publick Performance" of one kind or another. [104]

The second part of Chipman's manuscript essay moved from the embodied expression of emotions to the place of affections in the "body" of the church. [105] Even if feelings were located in the heart, they still had social contexts and public implications. In this section, Chipman intended "to make Some observations on the Conduct of those who Manifest great Satisfaction in the conduct and practice of those Preachers and Exhorters before mentioned in their Distortions, Agitations, and Gestures of Body in their Publick Performance in Divine Service, Saying they care not how they come, So they come in the Spirit of the Lord." [106] In other words, he rejected the claim that the public performance of emotion was a matter of indifference. He argued that it mattered a great deal "how they come."

Some pulpit displays of religious feeling were simply unsociable. Chipman apparently did not doubt the authenticity of the religious experiences of preachers like Dimock or the Manning brothers; he seemed willing to concede that their ecstatic affections had spiritual value. Nevertheless, in the social setting of public worship, uninhibited or unintelligible displays of emotion ignored the fact that feelings also had a corporate aspect. Chipman drew on the New Testament book of 1 Corinthians to argue that individual experience (however sincere) needed to be balanced with a concern to build up the whole body of the church. The principle was simply "that their friends might be Eddified as well as themselves."[107] Chipman's worries about "distortions" in the body of Christ at Cornwallis presented in microcosm the broader question implicit in the title of *Enthusiasms and Loyalties*: did the focus on private religious experience and judgment undermine or edify society? Were some religious passions *too* unsociable? Chipman urged New Lights to moderate their religious affections. He attempted to fashion an emotional community that cultivated personal religious experience *and* the social affections. "As the Christian Religion is in itself a Sober and reasonable thing, It Should not by the Ministers of it, be made to Look wild, Unintelligible or Senseless."[108]

"Infallible knowledge in thus knowing a real Christian"

What can – and cannot – be known from emotions? In a second manuscript essay, "A Discourse concerning The Resurrection of the Body of Mankind, ... also Sundry Matters about Errors in our Church here, called New Lights," Chipman addressed what he felt were several "Gross, Scandilous Errors" in the New Light church's teaching and practice. These erroneous views were being "hugged and spread abroad to an Amazing degree, and to the great prejudice and hurt of the Growth of Vital Piety among us here in this Town." Chipman wrote that some of the local New Lights were claiming that they had received "Infallible knowledge in thus knowing a real Christian." The basis for this certainty was "an Inward Impulse of their minds."[109] Chipman attempted to discredit such "enthusiastic" claims as a form of reliable knowledge, even as he insisted that *other* kinds of affections carried weight as rational evidence.

Membership in the New Light church was premised on evidence from the heart. Like other Congregational churches, the "covenant and articles" of the Horton-Cornwallis New Light Church expected members to give "satisfying Evidence of a work of grace In their Hearts whereby they are united to Jesus Christ."[110] Yet in this case, individuals were claiming to have certainty about a work of grace in the hearts *of others*, and were relying on their own emotions and special impressions as evidence.

Some of their choices appeared surprising. Chipman reported that such declarations were made to some who "never made the least pretentions to their being converted."[111] Even more unexpectedly, the New Lights "on a Sudding [sudden], Set their Eyes on Young Children, and told the Parents that Such and Such a Young Child would Infallibly Reign with them in Glory" – even when the parents denied the children had displayed any strong religious leanings.[112] These confident assertions were made on the basis of "neither the Relation of the Persons' Experience told [to] them, nor any tokens of Grace by their Life and Conversation," but on the basis of sudden, inward impressions.[113] This emphasis on immediate, esoteric knowledge finally led Chipman to label the New Lights' beliefs "wild Enthusiastic principles."[114]

And yet Chipman was not prepared to give up on the possibility of spiritual assurance. Although he vehemently opposed claims of "infallible knowledge," this section of his essay was replete with the vocabulary of evidence, knowledge, and certainty. As discussed above, assurance was one of the distinctive features of eighteenth-century evangelical Protestantism: Enlightenment empiricism meeting experiential piety. Assurance had also been an important theme in Puritan spiritual writing, but often by its notable absence, compared with the confidence of evangelicalism. Under the influence of teaching by the likes of Whitefield and Alline, for the heirs of the evangelical awakenings a degree of certainty about one's own spiritual state was usually an expectation rather than an exception. Chipman recalled remarks that these evangelical preachers had made in his hearing: "I once heard Mr. Whitefield Say, he had not had [doubts] for years, but added, but God alone only knows how Soon I may. And I have heard our dear Mr. Henry Allen [Alline] often Say the Same, with great thankfulness."[115]

Chipman also employed a biblical image, now obscure, of spiritual assurance – a "white stone of converting grace." The metaphor was drawn from Revelation 2:17, where it is written that Christ will give true believers "a white stone, and in the stone a new name written, which no man knoweth saving he that receiveth it." When such a "Certain assurance" is given, Chipman wrote, "they Seldom Scruple it or have even a doubt of it."[116] Both Whitefield and Alline used this metaphor in their preaching. Whitefield, for example, interpreted it to mean that a true believer exhibits characteristics such as joy, peace, long-suffering, and meekness. He said, "As for my own part, I had rather see these divine graces and this heavenly temper stamped upon my soul, than to hear an angel from heaven saying unto me, Son, be of good cheer, thy sins are forgiven thee."[117] The "white stone" was a changed heart rather than a sudden impulse. In other words, while he *did* believe a person could receive certain knowledge about their soul, he located the grounds for such confidence in a *transformation* of the affections rather than the kind of special heavenly revelation that the Cornwallis "new dispensationers" were claiming.

Chipman's essays appear to have been written in the months after the most explosive confrontations, though by then his own membership in the New Light community was in doubt. Chipman and his minister, Payzant, adopted very different strategies for negotiating the inflamed passions and animosities in the church. Payzant urged tenderness and thought that there was "no other way, but, let them get some expereance in their new scheme, which would convince them or some of them, the danger of it."[118] Payzant thought Chipman made the situation worse. He described Chipman as standing "so much against them that he drove [them] as far on the other hand," his lack of patience giving even greater strength to the group's "Schismatical notions."[119] By 1793, Chipman had requested his dismissal from the church, but he hoped that these essays would clarify the theological and emotional issues and perhaps persuade the church to return to a more moderate evangelical sensibility. He did so, however, from the periphery of the emotional community he had helped to form.

CONCLUSION

In Chipman's will, written months before his death in 1799, he directed, "All my Books printed and wrote I would have carefully preserved and kept in a Library for the families to read ... A list of them will be found among my wrote books in a little book by itself with a brown cover, being 25 pages."[120] Chipman's record of reading suggests that he and other Nova Scotians were active participants in early modern transatlantic print culture, including Protestant devotional culture and the eighteenth century's vigorous debates about passions, affections, and sentiment. His many "wrote books" are evidence that these transatlantic conversations were also local concerns, as Nova Scotians attempted to make sense of their experiences and reconfigure the boundaries of religious and emotional communities.

His will also created an endowment of fifty pounds to be equally divided among the township's Congregational, Anglican, and New Light churches, for the purpose of creating an annual memorial sermon; it was to be preached on consecutive days in the respective churches, from 31 August to 2 September. Most importantly, Chipman directed that the annual sermon be preached "in a very Soul Searching Scriptural manner," on a very specific theme: "against Quenching the Motions & strivings of the Holy Spirit of God, and the checks of Conscience (God's Vice-regent in the Soul) and more especially by those whom God hath brought home to himself by Regenerating Grace, &c, and that have been made to taste in deed and in truth that the Lord hath been Gracious to them, by the manifestation of his Consolating love to their Souls, whereby they bring double guilt on their Souls and for which God will sorely Chastise them sooner or later even in this Life." Chipman's directions strike some of the signature notes of his affectionate piety. His insistence that the sermon be addressed "in a very Soul Searching Scriptural manner" recalls his admiration for the "Close Soul Searching Comprehensive" preaching of George Whitefield.[121] His emphasis on God's "Consolating love to their Souls" echoes the New Light message of Henry Alline, addressing divine love to the "inmost Soul." And notwithstanding that some of the "wrote books" mentioned in his will attempted to curtail what he perceived as the enthusiasm of the New Light church, Chipman's directions for the memorial sermon insisted that the "Motions & strivings of the Holy Spirit" not be "quenched." Religious affections remained central to the evangelical message that Chipman wanted to perpetuate in Cornwallis Township.

The memorial sermon was, notably, to be preached in each of the town's three churches. Similarly, Chipman's pallbearers were to be chosen equally from the three congregations. Ultimately, Chipman's religious aspirations proved impossible for a single congregation to satisfy. Having attempted to foster a balance between orthodox theology and affectionate experience, between order and zeal, Chipman appears to have conceded, at least in death, that it was difficult for any single church to keep these emphases in equilibrium.

The affective piety of early evangelicalism emerged in the same contexts as the eighteenth-century culture of sentiment – sometimes in harmony, sometimes striking a discordant note, sometimes a complementary counterpoint. Likewise, Chipman's manuscript meditations, and the local emotional conflicts that provoked his manuscript polemics, were a form of local participation in transatlantic conversations and debates. But even in this one Nova Scotia locale, emotional communities intersected, overlapped, and conflicted. Setting Chipman's political and religious experiences and feelings alongside those of another New England migrant to Nova Scotia, Jacob Bailey, exposes the range of what was feelable during the period's upheavals.

3

"Enthusiasm in politicks, as well as religion": Jacob Bailey's Emotional History of the American Revolution

Enter Parson Teachum, attended with a Liberty Mob and a number of friends.

Teachum: Gentlemen, I am summoned before your tribunal as a very great offender. Pray let me know the crimes with which I am charged.

Joab, the Brigadeer and chairman of the committee, rises with an important face.

Joab: Hem, hem, Sir, hem, you are accused of being unfriendly to the cause, of having an undue attachment to Great Britain, and of being disaffected to the noble struggles of America for freedom.

Teachum: Sir, whatever accusations may be offered against me, I profess myself a friend to my country.

Joab: We shall make it appear even to demonstration that you are prodigious inimical, and approve all the proceedings of the British court. In the first place, you have been guilty of refusing to read a proclamation for a continental fast, out of a barefaced and daring contempt of the congress. 2. You read a proclamation from Tom Gage against vice, immorality & profanity. 3. You have advised people to continue quiet and peaceable and to mind nothing but their own business ...

Joab: What have you to say about advising people to be quiet and peaceable and to mind nothing but their own business?

Teachum: If this is a crime I must confess myself guilty for I have recommended the advice of St. Paul – "study to be quiet and mind your own business, lead quiet and peaceable lives in all godliness and honesty." Now, since it is my concern to preach the gospel of peace, I cannot think it out of character to urge the practice of this gentle virtue.

Joab: However proper a Sermon of this nature might have been formerly, in quiet and peaceable times, they are wholly out of season at present. It is a cursed doctrine at this day. What – advise the people to peace and quietness when we want to have them all fire and fury, when the welfare and salvation of our country demands the most vigorous and obstinate efforts of resistance, and when the resolves of congress call aloud for vengeance, blood, and slaughter?[1]

Passion dominates the dramatized version of the proceedings of the Committee of Correspondence, Inspection, and Safety from Pownalborough, Maine (then part of Massachusetts) in May 1776. Entitled, "The Humors of the Committee, or, Majesty of the Mob," the dramatic sketch was written by the Anglican minister Jacob Bailey (1731–1808), thinly veiled as "Parson Teachum."[2] Feelings are at the base of the committee's case that the parson is a "Tory"; they accuse him of "having an *undue attachment* to Great Britain, and of being *disaffected* to the noble struggles of America for freedom."[3] The parson's affection for Britain is "undue" because unnatural, an aberration of the hostility he should feel for a tyrannical power. Later in the play, the committee passes a similar resolve that he has "an undue attachment in his heart to the ministerial tools and Butchers … a secret and inward enmity to the glorious cause of liberty, and wishes from the bottom of his soul success to the british tyrant."[4] It is just as unnatural that he should be "disaffected" with the noble American cause of liberty. The parson denies this characterization of his feelings, but the committee is resolute in the inspection of the parson's heart, as well as his outward compliance with Congress's directives.

The binary representation of political feelings obscures the more complex emotional landscape of the colonies prior to the polarizations of the Revolution. Not many years earlier, it was possible to have natural attachments to both Britain and one's American locale, and to see the cause of American liberty in distinctly British terms. Loyalists like Bailey wondered in 1776 whether their affections to Britain and America could continue to run in the same direction.

Bailey's drama on the "Majesty of the Mob" also highlights his grave concern that a revolution organized by such "unfeeling committees" endangered the harmonious sympathies and "gentle virtues" that held a people together.[5] In the playwright's version of events, the chair of the Committee of Correspondence admitted that instead of "peace and quiet," the revolution required "fire and fury" and "vigorous and obstinate" feelings if it were to fulfill the Continental Congress's call to "vengeance, blood, and slaughter" in the cause of liberty. Historians of emotion have echoed Bailey's insight on this point (if not his barbed sentiments), that colonial leaders had to accomplish a revolution of feeling for their rebellion to succeed: weakening – indeed, stigmatizing – ties of sentiment with Britain and affection for the king, and embracing the fury of less refined passions.[6] In Bailey's telling, the trampling of gentle virtues and natural affections undermined the justice of the American rebellion; unfeeling committees could only give birth to an unfeeling, insensible people.

This chapter traces Jacob Bailey's emotional history of the American Revolution. It begins with a brief overview of Bailey's Loyalist ordeal, and examines the transatlantic culture of polite sensibility and sentiment that lay at the base of his version of loyalism. A cosmopolitan concept of connection allowed Bailey to cultivate his British loyalty *and* a strong sense of American belonging – without emotional contradiction. Bailey's polite cosmopolitanism was on display in his unpublished history of New England, written in the years before his Loyalist ordeal. By piecing together the remaining manuscript copies of this understudied history, this chapter highlights the centrality of political and religious emotions in his narrative. Enthusiasm and seditious passions, according to Bailey, were intertwined threads running through New England history, opposing polite religion and loyal affections and helping to explain the emergence of the American Revolution. The discussion concludes with a look at Bailey's reflections on what he perceived as the necessary connection

between refined feelings and civil society, and the threat that the
rough and unfeeling rebellion posed to both. The next chapter follows Bailey as a disaffected Loyalist refugee in Nova Scotia.

"THE UNHAPPY TEMPER OF THE TIMES": BAILEY'S LOYALIST DEAL

The American War of Independence intensified .Bailey's already-
conflicted experience as an Anglican missionary for the Society for the
Propagation of the Gospel (SPG).[7] Bailey was born in Rowley, Massachusetts, to a family of modest means, but the benevolence of patrons
enabled him to attend Harvard College (graduating class of 1755).
Two years after being approved as a Congregational minister, Bailey,
like a growing number of other New Englanders of his generation,
went down the Canterbury trail, converting to the Church of England.[8]
For Bailey, Anglicanism was the embodiment of the "polite Christianity" he had imbibed at Harvard. An eighteenth-century amalgam of
Reformed Protestantism, a Shaftesburian emphasis on the affections,
neoclassical aesthetics, and metropolitan manners, the transatlantic
culture of polite Christianity was expressed by English writers such
as Isaac Watts (1674–1748) and Elizabeth Singer Rowe (1674–1737),
and was fostered in New England by a coterie including Benjamin
Colman (1673–1747), Mather Byles (1706–1788), and the poet John
Adams (1704–1740). Historian David Shields says that the design of
polite Christianity "was to make society both religious and polite,"
and in words that could have been an epitaph for Bailey himself,
described it as a "synthesis of politeness and Reformed Christianity
[that] provided a middle way for those embarrassed at homespun yet
uncomfortable with courtly finery."[9] From this religious culture Bailey
shaped a faith that was orthodox and affectionate but decidedly not
enthusiastic, an aesthetic that emphasized the sublime, and a strong
commitment to cosmopolitanism. All these themes (and not merely
reactionary religious "Toryism") contributed to his expression of loyalism before the American Revolution.

In January 1760, Bailey travelled to London to take holy orders,
including the oaths that would shortly thereafter set him at odds
with revolutionary sentiments. His conversion to Anglicanism and
his journey to the metropolis neatly embody the anglicization of
eighteenth-century colonial life, as pre-revolutionary Americans
grew more closely tied to Britain through trade, consumer culture,

Figure 3.1 | Portrait of Jacob Bailey, undated.

religion, and polite society.[10] From London, Bailey wrote to one correspondent about the metaphorical, as well as literal, distance he had travelled: "At length, after encountering a variety of scenes, striving with a thousand vexations, and breaking thro' all the obstacles that surrounded me, I obtained a liberal education, conquered my prejudices, and by the assistance of a favourable providence am safely arrived – notwithstanding the cruel dangers that threatened me – to the Metropolis of Great Britain."[11]

"Cruel dangers" also awaited Bailey at Pownalborough (now Wicasset), in eastern Massachusetts, where he served as a missionary for the SPG. A number of factors conspired to make life difficult for him as he attempted to plant Anglicanism on the eastern "frontier" of New England. There was personal animosity between Bailey and two former Harvard classmates, Jonathan Bowman and Charles Cushing, prominent officeholders resentful of the community influence accorded to their social inferior. Bailey also appears to have been the victim of a political proxy war among the Kennebec Proprietors who invested in settling the region, with tensions between Bailey's Anglican patron, Silvester Gardiner, and Boston mercantile Whigs.[12] And as elsewhere in New England, there was a long-simmering tension between the Congregational establishment and the growing Anglican presence. Compounding those tensions were the relative scarcity and deprivations of a frontier community still struggling to establish itself. All these variables were intensified further by the imperial crisis of the 1760s and 1770s, and the growing anti-British and anti-Loyalist sentiment.

As early as October 1774, Bailey wrote to friends about his treatment en route to Boston, that he was "repeatedly insulted upon the road ... insulted, threatened, and mobbed."[13] He generalized about the role of popular harassment in the colony: "Nothing could be more dangerous than journeying on the road. The unhappy temper of the times, the perpetual mob ... the barbarous and bloody threatenings which are continually thrown out against all who have any dependence upon Great Britain must render it very unsafe to venture from home."[14] His daily diary more tersely, but no less fearfully, noted, "Abroad. Fled from the mob."[15] Closer to home, a liberty pole – that quintessential symbol of popular Whig politics – was erected near Pownalborough's Church of England.[16] Bailey also confessed that he was haunted by the spectre of betrayal among the townspeople: "We ... regard the approach of a neighbour with suspicion and timidity, least he should advance with some hostile message, or form a design of betraying us to the malignant powers."[17]

Nevertheless, the campaign against Bailey was largely fuelled and executed by Bowman and Cushing and the official means at their disposal, rather than the local populace. As the dramatization above suggests, Bailey was harassed as a "Tory" by the Pownalborough Committee of Correspondence, and ordered several times to appear before them. As elsewhere in New England, Bailey's performance of

Anglican worship was increasingly politicized; he faced pressure for continuing to pray for the king, and for his fidelity to the oaths that were part of his ordination vows. Although a 1777 town meeting voted that Bailey was "not inimical to the peace," the magistrates issued a warrant for his arrest. To avoid this arrest, Bailey left his young family in the night and began "roving about" New Hampshire for several weeks until the warrant expired.[18] Bailey expressed the extent of his ordeal to one correspondent in 1778:

> My own private circumstances are very distressing, for tho I am at this instant with my family, yet I am uncertain what may be my fortune the next moment. I am surrounded with a lot of surly & savage beings who have power in their hands and murder in their hearts, who thirst and pant and roar for the blood of those who have any connection with or affection for Great Britain. In recounting my vexations, not to mention, poverty, rags, hunger and perpetual anxiety of mind sufficient [to] wear down the most vigorous constitution, I have been twice assaulted by a furious Mob, four times hauled before an unfeeling committee, sentenced to heavy bonds and harried from one tribunal to another, three times have I been driven from my family by the fury of my persecutors, and obliged to preserve my freedom by roving about in distant parts of the country. Two attempts have been made to shoot me.

He continued by admitting, "I must confess that these trials, together with the appearance of publick affairs are sufficient to overthro' a courage and fortitude superior to mine. But as yet I have never yet been either allured or terrified to renounce my principles, so I have taken a firm resolution not to be guilty of treachery, rebellion, or treason to preserve myself from ruin." [19]

Despite his resolve, there appeared no prospect other than ruin or imprisonment should Bailey remain in Pownalborough. He obtained leave in 1778 to travel to Boston to petition the assembly for permission to leave Massachusetts for Nova Scotia. His petition emphasized his material circumstances rather than his principled loyalism. He explained that he had gone three years without salary from either the SPG or from his poor parishioners, with the result that he was "reduced to such poverty and Distress as frequently and for a considerable time to be destitute of even the Necessaries as well

as the comforts of Life and has been obliged to dispose of almost all
his moveable effects to Support himself to this time." He therefore
asked that "he may have Liberty to depart with his family (consisting only of his Wife and infant Babe) to some part of Nova Scotia,
and to Carry what few Effects he has left, the whole not amounting
to One Hundred Dollars and consisting of a few necessary Articles
of Furniture." The move to Nova Scotia would allow him, he hoped,
to resume missionary work for the SPG and to "get Bread for himself
and Family." He urged the assembly to consider his "Extreme neces-
sitous and distressing circumstances" in granting this liberty.[20] The
assembly did indeed issue Bailey permission for removal to Halifax.
During a long winter of waiting for passage, and under virtual house
arrest, he counted the days until he could finally escape "this region
of sturdy malice and implacable revenge."[21]

A "NARROW AND CONTRACTED SPIRIT": BAILEY'S EMOTIONAL HISTORY OF NEW ENGLAND

If Jacob Bailey's history of New England can be believed, the rebellion of the American colonies was no surprise. It was, according to
Bailey, only the latest (if most violent and divisive) expression of
deeply ingrained and self-interested resistance to royal authority.
The "passion for liberty" that animated revolutionary mobs was the
most recent example of a long American history of political and religious enthusiasm. Bailey traced this emotional history in his unpublished book manuscript *Compendious History of the most important
concerns in the history of New-England.* The book surveyed New
England's history from the seventeenth-century arrival of European
settlers up to the middle of the eighteenth century. Although it did not
make it to publication, most of the manuscript can be reconstructed
by piecing together several draft notebooks among Bailey's papers.[22]
The *Compendious History* provides a valuable Loyalist perspective on
New England history.[23] He, like other Loyalist historians, attempted
to isolate the themes of radical Puritanism and self-interested inde-
pendency from the larger narrative of British American history.[24] By
critiquing what he viewed as a parochial perspective, Bailey was advocating a more cosmopolitan set of political affections in which local
or national identity need not conflict with broader Enlightenment
sympathies. In place of such parochial self-interest, Bailey aspired to
the universal benevolence of the transatlantic culture of sentiment.

Neither was Bailey's loyalism defined by narrow Britishness, any more than it was by American separatism; rather, being a British subject made him a citizen of the world.[25]

As he neared completion of the manuscript in 1773–74, Bailey proposed its publication to Boston printer Ezekiel Russell, inquiring whether he thought it would be "acceptable to the publick." He described the project as "a short History of the most important transactions in New England, to which is prefixed a brief description and natural History of the country. I imagine it will contain about 300 pages duodecimo pretty close print."[26] At about the same time, Bailey was also working on a similar project on the Indigenous, settler, and natural history of the "Eastern Country" of Massachusetts (now Maine). He proposed this book, in two volumes, to Boston printers Mills and Hicks, as "an entertaining description of the Eastern Country ... the manners & customs of the indian inhabitants, together with the surprizing progress of the late settlements, interspersed with some curious anecdotes."[27] Bailey was confident that the manuscripts would make it into print. In December 1773, Bailey wrote to his brother, "Several printers in Boston have engaged me to prepare for the press a short history of N England, about 300 pages in 12° and a description of the Eastern country below Casco in another vol. containing about 200."[28] As it turned out, however, neither book was printed. Their publication was most likely interrupted by the War of Independence, for they expressed a political perspective that proved unsellable for most colonial printers.[29]

Bailey's *Compendious History* was written with a brisk style for a general readership. Its synthetic narratives drew on a range of contemporary sources and historical accounts, including publications by William Hubbard, Cotton Mather, Pierre-François-Xavier de Charlevoix, and Thomas Hutchinson. As he worked on more recent events, he also weighed evidence from contemporaries.[30] Unfortunately, the surviving drafts do not include a preface in which Bailey might have commented on his methods, perspectives, or the uses his history may have served. From his text, however, it appears that Bailey attempted to balance historical judgment, didactic lessons, and an entertaining narrative style.[31] As with much of his writing, Bailey's history is shot through with emotion: evoking sympathy for the victim of a violent mob, outrage at the merciless treatment of prisoners, or warm admiration for courageous underdogs.[32] Such emotives energize the narrative, but they also had the didactic purpose of shaping the feelings of readers. Not infrequently, Bailey inserted moral commentary, such as this aside: "Affection, benignity, and benevolence are chiefly due to our friends and the more worthy part of our fellow creatures, but Truth, Honour, and Integrity may be demanded by the most perfidious enimy."[33] It appears that Bailey wrote his history to persuade as much as to educate, addressing the current crisis by describing some of the historical tendencies that led to that moment.[34]

The New England of Bailey's *Compendious History* was no "city on a hill." Describing New England's Puritan errand to establish a more reformed society, he wrote, "It was the pride and ambition of our Ancestors to erect a pure church in the wilderness which might become the admiration and envy of the christian world and flourish with increasing glory to the remotest period of time."[35] But Bailey had no such admiration. He found New England Congregationalists intolerant of difference and he claimed that although they were jealous of their own religious liberty, they denied such liberty to others. As an early example, Bailey discussed how Puritan leaders of the 1640s received Samuel Gorton (1593–1677), a settler and leader of a religious sect. In what Bailey described as an overreach of their authority, Boston magistrates sent an armed force to compel Gorton to appear before them on charges of blasphemy. His possessions were seized, he was sentenced to hard labour, and was threatened with death for continuing to teach "heretical" views. Bailey remarked, "Mankind should be thankful that out of Spain and Turkey, we seldom meet with such severe exertions of spiritual tyranny and arbitrary power."[36] He went on to inventory the "severe persecution" of the Quakers, a group he condescendingly described as "deluded but harmless sectaries."[37] Despite repeated petitions from dissenters and even the directives of royal commissioners, New England leaders "had no inclination to allow Liberty of conscience."[38] It seems clear that Bailey narrated these and other instances of religious intolerance as the larger historical context for his experience as an Anglican missionary facing the resentment of establishment Congregationalists.

Bailey often commented on the emotional tenor of New England Puritanism, which he characterized as a "Narrowness of spirit and contracted disposition," or an "ancient rigid spirit."[39] He wrote sardonically about the Puritans' "solemn" strictures against matters of clothing or behaviour, such as "the heinous sin of wearing long hair."[40] He argued that while the infractions themselves should be matters of indifference to religious leaders, such legalism had serious consequences for personal virtue and for civil society: "Solemn stifness and gloomy severity is extremely favourable to the more pernicious vices of the mind – it produces uncharitableness and spiritual pride, renders men morose, unsociable, and ill natured, induces them to treat all mankind except their own party with contempt and frequently ends in the destructive exercises of hatred, revenge, and cruelty."[41] Ironically, Bailey's "polite" and "rational" critique of Puritanism was echoed by New Lights: that the focus on external conformity often left the heart untouched.

The *Compendious History* paid particular attention to the often-fraught relationship between Indigenous people and European settlers. Bailey suggested that had early settlers been more attentive to their professed concern to christianize Indigenous North Americans, there would have been "an union in religious sentiments and ... a lasting friendship and affection between the two nations" instead of the succession of wars and atrocities that he chronicled.[42] Bailey's attempt to write from a more detached viewpoint is evident in his discussion of King Philip's War (1675–78), and especially his portrait of Wampanoag leader Metacom, or King Philip (1638–1676). Of Metacom's plan to expel the English from his territory, Bailey wrote, "Had his success been equal to the vastness of his design, or the firmness of his resolution, he would have been represented by unconcerned writers as a mighty hero, and a generous deliverer of his country." However, this was not, according to Bailey, the Metacom of New England historiography: "It cannot be denied that our N. England writers have painted his character in the darkest colours, and this method they have generally observed towards all who opposed their interest or acted contrary to their inclinations, however great and worthy in other respects."[43]

Bailey was particularly critical when describing instances of the cruel treatment of Indigenous prisoners of war at the mercy of New Englanders. After the death of Metacom, a great many of his people ceased their hostilities and surrendered themselves to the settlers. Bailey catalogued the brutality of the settlers' response: "Many were killed upon the spot where our forces invested them, thousands were driven into captivity, and of those multitudes who surrendered upon a promise of preservation, as many as were actors in the late scenes of hostility were condemned [and] executed at Boston; and most of the remainder were harried from their native country and sold for slaves beyond [the] Sea."[44]

Bailey indicted these actions as "inhuman" and "barbarous." Drawing attention to his New England roots – but attempting to transcend that perspective – Bailey wrote, "I must acknowledge that tho' several of my Ancestors have perished in these conflicts with the Indians, I cannot embrace the sentiments of many people nor justify any acts of needless severity."[45] He claimed that the Wampanoag had just as much right to engage in this war "as any nation in Europe." Conversely, he charged that the settlers would be viewed "with detestation and horror" by disinterested observers for their cruel treatment of prisoners of war. The cruelty of early settlers toward native inhabitants also had an effect on their own hearts and colonial society. Bailey contended that "Tenderness is natural to the heart of man … [but] wanton cruelty is a science, and it requires a considerable degree of study and application to divest ourselves of those soft and tender affections which are so essential to simple and unadulterated nature."[46] Bailey was intimating that the violence of colonization, in addition to the havoc it wreaked on Indigenous communities, also had long-term consequences for settler society, making it insensible to social affections.

Written during the imperial crisis of the early 1770s, Bailey's *Compendious History* characterized New Englanders as unwilling to accept British authority, an "indisposition which prevailed thro the colonies to comply with the king's instructions."[47] One of the most striking episodes in Bailey's narrative is his description of the fraught administration of Governor Edmund Andros, when the colonies were reorganized as the Dominion of New England (1686–89). New Englanders resented the revocation of their original charters, the stricter enforcement of the Navigation Acts, and the imposition of the Church of England in Boston. Even as a royalist, Bailey appears to have had no love for Andros's strong-arm tactics, writing of his "arbitrary intentions," restrictions on the "liberty of the press," and his "despotic sway."[48] Nevertheless, what comes to the fore in Bailey's account is the role of the "mob" in overthrowing Andros's imperial authority. He wrote that after news of the Glorious Revolution reached New England, the people, "animated with one spirit, rose in arms … to suppress the growing authority of their tyrannical masters."[49] In breathless prose, Bailey reported that in Boston, "the multitudes poured along the streets like a mighty torrent, and nothing could resist their dauntless fury." He described the people as "an enraged populace" – "victorious insurgents," "ungoverned and restless." Bostonians successfully seized Andros and the instruments of government, and fired by that example, the people of Providence seized colonial administrator Joseph Dudley "with loud acclamations of riotous joy [and] carried him away." Bailey's summary remarks on the rout of Andros emphasized (with just a note of grudging admiration in this instance) what he considered to be an intransigent, reflexive opposition to authority as the defining characteristic of New England culture: "This undertaking is a striking instance of that daring and intrepid spirit for which this country has always been so remarkable. The emigration of their forefathers was occasioned by sullen discontent and a dissatisfaction to government and their descendants in every age have been rather disposed to despise rather than to reverence authority.[50] Bailey admired the new Massachusetts charter, judging that it "secured both the authority of the King and the liberty of the people."[51]

Enthusiasm was a flexible category of analysis for Bailey. He turned to "extravagant freaks of enthusiasm" to help explain the influence of Squando and Madockawando, Abenaki religious leaders of later seventeenth-century Maine. In fact, Bailey's interest in Madockawando (about whom he wrote at length elsewhere) may have been for the purpose of a comparative study of enthusiastic elements that he also observed among Protestant groups. He postulated that some kind of religious reverence was ingrained in human nature. "For this reason," he wrote, "the most wild, romantic and inconsistent impostures, who make solemn and confident pretences to visions, extacies, and revelations, never fail to secure disciples and prosilites."[52] Bailey was not skeptical of the supernatural elements of religion, but he was profoundly suspicious that enthusiasts were often appealing to the irrational passions for very unspiritual reasons. He also applied the idea of enthusiasm to the witchcraft trials at Salem in 1692–93, saying that "a kind of epidemic madness had seized the minds of people, which spread like some contagious disease or rather like the fire of enthusiasm, thro' every rank and order."[53] The phenomenon was marked by unsociable and irrational elements. On the one hand, people in Salem indulged their "private resentment[s]" and the "malignant passions."[54] On the other hand, he asserted that

a preoccupation with "the misteries of darkness ... arouses the attention, astonishes the mind, confounds the understanding, and drives
the imagination to the most extravagant excess."

There are few historical figures that did not merit at least a
line or two of moral commentary in the *Compendious History*,
but Governor William Phips's (1651–1695) unjust treatment by
Massachusetts's leaders exposed, for Bailey, their unfeeling character.
In reporting the sudden conclusion of Phips's administration, Bailey
stated that he was "of an open, generous and friendly disposition,
but of a warm and precipitate temper," unlike his enemies among
the colonial elite, with their "malignant designs," "deepest cunning, the darkest hypocrisy and the most phlegmatic insensibility."[55]
Bailey allowed that Phips's behaviour was not immune to criticism,
observing that "his passion was certainly in some instances unrestrained and hurried him into acts of unjustifiable imprudence."[56]
But he appears to have had a particular fondness for Phips, perhaps
because of his humble shepherding roots in Bailey's Kennebec region
of Maine.[57] As he described Phips's unlikely rise to prominence and
his subsequent treatment by Boston elites, Bailey almost seems to
have slipped into autobiographical reflections on his own aspirations and sad experience: "By courage and application, united with
a secession of fortunate accidents, he rose from the dust of obscurity,
from the very lowest condition in life to be the greatest man in his
country. But a man of this character must ever be remote from happiness and true enjoyment, since the meaner parts of mankind will
always regard him with envy, and those in higher stations with contempt."[58] Though a lifelong New Englander, Bailey perceived himself
as an outsider to the Congregational and merchant establishment, a
sense that coloured his narrative.

As Bailey's narrative turned to the early decades of the eighteenth
century, he remarked on the cultural changes – in manners, education, and consumption – that modern historians have described
as "the refinement of America."[59] "The inhabitants of New-England
were now greatly improved in knowledge and politeness, the language became more refined, wealth and elegance abounded and the
arts of luxury and genteel enjoyment began to prevail. The roughness of manners and pious deportment of our forefathers were now
dispised and frequently ridiculed as affectation and hypocrisy."[60]
He described a thoroughgoing set of transformations, including
a moderation of even the more severe aspects of Puritan piety to

which he had earlier drawn attention. What did *not* change, claimed Bailey, was the New England aversion to imperial oversight: "Little remained to distinguish us as [our forefathers'] genuine offspring except [for] that opposition to the authority of our parent country which so strongly marked their characters."[61]

The Great Awakening of the 1740s, which Bailey called the "religious commotions," embodied his greatest concerns about religious enthusiasm and social order. Bailey suggested that this religious revival was as astonishing as the Salem witchcraft trials, and even "more boundless in its extent and important in its consequences." He called it nothing less than a "revolution [in] religion."[62] Bailey argued that the lacklustre state of religion among Congregational churches helped explain the success of this revolution. He portrayed passive Christian hearers, content to "get to heaven with as little noise and disturbance as possible," and unexceptional ministers without any real understanding of either books or human hearts. He claimed that their sermons, though "plain and sensible," were "encumbered with a multitude of subtle divisions" and "were delivered to their sleeping audiences with a heavy uniformity of accent, void of all graceful action, and in a language rather calculated to lull the passions into profound repose, than to arouse and stimulate the heart."[63]

The contrast with George Whitefield, according to Bailey, could not be greater. Whitefield, that "celebrated rambler," "understood the secret of moving the passions, and urged the most weighty and striking subjects, with all the force of language, and a violence of action which nothing could resist."[64] Bailey described the sobering effect of Whitefield's preaching on the people of New England, who "continued under uncommon impressions of religious concern" and laid aside all kinds of secular enjoyments, as "vice became ... unfashionable."[65]

As a historian of New England's eastern frontier, Bailey described York, Maine (not far from his own Kennebec region) as the centre of this "religious commotion."[66] In forceful language, Bailey portrayed the "convulsions" of revival meetings as overwhelming sensory and physical experiences: "some screaming out under the most sensible agitations of distress, and confessing their guilt in the bitterest agonies of their soul, whilst others exclaimed in the wildest transports and loudest exaltations of joy." The more dramatic "visions, extasies, prophesies, trances and spiritual ravings" resulted when "the passions [were] presently roused and agitated into a violent fermentation, till all the faculties [were] incited to rebel against the authority of reason."[67]

Among Bailey's concerns about religious enthusiasm was his worry that the "religious commotions" intensified New England's existing resistance to authority. Comparing the religious and political upheavals, Bailey remarked that "enthusiasm, like sedition, is more contagious than the pestilence," and he worried that this movement "began to threaten religion with total anarchy and ruin."[68] Bailey argued that the spiritual liberty and self-righteousness engendered by the revivals was overturning social order, portending a dangerous disregard for social harmony, family government, and civil laws. In this "surprizing revolution" the settled clergy of New England "lost their influence, and a period was put to their dominion." Unsettling the very township structure of New England, "the most senseless itinerant, empty of all rational improvement and ignorant of letters – if he had assurance enough to plead an inward designation from heaven, and favoured with a potent pair of lungs ... had it in his power...to ruin the authority of the most prudent, learned and pious divine." Bailey considered the events of the 1740s as another troubling episode in the region's history, linking religious enthusiasm with political sedition.[69]

It is worth pausing here to compare Bailey's analysis of the Great Awakening with that of Handley Chipman, since both men felt first-hand the early heat of the movement in Massachusetts and Rhode Island, respectively, and then observed Nova Scotia laypeople fanning its flames from the 1770s through the 1790s. To a great degree, Bailey and Chipman agreed that the awakenings spread because preachers like Whitefield engaged the emotions of their hearers in a way that staid and doctrinaire Puritan sermons often failed to do, however orthodox they were. They also shared worries about what they perceived as the excesses of the movement – raucous, sensational worship services and unsettling social disorder. Bailey, as well as Chipman, acknowledged the importance of the affections in religious life, later preaching that "we must examine the secret emotions of our minds, enquire into the nature of our desires, inclinations, and governing passions."[70] Yet for all this agreement, Chipman and Bailey drew different conclusions. Chipman felt that Puritanism was worth renewing by means of the affective, personal piety of the awakenings, even if that required constant shepherding to prevent the movement from slipping into more extreme subjectivity. Bailey, by contrast, rejected both Puritan cant and evangelical fervour in favour of a polite Anglicanism that more straightforwardly affirmed a traditional social order. He contended that Whitefield and his New Light followers "establish[ed] their own feelings as the standard of Christianity and rashly ... condemn[ed] all who have not the same degree of ardor and zeal."[71] For Chipman, Whitefield represented the moderate balance of head and heart, while to Bailey, the Grand Itinerant was balanced only on the cusp of a slippery slope into enthusiasm.

Bailey's history of New England is a narrative of passions and interests – the passions of a populace easily stirred up to religious or political enthusiasm, and the narrow self-interest of Boston elites all too willing to manipulate them. Charging New Englanders with a "narrow and contracted spirit," Bailey contended that they were insensible to the bonds of affection with Britain that enlarged rather than restrained American prosperity.[72] The *Compendious History* expressed Loyalist convictions shaped *before* Bailey's revolutionary ordeal, when he still assumed America's future remained within the British Empire, and when he had no reason to doubt that he would continue to serve the people of the Kennebec. The timing is important because it helps to challenge the stereotype that loyalism was primarily reactionary. Loyalism was, for some, a part of a coherent set of beliefs about the world and America's place in it. Unquestionably, the onset of anti-British and anti-Loyalist sentiments in the years after 1765 lent a bitter edge to Bailey's writing. Yet, the *Compendious History* was completed before his encounters with the Pownalborough Committee of Correspondence, and as late as April 1774 he reported with gratitude, "Our people have been free from those publick commotions which have lately been so frequent and alarming in other places."[73] The book, then, was written as a historical intervention at a time when it was not at all inevitable how events would unfold. Bailey wrote to persuade would-be readers to abandon American parochialism (but not North American identity altogether), and to value cosmopolitanism and connection to the British Atlantic world.[74] His was the Britishness described by historian Michael Eamon: "Being loyal, indeed being British, meant being part of something larger: a subject in a world-wide empire, a member in a most sociable race of people boasting in a rich legacy of literature, political debate, legal precedents, scientific advancements, and folk customs."[75]

While Bailey wrote New England's colonial history as a narrative of unmitigated disloyalty and narrow self-interest, he did not altogether abandon his affection for America. Bailey expressed his American identity through other writings, especially natural history, the history of the Indigenous inhabitants of North America, and the history of Maine, including his own Kennebec region.[76] By focusing on sublime beauty in nature and ancient Indigenous nobility, he could identify a version of America untroubled by disloyalty and intolerance. By writing about the history of the "Eastern Country" of New England, both separately and as a recurring theme in the *Compendious History*, Bailey decentred Puritan Boston in his narrative, and reinforced his perspective as an outsider to the New England establishment.

"ALL LEARNING, POLITENESS, AND HUMANITY ARE ALMOST EXTINGUISHED"

Bailey was troubled by what he perceived as a radical shift in American public discourse during the Revolution: repudiating a culture of sensibility, refinement, and politeness for the sake of "manly roughness," plain speaking, and populism. "We are sinking with surprizing rappidity into ignorance and barbarity. Our conversation, our writings, and intercourse with each other are strongly tinctured with the roughness and severity of the times."[77] Revolutionaries felt they were embracing a style of language that, in its directness and common sense, was more suited to North American conditions. Bailey disagreed. He believed that civil society was only possible when learning and refinement flourished, when individuals increased their capacity for fellow-feeling, and when oaths were held sacred. While later revolutionary leaders adapted the language of sensibility to cultivate the virtue of the young republic, in the 1770s Loyalists like Bailey employed sentimental discourse to *critique* the Revolution and to urge Americans to retain the Enlightenment's commitment to universal benevolence, cosmopolitanism, and civil society.[78] Bailey worried that by abandoning sensibility, Americans were not only cutting themselves off from European learning, but were also eroding the ability to speak to one another with civility.[79]

Bailey feared that refinement of language and manners had been replaced by roughness. He lamented that "all learning, politeness, and humanity are almost extinguished, and nothing remains but a savage roughness of expression and a ferocity of manners truly shocking to those who have any gentle sensations or softness in their natures."[80] Whereas polish or refinement was achieved by polite social interaction, roughness resulted from remaining isolated or apart.[81] Likewise Bailey was concerned that what tied people together – their humanity and their innate capacity for feeling – was being extinguished by strong demarcations of difference. When he considered the literature and print culture of the Revolutionary Era, Bailey saw a similar roughness: "Our compositions are no longer debated and enervated by polished sentences and fine turned periods, but are dignified with a manly roughness which strikes the ear like the grating of rusty iron."[82] Sensibility was a capacity that had to be cultivated, but rough, unfeeling social interaction could only introduce "insensibility of heart," diminishing the possibility of fellow-feeling and civic discourse in American society.[83]

Bailey was particularly worried about use of the language of "liberty" to describe the Revolution. Mocking the rhetoric of the revolutionaries, Bailey wrote, "I write this epistle from the glorious land of liberty, from the free and independent states of America! Free from all the troublesome restraints of religion, goodness, and humanity, and independent of everything truly great, generous, and worthy ... We disdain from the bottom of our souls to be governed by the tyranny of law, equity, and reason! We entertain more dignified sentiments and have placed ourselves under the dominion of violence, rapine, and folly!"[84] From Bailey's perspective, Americans were not so much free as cut off, and not so much liberated as dominated by far worse tyrants. He asserted that some restraints were, in fact, salutary and were not opposed to liberty. Religion, reason, law, and human benevolence were only restraints in the sense that they curbed the worst excesses of social life and the most troublesome passions of the individual.

Bailey perceived that revolutionaries were self-consciously adopting a gendered style of rhetoric to contrast indulgent British and European milieu from homespun American culture. He sarcastically wrote, "We scorn as infinitely beneath our dignity, the gentleness, patience, and humanity of the Britons. We pride ourselves in being unfeeling, inflexible, and obstinate Americans." Rather than the "effeminate" ways of a dying empire, Americans adopted a "manly roughness ... more properly adapted to a race of Heros."[85] Bailey's letter provides some reportage on the weaponization of gendered emotions in revolutionary rhetoric, drawing a contrast between the "effeminate" refinement of European sensibility and the "manly roughness" of American passion. This is an unusually clear example of the historicist, contextual meaning of emotions – the reality that makes a history of emotions possible. Within a generation, American colonists reinscribed the meaning of masculine feelings, turning away from refined feeling and embracing revolutionary passion; the Early Republic witnessed a further change, promoting sympathies among men in the interest of building a national culture.

Bailey was particularly concerned with what he saw as "a disregard for the most solemn oaths."[86] And more than any other factor, Bailey's principled loyalty to his oath to the king contributed to his ordeal, and he honoured it at great cost. In a 1778 letter, he explained his convictions about oaths, sensibility, and society.[87] He wrote that his views on the connection between oaths and society were based on an extensive personal study "long before the commencement of the revolution." He condensed that historical examination by noting a nearly universal "sacred regard for oaths," and argued that "whoever attempts to lessen their obligations is an enemy to the welfare and security of civil society."

Bailey was keenly aware that not a few Loyalists, including some of his Anglican ministerial colleagues, had found a way to justify the exchange of their British for an American oath of allegiance, while others simply took the oath as a wartime survival strategy rather than out of any heartfelt allegiance. The underlying assumption of such oath-taking was that it was an external matter, unconnected to one's interior convictions. Bailey was worried about just such a disconnection. He wrote, "if [one] is induced to offend against conscience [by taking an imposed, unfelt oath], he must become ... hardened against future conviction."[88] By submitting to an enforced oath, "people will lose their reverence for oaths in general." The reverence for oaths – and for other kinds of words – was, for Bailey, the basis of the social ties that bound people into a virtuous society. Once the principle of avoiding sacrifice for one's oath is introduced, it was a slippery slope toward the cheapening of all oaths, words, and commitments: "they will regard them as matters of trifling importance, and in the conclusion the peace and foundation of society will be greatly weakened, if not wholly destroyed." By disconnecting words from feeling, Bailey contended, or by imposing oaths without regard for personal allegiance, governments invited trouble. He asked, "Will men who have been compelled to take this oath become more friendly? Will they consider it as binding?" There was no such guarantee. To ensure that oaths were expressions of conviction, and that they carried a strong sense of obligation, Bailey concluded that "oaths ought to be voluntary."[89]

As he did in his manuscript history of New England, Bailey critiqued the tendency of (some) Americans to be separate and independent, rather than connected, an inclination expressed in the revolutionary discourse of "liberty." On the one hand, Americans were cutting themselves off from the transatlantic culture of sensibility and politeness by which much of colonial society had become more refined. They were choosing populism over the moderate Enlightenment's cosmopolitanism. On the other hand, Americans were self-consciously adopting ways of speech that Bailey believed would undermine civic discourse, social harmony, and the negotiation of political differences present in culturally diverse democracies. Ironically, Loyalists like Bailey would have been far more at home in the republic during the 1790s, when revolutionary leaders began to employ (or recovered) the language of sensibility to encourage national fellow-feeling and republican virtue. During the 1770s, though, Bailey employed the language of sensibility to critique American isolationism and the breakdown of civil discourse.

"SPIRITING UP THE PEOPLE": EMOTIONS AND CONSPIRACY IN THE REVOLUTION

Bailey saw the American Revolution as a conspiracy – a scheme designed to manipulate the passions of the American people *and* the affections of the British Parliament. This surprising viewpoint is reflected in *A Letter to a Friend on the Present Situation of our Publick Affairs*, a manuscript he wrote sometime during the course of the War of Independence, and which apparently remained unpublished.[90] It is a remarkable document. There is, of course, the reader's prurient pleasure of discovering the identity of Bailey's alleged conspirators and the details of the scheme he perceived. More to the point of this study, the letter proposes an account of the role of political enthusiasm in the Revolution. It also reveals an aspect of Bailey's political affections articulated nowhere else so clearly. Janice Potter argues that many Loyalist writers similarly explained the Revolution with reference to the passions of the people – "easily swayed and vulnerable to appeals to their passions or baser instincts, [and so] were duped by a crafty and unscrupulous cabal."[91] Bailey's account is even more emotionally complex, involving British as well as American actors, and the affections of the members of Parliament, as well as the rank and file.

The conspiracy in brief: "some of our most zealous sons are directed in their motions by the ministry."[92] The conspirators: "F___k__n," "A__ms," and "H___k," *and* a tyrannical faction of the British ministry.[93] Bailey proposed that the Revolution was plotted in Whitehall as a pretense for decisive military action against the American colonies and the further reduction of their liberties, if not their enslavement. The leaders of the so-called "sons of liberty," chief among them Benjamin Franklin, John Adams, and John Hancock, agreed to be the "tools" of the ministry in return for indemnity from prosecution and, of course, considerable personal wealth. The role of the New England "junto" was to kindle "the flames of sedition and rebellion thro' the province," to encourage acts of resistance that were intended to "estrange the affections of the parliament from the colonies."[94]

For proof of the conspiracy, Bailey pointed to the plainly inadequate response of the British administration to early American rebelliousness, such as the destruction of the tea in Boston Harbour. The Port Bill, he wrote, was never intended to bring the colonists to submission, but only to provoke them to further insurrection. Likewise, the legislation that removed the provincial charter was a half-measure that intentionally did not prevent town meetings – venues that allowed the "seducers" to animate the people to "tumult, mischief, and sedition."[95] Most importantly, Bailey contended that no group as shrewd as these men would dare push the colonies into so mismatched a war, against so vastly superior an army, and in such defiance of common sense, without some ulterior motivation.[96] He urged his readers to inquire further, before it was too late: "I must now, Sir, express my humble and most importunate wishes that the eyes of my countrymen may be opened to discern that eminent danger which threatens them with speedy destruction, let them be persuaded to exert their native good sense and penetration to reflect a little upon the transactions of the present day, and seriously examine whether these very flaming patriots to whose guidance they have resigned their judgments, their consciences, and their safety, may not possibly in concert with a wicked and tyrannical ministry be engaged to compleat their ruin."[97]

Poignantly, Bailey wrote at a moment during the conflict when American victory still seemed unlikely, and the damage wrought by manipulated passions could still be undone.

In laying bare the mechanics of his conspiracy theory, Bailey made several comments on the role of political emotions in the Revolution. He contended that in the "cause of freedom," as with any other political goal, it was best not to place one's confidence in the "most noisy, precipitous, and furious" methods, but rather in "firmness with moderation, steadiness with secrecy, and humanity with earnest persuasion." He explained that the latter approach "engages both the reason and the affections." Relying on fury and impulsive action, on the other hand, "either conduces to excite a sudden tempest of passion without any lasting effect, *or* to estrange the hearts and inclinations of most of the people from a cause that requires such perpetual bluster and commotion to maintain it."[98] In Bailey's view, the Revolution was sustained *not* because ordinary colonists had been truly, rationally convinced that the "cause of liberty" required rebellion against Britain, but because their initial outrage at the so-called Intolerable Acts was constantly fanned into passionate fury by an unrelenting barrage of inflammatory rhetoric and mob tactics. Let the people cool their passions long enough to reconsider, however, and he believed they would choose a different course.[99]

Like many observers then and since, Bailey was astonished at how suddenly and thoroughly revolutionary sentiments spread through the colonies. He pointed to such factors as the influence of the Continental Congress, the activism of local committees of correspondence, and the "misrepresentations of facts" in print. Yet Bailey also suggested that emotions played a role, magnifying the effects of other causes: "It was really astonishing to observe the rapid progress of the contagion, the passion for freedom, spread from town to town, from city to city, from province to province till the whole continent was kindled in flame and combustion. Enthusiasm in politicks, as well as religion, catches like gun powder and like a torrent of lightning rushing from the clouds, [it] dazzles, confounds, and consumes with irresistible force."[100] As he often did with religious enthusiasm, Bailey argued that political wildfire can be ignited and fanned into fury, but it cannot be controlled. He believed that, under the influence of such strong passions, people were susceptible to manipulation by self-interested individuals. But it was impossible to predict the result of such a conflagration.

It is interesting to compare Bailey's analysis to more recent studies of the *emotional* revolution that enabled the political revolution. There are many points of agreement. Nicole Eustace, for example, argues as Bailey did (though without the element of conspiracy) that revolutionary leaders knowingly embraced the rougher passions since "they found that they could not advance in the cause of revolution without the aid of that immoderate emotion they had so recently eschewed."[101] Bailey spoke of "spiriting up the people," and Eustace of "the notion of *spirit*," to describe the intentional strategy of firing the emotions of the people. However, while Eustace argues that strong passion was, to a degree, combined with classical virtue, Bailey insisted that it was a cynical strategy designed to unleash destructive, rather than noble, forces. A key aspect of Eustace's assessment of Patriot emotions is that "They thus began seeking ways to combine the civility and respectability attributed to refined feelings with the force and might believed to stem from popular passions."[102] Bailey believed his experience as a Loyalist belied such a view. He argued that revolutionary passions *overwhelmed* civic affections, making neighbours insensible to the suffering they were inflicting upon one another. Perhaps speaking of his own experience with mobs and the Committee of Correspondence in Maine, Bailey wrote, "In these dreadful moments of assault and ravage nothing could soften or divert the *inexorable spirit*. The assailants *divested* themselves of everything noble, generous, and good, *disregarded* all the tender offices of friendship and benevolence, *banished every sentiment of tenderness* from their bosoms."[103] Bailey did not for a moment doubt that emotions were central in the unification of formerly disparate colonists, or that firing the passions was crucial in the spread of revolutionary sentiments. But, he asked, at what cost? What kind of society was created as a result? "Can we expect that harmony should prevail?" Will neighbours be willing to "unite their affections to those persons who offer such violence to their native freedom?"[104]

Finally, *A Letter to a Friend* offers a surprising glimpse at the kind of revolution against Britain that Bailey – the *Loyalist* – could have supported. As he wrote, Bailey believed that America faced "impending ruin" before Britain's superior military might.[105] And yet he offered a counterfactual possibility – an approach to revolution that he believed would have been successful "if these men had entertained a serious intention of expelling the British forces."[106] Bailey's revolution would have employed cool cunning instead of so much furious passion. He would have made extensive preparations (which he does not detail) "with the profoundest stillness and concealment," lulling the British army into inattention. Then, he said, "with these precautions our countrymen might have performed wonders and by an unexpected and fortunate blow, have so intimidated the administration as to have delivered themselves and posterity from European slavery." Bailey even went so far as to describe *that* scenario as a "pleasing and patriotic idea." In other words, Bailey agreed with the revolutionaries that a tyrannical, heavy-handed British administration (if not the king himself) was in a position to subject Americans to "slavery."

Bailey would have supported some version of passive or even active resistance to British authority. Almost unthinkably, Bailey the Loyalist would have cheered as "pleasing and patriotic" the striking of an "unexpected and fortunate blow" against Britain. All this would have been conceivable – *if* the Revolution had appealed to the reason, as well as the passions, of the people, if it had not trampled their affections and virtues. Bailey so often criticized the unfolding of the American Revolution that it has been possible to overlook his very real worries about British policy and his deep emotional identification with America. His unwillingness to countenance the roughness of revolutionary passions has made it possible to miss his American sympathies and the weakening of his British affections.

CONCLUSION

The writings of Jacob Bailey reveal, as it were, two possible histories of emotion in British America. On the one hand was the emotional history that might have been: a positive vision for the British and cosmopolitan identity of the American colonies. Granted, what Bailey stood *for* is often overawed by the vociferousness of his polemical rhetoric, but the negatives can be developed into a positive snapshot of his views. He envisioned an American future in which the colonies continued their refinement and became more integrated into British and European culture. North American identity, however, was not swallowed up in this scenario; Bailey hoped for a genuine exchange, in which the ancient dignity of America's Indigenous people, the sublime beauty of the New World's pristine landscapes, and the strength of character cultivated by labouring to settle the frontier, were all

unique contributions that his country of birth could offer to transatlantic culture. Reasoned emotions – sentiments – were the glue that
made it possible for people of diverse backgrounds and across vast
distances to be knit together into a refined British American civilization. Bailey's was a cosmopolitan version of loyalism. He understood
America's connection to the British Empire in expansive terms; more
than nationalism *per se*, loyalism was the vehicle for participating in
a refined, sentimental culture.

However, as he did in the *Compendious History*, Bailey often
expressed this cosmopolitan loyalism in a negative mode, criticiz-
ing what he perceived as American parochialism and separatism. He
narrated, that is, another history of New England: a long history of
American self-interest and recalcitrance before legitimate authority,
a deeply ingrained tendency that cut off the colonies from a world
of cultural exchange and refinement. In this account, Puritanism's
long-faced solemnity and the Great Awakening's enthusiasm seemed
likely to overthrow more polite expressions of Christianity. It was a
critique that only intensified as the imperial crisis unfolded. Bailey
saw the culture of sentiment overwhelmed by the rough manners
and violent passions of revolutionary agitators. He worried that
violent actions and words would render colonists insensible to the
very sympathies and affections that had made civil society possible.
One need not agree with Bailey's strident critiques to find him a
perceptive analyst of the role that emotion played in the American
Revolution. He understood, as historians of emotion now find, that
sympathy could facilitate transatlantic connections, and that passion
could motivate disruptive change in political systems.

Bailey's loyalism was undoubtedly changed by the American
Revolution, but it was grounded in a long history of intellectual
coherence and emotional resonance that preceded that climactic
event. The question for Bailey, taken up in the next chapter, was
whether that cosmopolitan version of loyalism and his hope for a
transatlantic culture of sympathy could survive the violence and
polarization of the Revolution.

4

"Not from any remainders of affection": The Disaffection of Jacob Bailey's Loyalty

> How is it possible for me to follow your advice respecting politicks, when I have continually before me such shocking and affecting examples of the folly, wickedness, and cruelty of British and congressional government. A man who can behold such objects as present themselves to my view without emotion must divest himself both of religion and human nature.[1]
>
> Jacob Bailey to Thomas Brown, 10 May 1783

The previous chapter began with a dramatized revolutionary Committee of Correspondence charging Parson Teachum, Jacob Bailey's alter ego, with "having an *undue attachment* to Great Britain, and of being *disaffected* to the noble struggles of America for freedom."[2] It is tempting to take the committee at its word, characterizing the emotions of Loyalists as primarily "British" – portraying them as unreconstructed anglophiles or "Augustan Tories."[3] And yet Bailey's emotions were unsettled by the actions of both the "British *and* congressional government." Though Bailey certainly nursed bitter resentment against the American rebels, his emotional connection to *Britain* also changed. It was not as if one aspect of his British-American identity suffered while the other remained constant; *both* underwent significant transformation during and after the Revolutionary War. His writings express feelings of anger, disillusionment, humiliation, and grief directed toward the nation that had once been the object of his devotion and for which he had suffered.[4] In short, Bailey became profoundly disaffected with Britain.[5]

And yet Bailey persisted in his loyalism. Disillusioned though he was, Bailey did not abandon his British allegiance. He did, however, have to ground that loyalism in something other than feelings: "If we continue our loyalty after such obvious and striking demonstrations of partiality, it must be from principles of conscience and not from any remainders of affection."[6] This chapter, then, traces Bailey's disaffection with Britain and the reconfiguration of his loyalism, and in so doing makes the case for the emotional complexity of loyalty and offers further evidence of the contingent, contextual meaning of human emotions.

The dislocating experience of being a refugee was central to Bailey's political disaffection, but it was not the only contributing factor. Even before his exile, he and other Loyalists were humiliated and disheartened by British overtures of reconciliation made to the American rebels beginning in 1778. In the spring of 1779, Bailey and his family sought refuge in Nova Scotia. After some months in Halifax, Bailey accepted the position as the SPG missionary at Cornwallis Township. He was soon disabused of his hope that the province would be a haven of loyalism. Instead, he found the former New England residents sympathetic to the Revolution; their hostility seemed to extend, rather than relieve, his Loyalist ordeal. Bailey remained at Cornwallis until 1782, when he moved to Annapolis Royal to minister to a growing Loyalist community. During the course of the War of Independence, Bailey witnessed successive waves of Loyalist refugees arriving in the province. Their desperate circumstances elicited Bailey's deep sympathy, even as he became disillusioned by the "unfeeling" British policy toward the Loyalists. As the terms of the Treaty of Paris (1783) became known, Bailey was incensed at the "inhumanity" of his nation's betrayal of her most loyal subjects. And yet in the years following the Revolution, Bailey remained committed to royal authority and the liberties of the British constitution, even if he expressed his loyalism with a more critical accent.

Bailey's writing in Nova Scotia was replete with complex emotions. He articulated the emotional experience of political exile – his own and that of other refugees – in hundreds of pages of letters and diaries. Whereas Bailey's New England writing was predominantly historical, in Nova Scotia he turned to satirical poetry in a Hudibrastic style that combined ludicrous humour and devastating critique of popular religion and political enthusiasm. Bailey also contended with other Loyalists about the role that passions should play in their wartime writing.

THE BEGINNING OF DISAFFECTION

The experience of dislocation within the British Empire began while Bailey was still living in New England – before his physical exile – in response to the 1778 peace commission led by the Earl of Carlisle. The commissioners offered terms of peace and a form of American self-rule to the Continental Congress; meeting with no success with that body, they had their *Manifesto and Proclamation* published and sent to each of the rebelling colonies.[7] Bailey felt sharp betrayal at the possibility of a pardon for the revolutionaries. He wrote, "Nothing could occasion greater surprise and anxiety to the friends of government, than the sudden alteration in the language and operations of the British court."[8] The offer of peace was profoundly disorienting to Loyalists. Of their emotional upheaval he wrote to his correspondent, "We recollected our former connection with blushes of confusion, and were almost ashamed of our steadfast adherence to an authority which had neither spirit enough to punish its enemies, nor gratitude sufficient to encourage its friends." He also began to worry that the friends of Britain would be abandoned: "instead of receiving any countenance, protection, and reward for our firmness and sufferings, we were now exposed as consigned victims."

Bailey rehearsed some of the ordeals he and other Loyalists faced for their attachment to Britain, their suffering devotion seemingly belittled by the peace offers: "We had long been suffering every indignity for our loyalty and attachment, from the sons of hostility and vengeance, daily exposed to the unexampled turbulence of their rage, and the bitter inflictions of their malice – our houses plundered, our fortunes ruined, our families undone, our freedom invaded, our consciences forced."[9] Loyalists had endured such suffering "rather than renounce[ing] their principles," and they had expected Britain's powerful, decisive military response. Instead, they learned about Britain's "most abject and humiliating" peace proposals. Bailey summed up his strong emotional reaction to the offer of pardon: "Every person who possessed any sentiments of duty towards his majesty or felt any affection for Great Britain was seized with a mixture of astonishment and indignation." He continued, "If we continue our loyalty after such obvious and striking demonstrations of partiality, it must be from principles of conscience and not from any remainders of affection." Bailey's comment provides an important insight into the nature of his loyalism, the composition of which eludes simple or static definition. His loyalty seems to have been a complex and changing amalgam, including British patriotism, cosmopolitan refinement, personal connections, and ideological convictions. Though it was never merely an affectionate or sentimental attachment, it was still a disorienting experience for Bailey to remake his loyalism without "any remainders of affection."

"NO REFUGEE CAN BE HAPPY"

As Bailey and his Kennebec companions crossed from American to British territory in June 1779, Bailey confessed to his diary, "It occasioned an abundance of regret and chagrin when we found ourselves departing from our native country to seek a refuge in a foreign region."[10] They were among at least 60,000 Loyalists who were eventually cast into the British world by the War of Independence.[11] As an early refugee with the support of the SPG, Bailey's experience was not necessarily typical of varied refugee circumstances. Nevertheless, as Bailey recorded his passage from Pownalborough, Maine, to Halifax, he attempted to generalize from his own emotional reactions to write sympathetically about a common set of refugee experiences and feelings.

Though Bailey identified closely with Britain – culturally, intellectually, religiously, politically – he was a lifelong New Englander. For almost two decades he had been in the Kennebec region, serving its people, studying its ancient history, and observing his natural surroundings. Bailey sought permission to leave the region for British territory only when it became painfully clear that the local Committee of Correspondence was intent on making his life and work there untenable. Departing by schooner in late May 1779, Bailey filled several notebooks with an account of their "expulsion," capturing the pathos of a journey that was simultaneously into freedom and into exile. He began his account with the question, "Must we after all the trouble, harassments, and cruel persecution we have endured for the cause of truth and virtue, must we leave these pleasing scenes of nature, these friendly shades, these rising plants, these opening flowers, these trees swelling with fruit, and yonder winding river?"[12]

Despite their sorrow at leaving and the worries of sea travel, the voyage was also a tremendous relief after years of poverty and political persecution. Of their feelings as their vessel came within "the long wished for" sight of Cape Sable, on Nova Scotia's southern coast, Bailey wrote, "It gave us immense pleasure to behold a country under the dominion of our lawful prince, and where the tyranny of republican villains had not yet extended."[13] As they sailed into Halifax Harbour and saw the naval ships "with the Britanic colours flying," they were inspired "with the most pleasing sensations." Bailey expressed his gratitude that his family had been conducted "to this retreat of freedom and security from the rage of tyranny and the cruelty of oppression."[14]

Bailey and the other Kennebec refugees arrived in Halifax with little more than the tattered clothes on their backs. When they set out from Maine, Bailey noted forlornly, "we carried our beds and the shattered remains of our fortune, the whole not worth 40 dollars."[15] Stepping onto the Halifax dockside, Bailey said that their "uncouth habits and uncouth appearance" attracted such looks of concern from the gathering crowd that he felt compelled to address them, saying, "Gentlemen, we are a company of fugitives from Kennebec in New England, driven by famine and persecution to take refuge among you, and therefore I must intreat your candour and compassion to excuse the meanness and singularity of our dress."[16] When a loaf of bread was set before the travellers at a friend's table, Bailey's young son, Charley, had to ask what it was since "the poor little fellow had never seen or tasted any bread made of flour" – one measure of the deprivations in Maine in the years before their eventual exile.[17]

From his own experience, Bailey reflected on the plight of a refugee in the early modern Atlantic world, including the emotional dimensions of that experience.[18] First, he said that refugees could expect an uncertain reception and were likely to be treated by strangers with "suspicion and jealousy."[19] In wartime, refugees often disembarked from their ships with immediate physical needs, unknown political views, and potential diseases. As a refugee himself, Bailey felt that he could expect hostility or suspicion from local inhabitants, whether or not he received government aid. On the one hand, "should the government to which they repair afford them any assistance or support, they immediately become objects of hatred and indignation, for the natives consider them as invaders of their own proper rights" – competitors for jobs, scarce resources, or emoluments. On the other hand, Bailey wrote, refugees who did not obtain official attention could also be resented: "If – as commonly happens – they are wholly neglected by government, they quickly become the most insignificant wretches in nature. They are everywhere treated with indignity ... tho' people at first, from that compassion and benevolence which is natural to the human heart, may console and relieve them, yet the hand of charity will soon be closed, and men will always have contempt for a fellow creature who depends upon their bounty for assistance."[20] Bailey believed that the condition of refugees stretched the capacity of people to respond with sympathy and compassion for others. His optimistic Enlightenment belief in the benevolence of human affections had its limits; when the need was too great, people became insensible. Mass dislocations of peoples created a humanitarian crisis to which only governments could respond. He would soon complain that nations, as well as individuals, could be unfeeling toward the plight of refugees.

While there are moments when Bailey's journal entries from Kennebec to Cornwallis read like a travel account, with attention to his natural surroundings, he observed that there is little pleasure in a refugee's journey "when they are expelled by faction or legal authority." He admitted that exiles "repair to the place of our banishment, however delightful and advantageous, with reluctance and aversion."[21] Bailey also noted the emotional effect of not knowing whether their exile would be temporary or permanent: "What rendered our situation still more distressing was the uncertainty of our return to our country, our friends, and habitation."[22] Indeed, until the conclusion of the war, Bailey, like other Loyalists, retained the hope that British victory would enable their safe return and the resumption of their former lives. This hope (however faint it became) made it difficult for Loyalist refugees to wholeheartedly identify with their new communities, and eventually the dashing of that hope compounded their bitterness.

Ultimately, it was the dependence of refugees upon others that rendered their situation so fraught. "On the whole," wrote Bailey, "I am convinced that no refugee can be happy, unless he is able to support himself by his own fortune, or some employment independent both of the government and the people."[23] Yet such self-sufficiency was difficult to attain. Having escaped the difficulties of war, Loyalists in Nova Scotia were soon mired in practical problems such as insufficient provisions, troubled land surveys, mediocre agricultural land, competition for scarce resources, and an unsatisfactory British claims process.

"WHO CAN BEHOLD SUCH OBJECTS ... WITHOUT EMOTION?"

Bailey's disaffection with Britain was also caused by his sympathetic, empathic response to the conditions of Loyalist refugees. The arrival of Bailey and the Pownalborough exiles was followed by waves of other Loyalist refugees, particularly at the end of the War of Independence. In all, 20,000 Loyalists would make their way to Nova Scotia, many of whom were driven from the uncertainties of war to the deprivations of refugee camps.[24]

In a striking inversion of the devotion to monarchy that characterized Bailey's earlier loyalism, Bailey expressed mocking bitterness toward a king whose tenderness toward his enemies only contributed to the suffering of loyal subjects. Shortly after arriving at his new missionary assignment in Cornwallis, Nova Scotia, Bailey sent a satirical poem of 120 lines to his brother-in-law, wishing that it would "be the humble means of reducing you to a little good humour."[25] Safely framed as a tale of a "famous king / who liv'd and reign'd in days of yore / a Thousand years ago and more," the poem was a thinly veiled description of what Bailey viewed as George III's unjust responses to the American rebels and Loyalists. The poem's humorous style did little to disguise Bailey's rancour and disaffection. Of the king's reluctance to punish his enemies, he wrote, "He can no injury resent / and hates the work of punishment / Had rather ruin half the nation / than give a rascal flagellation." Or again, the king did, "in his humble meekness choose / to lick the hand which gives abuse." The poem also captures the Loyalists' sense of disorientation at being abandoned by Britain; having suffered so much for their king, they found his silence perhaps more painful than their losses at the hands of American revolutionaries.

> But [those] who from virtuous inclination
> treat him with love and veneration,
> who labor with incessant pain
> his cause and empire to maintain,
> who with an honest fervor rose
> to stem the malice of his foes,
> who still remain with equal zeal
> to seek his honor and his weal,
> who leave their children, friends, and wives

and in his service spend their lives
these by their sovereign are neglected,
basely insulted and rejected.

He disregards their plaintive prayers,
nor salves nor relieves their fears,
sees them without the least concern,
pursued with hostile rage and scorn
sees them, for [their] truth and loyalty,
in dungeons doomed to rot and die,
or else expel'd [from] their cheerful homes,
in foreign lands condemn'd to roam,
exposed to causeless infamy
and grapes of pinching poverty,
where men employ their utmost power
them to keep under and devour.

It was painful, contended Bailey, for the Loyalists who had treated the king "with love and veneration … his cause and empire to maintain" to be so "neglected / basely insulted and rejected" by that same sovereign. Bailey levelled the devastating criticism that the king acted unsympathetically toward his loyal subjects in America – "without the least concern." If he saw them at all, he watched unmoved as they were pursued, jailed, exiled, and impoverished.[26] Bailey was moved to pity and compassion by the desperate conditions of Loyalist refugees arriving in Nova Scotia, and was angered by what he saw as Britain's insensibility and inhumanity toward them. "The Refugees in this province are under the influence of melancholy and dejection. The inflexible obstinacy of the rebel powers, the dilatory conduct of the British forces, and the ungenerous treatment they meet with in the regions of New Scotland, have broken the spirits of several worthy persons."[27] As Bailey intimated, when American Loyalists found that their place of refuge bore a troubling resemblance to the republican communities from which they had escaped, their Loyalist ordeal was extended.

Standing on a quay in 1783 to greet the arrival of more Loyalist refugees, Bailey described how their pathetic condition influenced his own feelings and the affections of the refugees themselves.[28] He admitted that it was "impossible to describe the hurry, bustle, and confusion that now prevailed at St. Johns or to communicate the feelings and agitations of mind." He recounted the people's profound disorientation on disembarking at an "unhospitable and wilderness shore" in the middle of a downpour of rain, without shelter from "the horrors of a cold and stormy climate," and lacking the reassuring presence of "friendly authority" to relieve their insecurities. As he walked among the refugees, offering what small comfort and assistance he could, Bailey asked about their individual circumstances. He heard the story of a wife whose husband died as the ship departed New York, and whose son died as the vessel arrived in Nova Scotia. A once-wealthy woman, now impoverished, claimed that rebels had plundered her house without cause. An orphaned boy described how his magistrate father was killed, how his mother had "died with a broken heart," and how he was separated from his only brother. "I am left alone in the desolate and horrid country without a single friend," he concluded. Everywhere children were shivering in their tattered, inadequate clothing. Bailey attempted to articulate the profound emotional impact of observing the condition of the refugees: "The various objects which engaged my attention and the different scenes which arose excited a thousand contending sensations in my breast, at this general and cursory view: anger and meekness, indignation and pity, grief and joy, rage and tenderness, esteem and contempt, anguish and laughter, alternately filled and agitated my mind."[29] As he listened to wives reproach their husbands for joining the "faithless Britons," just as much as they blamed the Continental Congress, and as he heard others "in the extreme bitterness of their spirits" cursing the British crown, Bailey reflected upon what such experiences must mean for their (and his) loyalties.

In Bailey's estimation, the exiles before him were the "unhappy outcasts" of Europe *and* America. He was hard pressed to see that this group owed affection to any country: "Should they be directed in the sentiments, by the dictates of reason, the precepts of christianity, and the feeling of human nature, they cannot regard the continent of their ancestors with affection, but must view every European nation, in its political capacity, with disgust and abhorrence, must they not despise the solemn justice of Spain, the boasted politeness of France, the pretended purity of Holland, the extolled humanity of Britain."[30] Britain's culture of sentiment had once been what attracted Bailey's political affections. Before the Revolutionary War, he had participated in a transatlantic culture of sympathy and cosmopolitan sensibility that helped him feel connected to Britain (and Europe)

from his location in provincial America. On the strand, surrounded by
desperate refugees, the same notions of sentiment and feeling, as well
as reason and faith, stood in judgment of the very nations that had
once seemed the epitome of polite culture. By disregarding the very
people who had exhibited sacrificial loyalty, Bailey charged, European
nations forfeited their claims to politeness, justice, or purity, and
Britain made a mockery of her self-portrayal as an empire of benevolent humanitarianism. In other words, the feelings and sentiments
that had once given shape to his loyalty now deepened his disaffection
from Britain. Bailey contrasted his own sympathy and distress over
the condition of other Loyalist refugees with Britain's *un*feeling, *in*sensible reaction; he claimed that anyone "who can behold such objects
as present themselves to my view without emotion must divest himself
both of religion and human nature."[31]

THE POETICS OF DISAFFECTION

Bailey was a poet before his revolutionary experience. But as a
Loyalist refugee in Nova Scotia, he began to write poetry in a genre
that reflected his sense of disaffection and dislocation: Hudibrastic
verse satire, a style that employed absurdity to expose enthusiasm in
religion or politics. While his *Compendious History of New England*
was certainly written in a minor key, sharply critical of what he perceived as the region's propensity to religious enthusiasm and political self-interest, Bailey nevertheless intended it to be printed for a
general audience, hoping that it would persuade readers to adopt
more cosmopolitan sentiments. In style and content – and even in its
more restricted manuscript circulation – Bailey's satirical poetry, by
contrast, seemed to reflect his chastened confidence about writing
for a single Anglo-American public. He used passion to fortify an
emotional community of Loyalists, rather than the broad society of
sentiment to which he had formerly aspired. Bailey's satire embodies
many of the features of "Loyalist poetics" identified by Philip Gould:
"its separation of virtue from politics, its uncertain view of the elas-
ticity of language ... it does not address a disinterested public sphere
nor does it attempt to connect with an abstract public through elo-
quent performance."[32] Rather than employing careful reasoning or
polite wit, his satire used mockery, stark accusations, and even ribald
humour to skewer American revolutionaries and to hearten or provoke the community of Loyalist refugees.[33]

Bailey's narrative verse imitated the style of Samuel Butler's *Hudibras*, a satirical portrayal of the topsy-turvy world of the seventeenth-century English Civil War.[34] Butler's long poem (published in three parts, 1662, 1663, 1677) was a burlesque epic featuring the Quixotic mock hero Sir Hudibras. The humorous inversions and exaggerations of the poem censured the religious and political dissenters whose rebellion led to regicide and the overturning of English society:

> When *civil* Fury first grew high,
> And men fell out they knew not why;
> When hard words, *Jealousies*, and *Fears*,
> Set Folks together by the ears,
> And made them fight, like mad or drunk,
> For Dame *Religion*, as for Punk.[35]

Written during the early years of the Restoration of the monarchy, *Hudibras* argued that the fragile order of English society was not yet sufficiently safeguarded. The poem asserts the fundamental untrustworthiness and disloyalty of dissenters.[36] Monarchy, in Butler's view, was the only rational check against the chaos of popular opinion; he believed that the alternative was the world portrayed by *Hudibras*, "a world of madness and mayhem, in which charlatans and knaves are unrestrained and authority is unasserted."[37]

Hudibras satirized the seventeenth-century Civil War, but more than a few eighteenth-century readers and imitators saw the poem as a tract for their own unsettling times. Both Loyalist and Patriot poets employed Hudibrastic verse style and themes to comment on the American Revolution; one scholar counted as many as seventy-seven poems, mostly unpublished, in the period from 1765 to 1783.[38] Bailey was not the only poet of Loyalist satire in the British Maritime provinces; Jonathan Odell (1737–1818), whom one scholar described as "perhaps the best satirist of the American Loyalists and among the best poets of the American Revolution," took refuge in New Brunswick.[39] Unlike Bailey, however, Odell's satire largely ceased after he left New York; by contrast, exile seemed to be the environment that incubated Bailey's barbed verse.[40]

Bailey was introduced to *Hudibras* in 1779 by fellow Loyalist Jeremiah Dummer Rogers.[41] Bailey wrote to Rogers, "I have been reading Hudibrass with a profusion of pleasure and perceive that it perfectly agrees with Lord Clarendon's account of the grand rebellion in England."[42] In the months after his introduction to *Hudibras*, Bailey continued to look for parallels between the two revolutions, ordering an unabridged copy of Lord Clarendon's *The History of the Rebellion and Civil Wars in England* (1702–04).[43] Like so many other readers, Bailey saw the similarities between the English Civil War and the American War of Independence: "I perceive a striking resemblance between the characters and proceedings in that time of confusion and those of the present day." If the seventeenth-century revolution's anthem was "The world turned upside down," Bailey experienced the eighteenth-century revolution as similarly disorienting; in one of his Hudibrastic poems, he declared, "the world is overthrown / And all its structure tumbl'd down."[44] Bailey asserted that *both* revolutions were characterized by "hypocrisy, lying, imposition, and disregard for oaths and the most sacred engagements, and the same contempt for authority and all established principles, and lastly the disposition for violence, rapine, plunder, and cruelty."

Hudibrastic poetry allowed Bailey to depict revolutionary leaders or New Light preachers as mock heroes, exaggerating their language to "expos[e] the vulgar, self-interested motives lying behind [their] grand pretensions."[45] To one correspondent, he explained why he portrayed "the insurrections and Heroes of the present day" with such an impolite, impassioned form of poetry: "If it should be deficient in point of elegance and politeness, you must remember that it aims at the manner of Hudibrass, and that licentiousness and rebellion supported by a solemn pretense to religion, are not very delicate subjects, and besides, it may be proper to expose hypocrisy and lewdness when united in the most odious colours."[46] In other words, the Revolution's violence had already shattered the possibility that elegant rhetoric could sustain civil society, or that polite discourse could harmonize differences of opinion in the Anglo-American body politic. Passion had already overwhelmed reason. All that remained was to expose the rhetoric of "liberty" for what Bailey thought it really was. Though Bailey freely admitted there was an element of private revenge in the acerbic humour of his satire, he believed it could still be "attended with public utility."[47] Yet its utility was to expose brokenness, rather than to mend.

Bailey employed his satirical poetry to expose what he perceived as the volatile mix of republican sympathy and religious hypocrisy in Nova Scotia's Planter townships. While he had hoped to find relief from his revolutionary ordeal, the hostile reception he received among former New Englanders in Cornwallis Township only extended it. As he told fellow Loyalist Samuel Peters, "I was quickly after my arrival surprized to find myself surrounded with Whigs, Independents, Anabaptists, newlights, and rebels."[48] In strident language, Bailey described the Nova Scotian sympathizers of the American rebellion with shades of the regicide of the English Civil War: "I am perswaded that the number of King Killers are in proportion ten times greater here than in the dominions of Congress." And just as Butler in *Hudibras* warned that religious dissenters undermined the liberties of England's monarchical constitution, Bailey asserted that the Congregationalism of the former New Englanders was subversive to British loyalty.[49] He claimed that it was only the presence in nearby Halifax of the British Navy that restrained the "saints of the high and mighty congress" from more publicly enacting their "rebellion and treason." As it is, he said, "they are unhappily constrained to fast, pray, mutter, growl, murmur, plot, conspire, and execute in secret chambers and cabals against the tyrannical dominion of Britain."

Along with these reflections, Bailey sent Peters a Hudibrastic paraphrase of "that whiggish maxim, 'the voice of the people is the voice of God'" – a motto that, to Bailey's view, was a rhetorical dressing gown over uglier truths. He worried that popular sovereignty, whether political or religious, very often slid into enthusiasm and social violence, and that "the people" were susceptible to the designs of self-interested populist leaders.

As for Religion, he could mix
And blend it well with politicks,
For 'twas his favorite opinion
In Mobs were seated all dominion.
All power and might he understood,
Rose from the Sovran multitude,
That right and wrong, that good and ill
Were nothing but the rabble's will.
Tho' they renounce the truth for fiction
In nonsense, trust, and contradiction.
And tho' they change ten times a day
As fear or interest leads the way
And what this hour is law and reason,

declare the next revolt and treason.
Yet we such doctrine must receive
And with a pious grin believe.

In ev'ry thing the people's choice
Is truly God Almighty's voice,
'Tis all divine which they've aver'd
However foolish or absurd.
If in a tumult they decree
That men from all restraints are free,
At Liberty to cut our throats
'Tis sanctified by major[ity] votes.
To bathe the sword in kindred blood,
When it promotes the public good.
That is, when men of factious nature
Aim with Ambition to be greater
Should they in mighty congress plod
To set up H – ck [Hancock] for a god.
A god in earnest he must be,
With all the forms of deity.

The high, the low, the rich, and poor
Must quake and tremble at his power,
And who denies him adoration
is Sentenced straightway to damnation.
Yea they have power to godify
An onion, turnip, or a fly
And some have even understood
To consecrate a pole of wood.
Then force their neighbours great and small
Before it on their knees to fall
Since from the people only springs
The right of making gods and kings
Whoe're derives authority
From any sovran powers on high
Is at the best a wicked dreamer
A stupid Tory and blasphemer.

From this we see 'tis demonstration
There's no supreme in the creation

Except that mighty pow'r the People,
That weathercock, which rides the Steeple,
That noisy and licentious rabble
Which storms ev'n heaven itself with gabble,
Should these give sanction to a Lie
'Tis plain that heav'n must Ratify.

In this poem and elsewhere, Bailey rejected the notion that the War of Independence was motivated by religion. Comparing it to the Puritan roots of the English Civil War, Bailey claimed that American revolutionary leaders in New England did not even bother with a "pretense of religion," discerning that "the predominant passion of the age and country was not for religion."[50] With a degree of cynicism, however, Bailey claimed that the revolutionary "hero" of his poem could *use* religion: "he could mix /and blend it well with politicks," to provide a holy veneer over mob violence. For Bailey, when the people were "sovran," there could be no religious or political truth, for the passion of the mob always overwhelmed its reason, and enthusiasm always trumped loyalty. "The People," he pointedly wrote, were "that weathercock which rides the Steeple."[51] In another Hudibrastic poem, Bailey contended that the Puritan leaders of the English Civil War used religion to stir up the passions of the population:

Our fathers by this instrument
Caus'd all the nation to ferment.
...
On words alone they lay the stress
Religion, Liberty, we find
Will work like magic on the mind,
And when their sounds are oft repeated
The multitudes are warm'd and heated.
...
For passion reason will deceive
And make us things absurd believe.[52]

Enthusiasm in religion, Bailey believed, slipped easily into enthusiasm in politics.

In Nova Scotia, then, Bailey embraced a poetics of disaffection. In Hudibrastic verse Bailey discovered the English Civil War as an interpretive framework for understanding the enthusiasms of the American Revolution. Using the form's exaggerated language, he sought to expose and provoke with passion, rather than to convince with wit and reason. Only occasionally publishing his satirical poems in newspapers, Bailey primarily circulated them in manuscript among a circle of fellow Loyalist refugees – expressing and shaping a circumscribed emotional community, rather than a larger public. As Philip Gould observes, "one of the great ironies of Loyalist writing is that it often exacerbates the very sense of isolation it is trying to overcome."[53] Nevertheless, Bailey envisioned other forms of writing as passionate interventions in Nova Scotia's print culture.

"IF ZEAL IS A VIRTUE, THIS IS A PROPER TIME TO EXERT IT"

Bailey may have become increasingly disaffected with Britain, but as the Revolutionary War continued to rage, he began to insist that loyalty demanded passion. Nova Scotians, he asserted, were entirely too sympathetic to the republican rebels, and sadly not compassionate enough toward the Loyalist refugees in their midst. Changing hearts would require passionate writing, not merely polite reasoning. When Bailey discovered that not all Loyalists felt the same emotional urgency, his loyalism was further disaffected. Bailey's reflections on the necessity of a mode of writing that appealed to political passions were occasioned by his interactions with John Howe (1754–1835), a fellow Loyalist refugee and printer resettled in Halifax.[54]

Bailey initiated a correspondence with Howe in December 1780, saying that he understood from mutual acquaintances that Howe was a printer "expelled from the metropolis of sedition, on account of your integrity." He thus wrote to him as a "brother exile."[55] Knowing that Howe would be seeking a means to support himself, Bailey wanted to suggest a "scheme" for Howe's "honour and emolument." He said that the province needed a skilled printer, and complained of the "deficiencies and blunders" in the work produced by current King's printer Anthony Henry – "ignorance and errors … so numerous as to discourage any persons of leisure and genius from contributing to the information [and] entertainment of the public." The arrival of Loyalists in the province marked an expanding and more discerning readership, and the time was ripe for a printer of quality to produce a new periodical.

But it was not only the quality of typesetting and style that motivated Bailey's proposal. He felt that the province needed a loyal counterpart to Henry's *Halifax Gazette*, one that was less sympathetic to the American cause.[56] As a Loyalist refugee, Howe could surely be expected to provide a voice for the "friends of government." Bailey outlined the editorial stance that he had in mind: "I should always be open to the distresses and complaints of the refugee. I have no design of dictating either to you or the public, yet from an honest attachment to the fortunes of my loyal brethren, I am induced to suggest the propriety of beginning every number, either with an essay relative to the times or some historical anecdote which may tend to display the malignity of rebellion." Bailey offered that he would be willing to furnish Howe with pieces from his "considerable collection of materials" on the Revolution, but only "upon condition of inviolable secrecy with pieces of this nature." He concluded the letter by expressing his willingness to help procure subscribers for such a periodical, and observed, "should it be printed in quarto it would make a decent volume at the close of the year." Having appealed to their common experience of suffering as Loyalist refugees, Bailey hoped that Howe would inject a passionately loyal voice into the print culture of a province that harboured too much republican sympathy.

Whether or not Bailey's proposal had any influence, Howe did indeed begin publishing the *Halifax Journal* in December 1780. Two months later, Bailey wrote to frequent Halifax correspondent Thomas Brown (who also knew Howe) about the tone that the publisher was setting for the *Journal,* and his reaction to pieces Bailey had submitted. He observed that Howe was "a sagacious, prudent, and cautious man."[57] Perhaps too cautious. Bailey was willing to concede that at least one of his pieces was too aggressive, and that he "too abruptly discovered [i.e. expressed] a design of attacking the impregnable fortress of rebellion." But attack he must, if Nova Scotians were to be convinced of the terrors of a revolution with which too many of them sympathized.

While Howe was attempting to "avoid political disputes" and take a non-partisan approach in contentious times, Bailey felt the stakes were too high. "That the horrid cause of rebellion should not be exposed because it has some advocates in Accadia ... is a doctrine to which I can by no means subscribe." Bailey admitted that he was disappointed by Howe's response. He had hoped that since Howe was, like him, a Loyalist refugee, he "would have opened his press to the distresses of his brethren," giving voice to "the children of expulsion and contempt." But Howe and Bailey disagreed about how to change hearts and minds.

Howe remarked to Bailey that "the way to a man's conscience is not by irritating his passions." Like many other Anglo-American readers of the polite publications inspired by the *Spectator*, Howe thought that "wit and humour" could be skilfully deployed to prick the conscience without recourse to less rational passions. Bailey, on the other hand, asserted that persons whose emotions were inured to the violence of the Revolution demanded something stronger than such a "casual" attack: "Those miserable vices which have strongly fortified the heart against gentler impressions and hardened the soul with the deepest malignity must be stormed with thunder bolts and when the passions of the guilty are aroused into a tempest without an opportunity of revenge, when the tumult begins a little to subside, he is open to conviction, reflection rushes in, conscience is alarmed, and shame and remorse unite to produce a reformation."[58] One could be forgiven for thinking Bailey sounded something like the New Light preachers he frequently disparaged: storming the heart with thunder to arouse a sense of guilt, awaiting the moment of conviction, alarming the conscience, repentance leading to reformation. Evangelicals and moral philosophers alike shared the belief that the passions could be deployed for moral ends.

Bailey contended that there were times – such as his own – when loyalty demanded zeal. Writing to Thomas Brown about Howe and the directors of his press, he claimed, "Their moderation in the affairs of government, at such a season as the present, is as inconsistent with true loyalty as indifference in matters of religion is with real piety."[59] While moderate emotions may be preferable during seasons of peace and when reasoned debate is possible, such a stance is unsuitable for the violence and polarization of rebellion. Moderation, in such circumstances, could even be considered a vice. On the other hand, Bailey wrote, "If zeal is a virtue, this is a proper time to exert it." Silence, moderation, and calm suggest that one cannot truly apprehend the horror of rebellion nor have sufficient sympathy for suffering. To his brother-in-law, also a Loyalist refugee, Bailey wrote, "We imagined that [Howe] would have attacked rebellion with that honest zeal which ought to distinguish a person in his situation."[60]

The rage of revolution removed the possibility of moderation. Bailey argued, "In such seasons, no medium will be allowed by either party between loyalty and rebellion."[61] Revolution polarized what had been a more complex spectrum of allegiances and affections; there remained only the stark binary of loyalty or rebellion. Figures such as Howe, though, were "trimmers," attempting to plot a course between the two choices, trying for personal or commercial reasons to avoid affronting either party. Bailey skewered this position in a satirical poem sent to Dummer Rogers, inspired by "the extreme caution of our printers, who it seems refuse to insert anything which tends to expose the guilt and madness of rebellion."[62] The poem begins:

> Men often play in politicks
> Like subtle Fox, their cunning tricks
> And when they see all in commotion,
> Like noisy waves in stormy ocean,
> They wisely aim in soft repose
> To keep Dear Self secure from blows.
> Careless of Prince or country's glory,
> They nicely trim twixt whig and tory,
> And gravely think that honesty
> Is out of date in policy.

He continues the tale of a "new fangled nation," in which a "man of wondrous moderation" was compared with those who suffered on behalf of their nation's "law's" and "freedom's cause." While they endured "madness, rage, and foam," the moderate man was at home in "indolence and ease / like mouse in belly of cheese." Indeed, this contrast between the suffering Loyalist and the self-interested moderate was at the heart of Bailey's quarrel with Howe and other so-called Loyalists:

> Nor love nor homage did express
> In word or deed towards King or Congress
> Resolved to sleep in a whole skin,
> Whilst others trug'd thro' thick and thin.

Despite his intention to remain aloof from the conflict, the subject of the poem was molested by the Committee of Correspondence as disaffected because of his evasions, and was likewise mistrusted by the British. His "trimming" came at the cost of his integrity, and for all that, turned out not to be a safe strategy during the conflict.

As Thomas Vincent observes, Bailey's perspective is somewhat problematic.[63] The poem plainly criticizes the "trimmer" for attempting to appease both parties, suggesting that such a balancing act would eventually be revealed as dangerous and untenable. Yet the poem also attacks the unfeeling committee for forcing such a choice upon an innocent citizen. The two-pronged attacks of the poem's satire creates an ambiguous moral message: it is not possible to remain neutral during times of rebellion, but this is itself a form of violence rather than a basic political good. Or to pose the problem a different way: in the poem, Bailey ends up insisting on the same political polarization as the rebel committee, when he in fact experienced this forced choice as coercive.

As they continued their correspondence, Bailey continued to press Howe on the question of appropriate emotions in the face of the rebellion and the condition of the refugees. In a letter of September 1781, Bailey dwelt on the theme of honesty in emotional expression. He did not mean, as in modern usage, that one should be transparent about one's feelings. Instead, Bailey argued that emotions should function like a moral compass, giving an accurate reading of the morality of civil society. Describing what he perceived as the injustices and cruelties of the American rebellion, he wrote, "Such scenes of wickedness and impiety cannot be regarded with *indifference* by an honest man, nor be properly described without some degree of *spirit* and *indignation*."[64] To respond unfeelingly – with anything less than "spirit and indignation" – would demonstrate a lack of moral understanding. To be sure, admitted Bailey, "candor and moderation is required towards all who differ from us in mere opinion." But the actions of revolution went beyond intellectual debate: "when actions are openly avowed, defended, and perpetrated which disgrace humanity, every honest man should be alarmed and be at liberty to express his resentment, under the control, however, of decency and prudence."[65]

Passion should be used in public writing, argued Bailey, to evoke the right public sentiments, whether outrage or sympathy. Certain genres or styles of writing conveyed such emotions more effectively. The pieces that Bailey submitted to Howe's *Halifax Journal* were short historical anecdotes, personal narratives, and satirical poetry. Of the latter, Bailey noted, "it may be proper to employ the force of ridicule and the most animated description in order to expose their vices to publick abhorrence."[66]

Although Bailey lamented what he perceived as the irrationality of the American rebellion, he believed that the intentional use of passion was necessary in public writing to overcome the strong prejudices or complaisant indifference of too many Nova Scotia readers. His goal in such feeling prose and poetry, he wrote to Howe, was "to elucidate the folly, the madness, the iniquity and impiety of this rebellion," and to "excite the compassion of conscientious loyalists towards the unhappy victims of political rage." Though his intent was not to "kindle the resentment of the disaffected by any unseasonable severity," he would rather err on the side of loyal zeal than over-cautious moderation.

Howe remained skeptical about Bailey's case for the effectiveness of passionate writing in winning over those "disaffected with government." It appears (from Bailey's side of the correspondence) that Howe replied with counter examples from Loyalist newspapers in New York and Newport. Despite Bailey's argument that "nothing but the rod of severity can correct [the American rebels'] native stubbornness or work any conviction on their minds," even the strongest writing did not appear to have convinced them to return to loyalty.[67]

Bailey insisted, however, that bold, zealous political writing *did* have an effect on other groups. "Tho' they had no proper effect upon the determined rebels, yet they gave amazing spirit and courage to the loyal party, confirmed the wavering, and ... greatly revived our desponding hearts, and abundantly fortified us against the attacks of persecution."[68] Bailey was convinced that Loyalists still in the American colonies, as well as those refugees in Nova Scotia, would be heartened by writing that confirmed their costly loyalty and expressed solidarity with them. He reckoned that the "timidity" of the British government and recent successes by the rebels rendered such passionate loyal print even more necessary.

In his exchange with Howe, Bailey outlined his justification for adopting the style of writing – more passionate and immoderate than polite – that the Revolution demanded of Loyalists. He hoped that emotional depictions of the violence of revolutionaries or heart-rending tales of refugees' losses would evoke a response from unfeeling hearts: to stir the indifferent, to shame the rebels, to induce sympathy for the refugees. His own ordeal appears to have shaken his confidence that reasoned, polite discourse could overcome disagreement and address a single public. In revolutionary times, it appears that only passion could have an effect. Howe's reticence to forsake moderation, even though a Loyalist refugee himself, contributed to Bailey's Loyalist disaffection.

"IT IS DIFFICULT TO LOVE AND ESTEEM THOSE WHO HAVE NO REGARD FOR ... THE SITUATION OF THEIR STEADFAST ADHERENTS"

The Treaty of Paris of 1783 stripped Bailey's loyalism of any remaining affection. The terms of peace recognized the independence of the United States but only managed to "recommend" the restitution and mild treatment of loyal British subjects.[69] To one correspondent, Bailey gave full vent to his anger and disappointment: "It is impossible to form expressions strong enough in condemning the peace. Neither can a parallel be found to the folly, meanness, injustice, and inhumanity of the British court in deserting her best friends, and delivering her warmest friends to distress and ruin. We may still be loyal from principles or conscience, but it is difficult to love and esteem those who have no regard for their own honor nor the situation of their steadfast adherents."[70] Even as he voiced these bitter reflections on the former object of his affections, Bailey reaffirmed that he intended to persevere in his loyalty. Having been bled of love, however, Bailey's loyalty would be "from principles or conscience."

Bailey remained committed to royal authority and to Britain's constitutional liberties, even if he regarded recent actions as a betrayal of those ideals. In addition to his ideological commitments, Bailey was able to maintain this dichotomy because he ascribed the British betrayal to specific individuals. He believed the American conflict was driven by corrupt officials in the British ministry (and their American co-conspirators). He wrote, "It is not my intention to reproach the nation, since I am convinced that a most wicked and daring faction have directed our public affairs."[71] As he did from the earliest overtures of reconciliation, Bailey laid much of the blame at the feet of George III. In a poem sent to Charles Inglis, then at London, Bailey poured out frustration that bordered on treason, impugning the Crown with vacillation, oppression of its subjects, and passivity unbefitting a monarch:

When I survey the refugees,
Camped under tents and spreading trees;
Along the fields and pastures spread
Without a house to screen their head
From the dire peltings and alarms
Of northeast winds and thunder storms;
From clime to clime obliged to stray
As freakish Britain leads the way;
Sometimes as friends and sons caressed
And them with every ill opprest;
The butt, the scorn, the insult made
Of those to whom they lent their aid;

When I those wretched wights behold
It brings to mind the Saints of old:
Forced o'er hills and dales to [trudge]
And forced in caves and dens to lodge.

But this difference we may see
Between a Saint and a refugee:
The first acknowledges the Lord,
The other bows to George the Third;
The former is Heaven's immortal king,
The last, a supple passive thing.[72]

While in principle Britain's constitutional monarchy should have offered stability and refuge for its subjects, in practice Loyalist refugees were in the most unstable, insecure of circumstances – exposed to the elements in refugee camps. And while they had escaped the "freakish resolutions" of revolutionary mobs, they were hardly better off being led by "freakish Britain." Most damningly, Bailey charged the king with passively bending before the Americans rather than exercising the kind of strength and resolution becoming a ruler. Little remained of the warm affection Bailey once had for the king, the admiration with which he regarded the metropolis, or the pride he felt from his connection to the benevolent empire.

Britain's wartime mismanagements and the betrayal of Loyalists, as he saw things, corroded Bailey's political affections. Instead of turning to republicanism, however, Bailey reconfigured his loyalism on the

basis of political ideology and personal integrity; royal authority and
fidelity to oaths still mattered to social cohesion, even if British leaders
had failed to live up to the promise of the British constitution. Robert
Calhoon has perceptively observed that some Loyalists were able to
channel their disillusionment and their self-understanding as "victims
of both American aggression and British incompetence" into something constructive – "a tough, realistic, and implacable determination
to surmount the difficulties of rebuilding their lives and constructing a
new political social order in British North America."[73] Bailey's determined application of these principles was evident as he put them to
work in a local political dispute.

"THE ENJOYMENT OF LEGAL HAPPINESS"

Bailey's personal feelings about loyalty and enthusiasm were intimately connected to institutional structures. His ordeal in Maine
was largely due to the local revolutionary Committee of Correspondence, which Bailey described as an "unfeeling committee." Despite
Bailey's disaffection with Britain, he remained committed to the
British Constitution as the most likely support for "the enjoyment
of legal happiness." Perhaps not every political institution was so
"unfeeling." This lingering political belief was demonstrated in Bailey's written representation to the Nova Scotia House of Assembly
about the controversial outcome of the 1785 provincial election.[74]

In Nova Scotia communities like Bailey's Annapolis Royal, the
election of 1785 laid bare the fault lines between Loyalists and
previous settlers.[75] The factions in the county were represented in
the election by pre-Loyalist Alexander Howe and Loyalist David
Seabury.[76] The residents of the county – "with prudence, coolness,
and impartiality," in Bailey's words – elected Seabury by a significant
majority.[77] Howe contested the election, alleging the partiality and
undue influence of the sheriff, a Loyalist. The legislative committee
annulled the election result on the sole basis of Howe's depositions.
Bailey considered the new election not only an egregious breach
of custom and rights but also a "cruel imposition by reason of the
severe weather at this season of the year." Despite the difficulties
to travel caused by the "deepness of the snow and the vast collections of ice in our rivers," the residents returned another majority for
Seabury. Bailey's written representation to the Assembly may have
been occasioned by a further appeal by Howe.[78]

What most incensed Bailey about the contest over the results of the elections was that the Loyalist supporters of Seabury were denied their opportunity to be heard by the Provincial Assembly. The basis for his representation was not the relative merits of Seabury or Howe, or even the minutiae of the election process. Instead, Bailey made his case on the basis of "the constitution of the British Empire" and "our established rights."[79] By refusing to grant Seabury and the electors of the county the opportunity to submit their petitions, the Assembly was denying a fundamental constitutional privilege. "Is it not," Bailey asked, "the custom of all polished nations, and the boasted privilege, the glory of British subjects, not to be condemned till after a candid and impartial hearing before their judges and accusers, and is not this custom founded in reason, nature, and religion"? However disaffected with Britain he may have been, Bailey did not hesitate to charge the Assembly: "You have … deprived us of our right as British freeholders." However bruised his faith in British polity, it remained central to his political convictions and the basis on which he and other Loyalists would attempt to build their future.

Loyalists, claimed Bailey, had a particular stake in whether the Assembly safeguarded British liberties or whether it exhibited the kind of arbitrary government they had just escaped. Would the provincial government maintain the constitutional structures that made it possible to enjoy "legal happiness, freedom, and tranquility"? He asked:

If our lawful protectors and guardians neglect to hear our just complaints, if those whom the constitution has appointed to be the supporters of freedom commence Tyrants and have recourse to partial and arbitrary measures, and treat their constituents as the worst of criminals, to whom shall we apply for redress. Where shall we, who have already fled from the horrors of democratic oppression and tyranny to the dominions of Britain for the enjoyment of legal happiness, freedom, and tranquility – where shall we, disappointed, chagrined, insulted and abused, find another retreat, in which we can enjoy the benign influence of royal authority under the best of sovereigns without feeling the malignant strokes of popular decision, or rather, Aristocratic Despotism?[80]

Bailey equated the "enjoyment of legal happiness" with enjoyment of "the benign influence of royal authority." But is it not remarkable that only two years after calling the king a "supple passive thing," Bailey here described him as "the best of sovereigns"? Perhaps the political emotions are not so contradictory as first appears. As this quotation suggests, Bailey had not lost the vivid sense of the refugee experience. His rights as a British subject, he had learned, must be asserted rather than assumed. At the same time, however, Bailey maintained that this sovereign was infinitely safer than "popular decision" or "Aristocratic Despotism." Bailey maintained his loyalty to "royal authority" in the face of the conspiracies of "the mighty" and the enthusiastic "madness of the people."

CONCLUSION

Historian Dror Wahrman has contended that the American Revolution unsettled the political identities of many Americans and Britons. However, Keith Mason adds that Loyalists complicate that thesis. "In the case of the Loyalists," Mason suggests, "the conflict itself actually hardened their sense of identity. It was the subsequent experience of exile that destabilized it."[81] Attending to Bailey's political emotions during his revolutionary ordeal and exile illustrates just this process of hardening and then destabilization, followed in his case by the reconstitution of his loyalism on different intellectual footing. Bailey was harried and beleaguered by the efforts of the Pownalborough committee to police his political affections, but throughout that experience he remained remarkably committed to his loyalty and his oaths. It was actually the *British* response to the Revolution and to its loyal refugees, as he saw things, that destabilized Bailey's sense of political identity and provoked his disaffection. He expressed that disaffection and uncertain identity through the barbed verses of Hudibrastic poetry, written more to commiserate with other disillusioned refugees than to address the kind of diverse, sympathetic British American public he had once envisioned. Bailey's correspondence with printer John Howe reveals that he was less optimistic than before about the power of reason to persuade, and was more willing to employ passion and zeal in his writing, to awaken those who had become insensible to the injustices of British policy.

And yet Bailey did maintain his loyalism despite this disaffection; by reflecting on just this agonizing experience, he clarified what perhaps should have been evident all along: that loyalism, at least for Bailey and others like him, was always about more than an anglophile's fondness for Britain's culture or king, and about more than reactionary conservatism. As he demonstrated in his representation to the Nova Scotia legislature about the disputed provincial election of 1785, Bailey's loyalism had intellectual content: a firm commitment to British constitutionalism and its moderation of the political passions of the moment.

"A good Degree of Affection in Things of Religion becomes us": Henry Alline, Jonathan Scott, and the Long Argument

Consider these statements about the place of emotions in religion, both made by evangelical preachers in Nova Scotia in 1783–84:

> I would be very far from speaking against the Exercise of natural Affection and Passions in Things of Religion ... I think that a good Degree of Affection in Things of Religion becomes us; seeing the Things of Religion are of the greatest Importance.

> But O how apt are young Christians to be led stray, being so fond of everything that has a zeal ... I heard men exhort that had nothing of the Spirit of Christ, but many of the Christians thought them certainly right, because they seemed to have a great zeal ... I believe if they have the spirit of God, [it] brings meekness, love and humility with the zeal.

One of these was written by Henry Alline (1748–1784), a tanner and farmer turned charismatic New Light itinerant who, from his base in Cornwallis Township, sparked a populist religious movement throughout the settlements clustered around the Bay of Fundy and along the St John River. Alline was charged by contemporary critics with fomenting enthusiasm and spreading a heterodox message confused by "reveries of mysticism."[1] The other was penned by Jonathan Scott (1744–1819), a fisherman turned Congregational minister who became Alline's leading critic, and who was seen as a moderating influence by Nova Scotia churches riven by the emotions stirred by the evangelist's ministry. Scott published a point-by-point rebuttal of Alline's theology, a message he claimed was "in direct Opposition to *Reason*, and the Sentiments of sober and considerate People."[2]

With those general positions sketched, it may be surprising to discover that the first statement, urging "the Exercise of natural Affection and Passions in Things of Religion," was made by Scott, while the judicious remark that true zeal must be accompanied by "meekness, love and humility" was offered by Alline.[3] Scott's religion, that is, was not so "rational" as to be unfeeling, and Alline's ministry encompassed emotional moderation as well as rapture. This chapter provides the context for those isolated remarks, arguing that the debate between Alline and Scott cannot be reduced to the "religion of the heart" versus "rational Christianity."

To be sure, the differences between the two Nova Scotia authors on the role of emotions were substantial. Scott charged Henry Alline with "imprudent Zeal and wild Enthusiasm."[4] Having spent time in Cornwallis Township near the beginning of Alline's preaching ministry, and later witnessing the effects of Alline's itinerancy in his own Yarmouth church, Scott complained that Alline's writing, as well as his preaching, was intended to inflame the natural passions rather than to cultivate godly affections. Of Alline's treatise, *Two Mites*, Scott exclaimed, "The whole Book is interspersed with *Poetry*, calculated to excite and raise the *Passions* of the Reader, especially the *young, ignorant*, and *inconsiderate*, who are influenced more by the Sound and Gingle of Words, than by solid Sentences, and rational and scriptural Ideas of divine and eternal Things."[5] Perhaps most painfully, when Scott was forced to resign as minister of the Yarmouth Congregational church, he blamed Alline and other New Light itinerants for sowing the unsocial passions that led to the "Disaffection and Disunion in Sentiment" within his congregation. Scott and Alline would appear to belong to two very different emotional communities.

And yet Alline and Scott had more in common than this rhetoric might suggest. Theirs was not really a New Light-Old Light debate, nor another instance of emotional versus rational religion. The two ministers, for example, shared a commitment to evangelical revivalism. When Scott underwent his own conversion in 1766 and was mocked by his acquaintances for his newfound religious

seriousness, he was willing to embrace the label "New-Light."[6]
Despite his opposition to the Allinite revivals, when he removed
from Nova Scotia to Maine, Scott himself acquired a reputation as
a New Light and a revivalist.[7]

In other words, the disagreement between Alline and Scott can be
seen as, among other things, one iteration of a long-running tension
within Anglo-American Protestantism – and even within the evangelical
movement – between individualistic and communitarian impulses. As
Stephen Foster has persuasively argued, what gave Puritanism its vital-
ity was a "long argument" between the laity's concern for purity and
the magistrates' emphasis on order.[8] While the former tended toward
insularity and separation, the latter embraced comprehensiveness and
was willing to use civil power for religious ends. In language that is
manifestly relevant to the debates about the passions of revival in Nova
Scotia, Foster contended that "The Puritans formed a vision of some
combination of *order* imposed from above and *enthusiasm* elicited from
below."[9] As historians of Puritan New England have demonstrated, the
tenuous balance between these concerns was irrevocably unsettled by
the breakdown (or in the case of new settlements, like Nova Scotia,
the absence) of the traditional town-church synthesis.[10] Scott and Alline
represented the continuation of this tension within evangelicalism in the
Age of Revolutions: how to maintain an emphasis on personal religious
experience without abandoning a comprehensive social vision. Both
writers emphasized conversion-centred piety, but they differed on how
to coordinate that personal emphasis with more communal concerns.
To maintain the purity of personal experience (if not doctrine), Alline
was willing to jettison all "externals," while Scott considered covenant
bonds the very sinews of religion and society.[11] Their polemics clarify
the boundaries between their two emotional communities. However,
looking beyond their rhetoric to the role that emotions actually played
in their thought and practice reveals that those boundaries were more
porous than they appear at first glance – that their emotional communities overlapped and held shared, if contested, convictions about the
public effects of private feelings.

At about the same time that North America's political elites were
attempting to mediate between liberal individualism and the republican vision for the "common good" in public life, the New Light heirs
of the Great Awakening explored various ways of balancing "heart
religion" and social order.[12] As Ruth Bloch has argued, evangelical
religion and sentimental culture, spheres less rarified than politics or

economics, could be mediating spaces between individualistic and communitarian impulses. She writes, "The individualism of evangelical religion and sentimental literature ... upheld the freedom of individual choice, but the choices described within these religious and sentimental frameworks were not those of individual autonomy but of identification with the communal groups of the church and family."[13] Although the emotional preaching of evangelicals was focused on individual conversion, the religious affections they cultivated – from humility to love – were embodied in social settings. And while evangelicals agitated for individual religious choice, they tended to separate into alternative church communities rather than remain isolated agents.[14] Emotions were not only the instruments of individual self-assertion or self-expression; individuals cultivated specific feelings in and for communal contexts.

Anglican critics of evangelicals like Alline, whether Inglis in Halifax or John Strachan (1778–1867) in Upper Canada, typically framed their polemics as "enthusiasm versus loyalty," arguing that evangelical individualism, populism, and egalitarianism fomented republican politics and strained social bonds.[15] But comparing Alline with Scott, as two points along the evangelical spectrum, introduces shades of grey. For despite their real differences, their common convictions about religion and emotion make their disagreement part of an ongoing tension *within* the larger emotional community formed by the heirs of the Great Awakening. Gordon Stewart and George Rawlyk once described Alline's theology, in part, as a "tortuous attempt" to reconcile the "communal religious traditions of the New England way with ... [an] emphasis on the individuality of the Christian experience," and while Alline's proposed reconciliation may indeed have been idiosyncratic, the tension itself was apparent in the evangelical tradition writ large.[16] And that attempt to bridge communitarian and individualistic ideas was just as tortuous and fraught throughout the Revolutionary Atlantic. What follows is a discussion of the role of emotion in Alline's and Scott's theological writings, especially Alline's *Two Mites on Some of the Most Important and Much Disputed Points of Divinity* (1781), and Scott's lengthy published rebuttal, *A Brief View of the Religious Tenets and Sentiments Lately Published* (1784). Particular attention is given to the way that each of them used affections to mediate individual and communal tendencies – how they attempted to avoid the opposite ditches of unsocial enthusiasm and unfeeling formalism.

The print exchange between Alline and Scott was also an instance of how local communities and middling religious leaders negotiated longstanding transatlantic debates about emotions, self-fashioning, and communities. If their literary productions set them apart from most other New Lights in their communities and gave them a measure of regional influence, still their humble origins (a tanner and a fisherman) and lack of formal education locate them at the margins of Anglo-American learned culture. Their close contemporary John Payzant offered a pretty accurate assessment of their formal qualifications when he observed, "It was evident, that Mr. A[lline] was as well educated as Mr. S[cott], for Mr. S[cott] was but a fisher-man – and had taking up Preaching without acadamical aducation."[17] Both authors wrote with the religious concerns of their own region in mind, but did so by adapting the discourses of, and participating in, transatlantic conversations about religious and political emotions. That two largely self-educated Nova Scotian ministers attempted such ambitious, if not always successful, forays into this transatlantic conversation demonstrates how pressing emotions – and ideas about them – were to communities throughout the Enlightenment Atlantic.

"THERE IS NOT ONE SPARK OF TRUE RELIGION IN ALL THE EXTERNALS": ALLINE'S INDIVIDUALISTIC PIETY

Beyond the observation that his New Light message was crackling with "highly charged emotionalism," as one historian put it, how did emotions actually figure into Alline's theological framework?[18] It turns out that he addressed a range of issues related to the affections, beyond the intensity of experience. Was human nature endowed with a capacity for certain affections and sensibilities? What were the obstacles to cultivating virtuous emotions, and how could they be overcome? How could enthusiasm be avoided without losing sight of affect in the religious life? And how did (or should) private feelings reverberate through society? With these and other themes, Alline was addressing many of the same questions as philosophers such as Shaftesbury and Hume, or theologians such as Wesley and Edwards. And if some of his proposals were less coherent or more esoteric than theirs, still his work represents a British North American and evangelical intervention into those transatlantic conversations.[19]

In his treatise *Two Mites on Some of the Most Important and Much Disputed Points of Divinity* (1781), Alline asked why it was that even among putatively religious people, the *"Externals of Religion and Ceremonies"* were regarded as essential to faith while, on the other hand, "the Power of Godliness, and the *Internals* of his Kingdom are either treated as Enthusiasm, or matters of no Importance?"[20] Such was Alline's focus on individual conversion and felt religious experience that his writings expressed ambivalence – and sometimes outright hostility – toward the communal church practices most associated with public morality and social order. "There is not one Spark of true Religion in all the Externals," he averred, "since all Religion is a Work of the Holy Spirit on the inner Man."[21] This interior, affective perspective was woven through his theological writings. Feelings were central to Alline's anti-Calvinistic account of free will and human agency. He described a more feeling God and asserted that happiness in salvation could only be rooted in felt consent. Alline portrayed human salvation as, in part, an awakening from unfeeling insensibility. Conversion was narrated as an exchange of one set of feelings and desires for another. This experiential piety became, in Alline's message, a principle of critique, challenging the authority of unfeeling ministers and dissolving traditional covenants to form congregations with more personal bonds.

"They could be happy no other way": Feelings and Agency

Alline proposed a more feeling alternative to the Calvinism of his New England background. From the divine side of the equation, Alline's God was motivated by love rather than (as he characterized Calvinism) by wrath or indifference. Human beings were created to find their true happiness by connection to that God, but such a love was meaningful only if rendered willingly, out of felt consent. Rather than being arbitrarily chosen, some for salvation, others for damnation, humanity was universally "endowed with such capacity and placed in such a Station, as to render [them] capable of acting as a free Agent."[22] Alline's anti-Calvinism has been cited as an instance of the populist resistance to elite intellectualism and clerical authority, and it was surely that.[23] It is difficult to hear his admonition, "Consent, Consent O Sinner!" and not think of the democratization of public discourse in the Revolutionary Atlantic.[24] Yet Alline's theology may also be seen as part of a more general tendency to moderate Calvinism and to make greater accommodation for individual human agency, even among those theologians who retained Calvinism. George Whitefield, for example, upheld Calvinism over against John Wesley's Arminianism, but Whitefield, as much as anyone, emphasized the capacity of his hearers to respond feelingly to the gospel message.[25] For Alline to emphasize happiness, love, and felt experience was a way of indicating that it really was the individual expressing their agency in receiving God's universal offer of salvation.

Even God, in Alline's theology, acts out of a depth of feeling. Loving benevolence, rather than reason or justice, is the motivation for God to act in creation or salvation. "For the very Nature of the DIVINE BEING," wrote Alline, "is to flow in LOVE and GOODNESS to all his Creatures."[26] Alline portrayed a deeply feeling God, contrasting sharply with the cool detachment of the Calvinist deity, who acted by rational necessity from eternal decrees. That is not to say that Alline perceived God to act on impulsive feelings or irrational passions, changeably moved by the actions of his creation; no, God was the ultimate free agent.[27] God, who was "happy in and of himself," sought to share this happiness with humanity.[28] "The great Design of Heaven," he declared, "was to make His Creatures happy."[29] Alline rejected the belief that God's judgment of sinful humanity was rooted in feelings of anger or wrath, for "such is the nature of the Divine Being, as can never be roiled, incensed, or stirred up to thirst for Revenge."[30] Penitent sinners, then, did not need to fear the changeable feelings of an arbitrary deity, nor rouse an indifferent God. Rather, Alline's God was happy by nature, with a steadily loving disposition toward humanity.

Alline asserted that love must arise from consent. Over against the Calvinist emphasis on God's priority in predestining individuals to salvation or damnation, Alline claimed that love could not be compelled; it must be *felt* to be authentic. Quoting Edward Young's "Night Thoughts," Alline wrote, "Heav'n wills our Happiness, allows our Doom, / Invites us ardently, but not compels."[31] Portraying humanity's original innocence as represented by Adam in Eden, Alline asserted that Adam was "yet a free Agent capable of sinning ... but by no Means compelled ... For if he had been so, he could never have been happy."[32]

Restoring Sensibility

For Alline, the common difficulties of arousing the right feelings and regulating unruly passions pointed to a fundamental problem in fallen human nature, and so he described salvation as an awakening from insensibility. Though he believed that human beings were created with free agency, Alline contended that original sin impaired human moral capabilities. He argued that in their sinful condition, individuals are in a "state of insensibility," a kind of spiritual numbness or slumber in which they are unable to enjoy communion with God, their true source of happiness, nor can they feel proper sorrow for their condition.[33] Humans, that is, are working with a restricted set of moral affections and cannot cultivate the higher emotions unaided. This differed, of course, from more optimistic Enlightenment assumptions about the natural human capacity to cultivate benevolent affections.

The question, then, was how such an impaired faculty would be restored by grace. Alline wrote that the incarnation – God stooping to become a human being in Jesus Christ – restored the human capacity to sense one's condition apart from God and to respond to the gospel message.[34] The incarnation gave to *all* people, on a probationary basis, the power to consent freely to the offer of salvation.[35] Alline did not say that all people have such a moral capacity *by nature* (what he described as the Arminian position). Nor did he propose (as did Calvinist thinkers such as Jonathan Edwards) that God elected to give *some* people a spiritual sense of divine things. Rather, Alline proposed a universal, but God-given, capacity to respond freely and feelingly to God's overtures of love in salvation: "Thus, my dear Reader, you are to consider yourself ... neither elected nor reprobated, but with electing LOVE all around you, and a reprobating Power within you, and with a Conscience capable not of growing a Christian by Degrees, as some vainly imagine, but of hearing the Voice of Redemption, and consenting to the offer when made you by the great Restorer of Mankind."[36] Or in phrasing used throughout his writings, he wrote that, "REDEEMING LOVE knocks at the Door of every Individual," and each person has been given the ability to respond freely to this invitation.[37] Alline, that is, approached the eighteenth-century preoccupation with cultivating virtuous affections and sentiments as a theological problem, and sought to sketch out a solution that mediated between grace and human agency.

Conversion: "The Exchange of an Object of Delight"

Alline narrated conversion, in part, as a transformation of the emotions, as "the Exchange of an Object of Delight" for another.[38] A convert traded a set of worldly passions and delights for new desires and affections. Alline contrasted this focus on an inward change with the adoption of external religious habits or with intellectual assent to specific doctrines. He said that people may be "rationally convinced of many important Points ... may join with some Church ... attend the House of Worship once or twice a Week, ... are very liberal to the Poor, spend once or twice a Day some Time in private Devotion, seem to be zealous in Prayer ... may appear great advocates for Morality."[39] And yet, claimed Alline, "all this may be without a Divine Change in the Heart."[40] The central turning of conversion took place in the affective, rather than the intellectual or moral, aspects of life. Conversion, one of the most characteristic emphases of the evangelical movement, was given a particularly emotional accent in Alline's telling.[41] No one can be truly "born again," he wrote, "if their Hearts and Affections are not redeemed."[42]

Feelings also marked the *stages* of one's conversion. In the first instance, "the great Work of the Spirit of God is ... to bring the Man to a Sense of his fallen Condition, and the Impossibility of Happiness or Redemption while in Love with the Enjoyments of this fallen World."[43] Once a person has been thus "awakened" from their spiritual indifference, according to Alline, he "not only hears of his being a Sinner, but *feels it* in his own Soul."[44] However, feelings could be deceptive, so a potential convert must not settle for "agreeable Frames" that too quickly relieve the discomfiting experience of feeling one's own sin and helplessness.[45] Alline also warned that a person seeking salvation might even experience some "Transports" or feelings of religious ecstasy, but still be misled, for people may have their natural passions or their "animal Spirits" animated in some settings.[46] How, then, is a sincere seeker to know if the feelings they experience are truly indicative of conversion, rather than some facsimile? Rather than any one experience or feeling, Alline counselled his readers that a "divine change of heart" would be accompanied by a more thoroughgoing set of new dispositions and changed emotions:

They will find the Burden of their Sin gone, with their Affections taken off of this World, and set on Things above, with their Hearts oftentimes drawn out after CHRIST, under a feeling Sense of the Worth of his REDEEMING LOVE; at the same Time, with a Sense of their own Vileness, and the Vanity of all Things here below, together with the Worth and Sweetness of heavenly Things, and the Amiableness of the DIVINE BEING, they find an encreasing Thirst after more Liberty from Sin and Darkness, and a continual panting after the Enjoyment of GOD, and a Likeness to the meek and lowly SAVIOUR; for their Hearts, which before were set on Things below, are now set on Thing[s] above.[47]

Conversion, that is, entailed a renovation of one's emotional life: new pleasures, new aspirations, and new dispositions.

To help readers assess whether such a conversion of feeling had taken place in their own hearts, he posed the question, "Where do you get your greatest Happiness, and enjoy the sweetest Moments, not only at some particular Time and Place, but Days and Hours, Weeks and Years?" Is it, he asked, in "the Things of Time and Sense," or is it "in the Enjoyment of CHRIST, the Vitals of Religion, and a feeling sense of DIVINE THINGS between God and your own Soul?"[48] Although Alline often drew attention to the heights of religious experience, he insisted that the evidence of true redemption was not "Fancies, Dreams, or Visions" or the ecstasies of the moment, but rather a change of desires through the course of one's life. This is worth lingering over a moment, because New Lights were known for the rapturous emotionalism of their meetings, as Methodists were shortly thereafter to be known for the raucous spirituality of camp meetings. Alline, however, assigned great importance to emotional experiences and the cultivation of affections that were more personal and that were evident over time, a theme explored in the next chapter. The evangelical message urged women and men, in the words of Phyllis Mack, to "shape their own subjectivity, not in a single cathartic moment at a revival meeting, but over a lifetime."[49]

To focus his message on the conversion of the heart, Alline sought to purge religious practice of what he perceived as distracting encumbrances. Even more than against the seductions of the world, Alline preached against the spiritual dangers of "faithless Prayers, Spiritless Duties, and Christless Christianity."[50] Alline recognized how radical his critique was: "You may think perhaps that I am oversetting all Religion by speaking so much against your Prayers: but let me tell you, that you will never know or enjoy one Spark of True Religion until all those recommending prayers are overset."[51]

Clerical Authority: "A feeling Sense of the Love of God"

For Alline, as for other early evangelicals, personal conversion became a principle of critique, a means for lay people to evaluate and even resist clerical authority. Traditional clerical qualifications, such as education and ordination, were relativized by the evangelical criterion: Did the minister have "a feeling Sense of the Love of God"?[52] "A Man may get his Head full of the Letter of the Word," wrote Alline, yet "his Heart never touched with the Spirit of the Word."[53] As Nancy Christie has observed, religious practice in North America was remade during the long eighteenth century as, among other changes, cultural authority was redefined "in terms of emotional persuasion and dramatic presentation" rather than traditional markers of learning or respectability.[54] Characteristic of this aspect of the Great Awakening was Gilbert Tennent's controversial sermon *The Dangers of an Unconverted Ministry* (1741).[55] Alline was no less provocative in Nova Scotia when, to the question "Whether or not it is absolutely necessary for a Man to be a Converted Man to be qualified for the Work of the Ministry," he forcefully answered in the affirmative.[56] He challenged the province's ministers, "whether or not you have been experimentally acquainted with those Truths in your own Souls."[57] He boldly charged that "the greatest Part" of Christian ministers were unconverted, did not display authentic religious affections, and were unqualified for their position.[58] Alline took his subjective critique of clerical authority to its logical conclusion, urging his hearers to separate from churches and congregations that did not give evidence of experiential piety and felt knowledge of the gospel they preached.[59]

"A chearful Conformity to the Externals of Religion"

Alline most often portrayed the religion of the heart as inimical to churchly or social "externals" – superficial distractions from the more necessary transformation of the affections. That Alline was self-consciously positioning his individualistic New Light message in opposition to the communitarian structures of New England Puritanism was nowhere more apparent than in his comments about church covenants. In the "New England Way," local churches were formed as voluntary covenants among individuals who were able to narrate an experience of personal conversion.[60] The ideal proved difficult to sustain after the first generation of idealistic Puritan settlers, as new migrants and young children began to change the spiritual complexion of New England communities. While church and town were a seamless unity for full members, it was not immediately clear how those who had not yet experienced (or who were indifferent to) a Puritan conversion related to those linked community institutions. How could the Puritan ideal of a reformed church *and* society be sought if some residents remained outside the church? A solution adopted by many churches, the so-called Half-Way Covenant, granted some of the privileges of church membership to those who had not (yet) been accepted on the basis of their personal conversion.[61] The Half-Way Covenant can be seen as a compromise on the side of individual piety in order to secure communal morality and order.

Alline asserted that too often, following this pattern, individuals were admitted to church communion without giving any evidence of a "saving Change" in their hearts, to the detriment of genuine religion. He excoriated the Half-Way Covenant, mockingly asking, "Where, or what Place it is half way to?" He bluntly avowed, "It cannot be half way to Heaven."[62] His attack on such churches as being held together by so many "Paper Covenants" is perhaps the clearest indication that Alline had a radically different social vision from the Puritanism out of which he emerged – determinedly individualistic, rather than communitarian.[63] To focus on sincere heart-felt piety and the individual's covenant with the local church, Alline was willing to surrender a more comprehensive understanding of the covenant as providing a "canopy" over church and society.[64]

By focusing on individualistic piety, Alline mainly communicated ambivalence about the communitarian and social dimensions of Christianity. He observed that a basic religious sensibility might motivate some people to avoid egregious social vices and to "practice some external [religious] performances." He acknowledged that when people change their outward moral behaviour, "it may be better for civil Society." But, Alline continued, "all that can be said of the Change (respecting their own State) is, that they have exchanged from the open profane to the Moralist, and from one Part of the Devil's Kingdom to another."[65] "True religion," for Alline, was defined by a change of the heart, and only incidentally with reference to virtue in civil society.

Yet occasionally Alline articulated an implicit assumption that personal piety would lead to godly sociability, that being heavenly-minded, as it were, could produce some earthly good. Alline remarked that "this internal Work of the Spirit of God will reflect a chearful Conformity to the Externals of Religion."[66] This was a rare acknowledgment that cultivating the emotions could bridge the inner life and social ethics. Although Alline discouraged reliance on external authorities and boundaries, he was optimistic about the ability of individuals (aided by grace) to regulate their social behaviour by "internal constraints on the self."[67] Regulating emotions was, in fact, a way of regulating society. Later evangelicals, such as Edward Manning, developed this tendency much further than Alline's implicit assumptions, finding in voluntary associations a way to combine individual piety and social reform.

"DISAFFECTION AND DISUNION IN SENTIMENT": EMOTIONS AND SOCIAL ORDER

Jonathan Scott was Henry Alline's most vociferous critic. He charged that Alline's singular accent on individualism in religion had serious disruptive social consequences, and he claimed that the passions of New Light spirituality overwhelmed the cultivation of more orderly affections. As one of the few remaining Congregational ministers in Nova Scotia during the American Revolution, Scott (who was settled in Jebogue, Yarmouth) complied with a request from the Cornwallis Congregational church, then without a minister, to spend three months in the township to quell the clamour caused by Alline's preaching. Before the Revolution was over, the wildfire of New Light revival was also kindled in Jebogue, and Scott witnessed a series of divisions within his congregation that eventually led to his resignation.[68] In 1784, Scott published *A Brief View of the Religious Tenets and Sentiments Lately Published and Spread in the Province of Nova-Scotia*, a lengthy rebuttal of the theology and methods of Alline and the New Lights.[69] He could hardly have been more censorious of Alline's treatise, condemning its anti-Calvinism and disavowing Alline's esoteric views on the spiritual, rather than cor-

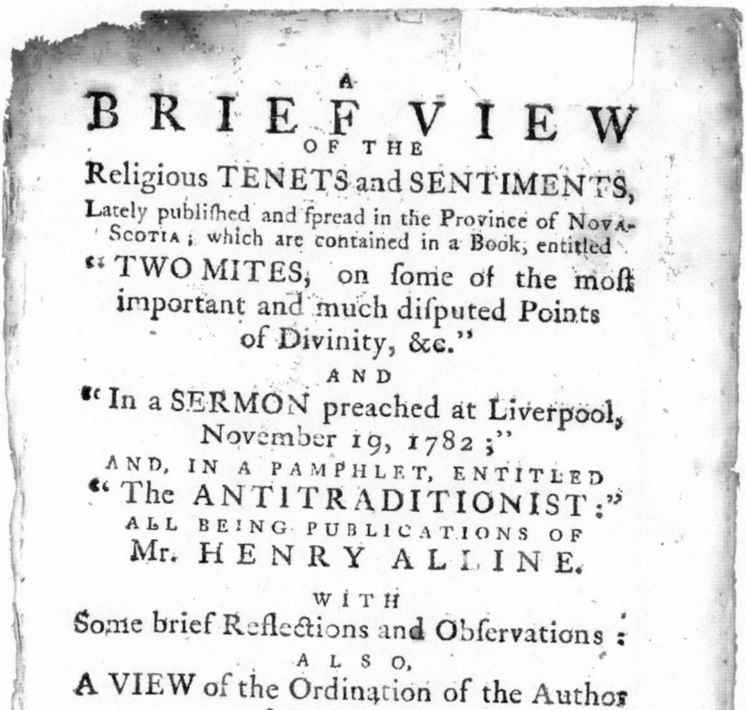

A
BRIEF VIEW
OF THE
Religious TENETS and SENTIMENTS,

Lately publifhed and fpread in the Province of Nova-
Scotia ; which are contained in a Book, entitled
"TWO MITES, on fome of the moft
important and much difputed Points
of Divinity, &c."

AND

"In a SERMON preached at Liverpool,
November 19, 1782 ;"
AND, IN A PAMPHLET, ENTITLED
"The ANTITRADITIONIST :"
ALL BEING PUBLICATIONS OF
Mr. HENRY ALLINE.

WITH
Some brief Reflections and Obfervations :
ALSO,
A VIEW of the Ordination of the Author
of thefe Books :
TOGETHER WITH
A DISCOURSE on external Order.

By JONATHAN SCOTT,
Paftor of a Church in YARMOUTH.

JUDE, verfe 3 *Beloved, when I gave all Diligence to write unto you
of the common Salvation : It was needful for me to write unto you,
and exhort you, that ye fhould earneftly contend for the Faith which
was once delivered unto the Saints.*

HALIFAX :
Printed by JOHN HOWE, in BARRINGTON-STREET.
MDCCLXXXIV.

Figure 5.1 | Jonathan Scott, *A Brief View of the Religious Tenets
and Sentiments lately published and spread in the province of
Nova-Scotia* ... (Halifax, NS: John Howe, 1784), title page.

poreal, nature of the original creation. Alline's thought lacked coherence, he claimed, and threatened to bring that same incoherence to the church: "This *Book*, entitled *Two Mites* ... abounds greatly with bold, barefaced Assertions, and mysterious, uncouth and unintelligible Sentences, which it is not at all likely that the Author understands himself; and the Sentiments and Sentences are, in a great many Instances, inconsistent, and in direct Opposition to each other, so as mutually to overthrow and destroy each other, as also all true Religion and Godliness."[70] For Scott, the unruly argument was of a piece with the havoc that Alline's preaching wreaked in church and society, stirring up dangerous passions more than godly affections.

The affections were central to Scott's long polemic against Alline. His goal, he said, was to help readers "in forming just Ideas concerning the religious *Affections* and *Exercises*, and the *Appearances* of *Religion* which [Alline] has been instrumental in exciting and promoting among People in this Province."[71] What did Alline's publications say about the affections, how did he employ the passions in his poetic style of writing, and what kinds of emotions did his ministry produce in Nova Scotia communities? Such questions, wrote Scott, get to the "Bottom and Foundation of the religion of our Author."[72] To be sure, Scott's analysis portrayed significant differences in the emotional styles of the two ministers. Yet Scott by no means disavowed the importance of the affections in religious life. Despite their many substantive disagreements and conflicting emphases, Scott and Alline did share important commitments about the affections and often employed similar vocabulary. The point is not that Scott and Alline were made from the same mold, or to suggest that Scott was simply a misunderstood revivalist, but rather that polemical rhetoric obscured their common convictions about the role of affections and about the contested meaning of emotions *within* evangelicalism. The terms of their internecine debate as conflicted heirs of the Great Awakening were different from the more familiar opposition between evangelicals and upholders of more "rational" or polite forms of Christianity. Although he contended that Alline's ministry was characterized by a "Spirit of wild *Enthusiasm*," Scott also maintained the centrality of emotions to religious life.[73] In fact, he insisted, "I would be very far from speaking against the Exercise of natural Affection and Passions in Things of Religion. ... And I think that a good Degree of Affection in Things of Religion becomes us; seeing the Things of Religion are of the greatest Importance."[74]

Writing in a polemical mode, Scott, of course, emphasized (and sometimes exaggerated) the differences between their views on the "root" and "fruit" of religious affections.[75]

"Right Affections in Things of Religion," wrote Scott, "have *Truth* for their Foundation" – that is, "the Doctrines and Instructions of the holy Scriptures."[76] Like other eighteenth-century writers on emotions, he understood affections to have cognitive content, rather than seeing feelings and reason in opposition. For evangelical writers, this meant cultivating certain feelings in response to a particular set of theological ideas, such as awe before God's holiness, sorrow at human sin, or gratitude for salvation.[77] Scott condemned the tendency, which he observed among some New Lights, to oppose experiential piety and biblicism. Some, he said, "have cryed up *Christ*, and the *Spirit*, and spiritual *Experiences*, while they have run down and cast Contempt on the Written Word of God, calling it only *Paper and Ink*, a *dead Letter*."[78] Those who downplayed the Bible as the source of religious affections tended to rely on more subjective experiences or idiosyncratic readings of scripture texts (decontextualized from larger theological narratives) – "sudden impressions" and "*Visions* and *Revelations* of Things."[79]

As Scott discussed the effect of conversion on the affections, he emphasized the sanctification of emotions more than the intensity of feelings. It was not enough simply to demonstrate "the greatest shews of *Zeal*," or that one's emotions were "excited and raised to a high Degree."[80] Not every religious feeling, after all, was necessarily an indication of divine activity. "The Affections and good Frames that many People have," contended Scott, might be "nothing but the Workings of natural Passions, or animal Nature excited and stirred up."[81] Grounding one's sense of assurance in the presence of heightened feelings or on moments of religious ecstasy might be misplaced confidence. Rather than occasional impressions, then, Scott described a suite of changed emotions as the fruit of conversion: "delightful Views of the glorious Excellency of God and *Jesus Christ*; Love to God for what he is in himself; universal Love to Mankind; a broken Spirit and constant mourning for Sin; Humbleness of Mind, Meekness, preferring others before Self; Patience under Trials and Losses; Abstractedness from the World, and Affections set on Things above."[82] Despite Scott's portrayal of the sheer emotionalism of New Light spirituality, however, Alline had offered a similar catalogue of changed dispositions as the evidence of a transformed heart.[83]

Scott, as well as Alline, sought revival and raised religious affections. Surveying the religious condition of Nova Scotia, he asserted that "There is a great Need of Reformation."[84] But he took a more moderate approach than what he observed in Alline and the New Lights, one that did not set affections at odds with scripture or reason, and did not overturn order in church and society: "The Truths of divine Revelation, the Order of the Gospel, and the Laws of Nature and Reason of which God is the Author, does not stand so much in the Way as that they must all be violated and destroyed to make Way for a divine Work of the Spirit of God."[85]

Despite his strictures against Alline, Scott was no "Old Light" in the mold of Charles Chauncy of Boston. In fact, Scott drew much of his thinking about emotions from the writings of Chauncy's sometime opponent, the pro-revival theologian of the Great Awakening, Jonathan Edwards. Scott acknowledged his admiration for Edwards, whose *Treatise on the Religious Affections* he regarded as "one of the best Books on *experimental Religion*, except the Bible, that I have ever met with," exhibiting Edwards's genius and "great Acquaintance with *vital Religion* and true *Godliness*."[86] Like Edwards, Scott sought to "distinguish between true and false Religion, between saving Affections and Experience, and those manifold fair Shews and glittering Experiences by which they are counterfeited."[87] Neither felt it was adequate to condone or to condemn all feelings. The contention between Scott and Alline, then, demonstrates two different approaches to emotions among the supporters of evangelical revivals.

Despite their overlapping, if distinct, beliefs about revival and affections, however, the breach between their respective followers was significant. Alline's preaching, Scott charged, was fomenting "Schism and Separation, Rents and Divisions" among Nova Scotia churches.[88] Despite, or perhaps because of, their focus on the religion of the heart rather than "externals," Nova Scotia New Lights were disrupting familiar religious structures and local churches. Citing examples from around the province, Scott claimed that, "there is scarce a Church or religious Community that I can hear of in this Province, but what our Author has broke in upon, and drawn off a Party from it by some Means or other."[89] Most bitterly, Scott recounted the divisions that he experienced in Yarmouth and that he witnessed in Cornwallis. He observed a pattern: soon after Alline or his fellow itinerants preached in an area, those who embraced New Light sentiments charged the settled minister with being unconverted or of preaching merely external religion, and began to separate from their congregations. New Lights, he said, "are flying in Haste, from their Covenants, Promises, Brethren, Friends, from God's House, Worship, Order, and Ordinances."[90] Scott saw the breaking of covenantal ties as an indication that these could not be godly affections.

Scott was particularly attuned to the *social* consequences of Alline's reorientation of religion around individual piety. New Light divisiveness was unravelling the covenants that held church and community together. Scott alleged that Alline had "done what was in his Power to break the Union and Relation that subsist among sober People, which is founded on solemn Covenant."[91] Alline's itinerancy was breaking down both the ties that held together local communities and the affectionate bonds between churches and ministers. When an embattled Scott finally requested a dismissal from the Jebogue church, he stated that Alline's New Light message had made them "a divided People in Things of Religion," alienated from one another by a "Disaffection and Disunion in Sentiment and Practice."[92] Scott also worried that the divisions and separations he saw "in Church and Society, and in Families" had troubling implications for the whole social order, and not only in the religious sphere.[93] The covenant, as was discussed above, represented the Puritan vision of a cohesive social and religious community. With the transplanting of New Englanders to Nova Scotia, with its frontier conditions, religious pluralism (relatively speaking), and centralized (rather than township) governance, it remained an open question how – or even whether – that kind of covenant community could be sustained.[94] So when Alline eschewed such social relations as so many "Paper covenants," and when "All Covenants, Vows, Promises, and Engagements, are trampled upon as the Dirt and Mire [and are] treated with open Contempt," Scott feared that an already-fragile form of community was in danger of fragmentation.[95] Scott's despairing question expressed the challenge that individualism posed to Anglo-American society: "If Men's own Covenant Engagements ... will not bind and hold them ... I know not what will."[96] By focusing on individual and affective piety, were evangelicals like Alline jeopardizing the very communal structures that nurtured that piety?[97]

CONCLUSION

There were both centripetal and centrifugal forces within the evangelical tradition. Just as those in political and economic spheres experienced the pull toward either liberal individualism or a communitarian approach to society, so the religious emphasis on personal experience strained the bonds of communities and made it difficult to sustain a comprehensive social vision. As the conflict between Alline and Scott suggests, religious emotions were one important site where this ongoing tension within evangelicalism was negotiated. Emotions were central to Henry Alline's individualistic New Light message, from his proposals for happy consent in salvation to the description of salvation as awakening from insensibility. Feeling also became a principle of critique, as he condemned the "externals" of unfelt religious practices and warned hearers away from unfeeling ministers. Jonathan Scott rarely admitted it, but he and Alline could agree that the transformation of one's emotions was the most important evidence of conversion. Yet Scott insisted that Alline and the New Lights focused too much on sudden emotional impressions and fleeting ecstatic experiences (which may, in the end, be nothing more than natural passions), instead of the steady transformation of one's dispositions and affections. Scott also worried that Alline and his followers were too careless of the social affections and covenants that knit together church and society, thereby fraying the bonds of the emotional community of which they both, despite their differences, were a part. The charge of "enthusiasm" polemically linked what Scott perceived as extreme individualism with its ripple effects in society.

Nova Scotians, like others in the Enlightenment Atlantic, wrestled with the meaning of sentiments and affections and wondered how self-fashioning and community-building could be reconciled. Alline and Scott, two self-educated ministers from different points along the evangelical spectrum, contributed to these transatlantic conversations and adapted them to their local circumstances. Without claiming that they belong on the same shelf as Hume or Edwards, they were, as J.M. Bumsted said of Alline, "attempting to come to grips with the important intellectual and philosophical issues of [their] time," which certainly included the role of emotions in self and society.[98] The long argument between Alline and Scott also demonstrates that "enthusiasm versus loyalty" is too simplistic, and that the categories of political (dis)loyalty or neutrality are not comprehensive enough to account for the myriad ways that people used emotions to work out the tensions between the personal and the communal.

6

Unfeeling Enthusiasts: Nova Scotia New Lights as an Emotional Community

Freely I hear the Son of God,
  For wretched sinners spilt his blood;
But I no Christ can feel or see,
  For other sinners or for me.

In midnight darkness here I dwell,
  While other souls of glory tell;
They say they feast on joys above,
  But I'm a stranger to their love.[1]

Feelings were not just a preoccupation of Nova Scotia New Lights, as their critics charged. They were a problem. While contemporary critics satirized their sensational excesses or fretted about rampant and unreasonable passion, New Lights themselves sang about their unfeeling hearts. Theirs was the problem, not of *too much* emotion, but of not enough, and of not the right kind. It was a deficiency they experienced at every stage of the spiritual life: newly awakened outsiders wondered if they would always be strangers to the pleasures of salvation; recent converts wanted to feel less "self" and more grace; and long-time pilgrims distrusted the authenticity of old sensations. It is not a little jarring to consider congregations of so-called enthusiasts, supposedly imagining themselves to be "the particular favourites of the divinity," singing lines as insensate as "I no Christ can feel or see."[2] More than tired tropes to be glossed over, the emotional conventions of aspiration and absence employed in New Light verse, narratives, and letters convey the affections that the community valued and expected New Lights to cultivate, however arduous this may have been in lived experience. Because the emotions that characterized their community – from the infrequent achievement of ecstasy to more workaday feelings like serenity – were not easily owned, New Lights spurred one another on through their life writing, their weekly songs, and in their letters.

Jonathan Scott, of course, attacked Henry Alline for the "imprudent Zeal and wild Enthusiasm and Imagination, which manifestly runs through all his Religion."[3] Though controversial during Alline's leadership, Nova Scotia's New Lights were even more likely to be charged as enthusiasts in the decade after his death, when a younger cadre of itinerant preachers led the congregations in a more emotionally demonstrative and perhaps antinomian direction. So concerned about this local movement was Bishop Charles Inglis that in 1791 his charge to the clergy was on the evils of enthusiasm. He contended that the province's New Lights were disseminating "wild notions, to the injury of society and rational piety."[4] Historians, too, have taken note of the emotional dimension of the New Light revivals. Maurice Armstrong described the New Light message as "a gospel which warmed men's hearts and stirred their deepest emotions." The excitement of the revival produced a contagion "among an isolated and emotionally starved people."[5] George Rawlyk emphasized their "exaggerated emphasis both on the emotions and on all sensory perceptions."[6]

Yet the witness of the New Lights themselves was that the right emotions were elusive. It turns out that the ecstasy of the moment had a long backstory. New Lights cultivated "spontaneous" feelings by intentional habits, repeated failures, and a community of concern. Even for so-called enthusiasts, emotions were what historian William Reddy has described as a "domain of effort."[7] As Rawlyk acknowledged, New Lights "sought the mountain peak of religious ecstasy but naively underestimated how difficult it would be for them to remain there."[8]

New Lights, that is, valued a constellation of particular emotions and they taught one another how to acquire and express those feelings. Generalizations about the sheer emotionalism of the movement obscure a whole range of religious affections valued and cultivated by New Lights. As Phyllis Mack says about another evangelical community, "Far from exhibiting mindless enthusiasm or an inchoate desire for contact with the supernatural, many people actually had trouble generating those emotions." Indeed, she continues, "The most cursory reading of unpublished sources shows not the unthinking

hysteria of people's emotional outbursts, but the conscious effort
that often preceded and reinforced them."⁹ Examining the emotional
aspirations of this community, then, sheds much-needed light on the
New Light revivals "as an emotional experience."¹⁰ Doing so also
begins to map the emotional terrain of the *daily*, lived experience
of evangelicals, for whom conversion or ecstatic raptures were only
occasional heights.¹¹ Religious affections were just as much a concern for New Lights when they walked through the arid plains or
dark valleys.

The diary, hymns, and letters examined in this chapter also invite
reflection on the gendered nature of the emotions that were valued in
this New Light community. What do we make of Alline's appropriation of the breathlessly erotic mysticism of the Song of Songs? Was
the New Light emphasis on putatively feminine devotional modes
such as surrender or selflessness at odds with the strong agency of
more masculine expressions of Enlightenment self-fashioning? And
how did conversation among women, in person or by correspondence, mediate the formation of emotional communities in ways
that were just as essential as the circulation of printed texts by male
authors? Examining these New Light verses and the epistolary conversation of awakened women complicates and historicizes any easy
correspondence between particular emotions and gender, as well as
identifying the broad range of religious feelings – both aspirations
and absences – that together marked out this emotional community.

"WHY IS NOT MY WHOLE SOUL RAVISHED ... MORE?"

A nineteenth-century biographer wrote that Alline was "converted in
a rapture; and ever after he sought to live in a rapture; and judged of
his religious condition by his enjoyments and raptures ... He looked
mainly to feeling, especially to rapturous feeling."¹² Indeed, the piv-
otal moment of Alline's life was his conversion, which he described
in this rapturous language: "My whole soul was filled with love,
and ravished with a divine ecstasy beyond any doubts or fears ...
I enjoyed a heaven on earth, and it seemed as if I were wrapped
up in God."¹³ Yet single-minded focus on "rapture" obscures a
whole spectrum of religious feelings – from distress to happiness
to humility – in Alline's experience and theology. Even more importantly, such emotional heights were not merely the gift of a moment;

THE

LIFE

AND

JOURNAL

OF THE

REV. MR. HENRY ALLINE.

BOSTON:
PRINTED BY *GILBERT & DEAN,* AT THEIR PRINTING AND
LOTTERY OFFICE, No. 78, STATE-STREET.
1806.

Figure 6.1 | *The Life and Journal of the Rev. Mr. Henry Alline* (Boston:
Gilbert & Dean, 1806), title page.

they required steady effort and cultivation, and even so were often Alline's aspiration rather than his daily reality. To be sure, being "wrapped up in God" was the *sine qua non* of New Light spirituality, but this state of selfless ecstasy was achieved only occasionally, and then after considerable attention to one's inner life. Alline's journal records the winding road *to* rapture, and then the daily process of emotional self-fashioning that prepared him for those ecstatic moments. Even for Nova Scotia's "mystic," rapture was as much longed-for as enjoyed. In addition, behind the public exuberance of New Light meetings was the more private and daily experience of emotional self-fashioning. Beyond rapture, Alline's journal also described the *other* affections valued in the emotional community of New Lights: certain assurance of their salvation, this-worldly happiness, and self-surrendering humility.[14]

Emotions structured Alline's conversion narrative.[15] His was an experience, not only of new doctrinal beliefs, but of new feelings. Alline described his conversion as a long journey through distress and despair to the joyful moment when redeeming love broke through. Like John Bunyan's Pilgrim, Alline was long stuck in the "slough of despond" before arriving at the desired country. In his memoir, Alline recalled that as a child in Newport, Rhode Island, he had been "awakened" by a thunderstorm to the danger of suddenly dying and being sent to hell.[16] He turned with greater attention to his prayers, catechism, and devotional reading. Rather than affording comfort, however, Alline's "awakening" unsettled him. Page after page of his early memoir is dominated by emotives registering distress: unhappiness, fear, despair, alarm, misery.[17] Such feelings in Alline's account led early psychologist William James to compare his "religious melancholy" to that of John Bunyan.[18] "Oh the distressing days and unhappy nights, that I have waded through!" he wrote. "Nothing but darkness, nothing but distress and slavish fear."[19] He was distressed as he examined his interior life, despaired as he studied and attempted to understand the mysteries of salvation, and was fearful and burdened with guilt when diverted by worldly pursuits.

Despair, however, did serve a purpose in the journey toward conversion. Alline hoped that the despair would win him some divine sympathy; he admitted that he "would sometimes think that my prayers and tears would prevail with God, and sometimes that my being so engaged, so affected, and so humble, would affect God, and cause him to pity me, and be willing to convert me."[20] Could the penitent's pathos change God's own feelings? As Alline came to understand it, despair *did* have a salutary, preparatory purpose, but it was not to appease God. Rather, it was meant to teach the would-be convert *not* to rely on more comforting religious feelings. He explained that an "awakened" person may readily cling to what contemporaries called "agreeable frames" – pleasing spiritual sensations or feelings of comfort – or they may feel their "passions moved" and hope they were closer to conversion.[21] Such feelings, warned Alline, provided only false confidence, a diversion from the divine source of salvation. He asserted that "their joys" were merely their "animal spirits [being] elevated with a prospect of happiness, when the *inmost soul* is never touched or redeemed."[22] The distressing period of preparation, then, is to wean one off the allure of self-confidence and to teach one to recognize superficially comforting emotions. Despairing of self-effort, the seeker, like Alline, could finally throw herself on God's mercy.

Alline narrated his conversion as an emotional hinge – a striking before-and-after moment. The climax occurred in March 1775 when, in anguish, he opened an old Bible to passages in the Book of Psalms that seemed, on the one hand, to describe his sense of sinfulness and brokenness, and on the other, articulated a plea for God to pull him out of his despair.[23] He recalled, "O help me, help me, cried I, thou Redeemer of souls, and save me or I am gone for ever." His prayer that night was "the last word I ever mentioned in my distress (for the change was instantaneous)."[24] Indeed, Alline's emotional vocabulary changed immediately, at least in his retelling. The distress had done its work of preparation, and it rarely occurred again.[25] He wrote of that change: "Redeeming love broke into my soul ... with such power, that my whole soul seemed melted down with love, the burden of guilt and condemnation was gone, darkness was expelled, my heart humbled and filled with gratitude, and my will turned of choice after the infinite God."[26] Conversion, for Alline, was an entire and almost instantaneous exchange of affections. Instead of feeling guilty and troubled, he registered new emotions: love, selfless adoration, humility, and gratitude. From a subjective point of view, this change of feelings served to certify the authenticity of the conversion.[27] These were precisely the religious feelings that he had for months despaired of ever experiencing, so their presence indicated to Alline that some spiritual change had occurred. In a similar vein, after being so long preoccupied with self-examination and the deficiencies of his own heart, he now found that he was less self-focused as his affections turned outward and heavenward: "Attracted by the love and beauty I saw in [God's] divine perfections, my whole soul was inexpressibly ravished with the blessed Redeemer; not with what I expected to enjoy after death or in heaven, but with what I now enjoyed in my soul: for my whole soul seemed filled with the divine being."[28] He was, he continued, "ravished with a divine ecstasy" and "it seemed as if I were wrapped up in God."

He recounted other moments of ecstasy over the next several years. Sometimes he alluded to a "blessed visit to my soul."[29] As an itinerant preacher, Alline's spiritual union sometimes occurred in the saddle: "Riding from place to place I was blessed with a sense of God's love to the world. My soul enjoyed happy hours with God."[30] Of one occasion in the pulpit, he wrote, "when speaking to the christians, my whole soul was so ravished with the love of Jesus, that I could scarcely speak; yea, my heart seemed melted with love."[31] The intensity and immediacy of his feelings in such moments of divine contemplation appeared to overwhelm his self: "Sometimes I had such a sense of his goodness ... Yea, sometimes I almost wish to be dissolved."[32]

And yet rapture usually eluded Alline. Despite the centrality of his rapturous conversion to his spiritual memoir, and despite his constant longing for that same intensity of emotion, his feelings often fell short of such heights. In verse, he expressed that aspiration: "I long to walk and live so near to God; / As *always* taste the sweetness of his word." But he then responded in prose, "O when I speak of those solemn and soul transporting truths, why is not my whole soul ravished with sacred joy and humbled at my Saviour's feet more than I am?"[33] On another occasion, he wrote that although he "enjoyed something of God this day," "yet I am so far from such a realizing sense of things as I think I ought to have, and my soul aspires after, that methinks I know nothing."[34] He complained, "I have seen such a disproportion ... between what I profess to believe and what I feel," and he exclaimed in frustration, "O this unfeeling heart of mine; why does it not melt?"[35] In other words, Alline often found himself unmoved and unfeeling. He aspired to those moments of unselfconscious surrender to divine presence, but these did not come as easily or often as he hoped. Alline regularly noted how difficult it was to maintain a feeling sense of divine things, to linger in those times of enjoyment, or to stay happy. He confessed that his feelings were "sometimes up, then down."[36] In the life of the quintessential New Light, the absence of intense religious feelings was as noteworthy as their presence.

How did Alline explain his difficulty with maintaining a feeling heart? Embodiment was one problem. An important strain in Alline's thought was the opposition of the spiritual and the corporeal. The spirit was imprisoned in the body, seeking heavenly liberation: "All things that were corporeal seem a clog ... a strong chain ... I seem as a wild bird in a cage."[37] He aspired to enjoy constant communion with God but confessed that he continued to struggle with more worldly passions: "I shall never get rid of all those chains, until I leave this mortal world."[38] Alline's language, of course, tended to minimize the extent to which his own religious emotions were embodied – expressed in tears, cries, laughter, and gestures. From his perspective, the physical was a limitation, and he anticipated the heavenly experience of "unmingled joys."[39] Alline also asserted that "zealous disputes about non-essentials" tended to dampen religious affections. He contended that "the life of religion" was "the love of God in [believers'] souls," while discoursing about questions such as the proper methods or subjects of baptism tended to preoccupy Christians when "religion grows cold."[40] He praised one nearby church for seeming to enjoy "so much of the vitals of religion and presence of God, as to lift them up above all sectarian zeal."[41] Others failed to cultivate a ravishing sense of God's presence because their ministers told them not to expect it. Alline claimed that "a number of anti-christian ministers are labouring night and day to prove that a feeling knowledge of redemption in the soul is not to be attained, and that all such pretensions are a vain imagination and a delusion."[42] The expectation that Christian converts should usually and immediately *feel* an assurance of their salvation was one of the central emotional dimensions of the Great Awakening, setting early evangelicalism apart from Puritanism.[43] Yet some ministers hesitated to ascribe such significance to subjective feelings, considering assurance a more elusive prize.

It was not only the *intensity* of feeling that mattered to Alline but also the day-to-day cultivation of specific affections, including happiness, love, and humility. Attending to the particular meanings that Alline invested in each of these terms, rather than assuming unchanging definitions, illuminates some of the values of the New Lights as an emotional community. Perhaps the most prominent of those emotions are happiness and pleasure. On almost every page of Alline's journal (after his conversion) are references to enjoyment and happiness:

> Christ is ... the source of happiness ... the joy of my life.[44]

> I enjoyed something of God this day.[45]

> As I was riding through the woods, my soul enjoyed that which the world cannot give nor take away.[46]

> [I] enjoyed some happy hours in my own soul.[47]

> I enjoyed some happy moments this day while travelling.[48]

> O the happiness of living near the Lord Jesus Christ![49]

As innocuous as these references may seem to modern readers, Alline's emphasis on *present* happiness and enjoyment is noteworthy. Echoing a sentiment famously expressed in the American Declaration of Independence, Alline took it as a given that humanity was "of an aspiring Nature and must always be in Pursuit of Happiness."[50] In this emphasis, Alline reflected the Enlightenment's optimistic belief that pleasure could be found in *this* and not only in a future heavenly life. His was not a deferred happiness, but could be a quotidian pleasure: "It was a heaven whenever or wherever I enjoyed my God."[51] Though religious writers such as Alline differed from some Enlightenment philosophers by maintaining the necessity of divine grace in human happiness, they participated in a fundamental shift in expectations, "presenting happiness as something to which all human beings could aspire *in this life.*"[52]

Another specific emotion that Alline sought to cultivate was humility: "O for humility, humility."[53] Alline often linked his desire for humility with the image of sitting "at the feet of Jesus," a posture of learning and surrender; "O that I had an humble place near his blessed feet to be swallowed up in God."[54] Humility sits uneasily in Enlightenment accounts of self-fashioning, in which assertions of agency and individual choices predominate. Cultivating humility and other forms of self-denial or self-surrender (themes taken up below in New Light hymns) seems the opposite of such assertiveness.

Yet as historian Phyllis Mack has observed, evangelicals did indeed aspire to feelings that seemed to surrender, as well as to fashion, the self. She proposes that historians recover "a conception of agency in which autonomy is less important than self-transcendence and in which the energy to act in the world is generated and sustained by a prior act of personal surrender."[55] Alline's desire, "O that I was more humble!" then, represented his aspiration to fashion a self that was not self-centred.[56]

In addition to any single feeling, Alline framed the process of sanctification as a fundamental reorientation of the heart: what the Christian loved and hated, what they were attracted to or recoiled from, how their passions were inclined. He described this continuing conversion of feelings in this way: "He that has the turn, that is after God's own heart, is also humble, and longs greatly to be free from sin, yea, from all sin whatever, and to be made perfectly holy: while those of the other turn do not wholly hate sin. O happy, happy souls, whose treasure is above; their love and holiness centre there, constrained by the ties of love."[57] Such a radical emotional transformation was one of the most convincing kinds of evidence that redemption had touched the inner person. Notice, too, that *longing* for a change of heart, and not only its perfection, was, for Alline, a sign of grace. The steady drumbeat of emotional aspiration in Alline's journal – the desire for more love, more humility, more enjoyment, more happiness – was itself an indication of a transforming heart.

Alline's journal not only recorded his other attempts at emotional self-fashioning but was also *itself* a medium to shape his religious affections. The habit of reporting his feelings was another means of paying attention to them. Of one such experience he wrote in his journal, "Employed some time in writing this day; and blessed hours, I have often, being thus employed, enjoyed, when I could feel what I wrote, and feast my soul on the glorious plan of life."[58] Writing his experiences (or the feelings to which he aspired) could change or intensify those feelings. Alline used his journal "to pen down the travels of my soul," but he did not only climb the heights of ecstasy; he also sojourned in the valleys of despair and across the unfeeling plain.[59] Though he certainly sought moments of spiritual rapture, he also sought to cultivate a range of religious affections and regarded his daily emotional transformation as evidence of conversion and sanctification.

"O LET ME FEEL THY LOVE DIVINE":
ALLINE'S HYMNS AS EMOTIONAL TEXTS

The hymns of Henry Alline were the texts by which Nova Scotia New Lights weekly proclaimed not only their faith but also the religious emotions that they valued most.[60] Literary scholar Thomas Vincent called attention to Alline's ability as a hymn writer to "communicate the emotional reality of religious experience," remarking that Alline's poetry did this "within the range of the sentiments and affections of ordinary [people]."[61] In 1791, when a young Edward Manning was struggling with the problem of his own unfeeling heart prior to his conversion, a neighbour gave him some lines from a hymn by "Dear Mr. Alline." Those verses, which began "O Hardened, Hardened heart of mine," Manning later recalled, "set forth my condition as it really was."[62] As this example suggests, Alline's hymns did not only focus on the relief of conversion or the glories of heaven; like his journal, the hymns, too, reflected the difficulties of shaping one's emotional life. Examining his large collection of hymns reveals some of the dominant themes in the emotional style of Nova Scotia New Lights: the problem of the unfeeling heart, the goal of self*less* affections, feelings as evidence of spiritual transformation, and the present enjoyment of religious happiness.

Hymns played an important role in shaping the affective spirituality of dissenting Protestant and evangelical churches.[63] As Alline asserted in the preface to his hymnal, singing could be useful to raise religious affections: "the heart may be alarmed, and stirred up to action, by local objects or vocal sounds."[64] He suggested that hymns were "far more likely to stir up and engage the heart (especially souls enlightened and groaning for liberty) when they express the state, groans, and desires of their own souls."[65] For that reason, Alline wrote hymns that were, he believed, "adapted to almost every capacity, station of life, or frame of mind."[66] His large collection of hymns was organized into five books, each of which reflected such a stage in the spiritual life, from awakening to conversion to the trials of the Christian to heavenly joys. Laid out in this way, the hymns can be read as a guide to fashioning the affections through each of those stages of the religious life.

The Problem of the Unfeeling Heart

Other souls his love have felt,
Will it not my hardness melt?[67]

The conversion of a person's emotions, according to New Lights, began with a growing awareness that the unconverted heart has a limited range and capacity – there are many feelings that one simply cannot experience. Many of the hymns in the first part of Alline's hymnbook, written in the "language of awakened sinners," reflect this experience of being caught between *knowing* and *feeling* the message of salvation.[68] Awakened sinners, who are just becoming "sensible" of their spiritual condition, begin, paradoxically, to feel sharply their *lack* of feeling, or, as many of these hymns put it, the "hardness" of their heart. [69] Having cast off spiritual indifference or the enjoyment of "sensual joys," the awakened person experiences the frustration of lingering sin and habitual stubbornness: "O what a harden'd wretch am I! / Will nothing melt my hardened mind? / ... my heart's so hard in sin / I neither feel, nor melt nor move."[70] The inability to feel, or to be moved or "melted," was an epistemological, as well as soteriological, concern; that is, unfelt knowledge was only partial or merely intellectual, in the same way that one can only *know* that honey is sweet by tasting it. The hymn entitled "A sinner convinced of a hard heart," drew together many of these themes:

1 Was e'er a wretch so hard as I
    My heart will neither melt nor cry,
I'm griev'd because no more distress'd,
    And wonder I so easy rest.

2 My stubborn will, will not relent;
    Nor my obdurate heart repent;
O might some pow'r of love divine,
    E'er melt this rocky heart of mine!

3 Come mighty God, these foes subdue,
    Form my benighted soul anew;
O let me taste the joys above,
    And join to sing redeeming love.

4 Give me one spark of heav'nly day,
    To scatter all those clouds away;
Nor shall I ever happy be,
    Till from these chains I am set free.[71]

The hard heart of the awakened sinner was not the result of indifference but of natural inability. Only "some pow'r of love divine," wrote Alline, could "melt this rocky heart of mine"; only God could form a "benighted soul anew" so that the awakened sinner acquired a "taste" for heavenly joys. Godly feelings, according to New Lights, did not come naturally or easily to sinful human beings; evangelicals did not share the optimism of sentimentalist moral philosophers who believed it was in human nature to express moral sentiments or benevolent affections. Over against the innate "moral sense" postulated by Shaftesbury and Hutcheson, for example, evangelicals like Alline asserted that unconverted humanity was "insensible" until "awakened" to new senses, new feelings, by grace. Only then might a hard heart be melted.

Desire

O Lord, methinks I feel thy love
And long to love thee more.[72]

Perhaps the most fundamental emotional transformation for New Lights was the conversion of desire – the reorientation of the heart toward new loves, new pleasures.[73] At the heart of these new desires was the desire for God, a longing expressed in Alline's hymn "Desiring Christ above all things":

1 Methinks I long to see thy face,
    O thou indulgent God,
To taste the sweetness of thy grace,
    and spread thy name abroad.

2 Jesus let thy heav'nly arms,
    Encircle me around,
And lift my heart above the charms,
    Of this enchanted ground.

3 Let lofty themes my soul inspire,
   To soar for joys above;
My heart inflame with the sweet fire
   Of thine immortal love.

4 O let the glories of thy name,
   My life and breath employ,
And ev'ry pow'r of thought inflame
   With pure seraphic joy.[74]

In contrast to the "insensibility" of those not yet converted, this song employed the vocabulary of the senses: sight, taste, sweetness. The lines convey experience and pleasure, but also a desire for a deeper spiritual communion. For the new convert, desire for God was kindled, rather than satisfied – a theme expressed by Alline's use of fire imagery: "My heart inflame with the sweet fire / Of thine immortal love," "ev'ry pow'r of thought inflame," or, in the words of another song, "O let thy love our souls inflame."[75] The prayer to be "inflamed" suggests emotional intensity, but also a willingness for the self to be consumed by the divine Other.

This language of selfless desire is the context for understanding the New Light preoccupation with moments of spiritual communion and ecstasy; rather than a yearning for sensation per se, the hymns taught them to aspire for more of God's presence. As New Lights sought to fashion their emotions, they attempted to do so with less of *self* at the centre of their experience. In the words of the hymn "Longing to be wholly for God," they prayed:

   I want all self to be subdu'd

   I want my will to be resign'd

   I want my soul bound up in God.[76]

And in a desire that confounds Enlightenment definitions of self-fashioning, they prayed, "O let me and thy self be one."

Feelings and Assurance

> When e'er I feel that faith divine
> I climb to realms of bliss;
> I feel the blessed Lord is mine,
> And *know* that I am his.[77]

The presence of certain religious feelings provided New Lights with
assurance of their salvation; the absence of those emotions provoked
uncertainty and doubt. Like other evangelicals, Alline sought to inject
an emphasis on personal experience into a religious tradition that he
felt had become too reliant on "externals" such as outward morality
or nominal intellectual assent. The presence – or the intensity or duration – of "felt knowledge" provided the subjective means of convincing oneself and others that an interior change had occurred.[78]

> O might I always feel thy pow'r
> Of that eternal life divine!
> Then could I say at every hour,
> That I was his and he was mine.
> ...
>
> Long as I felt the heav'nly charms,
> And tasted the immortal food,
> I would not leave my Saviour's arms,
> For countless years of earthly good.[79]

Not only the intensity, but also the consistency, of feeling provided
New Lights with the assurance that they had been, as they believed,
united with Christ. Another hymn has them sing, "O let me *feel* thy
love divine ... until I *know* that thou art mine."[80]

Not surprisingly, perhaps, such a subjective form of evidence often proved fleeting. Feelings were notoriously difficult to
sustain amid the changes of daily life. In "The travels of a doubt-
ing Christian," Alline articulates that experience of uncertainty. The
song confesses, "Once ... I thought the Lord had set me free, / And
all my doubts were over."[81] But that certainty dissolved when the
narrator wrestled with competing emotions:

But O! I left my heav'nly friend,
  And follow'd false delights;
Soon did my joyful moments end,
  In long and tedious nights.

While the hymn's closing lines expressed some confidence that their
desires for God could be renewed, they also retain a degree of ambiguity, stating how dependent New Lights were on feelings for their
identity: "Unless I *feel* that thou art mine, / I cannot think I'm blest."
In another hymn, singers second-guessed those feelings that once
seemed to assure them of spiritual security:

1 O that I *knew* it was the case
My soul was born of God,
And found myself among that race,
Washed in the Saviour's blood!

2 The time has been, *I thought I knew*
The bless'd Redeemer's voice;
I thought I lost my burden too,
And *felt* my heart rejoice.

3 *I thought* my will was then resign'd
To the Redeemer's ways,
And *felt* my inmost soul inclin'd
To tell the world his grace.

4 But O! *too soon* the scene was turn'd
I lost that pleasing view;
I lost the sweetness once I found
Lost earthly pleasures too.[82]

The hymn is a frank admission of the difficulties of using emotions
to ground religious certainty. The loss of feelings was not only troubling in the present moment but also introduced doubts about *previous* affections and assurance: "I thought I knew ... I thought I lost
my burden ... I thought my will was then resign'd." The implication
is that true feelings were lasting feelings. The emphasis in Alline's

verse was on feelings of intimacy and nearness to God. While New
Lights gave considerable thought to maintaining these feelings of
spiritual union and assurance, their sung theology did not obviously
teach them how to persevere through changing or absent emotions.

Feeling Heavenly Joys on Earth

> No distant God I know
>> Or future heav'n can trust;
> I want my heav'n *begun below*;
>> I want a *present* Christ.[83]

New Lights certainly retained a strong preoccupation with the joys
of heaven. The last section of Alline's hymnbook consisted "chiefly
of infinite wonders, transporting views and christian triumphs."[84]
Heaven, New Lights believed, will be the future realm of unend-
ing rapture, unmediated intimacy, and "unmingled joy."[85] Yet New
Lights insisted that their happiness was not entirely deferred until
the afterlife; they sang about "Heaven on earth."[86] That is, feelings
of spiritual communion, delight, and love in the present life were a
genuine foretaste of what awaited the resurrected Christian.

> 1 O for a taste of life divine
> To feed this hungry soul of mine!
> I want the Son of God to know
> And taste of heav'n while here below.

> 2 If I were sure that I should have
> A crown of joy beyond the grave,
> Yet that alone won't do for me;
> I want while here with God to be.[87]

While some contemporaries exchanged the happiness of a future
heaven for the "pursuit of happiness" in this life, New Lights did not
feel the need to choose. Rather than delayed joy, they believed that
the very essence of the Christian life was to experience *in the present*
a taste of the delights that awaited them: a "taste of heav'n while
here below." "On earth," they sang, "my soul enjoys a heav'n."[88] By
making the feeling experience of God's presence the essence of both

future hope and this-worldly spirituality, Alline could write – in the words of the title of one hymn – "Heaven not promised, but possessed." In striking language, New Lights proclaimed:

> It's not a heav'n to come
>   My soul can satisfy;
> Nor can I find myself at home
>   But with my Jesus nigh.
>
> O God thy heavens bow,
>   These parting walls remove,
> Let me begin my glory *now*,
>   And *here* enjoy thy love.[89]

The hymns of Henry Alline, sung by New Lights in Nova Scotia churches (and beyond), expressed the emotions that were valued in their community. Alline structured the hymnbook, like his conversion narrative, to articulate the emotional transformations of the Christian life – from the hard, unfeeling heart of the awakened sinner to the convert's growing desire for God to feelings of intimacy that, when present, provided the grounds for their assurance. The emotional "transports" that they experienced (or sought) in the present were, for Alline and the New Lights, a taste of heaven on earth.

"I THINK I FEEL NEW DESIRES": THE EMOTIONAL SELF-FASHIONING OF NEW LIGHT WOMEN

"Dear Sister in Christ," wrote Charlotte Prescott to Sarah Brown on 23 May 1790, "For So I trust ... I may call you; and tho' we are Strangers in person yet not in heart, but Join'd in the Everlasting Love of Jesus, which I find at times to draw my mind away from all Created Good."[90] Prescott's letter is one of several dozen written by Nova Scotia New Lights in the decade after Alline's death in 1784 and collected in a manuscript notebook by contemporary correspondent Thomas Bennett.[91] Like Prescott and Brown, the New Light correspondents thought themselves to be joined in heart – an emotional community sharing common experiences and aspirations. Though the circulation of the diary and hymns of Alline was crucial to the creation of a New Light community spread throughout scattered settlements, it is the letters that reveal the sinews of this emotional community as also a *textual* community.[92] Joseph Dimock, writing to Bennett on one occasion with revival news, claimed, "It warms my Heart while I write ... [and] while you read your Heart longs to be [here]." Joseph Baily simply confessed in another letter, "I feel as I write."[93] Beyond this sense of an affectionate connection, the letters, particularly the many between New Light women, were also the sites of mutual emotional fashioning. The correspondents expressed their aspirations, articulated their shortcomings, and offered advice or encouragement to one another about how to cultivate the emotions valued by the New Light community.

Recent scholarship has identified conversation and correspondence among women as an important site for Enlightenment culture, whether the French *salonnières* or the English bluestocking circle, expanding engagement with Enlightenment ideas beyond a small coterie of philosophes.[94] Nova Scotia New Lights were certainly not bluestockings, but their correspondence reveals the wide range of citizens – especially women – thoughtfully engaged in the era's debates and preoccupations, including questions about the public meaning of emotions and the intentional cultivation of particular affections and sentiments.[95]

"I dont know that I ever felt any thing"

Emotions could be a source of profound uncertainty and doubt. Charlotte Lusby, a New Light in Amherst, Nova Scotia, wrote to Thomas Bennett of her struggles to make sense of her religious feelings and her doubts about whether she had truly been converted.[96] With a sense of exasperation, she wrote, "I wish I knew what or where I am."[97] In one letter, she complained of her insensibility and cast doubt upon such religious feelings that she did have:

> Sr
> I take this opportunity to write to you to let you know
> Something of my Mind. I Can tell you how Stupid I am. It Seems
> to me that I am more hard and Stupid than ever I was in my life.
> I dont know that I ever felt any thing of the Love of God in my
> life. I doubt it greatly Sometimes and do at present. I thought
> Once and more than once that I felt happy, But I am so Stupid
> and hard that it Seems I am unmovable. It Seems to Me I have

got Secure and Insensible, and In a manner Contented; for I feel
Such a Wicked Heart that is almost Reigns Master. You must
pray for me when you Can, And when you are happy you must
write. – I was at Meeting this day And I felt my Heart as hard
as a Stone. Could any one feel so that ever was happy Before,
for I am so uneven it Seems to me I must be a Stumbling block
to poor Sinners. I realy wish Sometimes I was out of their way
for I do hurt. Remember me to all the Girls over there. I must
Conclude least I weary your patience
    I Conclude yrs C.L.[98]

Lusby used several terms to describe what she perceived as her
inability to feel the kinds of emotions that she associated with a
true conversion: stupid, hard, unmovable, insensible. She admitted
her frustration, for example, that at a New Light meeting "I felt
my Heart as hard as a Stone" – apparently unmoved by what she
observed.

Such insensibility made Lusby doubt the authenticity of her past
feelings, and therefore of her conversion. She confessed, "I dont
know that I *ever* felt any thing of the Love of God in my life" and
"I *thought* ... that I felt happy."[99] It could be difficult for New Lights
to gauge the sincerity and the meaning of their emotions. Such interpretation, moreover, was not the task of a moment only, since Lusby
expected a sense of consistency over time: her current feelings cast
doubt on her previous emotional assurances.

Counterintuitively, at least for modern readers, Lusby identified the
feelings of security and contentment as obstacles. Writing disapprov-
ingly, she said, "It Seems to Me I have got Secure and Insensible, and
In a manner Contented." New Lights, it seems, did not want to be
relieved of their emotional longings too easily; living with restlessness
was preferable to what they felt to be false comfort. As she put it in an
earlier letter, "Sometimes I think I am resting Short of Christ, O and
unconcerned about my Soul."[100] Even *religious* feelings could be problematic. Harris Harding warned another correspondent to be vigilant
about a "Natural Passion for Religion" – feelings of relief, contentment, or security that focused too much on self, and not enough on
God.[101] Staying "sensible" apparently demanded a continuing degree
of uncertainty, examining the source and effect of one's feelings.

Lusby concluded her letter with the worry that her uneven emotional life would prove as confusing to others in the New Light

community as it was to her. New Lights modelled their feelings and emotional responses on those of others, but as Lusby's example illustrates, interpreting the affections of others was just as subjective and uncertain an endeavour as knowing one's own heart.

"Ravish'd with his Beauty"

The same year that Charlotte Lusby was writing to Thomas Bennett, her sister, Betsy (or Elizabeth) Lusby, received a letter from Elizabeth Blair. Conveying the intense emotions of selfless contemplation, the letter read in part:

> I have Cause to bless and adore him for what he is in himself – infinitely Holy in all his ways and Righteous in all his Judgements. O go on in the Strength of your Lord and Master, Stand in that Bless'd Cause which is Stronger than Death, for Methinks The happy day hastens when our Souls shall be disentangled from the Clogs of Mortality and we Shall awake in his Likeness And be Satisfied. – O Can it be possible that Worms of the dust will be so ravish'd with his Beauty – Thou art fair my Love, Thou hast dove's Eyes. O Soul-Transporting Word, *God Man Mediator*, "The Bright and Morning Star that leads the way." Methinks my imprison'd [soul] longs to be gone, But O why Should I think the time long when I feel his Love and will Carry me thro all my Trials, and how fair is my love, my Sister, my Spouse. When I feel his Smiles I Can Say he is my friend in time, and will be thro Eternity; And why Should I be Impatient to be gone for he has promis'd me never to leave me nor forsake me. O that he may Empty me out of Self, for I know this Bless'd Robe of Righteousness will – and that, and that alone will – stand when Heaven and Earth shall pass Away.[102]

Compared with the self-conscious uncertainty of Charlotte Lusby's letter, Blair's heightened language pointed away from herself, contemplating the person and work of Christ, a New Light version of the "Beatific Vision." She anticipated a future (but hastening) day when she would be "ravish'd with his Beauty" and finally be satisfied.

The sensuous language of ravishing, so central to New Light emotional discourse, was inescapably gendered. For Blair, both female and male New Lights were "lovers of Jesus," her letter drawing upon

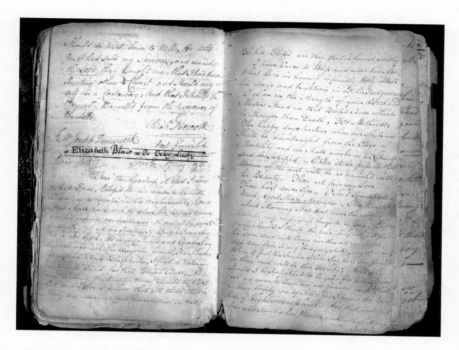

Figure 6.2 | Elizabeth Blair to Betsy Lusby, Letter, 17 August 1790.

the erotic imagery of the biblical book Song of Songs: "Thou art fair, Thou hast dove's Eyes," "How fair is my love ... my Spouse."[103] Like a lover, Blair's contemplative preoccupation was with the beauty of her beloved, adoring Christ "for what he is in himself" rather than the benefits she received. With this mystical use of the Song of Songs, these female correspondents joined a long devotional tradition – dating back at least as far as Bernard of Clairvaux (c 1090–1154) and Teresa of Avila (1515–1582) – using the language of matrimony for the mystical connection of the believer's soul to Christ, the Beloved.[104]

This "Soul Transporting" experience of surrendering oneself to a vision of the glory of Christ was the most desired, if often elusive, stage of New Light spirituality, and was often cultivated – as it was for Blair – by reflecting on the sharp divide between the heavenly and the earthly. Sarah Brown of Newport, Nova Scotia, wrote in ecstasy, "My Tongue fails to Express the Views of Eternal Glory ...

O, a field of divine Light transports my Soul to a paradice of Joy and wonder ... O Transporting View ... O Love transporting." And Elizabeth Prescott simply declared that she "often found [God's] Love to transport my Soul Beyond itself."[105] So God-directed, rather than self-centred, was this "transporting" experience that Blair declared, "O that he may Empty me out of Self."[106] Once again, New Lights decisively asserted that the "pursuit of happiness," that quintessential eighteenth-century preoccupation, could lead *away* from oneself.

Could such emotional self-surrender be *cultivated*? To New Light preacher Harris Harding, *less* control and regulation was required. He advised a Horton correspondent, "When you feel your Soul drawing after [Jesus], dont fear to let it go freely, dont Stand to examin whither it be right; nor yet to Stop here, because you have got as far as ever you did before; but let your mind Soar away to the Blessed Shore."[107] To other New Lights he wrote, "When you feel your minds Soaring away: dont fear to let them go ... O my sisters Launch out into the Great *Deep* of God's *Nature*."[108] Harding appears to have been advocating emotional passivity: encouraging New Lights to simply lean back, as it were, as their mind was carried along in divine contemplation. This kind of yielding advice seems to run counter to much eighteenth-century writing about the affections, which stressed the careful regulation of the passions so that one was *not* carried away. Harding, by contrast, asserted that too much reasoned examination would prevent the soaring of the soul: "dont Stand to examin whither it be right." And yet, even these moments of soul-transporting ecstasy required preparation; Harding's own letter assumed a kind of emotional apprenticeship, instructing fellow converts how to respond to common hesitations and how to overcome self-consciousness.

"All our desires, inclinations and pursuits must be turned on another way"

A letter by New Light Nancy Lawrence described the everyday emotional renovation envisioned by the New Light community. Lawrence was converted to New Light religion while on a visit to Nova Scotia, despite her staunchly anti-revivalist family background, and shortly thereafter married a New Light merchant not far from Cornwallis Township.[109] One of her letters expressed a nuanced understanding of the relationship between natural passions and religious affections.

What is required, she wrote, was nothing less than a change of heart, the transformation of nature by grace. While all eighteenth-century writers on the affections were convinced that particular emotions could be cultivated, evangelicals did not share Enlightenment optimism that this was a change automatically within everyone's reach. Lawrence said that, left to ourselves, "we partake of the fallen nature," in need of being "reinstated in that Image of God which we lost by the fall."

> We must have our nature, our hearts changed by regenerating Grace by the opperations of the spirit of God with our Spirits or never enter the Kingdom of Heaven ... I dont mean that the animal nature must be changed; but that all our desires, inclinations and pursuits must be turned on another way – or wills & affections renewed, and the chief end and aim of all our actions be to Glorify God and enjoy him, by this change we are brought to delight in holyness and conformity to the will of God and have a foretaste of Heaven while on earth which must be or we never shall behold his face in love in an unregenerate state. Heaven would not be a seat of happiness to us – but the reverse for we would not have all the faculties of our souls engaged & delighted in praising God and beholding the spotless purity and holyness of his nature in admiring the Glorious plan of salvation, the wonders of redeeming love and the riches of free grace.[110]

The emotional work of conversion, she said, was meant to achieve nothing less than that "all our desires, inclinations and pursuits must be turned on another way." Rather than simply a display of some feelings at some times, all the affections must be renewed.

Lawrence suggested that a key measure of such a change of affections was what a person most enjoyed. She drew on the language of the 1646–47 Westminster Shorter Catechism's first statement – "The chief end of man is to glorify God and enjoy him forever" – and used a vocabulary of delight, admiration, and enjoyment. Such a change of affections, wrote Lawrence, is a "foretaste of Heaven while on earth." It anticipates the more complete transformation of persons when they come face to face with God, since contemplation in this life at least begins to transfigure the heart and will.

In the short compass of this letter, Lawrence articulated themes that were central to works such as Jonathan Edwards's *Treatise on the Religious Affections*, especially the idea that renewed affections were evidenced by the inclination of the heart, as well as the emphasis on delight. Lawrence, that is, wrote as one familiar with the affective strain of Puritan teaching and the theological works of moderate evangelicals, and she did not find their emphases inconsistent with the teachings of the New Light community in Nova Scotia.

Although Lawrence's was a theologically moderate view of the religious affections, emphasizing a long-term emotional transformation as well as moments of ecstasy, she was conscious that her stress on grace to effect such a change of heart rendered her suspect, even among some religious communities. "I am well aware," she admitted, "this will be stiled inthusiasm, perhaps hypocricy or insanity."[111] While she shared the eighteenth-century's preoccupation with the affections, Lawrence and other evangelicals did not adopt the Enlightenment's optimism about unaided human nature or the individual's ability to redirect their passions in a new direction.

"I think I feel new Desires"

The cultivation of particular religious emotions was a defining communal activity for Nova Scotia New Lights, one performed by laypeople and not only by their ordained leaders. To return to the example of Charlotte Prescott, she gratefully responded to Sarah Brown, with the wish, "D[ea]r Sister, that I may be able to follow the Good advice you give me in your letter."[112] Prescott's letter picked up on several of the themes identified in other New Light correspondence. New Lights, she stated, were "Join'd in the Everlasting Love of Jesus, which I find at times to draw my mind away from all Created Good." There were moments, that is, when she found herself unselfconsciously contemplating divine love. But like most of the other letter writers, Prescott experienced the transformation of her emotions as a struggle and a field of effort. She continued, "I think I feel new Desires ... But O I find a Heart that is deceitfull above all things, Desperately wicked, prone to wander from Heavenly friend and often do in by[roads] and forbidden paths. Yet like a tender parent does he bring me back and Cause me to Rejoice in his Unchangeable Love which I find to be the Same yesterday, to Day, and for ever."[113] Her hesitant perception that she felt "new Desires" points to her understanding, like that of Nancy Lawrence, that conversion included a new inclination of the heart, the renewal of the affections.

She expressed the notion that her own feelings, unlike divine love, were quite changeable and therefore required both God's grace and her own constant attention. She admitted, "tho I Cannot Say my mind is in that happy frame that I have in times past, Yet I know he is faithful who has promis'd never to leave me nor forsake me." Prescott aspired to selfless contemplation and steady emotional transformation but understood this as finally a heavenly goal, realized only partially in this life, and as a struggle best attempted in community.

CONCLUSION

The thoughtful concern with which New Lights reflected on their emotions, the effort they invested to cultivate specific affections, and the extent to which their homespun advice mirrored themes in more refined sentimental culture, belies the simple polarization that historian George Rawlyk expressed in his comment that "New Light Christianity is a religion of the heart, not the head."[114] To be sure, New Lights were particularly concerned about heart-felt faith and aspired to moments of rapture. Yet New Lights were not unthinking or merely impulsive in the cultivation of their affections. To the contrary, they approached their emotional self-fashioning reflectively and intentionally, if not always with refinement. The writings of theologians and philosophers on affection and sentiment, in turn, had resonance because they addressed issues that concerned ordinary people in their daily lives.

Paying more detailed attention to the emotional lives of so-called enthusiasts also decentres revivals in historical accounts of evangelical religion. That is not to gainsay the importance of conversions or camp meetings; it is a recognition, rather, that there was a wider spectrum of lived emotional and religious experience apart from those events. And as impulsive as those moments of religious ecstasy may have appeared, even they were usually achieved only when individuals cultivated, worried about, and reflected upon the emotions that helped to define their community.

From Enthusiasm to Sympathy: Edward Manning, Heart Religion, and Society

"I am a lover of peace and order, both in church & state, and firmly opposed to all usurpers & disorganizers in either." So wrote Stephen Jones, a judge and Congregational layman in Machias, Maine, in an October 1796 letter, in which he charged New Light itinerants from Nova Scotia with being usurpers, overturning that very peace and order.[1] To Edward Manning, his brother James Manning, and fellow preacher James Murphy, he asserted, "I believe that you ... are men of warm imaginations, that your minds have been wrought upon, and that a spirit of enthusiasm has seized you, and that you have worked yourselves up into a religious frenzy."

Jones's letter described the Nova Scotians as possessing some of the most typical features of early modern "enthusiasm." He alleged that the New Lights presumed that in their preaching on "the extraordinary influences and ministrations of the Spirit," they had special access to the mind of God. Jones bluntly pointed to what he thought was the real source of their ministry: "Through an intemperate zeal, you have worked yourselves into a belief that you are the first favourites of Almighty God, and that he does and must work by your instrumentality ... your extraordinary feelings arise from the force of your own wild imaginations." Rather than divine inspiration, Jones asserted that the "extraordinary feelings" on which the enthusiasts boldly based their authority arose merely from undisciplined imaginations and unregulated emotions. And like other early modern commentators, he thought their alleged enthusiasm bordered on insanity; Manning and his associates spoke in "a jumble of words, not half articulated, and bellowed out with all the violence of a madman." The Nova Scotians also presented a populist challenge to the authority of the local minister. Jones contended that one of them, Murphy, "declared that no minister ever went to heaven who penned his sermons and preached by notes, or that had received a liberal Education," and that Edward Manning described the incumbent minister in his public prayers "as an unconverted person." If only, Jones enjoined, their minds could "be improved by reading and study" and "brought to reason on Divine things," they would surely discover the disordered passions that actually motivated their actions.

Manning's letter of response a few days later complicates Jones's portrayal of him as an enthusiast. On the one hand, Manning clearly expressed an individualistic, highly affective version of Christianity: "I believe that True Religion is in the heart, that it is a divine Principle implanted there By the finger of God"[2] – rhetoric that did position Manning's evangelical faith as a challenge to forms of religion that he judged to be more concerned with "externals." And against Jones's claim that Manning spoke of God in irreverent, overly familiar terms, Manning countered that personal, experiential piety was essential: "Nor can there be True Religion without a Praying heart." On the other hand, Manning rejected the charge that "it is a great Piece of Inthusiasm" for him to be so sure of his calling or to be certain of his salvation. To demonstrate that seeking such emotional assurance was not an innovation or aberration (and perhaps to rebut Jones's claim that Manning was unencumbered by any learning), he quoted three Calvinist authorities – Puritan John Flavel, the Westminster Confession of Faith, and George Whitefield – to bolster his sentiments (though including Whitefield would not have allayed Jones's concerns). While he allowed that Murphy himself may have spoken imprudently, Manning denied the claim of anti-intellectualism and wrote in the strongest terms of their esteem for "divines who many Times Preached by Notes, and men who have been Liberally educated." And though he did not deny that their itinerant preaching fomented separations and divisions in Machias churches, he rejected the charge of enthusiasm and the indictment of their actions as self-interested or for pecuniary gain.

Manning still sounded like an enthusiast, at least to listeners like Jones – employing the language of the heart, and relying on an impassioned, extemporaneous, and persuasive preaching style. As an itinerant, he and his New Light associates presented a real challenge to established church authorities and boundaries, preaching an unsettling message of radical interiority.[3] Yet Manning's willingness to praise learned theologians and to identify with Calvinist writers, and his jealous defence of his reputation and sentiments, suggests that Manning was also more than an enthusiast.

As it happens, in 1796 Manning was midway through a striking emotional and religious transformation.[4] Despite his marked differences from Jones, within less than a decade Manning would set aside his populism and antagonism to learned culture, and for the rest of his long life he was a prolific reader, established an extensive correspondence network of authors and publishers, and was involved with the founding of two colleges. Notwithstanding the emotional intensity, heterodoxy, and divisiveness of Manning's early itinerant preaching, he became a firm advocate for orderly worship and orthodox Calvinism and the Baptist minister for Cornwallis Township, and was instrumental in the emergence of the Baptists of the Maritime provinces as a respectable denomination.

Historian George Rawlyk emphasized sharp discontinuities in the religious and emotional development of Manning and his former New Light peers: "Thus, in their search for respectability and order, the Nova Scotia Baptist leadership jettisoned much of the emotionalism and evangelical spirituality which was at the heart of Alline's message."[5] Manning's message, Rawlyk claimed, "no longer emphasized – as it had – the central importance of feelings and impressions."[6] To be sure, the Manning of the 1830s is almost unrecognizable from the enthusiast who confronted Jones in the 1790s. And yet, there were important continuities underlying Manning's religious experiences. Daniel Goodwin has persuasively argued, against Rawlyk's declensionist narrative, that Manning and other nineteenth-century Calvinistic Baptists retained a strong emphasis on experiential piety, even as they sought order and built respectable institutions.[7] Nor were they any less feeling.

This chapter shows that feelings and emotions did, in fact, *continue* to have central importance for Manning, but in a different way. Manning continued to emphasize the religious affections, although – rounding off the rough edges of his earlier enthusiasm – he downplayed the ecstasy of the moment in favour of longer-term emotional habits. He also cultivated new social passions. *Sympathy* became crucial to Manning as he imagined his place in expanding emotional communities. Fellow-feeling helped him to identify with a transnational evangelical community, and his tearful, intensely emotional reading demonstrates how evangelicals used sympathy to respond to missionary and imperial expansion. Without surrendering his emphasis on heart religion and experiential piety, Manning cultivated more communal affections.

Manning's emotional transformation and lachrymose experience can be read as a coda to the argument *Enthusiasms and Loyalties* has been making, bridging the revolutionary period and the expansion of both the new British empire and the American republic, and the transition from Enlightenment to Romantic cultures of sentiment. His British loyalism was a given in a way that it had not been for Chipman, Bailey, or even Alline, but Manning became assiduous in shaping an evangelical emotional community that was feeling and sympathetic, but no less orderly because of it. Manning was both a self-consciously loyal British subject and a participant in a transatlantic religious community, even during the cross-border tensions of the War of 1812. And while he cultivated a warm (if tempered) evangelical piety that shared much in common with George Whitefield or Henry Alline, he also provides a striking illustration of his generation's expansive optimism about the ability of voluntary religious organizations to transform society as well as individual hearts.[8] A study in both continuities and discontinuities, Manning is an amalgam of the public feelings exhibited by Chipman, Bailey, and Alline, blended in ways that any of them would have found surprising.

THE MAKING AND REMAKING OF AN ENTHUSIAST

Manning narrated his New Light conversion as a prolonged, overwhelming emotional experience.[9] But his experience was also another illustration of how difficult it could be, even for "enthusiasts," to feel the emotions to which they aspired, and the disconcerting uncertainty about how to read their own affections. Manning, who emigrated with his family from County Monaghan, Ireland, to Nova Scotia in about 1770, was still a boy when Henry Alline began to kindle the province's New Light revivals. He later recalled Alline comforting him, then aged ten years, on the execution of his father, Peter Manning, for murdering a neighbour. "I well remember his addressing me, though but a child, and the tears dropping from his face upon mine, while he exhorted me to flee from the wrath to come." Though Alline cast a long shadow over Manning's life,

Figure 7.1 | Engraving of Edward Manning, [18-?].

it was not until after the evangelist's death that Manning under-went what he described as his conversion. In 1789, when he was twenty-three years old, a period of "reformation" was sweeping through Falmouth, led by local New Light preachers such as John Payzant.[10] Manning wrote that "at meetings, many times, when poor Souls would cry out under concern for their Souls' Salvation, my heart would be affected." Over the next several months, he oscil-lated between awakened affections and periods of "dulness" and even mocked others under religious conviction.

But then one Sabbath morning, Manning was particularly affected by the emotional displays of others in the meeting house – by "tears Rolling down [their] cheeks like rain" and by sinners "crying for mercy." "Every Word, Sigh or groan" which was uttered in the con-gregation, Manning said, "were as daggers to my Heart, and brought Tears from my Eyes in abundance." This "was the first time I ever did the like in a public Congregation." In vivid language, he recalled, "The World wore a different aspect in my view from what ever it did before," and "all my desire now was to be converted." For sev-eral more days, Manning endured many "melancholy moments" and was in an "agony of ... soul." He reflected that the words of one of Alline's hymns articulated the emotional dilemma in which he was experiencing: "O Hardened, Hardened heart of mine ... / The greatest grief that I endure ... Is that I am distressed no more, with this unfeeling mind. / I mourn because I cannot mourn." More than anything else, Manning agonized about not being able to generate the feelings of sorrowful repentance that he thought should mark a sincere convert. The moment of relief finally arrived at another meeting not long after when, as he later described it, he relinquished the belief that he could save himself, confessing that "*God* must do the Work at last." "That instant I let go my hold," he wrote, "I felt a Ray of Light Steal into my Soul, And I felt glad," and for about a half an hour he was "lost to the things of Time and Sense." An "unusual peace Seemed to swallow up My whole Soul with wonder and admiration."

Despite the intensity of that moment, Manning still doubted his religious feelings. He thought that *perhaps* he "felt a particular Love to the Christians which I had never felt before," but then wondered if this was nothing more than "natural affection." His heart was, he said, "melted with A sence of the Love of God," but he was inclined to distrust these impressions. Expressing the uncertainty that New

Lights could experience as they attempted to interpret their own emotions, he asked whether there was "a possibility of my being converted and not knowing it." He admitted his confusion about these new sensations to one woman, saying, "I felt strangely and could not tell the meaning of it." In the end, it was talking to others who had previously experienced conversion, comparing their changes of feelings with his own, that finally allowed Manning to turn from self to God: "This I know: my Soul was wrapt up in God's Eternal Love. I felt nothing but that Glory." Manning's conversion narrative certainly had the ecstatic climax that seemed quintessential of the emotional style of the New Lights. But the emotional tumult of the months leading to that transformation also illustrates how fraught religious feelings were, and how difficult it was for ordinary people to make sense of those feelings or to generate the affections to which they aspired.

Within a few months of his conversion, Manning had joined a cadre of young New Light itinerants who preached throughout Nova Scotia, New Brunswick's St John River valley, and into Maine. For a period of about two years beginning in 1791, Manning was prominent among a group within the New Light community who believed they were privy to a "new dispensation" from the Holy Spirit – the movement that provoked Handley Chipman to write his 1793 essays on emotions, bodily gestures, and reading feelings as moral evidence (see chapter 2). According to John Payzant, the minister of the New Light church in Cornwallis, Manning and his brother, James, said in a church meeting that "all orders were done away, and that the Bible was a dead letter, and they would preach without it."[11] Manning "in perticular, was insinuating these Eronious Sentiments in yong people minds." Payzant contended that by disavowing religious authority, order, and orthodox doctrine, the "New Dispensation" party had "cut off the reins of govement." Chipman wrote in 1793 that "Mr. Ed[ward] Manning used frequently to make Such a noise in his Preaching and Praying that perhaps not half his Sentences could be understood. But he Seems to be got over it in some measure."[12] He may have "got over it," but Manning's was not an immediate change. Manning was ordained by the Cornwallis New Light Church in 1795. Despite this apparent nod to order, however, in 1796 his intensely emotional preaching and lingering elements of his religious populism still elicited the charge of enthusiasm from Stephen Jones of Machias.

In the decade following the 1796 Machias encounter, Manning and many of his New Light peers underwent a series of linked changes in their piety, embracing Baptist ecclesiology, moderate Calvinist theology, a concern with order, and the necessity of a more learned ministry. Manning's diary, extant for the last half of his life, offers evocative evidence of his prolific reading. Sounding very much like Stephen Jones, Manning came to write that "Reading and good literature" and intellectual "improvement" constitute a "necessary hand-maid" to religion.[13] Manning also participated in an extensive correspondence network throughout New England and the Maritime provinces, contributed regularly to religious periodicals, was involved with the founding of schools that eventually became Colby College, Maine, and Acadia University, Nova Scotia, and acquired a reputation as "a man of abilities and great reading."[14] The piety he sought to cultivate was, as he once expressed it, "learned, and yet truly evangelical."[15] Daniel Goodwin argues that Manning "attempted to direct the New Light movement into a more balanced form of evangelicalism where ecstatic religious experience would always be tempered by order."[16] Manning, it seems, was an enthusiast no more.[17]

The distance Manning travelled from his earlier views might also be measured by his reaction, in the early 1820s, to the writings of Henry Alline and Jonathan Scott, and to the rapturous worship of John Payzant's New Light congregation. Years after his own change of sentiments, Manning reread Scott's *Brief View*. His reflections in his diary on that reading express how completely he disavowed his former views: "Have been reading Mr. Scott against Mr. H. Alline. Scott is in the right, and A. of course is in the wrong. Hope they were both good men, tho' both in some things it is probable were wrong, but I think I could seal Mr. S.'s sentiments generally with my blood!"[18] The next day he expressed sympathy with the disruptions that Scott experienced in the face of the New Light revivals. "Spent this day pretty much in reading Mr. Scott's publication. Poor man, he had much affliction on account of Mr. Alline. Mr. A. was verry erronious, but I hope is gone to rest, but his errors did not die with him. NO, they live to the Sorrow of many, and me among the rest."[19] Manning was troubled, rather than heartened, by the persistence of New Light or Allinite beliefs and practices in the township.[20]

In the early 1790s, John Payzant had attempted to moderate Manning's antinomian enthusiasm. But three decades later, it was

Manning who found Payzant suspect. He thought that Payzant interpreted the scriptures too "mystically" and that his focus on interiority tended to allow "contempt of the visible ordinances of the Gospel."[21] Calling Payzant's sermons "good generally, though somewhat confused for so great a man," he admitted, "I wish for clearer preaching." In September 1821, Manning visited Payzant's Liverpool congregation. Unlike many of his New Light peers in Nova Scotia, Payzant had not become a Baptist. Manning was discomfited by the sensory experiences of a once-familiar New Light service, punctuated by demonstrative gestures and intense emotions. He described sitting in the gallery of the meetinghouse following the observance of the Lord's Supper, when a number of females "screamed out ... [with] an extravagancy of Voice, and such uncommon gesticulations, leaving their seats, running round the broad [a]isle, Swinging their Arms, bowing their heads to the Ground."[22] Manning commented, "I hope they are good, but I truly wish they were more orderly." Indicating how much his emotional responses had changed from his own New Light days, he confessed, "surely I would freeze to death before that would warm me"; his affections would be raised, rather, by "a few words of evangelical Truth," even if delivered by a child. After two more days of meetings in the Liverpool area, Manning concluded, "O how much I esteem the Solemn devotions of the truly pious, and well-informed Christian assemblies I have Seen. I decidedly prefer the Solemn exercises of the pious in Cornwallis to the uncommon Vociferations of these Persons in and about Liverpool. They seem to know no better than that they are never in the liberty of the Gospel but when they are all agitated and their Voices extended so that you can hear them a Mile."[23] In Manning's assessment, New Lights continued to equate spiritual liberty with a full and free expression of emotions, particularly with their voices and bodies. He, on the other hand, had embraced the more restrained "Solemn devotions." Despite Manning's framing of the difference between the two pieties as "informed" versus those that "know no better," both emotional styles – restraint as much as demonstrativeness – entailed intentional cultivation in the context of their communities. That Manning was repelled by emotional expressions that had once come naturally to him suggests the extent of the transformation of his habits of feeling.[24]

"I AM HAPPY, HAPPY, HAPPY ...
BUT I DO NOT DEPEND ON RAPTURES"

In leaving behind his enthusiasm, Manning did not disregard emotions altogether. His extensive diary, from 1810 to 1846, portrays the affective dimension of his religious life to be one of Manning's greatest preoccupations, and emotional self-fashioning as one of the main purposes in his reading and journaling. To be sure, he sought to rein in and regulate the more enthusiastic passions of his New Light years. Yet emotional experience remained central, even as Manning adopted different theological frameworks for understanding his (and others') feelings. He still expected occasional moments of spiritual ecstasy, but the emphasis was different: "I am happy, happy, happy, in the blessed Jesus, the God-Man Mediator, God's Eternal Son, and My Eternal Surety. O, [I] want all to know how much comfort I have and do find in this blessed PLAN. But I do not depend on Raptures, but on Christ, but this trust produces Raptures sometimes, but they are not so much an evidence of Grace as holiness."[25] Manning no longer believed, as he had in the 1790s, that religious feelings could be read as certain evidence of one's salvation. The older Manning regarded changed affections as one aspect of the growth of holy character after salvation. In theological terms, emotions shifted from being a marker of conversion to being evidence of sanctification. Manning also came to believe that Christians should expect a variegated emotional life; he did not always expect raptures. In the words of author Charles Buck, in a book that Manning read with warm approval in the 1830s, "Let it not be understood, however, that by happy experience I always mean remarkable high emotions, ecstatic pleasures, or ravishing transports."[26] Or, as Manning put it, he could be "happy, happy, happy," without depending on raptures.

Manning was particularly drawn to authors who also wrestled with the affective dimension of religious life. From a friend in Halifax he borrowed Puritan books such as John Owen's *The Grace and Duty of Being Spiritually Minded* (1681) and John Flavel's *Treatise on Keeping the Heart* (1691).[27] Such reading, he said, "tends to solemnize my mind."[28] He read the affectionate writings of eighteenth-century English dissenters Philip Doddridge and Isaac Watts, including the latter's *The Use and Abuse of the Passions in Religion* (1729).[29] Manning thought that these "old puritannical divines" were so valuable because they combined robust Calvinist orthodoxy with a devotional emphasis on the "enjoyment of the comforts of religion."[30] In Jonathan Edwards's *Treatise on Religious Affections* (1746), Manning found the theological framework that made sense of his own religious affections, and the moderate Calvinism he had adopted. As he put it on 22 October 1822, "Reading Edwards on the Affections again. Confirms me more and more in the truth of what I have been endeavouring to exhibit for these many years."[31]

Edwards formulated his ideas about the religious affections at the intersection of Enlightenment philosophy and controversial religious awakenings. In one direction, Edwards looked toward the Lockean emphasis on sense perception, and then to the sentimental responses to Locke by the Third Earl of Shaftesbury and Francis Hutcheson. Edwards maintained their emphasis on the affections but denied that virtuous feelings could be naturally generated. Instead, they must be supplied by grace – a "spiritual sense."[32] Looking in another direction (one particularly relevant to Manning and Nova Scotia's reconstructed New Lights), Edwards's theology of the affections addressed the controversies provoked by the emotional displays associated with the Great Awakening. Not only did opponents of the revival, such as Boston's Charles Chauncy, decry the spread of "enthusiasm," but Edwards himself was horrified by excessive passions or fervour that did not result in lasting transformation of character. Edwards attempted to articulate a theology of the affections that affirmed their centrality to religious experience but also distinguished between "gracious" and "false" affections. Like Manning, Edwards sought a way to cultivate religious affections without encouraging enthusiasm.

Manning thought that Edwards's treatise was "verry clear in discriminating between true and false fear and joy" and that it was a "Sifting, Doctrinal, and Experimental and deep publication."[33] He did worry, though, that it might be "beyond the capacity of many Zealots for experimental religion."[34] By this, he was not implying that Edwards's work was intellectually impenetrable to those who focused so much on religious experience. Rather, he thought that they would be impervious to a book that "goes directly to condemn their flights." Manning admitted that reading Edwards not only gave him the intellectual framework he needed but also affected him personally; his work, he wrote, "I think has a tendency to make me more devotional."[35]

Manning also drew upon the work of Andrew Fuller (1754–1815). The most influential British Baptist theologian of the late eighteenth century, Fuller articulated a moderate Calvinism compatible with evangelical revivalism that also provided the theological rationale for missionary activism, such as the mission to India initiated by Fuller's close friend William Carey.[36] As Daniel Goodwin has argued, Manning and other Maritime Baptists found in Fuller a respectable theological framework and an emphasis on social reform that did not require them to sacrifice their evangelicalism.[37] Fuller himself was profoundly influenced by Edwards's writing on the affections and warned ministers against preaching an "unfelt gospel."[38] In a sermon on the importance of "an intimate acquaintance with divine truth," Fuller contended that feeling and doctrine were complementary rather than opposed. He wrote, "Knowledge and affection have a mutual influence on each other … Affection is fed by knowledge … By the expansion of the mind the heart is supplied with objects which fill it with delight."[39] When Manning read that sermon in 1822, he professed, "I find … the sentiments of my own heart better expressed than I could express them myself."[40] More than twenty years later, Manning was still reading Fuller regularly, and wrote, "I am much taken with [his] sentiments and heart religion."[41] As discussed below, Manning also read Fuller's biographies through the lens of his own emotional self-fashioning.

There was a fine line between evangelical heart religion and enthusiasm. It could be difficult to maintain an affective piety without succumbing to subjectivism or sheer emotionalism. Yet by avoiding the ditch of enthusiasm on one side, it was possible to fall into cold rationalism on the other. Commenting on one Church of England author, Manning explained the dilemma: "He has to soften many points to keep from the charge of enthusiasm that it rather tends to blunt the edge of evangelical truth."[42] While it was easy to distinguish between enthusiasts and rationalists, Manning constructed an approach to religious emotions that attempted to maintain the tension between experience and reason. He continued to seek "raised affections [and] true zeal."[43]

"A SWEET UNION":
EMOTIONAL COMMUNITY ACROSS BORDERS

In the 1790s, Charles Inglis worried that the religious passions of New Lights like Manning would be a solvent to social order. He insisted that loyalty and enthusiasm ran in opposite directions. In a way, he was right. Henry Alline's message, spread while the American Revolution was waged, was never overtly republican – if anything, it was indifferent to political events and allegiances – but its strong individualism did challenge the traditional supports of community life. The later Edward Manning, by contrast, maintained both the personal heart religion of evangelicalism *and* a broad set of social concerns, including education, temperance, and global missions. But if Manning was not so indifferent to social order and social reform as Alline, neither did his social affections neatly align with nationalist or imperial loyalties. By virtue of his itinerancy, correspondence, and consumption of print, he participated in both American and British cultures. He wrote with gratitude that his "Nation and Province" was blessed with "civil and religious liberty in an eminent degree," but he also described the United States (with apparent sincerity) as the "Land of light and Liberty."[44] Manning's political feelings, at least those expressed in his spiritual journal and correspondence, tended to be subordinated to his evangelical sensibilities. Largely silent about politics in the existing record, Manning did offer a few reflections during the War of 1812 and at the defeat of Napoleon that provide insight into how his political and religious feelings intersected.

The War of 1812, for many North Americans on both sides of the border, was a period of intense nationalistic feeling. Indeed, Nicole Eustace has observed that for many American war supporters, "emotional arousal was ... the central achievement sought by American belligerents."[45] If the war's military gains were dubious, the widespread sense of patriotism and national purpose was itself a kind of victory, ushering in what has been called the "Era of Good Feelings." British North Americans also had an emotional investment in the conflict. Manning's near contemporary, Beamish Murdoch, reflected on the feelings of Nova Scotians: "The effects of the war upon this province, and particularly upon the people of Halifax, were very marked. Always sympathizing closely with the national glory of Great Britain, they were now drawn more than ever to feel a lively interest in military and naval transactions."[46] But for Edward Manning, the tension between nations was an occasion for him and his American correspondents to reaffirm their participation in a transnational affective community, sharing a common religious identity and mission. They intentionally cultivated feelings that superseded nationalistic fervour. Gordon Heath has argued that this cross-border spiritual community weathered the experience of war because of shared ideological commitments, "regardless of national or imperial loyalties."[47] On 9 January 1813, Manning recorded in his diary, "This day felt uneasy in the morning and unpleasant sensations. But in reading and meditation found my mind sweetly led out after God and a sweet union to American brethren, notwithstanding the dreadful war that exists between the two powers."[48]

Manning's New England correspondents concurred with this cross-border affection. On the eve of the conflict, Daniel Merrill, a Baptist minister, author, and member of the Massachusetts State Legislature for 1812–13, remarked to Manning, "I wish the differences between your government and ours may be so accommodated, as to promote the good of both, and subserve Zion's best good. But I fear a contest is before us."[49] He continued, "However the differences may be between the governments among men, be it our concern to be in obedience to the government of God." Rhode Island minister and author David Benedict aptly summarized the sentiment, writing to Manning, "While there is War among the nations, I hope there will be peace among the Saints."[50]

National interests were ultimately relativized by common evangelical hopes for revival in the short term and an eschatological approach to history over the longer term. Patriotism was swallowed up in larger spiritual hopes for all nations. Partway through the conflict, Manning prayed, "O that the American people may be induced to come upon pacific terms, that they may not return themselves to continuing a war that they precipitated themselves into lest their obstinacy prove their ruin."[51] Nevertheless, he expected that wars would continue until "the commencement of the Millennium," when peace would prevail among the nations, and there would no longer be "divisions among the professing people of the Lord." Political differentiation did not ultimately define or supplant their sense of belonging to a transnational evangelical community. Even at the height of political tensions, the correspondents expressed mutual affection and a fervent commitment to their common missionary project.

Manning's response to news about the Napoleonic Wars also eschewed simple nationalism, adopting a spiritual and eschatological perspective. In late May 1814, he recorded in his journal, "Heard of the Defeat of Buoneparte and the Coronation of the French King and the success of the British Arms on the Continent of Europe. O that these successes may be a means of the establishing a general peace and permanent all over the world."[52] He continued with a prayer that suggested that triumphalism had no place among Christian feelings for their nation: "O that the successes of the British Nation [may not] tend to puff them up with pride lest they fall into ruin and disrepute. For Righteousness exalteth a nation but sin is a reproach to any people." While Manning did interpret military victories in terms of divine providence and eschatology, emphasizing God's apparent superintendence over the events of history, this tended to impose a sobering moral obligation on the nation rather than justifying its every deed.

The same chastened sense of national feeling was evident three days later, when Manning led the church and community in a service of thanksgiving for the military victory in France.

> On application being made to have the Meeting House illuminated this evening as a token of joy and gladness on account of the victory of combined armies of Great Britain and the other confederate powers of Europe over Buoneparte and the French nation, accordingly the house was illuminated and the neighboring houses. The concourse that attended behaved discretely in the Meeting House, and, at the request of some of the respectable inhabitants of the town, I sang an appropriate hymn or two and publically acknowledged the good hand of God to our nation. Gave a short address and dismissed the people who retired from the house. Continued firing until late but which of itself would have been well enough but to spend the evening as some (I fear) did is no honor to the God of Peace, but manifest dishonor. O when will people be rational, be discreet, and be religious. Alas, not until man has done sinning. O that the Lord [would] hasten the time when nations shall have done with sinning, and then wars will cease.[53]

Citizens of Cornwallis Township celebrated the martial success of Britain and her allies by lighting up the windows of the meetinghouse and private homes, by singing and praying in gratitude, and then by firing their guns long into the night. As Gordon Heath observes, even as he led in this public fête, Manning was reluctant to condone the "unbridled passions that often went hand-in-hand with celebrations."[54] Despite Inglis's fear that Nova Scotia New Lights were fomenting support for the republican passions of the French Revolution, as the long conflict in France came to a close, Manning had become as eager as Inglis to avoid *any* kind of enthusiasm, whether religious or political. Unwilling to give nationalism free reign, he was also communicating that for him, political loyalties were circumscribed (though not undermined) by religious identities and sentiments.

"FOUND MY HEART MUCH INLARGED": VOLUNTARY ASSOCIATIONS FOR REFORMING SOCIETY

Manning expressed a restrained sense of imperialism, reluctant to allow national pride or political passions to overwhelm religious propriety. Yet it would be a mistake to assume that Manning, in his concern for personal salvation, exhibited the same ambivalence to society as Henry Alline. To the contrary, Manning was very optimistic that heart religion and social reform could be complementary.[55] He no longer assumed, as Handley Chipman or Jacob Bailey had done, that an established church (whether Congregational or Anglican) would be the means of promoting religious virtue in society. Rather, Manning believed that the way to reform society was for individuals, stirred in their hearts, to join voluntary associations to address a web of linked religious and social causes such as temperance, Bible distribution, education, and international missions. Whereas Charles Inglis had asserted that enthusiasts cared so much about the heart that they disrupted social order, Manning and many evangelicals of the early nineteenth century saw voluntarism as the means to focus on individual religious experience and social reform without contradiction. The voluntary nature of these benevolent organizations meant that leaders such as Manning appealed to the affections as well as the reason of individuals in their communities. As Manning's experience suggests, the apparent progress of these associations was perceived to be of historical and eschatological significance, freighting them with powerful emotional meaning. Reading about these societies, Manning once remarked that he "found [his] heart much inlarged."[56]

Around the turn of the nineteenth century, evangelicals in the Anglo-American Atlantic turned to voluntary associations as the vehicles for religious and social activism, addressing causes as diverse as Bible and tract distribution, the promotion of Sunday schools, temperance, the abolition of slavery, international missions, prison reform, and the alleviation of poverty.[57] While these societies focused on single issues, their leaders and participants tended to be linked. Contemporaries provided the term "the Benevolent Empire" to describe the web of such Protestant societies in the early nineteenth-century United States, including the American Tract Society, the American Bible Society, and the American Temperance Society. "Benevolence" was the humanitarian disposition of the heart that motivated individuals to sympathize with others and turn to activism. This voluntarist, joining impulse in Protestantism mirrored developments in the wider society, as an increasingly informed and active citizenry depended less on state power, political parties, or religious establishments to cultivate virtue in public life.[58] Manning's extensive journal provides an unusually detailed account of one British North American's wholehearted participation in this movement.[59] In the brief compass of this discussion, it is possible only to illustrate his involvement in voluntary societies and to highlight the intense emotions that their progress evoked.

Manning was an early advocate in Nova Scotia for the British and Foreign Bible Society (BFBS), which he called "this incomparable Society."[60] Founded in England in 1804, the goal of the BFBS was to print Bibles in English without explanatory notes (therefore avoiding theological difference) and to distribute them at little or no cost.[61] In 1813, Manning was invited to represent the Baptists on the committee of the Nova Scotia Bible Society, and by October 1814, an auxiliary of the BFBS was formed in Cornwallis Township.[62] Shortly after the launch of the Cornwallis auxiliary, Manning reflected on the relationship between the nation, religious associations like the BFBS, and broader society. He wrote that Nova Scotians had been given "civil and religious liberty in an eminent degree."[63] However, he hastened to add, "those liberties are lamentably abused." Much-vaunted British liberties were not adequate on their own to cultivate national virtue; they imposed an obligation on individuals to "improve" the national blessings they enjoyed. But it would be voluntary societies like the BFBS, rather than the state itself, that would be the "instruments" of social and religious reform. That same year, Manning wrote a circular letter to the Baptist churches of Nova Scotia and New Brunswick in which he reiterated the sense of obligation they should feel because of the constitutional liberties they enjoyed as British subjects. He asserted that their affections should be stirred, motivating them to action on behalf of the BFBS and other benevolent associations: "We think that the institution of the British and Foreign Bible society is the most benevolent institution ever formed by man. Its motive is so pure, its object so great, and the plan so well calculated (under God) to accomplish the great event of general illumination, that it must attract your attention; and we wish it may excite a spirit of benevolence in the heart of every lover of the Lord Jesus to contribute freely in aid of this Godlike institution."[64] Manning appealed to their affections, and like many other reformers during the late Enlightenment, he intended to cultivate benevolence among the people. "This," he said, "is a favourable time to show our zeal for God."[65]

As discussed below, alongside the distribution of Bibles, Manning was also intensely interested in the wave of foreign missions that had begun in his lifetime. He was a key regional figure in the formation of missionary societies and, in 1845, the sending of New Brunswick Baptist Richard Burpee to Burma.[66] Manning recorded in his journal that he was "much affected" as he read about "the many benevolent institutions found in the world."[67]

Reading Manning's diary, it is striking how suddenly he became persuaded by arguments for temperance, and how thoroughly he became an advocate for the movement. In the early months of 1829, when he first read temperance pamphlets and sermons by Lyman Beecher, Jonathan Kittredge, and Heman Humphrey, among others, temperance became an almost-daily preoccupation, so that it was no exaggeration for him to declare, "The subject of intemperance greatly engrosses my mind."[68] Manning read temperance tracts and periodicals in a variety of public settings – from family hearths to wedding receptions to labourers in farm fields – and was instrumental in the spread of local temperance societies.[69] One might even compare Manning's growing concern with intemperance to his anxieties about religious enthusiasm. Years later, Manning reflected on the extent to which temperance ideas had been adopted in his community, reflecting his broad reforming social vision: "I bless the Lord that I have lived to see so much done to prevent crime, and wretchedness by the formation of Temperance Societies, the publishing [of] temperance sermons, tracts, etc."[70]

As has already been mentioned, Manning the populist itinerant who was reckoned in Machias to be an opponent of liberal education became a strong supporter of education societies (later universities) in Maine and Nova Scotia. Manning's itinerancy in Maine brought him into the orbit of the Baptists who had formed the Maine Literary and Theological Institution at Waterville (later Colby College). Manning visited the institution in 1819, was made an agent for the purposes of raising support, and was invited to move to Waterville to take a more prominent role – an offer he considered at length.[71] Less than a decade later, the self-educated Manning was instrumental in the formation of the Baptist Education Society for the churches of the Maritime provinces, serving as its president for the rest of his life. That society supported the creation of Horton Academy, which eventually became Acadia University.[72] From his initial ambivalence about education, Manning came to declare, about the expanding college in Wolfville, Nova Scotia, that "the cause of true religion needs such an institution."[73]

Manning and many of his contemporaries perceived the remarkable expansion of religious and benevolent associations to have unparalleled theological significance, interpreting them in a frame of optimistic millenarian eschatology.[74] Their view was that the message of the Bible would increasingly spread, and that a great part of humanity would receive salvation. Basing their understanding of history, in part, on the Book of Revelation, chapter 20, they believed the success of such missionary efforts would inaugurate a millennium of global peace and blessing, culminating in the victorious return of Jesus Christ. The events of history, political as well as religious, could be read as signs of progress, portending the millennium. Reading about the defeat of Napoleon, as we have seen, Manning wrote, "O that these successes may be a means of the establishing a general peace and permanent all over the world." Wars, he contended, would end with "the commencement of the Millennium ... Then shall the curse be removed and the earth be a paradise again."[75] Most importantly for Manning, the success of the missions movement, widespread Bible distribution, the advance of the temperance movement, and even nearby revivals, could be read as signs of spiritual progress, soon to be followed by the Millennium. Reading of such developments in the *Baptist Magazine*, Manning declared that he was "much delighted" and fervently hoped that "Those missionary exertions and the Bible Societies and other similar institutions

equally benevolent will be owned and blessed of God for the introduction of [the] Millennial State and Glory."[76] Little wonder, then,
with such an interpretation of their historical significance, that
Manning was often emotionally overwhelmed when reflecting on
the progress of benevolent associations. Without abandoning his
concern for evangelical piety and heart-felt experience, Manning
had travelled a considerable distance from New Light ambivalence
about "externals" in religion and society.[77]

"O HOW MANY THINGS BROT TEARS FROM MY EYES": SYMPATHY, READING, AND IMAGINED COMMUNITIES

Reading was an intensely emotional experience for Edward Manning.
He confided to his diary in January 1821, "Reading the Intelligence
from Burmah: the death of the King, the conversion of Maung Nau,
the Death of Mr. Wheelock, ... all tend to excite various immotions."
And later the same day, "Have been reading the Magazine this day
... Many pieces have struck my mind and moved my affections ...
my heart hath quite overflowed. Various have been my immotions."[78]
In November 1830, he and his wife read and discussed the latest
missionary news. He wrote, "I was so overcome that it was with
much difficulty that I could keep from crying out loud; from tears
I could not. My heart hath been rather soft ever since."[79] And of
that quintessential evangelical biography, Jonathan Edwards's *Life
of David Brainerd*, he wrote, "O how many things brot tears from
my eyes, and blushing in my face, and groans from my heart."[80]
Only a few volumes of Manning's library are still extant, but one
strongly suspects that were more to be found, many of them would
be tear-stained.

Manning's tearful approach to certain kinds of reading is further evidence that he did not become less feeling as he attempted
to leave aside his enthusiasm. The extensive record of his reading
suggests that he sought a new framework for understanding affections in religious life, reconciling them with learned culture rather
than marginalizing them. Paying attention to his tears while reading
is another way to measure the importance of emotion in his religious experience. In particular, his tears expressed the *sympathy*, the
sense of empathetic connection, that linked Manning to religious
and emotional communities beyond his Cornwallis locale.

Admittedly, such intense emotional responses to texts might seem
unthinkable to modern readers. It could reasonably be asked, did he
actually cry so much over his books, and if so, was such emotionalism primarily a product of an overwrought psyche? The hanging
death of his father and Manning's various insecurities certainly
leave room for such speculation. However, Manning does not seem
to have been constantly in tears; his descriptions were consistently
connected with particular kinds of reading. Or perhaps he was writing figuratively? To be sure, there could be some exaggeration or
conventions of speech at work, but on the other hand, Manning's
descriptions appear to be detailed and physical rather than generalized. Additionally, Manning recorded these lachrymose episodes
in his private diary, which he had no expectation of publishing.[81]
Yet even supposing that he was, at least sometimes, writing metaphorically or conventionally, that too would be interesting, and
useful as a gauge of what sentiments he thought he *should* have. As
historian Barbara Rosenwein says of formulaic emotional phrases,
"Commonplaces are socially true even if they may not be individ-
ually sincere." "The sources," she says, "tell us at least what people
thought other people would like to hear (or expected to hear)."[82] It
seems likely, based on the many instances of tearful reading, that
Manning really did respond so viscerally to many of his religious
texts, and that on other occasions he expressed the emotions he was
attempting to cultivate (even if not always easily). In both kinds
of situations, it appears that evangelicals expected to be moved by
what they read. Manning's reading also makes it possible to recover,
at least in part, the felt experience of participating at a distance in
the early events of missionary expansion. Neither were such effusive
male tears idiosyncratic in the context of early modern reading and
religion – they, too, have a history.[83] Contemporary commentaries
considered tears a gauge of a man's selfless ability to feel and exert
himself on behalf of others.[84] James Fordyce claimed that by "tender tears" one can detect "the feeling heart." Hugh Blair contended,
"Manliness and sensibility are so far from being incompatible, that
the truly brave are generous and humane."[85] Manning's tears help us
to see the changing gendered meanings of tears.

Manning tearfully read *memoirs* and *missionary literature*. These
newly abundant genres of religious print gave evangelicals a common emotional experience, and they also, by offering models of
evangelical feeling, provided a means of fashioning particular

emotions. Manning read memoirs with deep sympathy, identifying with an evangelical textual and emotional community that transcended denominational affiliation. His reading of missionary literature reveals how Manning experienced imperial expansion – how emotions such as sympathy, pity, and belonging helped him locate provincial Nova Scotia in changing global relationships. Paying attention to his tears makes it possible to examine the emotional experience of evangelical and imperial identities from one reader's perspective. Manning's religious, readerly, male, and imperial tears, that is, can be historicized, their meaning rendered less strange in context.

"HOLY SIMPATHY": IDENTIFYING WITH AN EVANGELICAL COMMUNITY

Manning was "melted to tears" by reading, among many others, the memoirs of David Brainerd, Ann Judson, and William Wilberforce – religious biographies that were among the period's most popular, included in an informal canon of evangelical texts.[86] By far the most tears dropped onto the pages of the biography of his "favorite author," Andrew Fuller, and of Fuller's memoir of Samuel Pearce.[87] Biographies were ubiquitous in late eighteenth- and early nineteenth-century print, and as Scott Casper has demonstrated, most biographies published in the period were didactic in orientation. Memoirs of the great and the obscure were read to shape character and feeling, whether republican virtue, domestic sentiment, or evangelical affections.[88]

Sympathy was central to Manning's reading of these biographies, as he strongly identified with the circumstances – and feelings – of their subjects. Of David Brainerd, Manning wrote, "I feel much simpathy for him ... I have experienced much of that gloom, and temptations he has experienced ... The feelings he endured ... I have felt in my soul."[89] Of the memoirs of Samuel Pearce, he wrote, "[I] find so many things that I have experienced that I feel truly an affection for [him]" – an affection, he says, that "would warm me in Greenland, comfort me in New Zealand, and make me happy in the Valley of the Shadow of Death."[90] Manning found connections between his own biography and those he read, observing common trials, interest in the missionary cause, and even similarities in health complaints. Although Manning was certainly moved by extraordinary events or exceptional characters, he proposed that what made biographies "most useful" was "their plainness and simplicity, or being common to all Christians."[91]

Evangelicals were not the only nineteenth-century readers to emphasize feeling and sympathy. Manning was reading at the trailing edge of the "culture of sensibility."[92] Elizabeth Barnes summarizes the literary and emotional milieu: "Sympathetic identification emerges in the eighteenth century as the definitive way of reading literature and human relations."[93] Rather than being an aberration, then, Manning's response of being "melted to tears" was actually, in the period's culture of sensibility, an expression of "the highest form of reading."[94]

Religious memoirs as a genre elicited sympathy and shaped sentiment through narrative techniques that mirrored those of novels.[95] Though novels are conspicuously absent from Manning's record of reading, he approached memoirs in a way that would be familiar to historians of sentimental novels. That the title of the first American novel was *The Power of Sympathy* indicates that Manning's "holy simpathy" had fictional counterparts. Manning and fellow evangelicals read memoirs in the same way that some of their contemporaries read sentimental novels: they identified with the central characters, sought to imitate their virtues, and read these texts with intense emotions. As with the more didactic novels, readers of evangelical biographies sought both religious sanctification *and* readerly satisfaction. The editors of the *Baptist Missionary Magazine of Nova Scotia and New Brunswick* encouraged that very comparison, describing the emotional and spiritual utility of missionary memoirs: "to read their journals is indeed delightful, they possess all the deep interest of a romance, and one is continually obtaining knowledge of other men, and countries, and manners, while his heart dilates with religious emotions, and his gratitude and joy are awakened by the success of the cross."[96]

Yet Manning did question the religious nature of this sympathetic identification. He recorded one particularly heightened response to reading about an author's death: "My feelings have been wrought up to such a degree that I suppose 20 times I could scarcely contain myself." He reflected, "Surely this cannot be all religion, but a sort of sympathy. If it was real evangellical Religion, why not when I think of the Dying of the dear Lord Jesus."[97] Were his tears symptomatic of a religious inclination, he wondered, or of some baser response of the passions? In his pious reading, Manning sought to cultivate what he called "the holy simpathy the gospel produces in the poor soul," but he did worry about excessive or misplaced sympathy.[98]

Indeed, sentiment in late eighteenth- and early nineteenth-century print was contested terrain. Manning's occasional worries about excessive sympathy reflect wider concerns about readers becoming too absorbed by sentimental novels. At its most extreme was the European phenomenon described as a "reading mania," or what Robert Darnton called an "epidemic of emotion," as readers were overwhelmed by sentiment in novels by Rousseau in France, and earlier, by Richardson in England, and Lessing in Germany. The rise of sentimental fiction generated worries about a dangerous surplus of emotion, ungoverned by reason. Others believed that the emotional satisfactions of "escapist" literature discouraged readers from attending to less fictional obligations.[99] Sympathetic and tearful Edward Manning, then, was not the only early nineteenth-century reader to use texts for emotional self-fashioning or to worry about excessive sympathy while reading.

Manning not only sympathetically *identified* with the subjects of biographies; he aspired to *emulate* their particular affections. Reading was used to fashion emotions. Reading the memoir of Brainerd, Manning exclaimed, "O that I could feel as that dear man of God did!"[100] Of another, Manning wrote, "O that I could feel the composure of Pierce, and feel the happiness he enjoyed."[101] One particularly poignant example of the way memoirs were employed for emotional self-fashioning was the deathbed conversations between Manning and his ill adult daughter, Nancy. Over several months, from November 1819 to March 1820, Manning's diary entries were shot through with the vocabulary of particular emotions – joy, terror, resignation, composure, happiness, pleasure – feelings that both Manning and his daughter carefully attempted to regulate.[102] The emotional intensity of the conversations that Manning recorded in his diary reveal the emotions that were particularly valued by the transatlantic evangelical community, affections that were modelled or admonished in texts and that individuals like Manning and his daughter attempted to emulate in their own situations, often with great difficulty.

Early in her illness, Manning talked with Nancy and "enquired [about] the particular feelings of her heart ... and read to her the piece in the 4th No. of the American Missionary Magazine upon being prepared for death."[103] The article that Manning read to his daughter emphasized the emotional preparation for one's last days, suggesting that "We cannot love that which is unwelcome to us."[104] Feelings such as anticipation of heaven, "a tender sense of [God's] authority," or a "contrite heart" would be evidence of a divine work of grace in one's heart.[105] Finding one's way not only to doctrinal understanding but also appropriate feelings about those beliefs was an important part of evangelical spirituality. Manning said that Nancy worried "that she does not sence [such feelings] as she aught."[106] Without discouraging the attempt, Manning told Nancy that such an emotional struggle was as inescapable as it was important: "Says she has a hope, feels composed, and longs to go, but still she does not feel as she wants to feel. She wants to feel more reconciled, more holy, and more happy. I told her she never would feel as she wanted to feel until she got home."[107] Perhaps more than any other setting, these deathbed moments reflect how, for these nineteenth-century evangelicals, emotional life was, as Reddy puts it, a "domain of effort."[108]

Manning admitted that he, too, had difficulty generating the feelings he thought he should. While he attempted to be composed with the thought of Nancy's eternal home, he confessed that he found the "sympathy of nature" at times overwhelming; "I am much affected, but I guard against it."[109] He recognized that there was an apparent contradiction between his natural and his religious feelings, and even in the private space of his diary, he did not want to leave the impression that he was not moved by the suffering or imminent death of his daughter. He explained, "I feel comfortable and happy, and not because I do not love my child, for I never loved her so well. But the thought of the Goodness and Sovereignty of God, and what he has done for my child, and the Glory that awaits her, fills me with consolation."[110] Or at least he hoped that he could maintain that sense of consolation while other feelings threatened to discompose him.

Throughout the illness, Nancy and her father relied on texts to help them shape their emotions. In addition to the Bible, they sang hymns (especially those by Isaac Watts) and reflected on the dying experiences of others as represented in popular evangelical memoirs. Manning, for example, wrote one evening, "Have been just reading the death of the incomparable Harriett Newel [missionary in India and Burma]. I suppose it prepared my mind for this struggle. I hope, I pray, that I may be calm."[111] More than once they spoke of

the memoir of Samuel Pearce, who, in a long illness, described himself as feeling "hot but happy." Manning wondered if his daughter
could make such a declaration in her fevered state. He recorded the
exchange: "'Can you say so, Nancy?' She paused, and said, 'Yes,
I think I can. I do not feel raptures as I have read of some feeling, but
I feel composed and think I feel happy.'"[112] Nancy's response illustrates how consciously evangelical readers used memoirs to shape
their own emotional reactions, her hesitancy perhaps also speaking
to how difficult such self-fashioning could be. The comments also
demonstrate the complexity of the religious and natural affections
that they sought to cultivate – not only raptures, but also composure,
happiness, and a sense of calm. By sympathizing with the figures in
evangelical memoirs, individual readers attempted to fashion their
affections according to the transatlantic emotional community of
which they imagined themselves a part.

IMPERIAL EMOTIONS? FEELINGS AND THE EXPERIENCE OF EMPIRE[113]

Missions literature, as well as memoirs, brought Manning to tears.
In January 1825 he wrote, "I spent the evening reading Baptist magazines and read out loud so that Mrs Manning and Mary might
hear, and partake of the feast. O how many times I wept for joy, and
I trust holy sympathy, with the many preacious souls and in knowing
what God is doing in our world."[114] Again, he records, "Received the
American Baptist Missionary Magazine, 131st number. The conversion and suffering of the converted Jews at ... Constantinople,
the conversion of two Buddhist priests ... the 10th Anniversary of
an Association in Connecticut ... seems almost to overwhelm me."[115]
These, and many other instances, capture the emotional experience
of evangelicals interpreting the early decades of the missionary movement and struggling to find their place in new imperial relationships.
   Manning's sentimental reading also raises questions about the
emotional and religious experience of empire and colonization.
Reading the outpouring of missionary literature was the primary
means of "bringing the Empire home."[116] British subjects – like
Manning – experienced the expansion of the British Empire as "missionary intelligence." As Susan Thorne observes, missionary print
culture "encouraged Victorian evangelicals to think about colonized
people on a regular basis."[117] It is striking how much Manning, a

self-educated reader living in rural Nova Scotia, came to know and care about events in India and Burma. Benedict Anderson has influentially argued that expanding print made it possible for readers to see themselves as members of an "imagined" national community.[118] Missionary periodicals helped readers to imagine, or perhaps *feel*, their connections in the global community that was the British Empire.

With an imperial context in mind, at least three kinds of tears can be identified from Manning's diary: tears of sympathy, tears of pity, and tears of grateful belonging, together suggesting that the experience of empire was emotionally complex. First, Manning sympathetically identified with the evangelistic work and personal suffering of the missionaries about whom he read. Despite the many differences between the locales, Manning felt connected: "Have been reading the sufferings of the missionaries in Burmah. My heart hath sympathized with them."[119] As with other varieties of eighteenth- and nineteenth-century humanitarianism, *sympathy* underpinned the missionary movement.[120] It was by this identification that Manning felt close to far-flung places and peoples.

Yet, as Laura Stevens has observed, missionary texts tended to place Anglo-American missionaries – rather than Indigenous inhabitants – at the centre of their narratives, and therefore as the primary objects of sympathy.[121] So while he wept tears of sympathy for *the missionaries*, Manning also cried a second kind of tears – of *pity* – for the colonized people. "Why," he wrote, "do [we] not *feel more* for the heathen, buried in horrible idolatry[?]"[122] Pity, compared with sympathy, was a feeling of *difference* rather than identification.[123] Note the complex combination of affection and superiority in Manning's diary entry for 3 October 1834: "This day rec'd the … Magazine for September, and am much affected with the acc't of the success of the missionaries … O how shocking, and how horrible is heathen idolatry. It melted me to tears today to think of our superior privileges."[124] Manning's feelings, that is, expressed the racialized assumptions of difference between Anglo-American missionaries and colonial subjects.

That same diary entry also identifies a third category of imperial tears: "tears of gratitude" for "<u>our</u> … privileges." It may be that reading helped Nova Scotians to feel more closely tied to Britain and belonging to something larger. The reading of missionary periodicals gave Manning and other British North Americans (and provincials in places like Edinburgh and Manchester) a common emotional experience that helped them to *feel* themselves to be full participants in the British Empire, aligned sentimentally with the metropole.[125]

Examining Manning's reading through his diary, we might observe, as Robert Darnton did of readers of Rousseau's *Nouvelle Héloïse*, that "one is struck everywhere by the sound of sobbing."[126] It is difficult for modern readers to recover this experience of reading. Yet Manning's intense emotional encounter with texts is far more understandable, and not so strange, in the context of the period's preoccupation with sympathetic reading, the emotional impact of expanding print and missions, and the felt experience of imperial belonging and colonial difference.

CONCLUSION

For some early nineteenth-century evangelicals, such as Edward Manning, discourses of affections and sentiments changed, but feelings were no less prominent in their experience and theology. Manning's conversion narrative certainly affirms the importance for New Lights of having one's soul "wrapt up in God's Eternal Love." But when we step back from that climactic moment, Manning's experience also illustrates how very problematic feelings could be – the difficulty of generating and maintaining the right emotions and the uncertainty of "reading" one's feelings properly as evidence of religious change. His reliance on sensations and impressions, to the exclusion even of the Bible, during the "new dispensation" tumult of the early 1790s, was an example of how emotions were contested by ordinary people in local communities and not only by philosophers and theologians in treatises.

Although by the late 1790s Manning and many of his New Light peers had repudiated their more "enthusiastic" practices and demon-strative emotional displays, they did not cease to regard affections as central to their evangelical piety. They continued to emphasize the religion of the heart and felt experience. Manning sought new theological frameworks and emotional discourses, finding them in Puritan devotional works, the Great Awakening theology of Jonathan Edwards, and the moderate Calvinism of Andrew Fuller. Together these provided Manning with an approach to religious affections less at odds with doctrine and order. Rather than emphasizing the suddenness of feelings, he sought a changed disposition – happiness, but not necessarily raptures. Manning's diary provides extensive evidence for his daily preoccupation with emotional self-fashioning and regulation.

Unlike the other figures in this study, Manning came to maturity after the upheavals of the American Revolution. He displayed little anxiety about national identity, at ease on both sides of the border between British North America and the fledgling United States. Even during the period of heightened national and imperial feelings during the War of 1812 and the wars in France, Manning was careful not to let political passions run free – he seemed to guard against any form of enthusiasm, political or religious. He built an affectionate transnational network through his itinerancy and correspondence, fashioning an identity that was probably more religious than political.

That is not to say, however, that Manning was indifferent to society in the same way that Alline had been. Indeed, Manning was an energetic advocate for a variety of social reforms, including education, the distribution of religious print, temperance, and international missions. He found no contradiction between the interiority of evangelical conversion and the "externals" of social institutions. In the era of religious disestablishment (uneven though it was), Manning and many other early nineteenth-century evangelicals acted on a voluntarist impulse for social reform – working through voluntary associations, stirring the passions of individuals to become active in various causes that had far-reaching social import. While later in the nineteenth century activists would employ associations without evangelical motivation, or work to achieve their social goals through the use of legislation rather than moral persuasion, for the decades of Manning's involvement, heart religion and social reform went hand in hand. Manning interpreted the progress of these various social and missionary initiatives as being momentous in human and divine history. The emotional impact of these reforms is captured in his often-tearful diary.

Those tears also provide a window into the importance of sympathy for Manning's religious (and imperial) experience. The unprecedented abundance of religious print allowed Manning and at least some of his Nova Scotian parishioners to *feel* themselves as part of evangelical and denominational communities that transcended their locale. As Manning read the burgeoning works of evangelical biography, he sympathized with their subjects' experiences and consciously (through writing and conversation) emulated their religious affections. Manning's tearful reading of missionary accounts provides historians (now accustomed to viewing missions with a degree of deserved skepticism) with a sense of how emotionally overwhelming those events could be for evangelicals – experiencing a flood of printed literature and news, interpreting missionary expansion in eschatological terms, and riveted by the pace of developments. Sympathy helped Manning to feel connected to missionaries, to far-flung peoples, and perhaps to the project of British (and American) imperialism. From enthusiasm to affections to sympathy, feelings remained central – though not unchanging – in Manning's evangelical experience.

Conclusion

As this book on emotions draws to a close, are there feelings – *pathos*, as well as ideas – that the author hopes his readers have experienced? As I immersed myself in the archive of this British North American community, I was repeatedly struck by at least three kinds of feelings that I hope have been elicited in these chapters.

First is a sense of respect for the significant effort that ordinary people invested in fashioning their own emotional lives with intelligence and intention. To be sure, we may find some of their sentiments strange or even objectionable, but no one who has made an effort to regulate their own inner life or their mindful response to the world can fail to acknowledge that this is an arduous part of working out one's identity. Their feelings, like our own, were contingent, and their meaning contextual.

Second, I hope that readers identified with the strong sense of connection that residents of this one provincial community felt to the Enlightenment Atlantic and their own far-flung emotional communities. Though in some ways quite removed from major centres, Cornwallis Township was also a node in overlapping networks, and through print, Handley Chipman, Nancy Lawrence, Edward Manning, and their neighbours not only followed but actively participated in intellectual conversations, devotional cultures, political movements, and emotional communities. It seems to me that attending to big ideas in small places is now a crucial aspect of the history of ideas and culture, and Nova Scotia is one compelling site from which to do this work.

Third, I hope that readers were surprised here and there by the complexity of the real people and emotions that lay behind the terms "enthusiasm" and "loyalty." Indeed, I used the plural form of both words in the book's title to signal the spectrum of emotional styles and experiences that existed across different communities and over time. These were contested and changing concepts, and historicizing these feelings reveals surprising affinities and paradoxes. Interrogating supposed polarities – loyal and Whig, evangelical and enlightened, or, of course, enthusiasm and loyalty – seems to be one effective way to get at lived realities, however messy.

To bring one implicit theme of the book to the foreground, it is hard to overstate the importance of *book culture* in the formation or fragmentation of the emotional communities that overlapped in Cornwallis Township. To be sure, in the absence of direct psychological access to the emotional states of past actors (whatever that would look like), texts are one of the few sources we have to reconstruct the history of feelings. Yet more than this, we have seen how these eighteenth- and nineteenth-century Nova Scotians actively interacted with specific texts – printed or of their own making – to fashion their personal feelings or to mark out emotional communities. People in this provincial community increasingly had fairly impressive access to metropolitan print, despite their distance from publishing hubs in London's Paternoster Row or Boston's Cornhill. The availability of books and periodicals ballooned in the early nineteenth century, but even before then, texts and ideas circulated through the region's personal and commercial networks: borrowed, purchased, shared, or copied into commonplace books. Nova Scotians selectively and reflectively used these texts, whether panegyrics to British liberty or prompts to awakened piety, as one means of shaping their own political and religious emotions. Recall Handley Chipman's conscious choice to compile chronologies of British progress on the eve of the Revolution, despite his misgivings about imperial policy, or Edward Manning and his daughter Nancy relying on evangelical memoirs as models for their own feeling responses to illness. No less important were the texts that they created themselves. Sometimes their writing lent emotional coherence to their communities, as when female correspondents guided one another toward the feelings their New Light churches valued most. At other times, strong feelings threatened to overwhelm the very possibility of unity, as in the case of Jacob Bailey's flaming newspaper articles or his biting satirical verse, despairing of his earlier confidence that civic society could be founded on common sympathies. Print made it possible to record, communicate, reflect upon, and debate the meaning of the feelings that characterized their communities.

Enthusiasms and Loyalties is about the public history of "private" feelings. In British North America, as elsewhere in the early modern Atlantic world, passions, affections, and sentiments did not merely move the heart; rather, they were a "causal factor in history," a "moving force" in realms such as politics, economics, and religion.[1] Few terms in the taxonomy of early modern emotions convey their potent impact as does "enthusiasm." From Civil War sectaries to French revolutionaries, enthusiasm represented the worry that the subjective would escape the bounds of reason and turn the social order upside down. Though sometimes ridiculed, enthusiasm was feared for its very public power. "Loyalty," likewise, transferred the inclinations of the heart to the rough and tumble world of politics. During the American Revolution, for example, committees of safety regarded disaffection as a threat to the cause of liberty, forcing emotions into the public square and policing the allowable spectrum of wartime feelings. No surprise, then, that as Nova Scotians reconfigured their political and religious communities during and after the Revolution, they gave particular attention to the public consequences of their feelings. What, then, of the emotions of the book's title?

Enthusiasm was an epithet that declared certain private feelings a public menace. The term brings to the surface the role that emotions played in the construction and contested nature of early modern communities – especially religious communities. Deployed by critics or avoided by self-censorship, enthusiasm as a smear was intended to fence the religious or imaginative sensations that elites deemed compatible with Enlightenment rationalism and polite society. In other words, it was (and remains) tempting to make "enthusiastic" and "enlightened" mutually exclusive categories. Yet the emotional communities of Cornwallis Township defy such easy polarization. Their preoccupation with feelings meant that people here took up many of the same questions as better-known philosophers: where feelings came from, how passions could be regulated, how affection could be cultivated, if emotions were reliable sensory evidence, whether sentiment could motivate moral behaviour, and what effects personal emotions had on society. To be sure, the answers at which

they arrived were anything but unanimous, but their local controversies involved even "enthusiasts" as participants in the debates of
the Enlightenment Atlantic.

Paying attention to religious affections also adds nuance to the
perception of the "emotionalism" of evangelical Protestantism. Even
so-called enthusiasts worried about unfeeling hearts. Revivalists,
true to form, aspired to the heights of spontaneous rapture, but
they also agonized over their failure to maintain more quotidian
affections and sympathies, and this often led them to reflect on the
meaning of their emotions. This book has argued that just as loyalism is about more than reaction to the Revolution, so evangelicalism
is about more than the raptures of revivals. Attending to the whole
spectrum of affections that were valued in these communities has
made it possible to learn something new about the everyday, lived
experience of eighteenth- and early nineteenth-century figures who
are usually defined by a few remarkable events.

The meaning of "enthusiasm" changed over time, retaining its
Civil War sense of the topsy-turvy to figures like Charles Inglis during
the French Revolution, but it then took on more positive shades of
meaning connected to Romantic creativity.[2] As Edward Manning's
story illustrates, by the middle of the nineteenth century, Protestants
in British North America and beyond who sought to distance themselves from the more enthusiastic elements of their faith made other
sentiments and affections integral to Victorian evangelicalism.[3] The
question is not if they remained "emotional," but in what way.

Loyalism encompassed a wide affective range. This book has
taken a sounding of the diverse emotional styles that constituted or
were compatible with loyalism. By expanding the historian's pal-
ate for political emotions – giving us a better sense of what was
feelable during the late eighteenth and early nineteenth centuries –
Enthusiasms and Loyalties adds to recent scholarship describing
a spectrum of loyalties, encompassing neutrality, pacifism, indifference, opportunism, and pragmatism, as well as more familiar
tropes such as ideological Toryism, irenic reconciliation, or refugee
displacement.[4] Paying attention to the affective element of political
identities helps to historicize and better see past the polarization of
heated rhetoric to appreciate the plurality of loyalties in the period.

If loyalism has a broad emotional register, it also has a long history reaching back to at least the end of the seventeenth century

and carrying on into the nineteenth century (and beyond). The emotional story of loyalism that this book has been telling emphasizes continuities as well as changes – affected by the American Revolution, but not entirely defined by it. In Jacob Bailey's moderate Enlightenment cosmopolitanism and Handley Chipman's provincial and genteel Britishness, we see versions of the loyalism that was the default political posture of British North Americans until the eve of the Revolution. In their voices, recorded before the din of conflict, we hear, among other things, the American accent and Whiggish cadences of their loyalism, both without a trace of contradiction. Unlike recent histories of Patriot passion and sensibility that emphasize the independence of American feelings during the revolutionary period (only returning to a transatlantic history of sentiment with the Federalist movement of the early republic), *Enthusiasms and Loyalties* argues that many Loyalists remained committed to the ideals of that emotional community without interval. The history of loyalism, that is, was coordinated with the "Long Age of Sensibility" as well as the Age of Revolutions.[5]

Yet that is not to say that loyalism was unchanging. Loyalist emotions reflected the range of their experiences and (dis)locations, their feelings sometimes galvanized by suffering and at other times muted by the surveillance of neighbours. To take just one example, a complex emotional story can be told by attending to the uses of "disaffection." Committees of safety deployed the term to rebrand the political affections of Loyalists, by their policing rendering a ubiquitous British American political sensibility into something subversive. Changing the label and cultural meaning of those emotions, however, was not the end of the transformation. In the face of what they perceived as British betrayals, and because of their experience as refugees, Loyalists like Jacob Bailey also became disenchanted – *disaffected* – with their identity as British subjects. Accused of being disaffected with an American homeland he still identified with, and disaffected with the British crown for which he suffered, Bailey stubbornly retained his loyalty, but it was undoubtedly a loyalty with a very different emotional cast. Loyalty continued to be a contested and multivalent set of affections well into the nineteenth century, a complex amalgam of memory, imperial patriotism, and reform.[6]

We began with Charles Inglis's warning that "a spirit of enthusiasm" was antithetical to true religion and loyalty, "malignant to government, and subversive of the peace and welfare of society."[7]

For revolution-weary Inglis, the enthusiasm and loyalty of the book's title were necessarily in conflict. And historians of British North America have – if with considerably less heat – framed the issue in similar ways, emphasizing the republicanism and disruptive potency of evangelical Protestantism: "evangelical voluntaryism" over against "Christian loyalism."[8] Yet perhaps they have hewed too closely to Inglis's polemical rhetoric. One of the findings of this study has been a broader gamut of engagement between religion and loyalism. As Katherine Carté and Denis McKim have convincingly argued, so-called enthusiasts benefited as much as anyone from their place in the British Empire: operating within its stable polity, protected by its pluralism, proselytizing apace with imperial expansion, or using loyalty as a badge of their respectability.[9] Indeed, the Protestantism that was such an essential aspect of loyal imperial expansion during this period was intentionally a big tent, encompassing, among many other groups, the Church of England, New England Congregationalists, and awakened evangelicals. Until the fissures of the Revolution, all of them were committed to the same British social order, even if they expressed their loyalty in different emotional registers.[10] Anglican Jacob Bailey would have been surprised to find that Handley Chipman – a latter-day New England Puritan if there ever was one – read the same polite metropolitan magazines that he did, or that he filled his diaries with paeans to British liberty. Henry Alline's spiritually levelling rhetoric never translated into political republicanism; to the contrary, he considered Nova Scotians a "people highly favoured of God" because they remained on the outer margins of "the dreadful calamity" of revolutionary conflict.[11] There, in a less polarized environment than New England, neutrality, pacifism, Whiggish loyalty, or even otherworldly ambivalence remained viable political and emotional postures. And contrary to the expectation of critics, Edward Manning demonstrates that many Protestants in the early nineteenth century turned their evangelical voluntarism to a panoply of social and religious causes that were eminently compatible with loyalty and order. Few evangelicals felt the need to choose between individualistic piety and communal commitments, though they did resolve the tension between enthusiasm and loyalty in different ways and with several affective styles.

Nevertheless, Inglis's worries about enthusiasm and loyalty do convey the belief in the potent agency of emotions in the most consequential public events of the eighteenth and nineteenth centuries. His comments remind us of the disruptive potential of emotions to divide and reconfigure – to make and unmake – political and religious communities. As all these case studies illustrate, colonial Nova Scotians used emotions to construct and mark out their communities, only to have them blasted and fragmented by the passions of the Revolution. However, when it came time to reconfigure new political and religious communities, they would turn again to feelings and sentiments to undertake that work of re-formation.

Notes

INTRODUCTION

1 Inglis, *Steadfastness in Religion and Loyalty*. On Inglis in Nova Scotia, see Fingard, *The Anglican Design*, esp. ch. 1; and Cutherbertson, *The First Bishop*. See also Hebb, *Samuel Seabury and Charles Inglis*.

2 Inglis, *The True Interest of America Impartially Stated*, quotations at v and vi. Paine, *Common Sense*. On Inglis's response to *Common Sense*, see Bell, *A War of Religion*, 149–55. To retain the sense of eighteenth-century language, primary sources are quoted here without correcting spelling or grammar, and without using [*sic*]. Necessary clarifications are included in brackets, and, in rare cases, there are silent corrections.

3 Inglis, *Steadfastness in Religion and Loyalty*, 16–18, emphasis added. On enthusiasm as a form of unsociability, see Klein, "Sociability, Solitude, and Enthusiasm," 153–77. For the application of the term to the French Revolution, see Mee, *Romanticism, Enthusiasm, and Regulation*, ch. 2. On the sermon literature of British North America during the French Revolution, including Inglis, see Wise, *God's Peculiar Peoples*, 7–15, 28–36.

4 Inglis, *Steadfastness in Religion and Loyalty*, 24, note.

5 Ibid., 24. Parker, *Beginnings of the Book Trade in Canada*, 29.

6 Inglis, *Steadfastness in Religion and Loyalty*, 21.

7 Ibid., 24, note, 16; emphasis in original.

8 Ibid., 5; emphasis added.

9 Ibid., 6.

10 Ibid., 8–10, 25–6, quotation at 16.

11 Ibid., 29.

12 Ibid., 19–20, 24, 30.

13 On sensibility and the culture of sentiment, see Barker-Benfield, *Culture of Sensibility*; Todd, *Sensibility*; Van Sant, *Eighteenth-Century Sensibility and the Novel*; Mullan, *Sentiment and Sociability*; Howard, "What Is Sentimentality?"; Vincent-Buffault, *History of Tears*; and Pearsall, *Atlantic Families*, ch. 3.

14 Hutcheson, *An Essay on the Nature and Conduct of the Passions and Affections*. A recent introduction to eighteenth-century moral philosophy, including Shaftesbury, Hutcheson, Hume, and Smith, is Frazer, *Enlightenment of Sympathy*.

15 Hume, *A Treatise of Human Nature*, 415. See Dixon, *Weeping Britannia*, 72. For a helpful discussion of Hume on passions and sentiments, see Mullan, *Sentiment and Sociability*, 18–56.

16 Smith, *Theory of Moral Sentiments*. For an extended discussion of the repression and then rehabilitation of the passions in relation to economic self-interest, see Hirschman, *The Passions and the Interests*.

17 Edwards, *A Treatise Concerning Religious Affections*, 95.

18 See especially Dixon, *From Passions to Emotions*, chs 3 and 4; Eustace, "Toward a Lexicon of Eighteenth-Century Emotion," in *Passion Is the Gale*, 481–6; Frevert, *Emotional Lexicons*; and Rorty, "From Passions to Emotions and Sentiments."

19 There is an ongoing debate about whether "emotion" can be usefully distinguished from "affect," the former designating *intentional*, culturally conditioned responses, and the latter implying neurological/somatic reactions *without* conscious agency. For an exchange that raises many of the key issues, see Leys, "The Turn to Affect"; Connolly, "Critical Response I: The Complexity of Intention"; Leys, "Affect and Intention." See also Gregg and Seigworth, eds, *The Affect Theory Reader*.

20 Reddy, "Historical Research on the Self and Emotions," and *Navigation of Feeling*; Dixon, *From Passions to Emotions*; Eustace, Lean, Livingston, Plamper, Reddy, and Rosenwein, "AHR Conversation: The Historical Study of Emotions"; Liliequist, ed., *A History of Emotions*; Matt and Stearns, eds, *Doing Emotions History*; Plamper, *The History of Emotions*; Rosenwein, *Generations of Feeling*; and Boddice, *A History of Feelings*. Research centres have been important in the development of the field; see the Australian Research Council Centre of Excellence for the History of Emotions (http://www.historyofemotions.org.au); the Queen Mary Centre for the History of the Emotions, University of London (https://projects.history.qmul.ac.uk/emotions/); and the History of Emotions at the Max Planck Institute, Berlin (https://www.mpib-berlin.mpg.de/en/research/history-of-emotions).

21 Rosenfeld, "Thinking About Feeling," 699–700.
22 Anderson, *Imagined Communities*.
23 Ibid., 51.
24 Ibid., 141, 52–3; emphasis in original.
25 Ibid., 143. Nicole Eustace insightfully compares Anderson's work on
    nationalism with Jürgen Habermas's on the public sphere: "Whereas
    Habermas stressed rationality, Anderson made clear in his discussion …
    that the emotional element of public life is fundamental and cannot be
    denied." Eustace, *1812: War and the Passions of Patriotism*, 239n7;
    Habermas, *The Structural Transformation of the Public Sphere*.
26 On the creation of "Britishness," see Colley, *Britons*; Wilson, *The Sense
    of the People*; and McConville, *The King's Three Faces*. For the formation
    of an American national identity in the early republic, see Waldstreicher,
    In the Midst of Perpetual Fetes; and Freeman, *Affairs of Honor*. Jeffrey L.
    McNairn observes that "Historians of early Canada have as yet paid scant
    attention to morality and emotion in relation to law and politics," though
    noting that "this is less true of studies of gender, family, and religion."
    See McNairn's important intervention: "The Common Sympathies of
    Our Nature," quotations at 50. Other recent forays in the Canadian
    history of emotions include: Kenny, *The Feel of the City*; Gregory and
    Grant, "The Role of Emotions in Protests"; Morgan, *Travellers through
    Empire*; Bannister, "Liberty, Loyalty, and Sentiment"; and Reiter,
    Wounded Feelings.
27 Adams to Hezekiah Niles, 13 Feb. 1818, in *The Works of John Adams*,
    10:288.
28 Eustace, *Passion Is the Gale*, 388. See also, Eustace, "A Feeling for
    History."
29 Eustace, *Passion is the Gale*, 387–8, 479.
30 See especially Barnes, *States of Sympathy*; Burstein, *Sentimental
    Democracy* and "The Political Character of Sympathy"; Wills, *Inventing
    America*, esp. part 4; Lewis, "Those Scenes for Which Alone My Heart
    Was Made"; Ellison, *Cato's Tears and the Making of Anglo-American
    Emotion*; and Smith, *American Honor*. On how sensibility was employed
    and debated in *British* politics and culture, see Barker-Benfield, *Culture of
    Sensibility*; Ellis, *The Politics of Sensibility*; and Jones, *Radical Sensibility*.
    The emotional history of the French Revolution certainly includes the
    theme of sentiment, but tends to emphasize the emotional discontinuities
    of fear and terror. William Reddy's pioneering work on the history of
    emotions was grounded in his scholarship on the French Revolution.
    Reddy, "Sentimentalism and Its Erasure" and *Navigation of Feeling*. For

recent overviews of the field, see Rosenfeld, "Thinking About Feeling";
and Andress, "Navigating Feelings in the French Revolution."

31 Landsman, *From Colonials to Provincials*; and Shields, *Civil Tongues and Polite Letters*.

32 Knott, *Sensibility and the American Revolution*, 4, 16; see 17.

33 Errington, "Webs of Affection and Obligation" and *Emigrant Worlds and Transatlantic Communities*.

34 Pearsall, "The Power of Feeling," 670.

35 Ibid.," 665, 669–71. See Gould, *Writing the Rebellion*, 8.

36 Calhoon, *The Loyalists in Revolutionary America*, esp. ch. 28; quotation at 317.

37 Potter, *The Liberty We Seek*, 40–6, quotations at 45.

38 Ibid., 42. Potter cites a study that attempted to determine whether Loyalists and Patriots displayed consistent personality differences. Based on the analysis of eighty individuals (for whom sufficient biographical information was available) using standard personality instruments, the authors concluded personality did indeed affect political choice. Hull, Hoffer, and Allen, "Choosing Sides."

39 Bannister and Riordan, "Loyalism and the British Atlantic," 9.

40 In addition to the many studies of loyalism and Loyalists that are cited throughout this study, on that distinction between loyalism and Loyalists, see especially: Bumsted, *Understanding the Loyalists*, 48–9; Bannister, "Planter Studies and Atlantic Scholarship," 30–2; Bannister and Riordan, "Loyalism and the British Atlantic"; Mancke, "Idiosyncratic Localism, Provincial Moderation, Imperial Loyalty," 176; and Eamon, *Imprinting Britain*, 189–90. For other studies that propose reconsiderations of loyalism from various perspectives in the Atlantic world, see Larkin, "What Is a Loyalist?" and "The Cosmopolitan Revolution"; Mason, "The American Loyalist Diaspora" and "The American Loyalist Problem of Identity"; Blackstock and O'Gorman, eds, *Loyalism and the Formation of the British World*; Brannon and Moore, eds, *Consequences of Loyalism*; McKim, "Anxious Anglicans, Complicated Catholics, and Disruptive Dissenters"; and Tillman, *Stripped and Script*, 6–11, 50. Two recent dissertations explore new emotional and gendered dimensions of the Loyalist experience. Timothy Compeau examines Loyalist conceptions of (dis)honour and manhood; "Dishonoured Americans." Patrick O'Brien's study, "Unknown and Unlamented," is an insightful examination of the way Loyalist women used their emotions in refugee homes and communities.

41 John Corrigan has been at the forefront of integrating a more established body of literature on the history of *ideas* about emotions with the newer

(more theoretically informed) history of religious *experiences*. Compare his monograph *The Hidden Balance* with his edited collection *Religion and Emotion*. On a specific emotional experience, see his *Emptiness: Feeling Christian in America*. On religious experience, see also Hall, ed., *Lived Religion in America* and "What Is the Place of 'Experience' in Religious History?"; and Orsi, *Between Heaven and Earth*.

42 Ryrie and Schwanda, eds, *Puritanism and Emotion in the Early Modern World*; Roberts, *Puritanism and the Pursuit of Happiness*; Ryrie, *Being Protestant in Reformation Britain*, esp. 17–95; White, *Puritan Rhetoric*. A previous generation of psychologically informed studies included Cohen, *God's Caress*; and Leverenz, *Language of Puritan Feeling*. For Reformation and early modern studies, see Karant-Nunn, *Reformation of Feeling*; Cummings and Sierhuis, eds, *Passions and Subjectivity in Early Modern Culture*; Paster, Rowe, and Floyd-Wilson, eds, *Reading the Early Modern Passions*; James, *Passion and Action*; and Ryrie, *Unbelievers*.

43 Van Engen, *Sympathetic Puritans*. Van Engen's argument is usefully read alongside the work of Ruth Bloch and Claudia Stokes on later religious adaptations of the culture of sentiment; Bloch, "Religion, Literary Sentimentalism, and Popular Revolutionary Ideology"; and Stokes, *Altar at Home*.

44 In the present study, the term "evangelical" is typically used to describe the religious style emerging from the Protestant Awakenings of the late seventeenth and early eighteenth centuries. David Bebbington's influential description of the movement identifies four main cultural and theological characteristics: a particular emphasis on the cross of Jesus Christ, personal conversion, the authority of the Bible, and an activist or missionary impulse; Bebbington, *Evangelicalism in Modern Britain*. For narrative and intellectual histories of early evangelicalism, see, among others, Noll, *Rise of Evangelicalism*; Ward, *Early Evangelicalism*; Winiarski, *Darkness Falls on the Land of Light*; and Hindmarsh, *Spirit of Early Evangelicalism*.

45 Taves, *Fits, Trances, & Visions*; Rivett, *Science of the Soul*; Rivers, *Reason, Grace, and Sentiment*, 2 vols; Fiering, *Jonathan Edwards's Moral Thought*; and Crawford, *Seasons of Grace*, 81–97.

46 Mack, *Heart Religion in the British Enlightenment*. See also Taves, *Fits, Trances, and Visions*, 4, who observes that in the historiography, "educated elites are typically depicted as explaining (away) religious experience in abstract terms, while ordinary people, embedded in traditions of faith and practice, are depicted as having them" – a set of assumptions she attempts to avoid by incorporating elites and ordinary people in the same narrative, an approach this study adopts. See Eustace, *Passion Is the Gale*, 6–7.

47 Hollett, *Shouting, Embracing, and Dancing with Ecstasy*. Also see Westfall on the exchanges between the two religious cultures of Protestant Ontario – those of (Anglican) order and (Methodist) experience – in *Two Worlds*, 19–49.

48 Brown, *Word in the World*; and King, *Imagined Spiritual Communities*.

49 Van Gent, "Sarah and Her Sisters"; Van Gent and Young, "Introduction: Emotions and Conversion"; Haggis and Allen, "Imperial Emotions"; Ballantyne, *Entanglements of Empire*; Elbourne, *Blood Ground*, chs 1, 4; Stevens, *Poor Indians*; and the essays in McLisky, Midena, and Vallgårda, eds, *Emotions and Christian Missions*.

50 The classic study of enthusiasm is Knox, *Enthusiasm*. More recent studies examine how the term was employed in changing discourses through the early modern period, including those of religion, medicine, polite aesthetics, and Romantic literature. See Tucker, *Enthusiasm*; Lovejoy, *Religious Enthusiasm in the New World*; Rivers, "Shaftesburian Enthusiasm and the Evangelical Revival"; Heyd, *Be Sober and Reasonable*; Klein and La Vopa, eds, *Enthusiasm and Enlightenment in Europe*; Mee, *Romanticism, Enthusiasm, and Regulation*; Rosenberg, "Accumulate! Accumulate!"; Taves, *Fits, Trances, and Visions*, 13–117; Dixon, *Weeping Britannia*, 69; and Laborie, *Enlightening Enthusiasm*.

51 Johnson, as quoted in Tucker, *Enthusiasm*, 17.

52 See Krysmanski, "We See a Ghost: Hogarth's Satire on Methodists and Connoisseurs," 292–310; and Dixon, *Weeping Britannia*, 92–4.

53 Klein, "Sociability, Solitude, and Enthusiasm," 162.

54 Pocock, "Enthusiasm: The Antiself of Enlightenment," 9–10.

55 Heyd, *Be Sober and Reasonable*, ch. 6.

56 Mee, *Romanticism, Enthusiasm, and Regulation*, 24.

57 Rothschild, *The Inner Life of Empires*, 4.

58 On the *interaction* between elite and popular culture, see Burke, *Popular Culture in Early Modern Europe*, especially 95–101. "The minds of ordinary people," Burke argues, "are not like blank paper, but stocked with ideas and images" (96–7).

59 Taves, *Fits, Trances, and Visions*, 4.

60 LCOLL Jacob Bailey Papers, MG 1, 94–10 (Reel 4). Letterbook, 2 May 1781, Bailey to Mrs Domett.

61 Gwyn, *Planter Nova Scotia: Cornwallis Township*, population at 58; and Eaton, *History of Kings County*. There is a rich body of scholarship on the New England Planters that resettled in Nova Scotia from the 1760s, especially the edited volumes in the Planter Studies series: Conrad, ed., *They Planted Well, Making Adjustments*, and *Intimate Relations*; Conrad and

Moody, eds, *Planter Links*; Henderson and Robicheau, eds, *Nova Scotia Planters in the Atlantic World*. See also Campbell and Smith, *Necessaries and Sufficiencies*; and Jaffee, *People of the Wachusett*. Elizabeth Mancke proposes reframing the post-1749 history of Nova Scotia, which was "not about creating a new New England but about securing an imperial periphery with the settlement of loyal subjects"; see "Idiosyncratic Localism," 169–81 (quotation at 176) and *Fault Lines of Empire*.

62 Jacob Bailey to Samuel Peters, 31 Oct. 1784, as quoted in MacKinnon, *This Unfriendly Soil*, 53.

63 On examining Atlantic history from a particular or "cis-Atlantic" perspective, see Armitage, "Three Concepts of Atlantic History," 23–8.

64 Clark, *The Siege of Fort Cumberland*; Brebner, *Neutral Yankees*.

65 Jerry Bannister argues, "Far from being on the periphery of the British Atlantic, or merely part of a regional borderland, Nova Scotia is now seen as occupying the centre of a larger struggle for supremacy in the Atlantic world." Bannister, "Planter Studies and Atlantic Scholarship," 21. Similarly, see Huskins, "Shelburnian Manners," 153. Seeing Nova Scotia as fundamentally connected to the Atlantic world is at odds with an older scholarly view of the province as peripheral and isolated, expressed in the title of Brebner's *New England's Outpost*.

66 Mack, *Heart Religion*, 134.

67 Eustace, in Eustace et al., "AHR Conversation," 1490; drawing on Reddy, *Navigation of Feeling*, ch. 3.

68 Rosenwein, in Eustace et al., "AHR Conversation," 1496.

69 Reddy, *Navigation of Feeling*, 55; Mack, *Heart Religion*, 6–7, 15–18. For a related discussion of emotions as a *habitus* shaped by a combination of personal agency and cultural norms, see Scheer, "Are Emotions a Kind of Practice."

70 Rosenwein, *Generations of Feeling*, 3, and *Emotional Communities in the Early Middle Ages*, 2. Also see Rosenwein, "Worrying about Emotions in History"; Broomhall, "Introduction," in Broomhall, ed., *Spaces for Feeling*, 1–11; Reddy, *Navigation of Feeling*, 330–2; and Wigginton and Van Engen, "Introduction," in *Feeling Godly*, 7. Feminist theorist Sara Ahmed describes the "sociality," rather than interiority, of emotions, arguing that feelings "are produced as effects of circulation"; *Cultural Politics of Emotion*, 8–10.

71 Rosenwein, *Generations of Feeling*, 3.

72 On microhistories and larger stories, see Rothschild, *Inner Life of Empire*, 4–8; Putnam, "To Study the Fragments/Whole"; and Brown, "Microhistory and the Post-Modern Challenge."

CHAPTER ONE

1 NSA MG 1, Vol. 218 (Microfilm 10154). Chipman Family Fonds,
   Commonplace Book (1776), 5.
2 McConville, *The King's Three Faces*; Nelson, *The Royalist Revolution*,
   esp. 239n29. See also Bushman, *King and People in Provincial
   Massachusetts*; Mason, "Loyalism in British North America," 165;
   Bumsted, *Understanding the Loyalists*, 48–9; Bannister, "Planter Studies
   and Atlantic Scholarship," 30–2; Bannister and Riordan, "Loyalism and
   the British Atlantic"; and Mancke, "Idiosyncratic Localism," 176.
3 On the need to examine British and Loyalist, and not only Patriot,
   emotions, see Pearsall, "The Power of Feeling?" 665, 669–71.
4 On Chipman's biography and genealogy, see Davison, *Handley Chipman:
   King's County Planter*; Miller, "Chipman, William Allen"; Chipman,
   Chipman Family; Chipman, *A Chipman Genealogy*; and Eaton, *History of
   Kings County*.
5 NSA Chipman, Commonplace Book, 1. On the significance of such
   genealogical connections, see Wulf, "Bible, King, and Common Law," and
   Hattem, *Past and Prologue*, 53–4.
6 Bartlett, ed., *Records of the Colony of Rhode Island*, 161–2.
7 ECW Chipman Family Fonds, 1931.005–CHI/4/1.25. Handley Chipman,
   Family Memoir (1796), 14, 30–3.
8 ECW Chipman, Family Memoir, 52; and NSA Chipman, Commonplace
   Book, 1. Thanks to Prof. Sylvia Brown, Department of English, University
   of Alberta, for this observation.
9 The classic discussion of anglicization is Murrin, "England and Colonial
   America," reprinted in *Anglicizing America*, 9–19, and see the other essays
   in the volume for historiographic context and reconsideration. See also
   Breen, "An Empire of Goods" and *Marketplace of Revolution*; and
   Landsman, *From Colonials to Provincials*. The most thoroughgoing
   dissent from this view is expressed in Butler, *Becoming America*.
10 The "new" British history has emphasized that ideas such as "Britain" or
   "Britishness" were not givens; they had to be consciously constructed and
   maintained through culture and policy. The literature is vast, but see
   especially Pocock, "British History: A Plea for a New Subject"; Colley,
   Britons; and Wilson, *Sense of the People*. In a wide-ranging essay, Nancy
   Christie explores how British North America can be located in this
   historiography; "Introduction: Theorizing a Colonial Past: Canada as a
   Society of British Settlement." For the complexities of defining Britishness
   in Nova Scotia, see Eamon, *Imprinting Britain*, 16–18.

11 McConville, *The King's Three Faces*, 105.

12 NSA Chipman, Commonplace Book, xii and 244. In his will, Chipman made provisions for all his books, "printed and wrote," to be "carefully preserved and kept in a Library for the families to read," planning for their further circulation; ECW Chipman Family Fonds, D1900.001.1. Handley Chipman, Will and Codicil (1799). Jacob Bailey reported seeing a "huge volume in folio" of Chipman's poetry, though Bailey mocked the verse for its simplicity and lack of sophistication; LCOLL Jacob Bailey Papers, MG 1, 94–7 (Reel 4). Letterbook. 2 Feb. 1781, Bailey to Mr Brown, and 7 Feb. 1781, Bailey to Sally Weeks.

13 Anderson, *Imagined Communities*; Wilson, *The Sense of the People*, 27–54.

14 Eamon, *Imprinting Britain*. See also Landsman, *From Colonials to Provincials*, 32–4.

15 Allan, *Commonplace Books and Reading*, 226.

16 On commonplace books, see Colclough, "Recovering the Reader"; Allan, *Commonplace Books and Reading*; Dacome, "Noting the Mind"; Berland, Gilliam, and Lockridge, eds, *Commonplace Book of William Byrd II*; Blecki and Wulf, eds, *Milcah Martha Moore's Book*; Burke, "Recent Studies in Commonplace Books"; Darnton, "The Mysteries of Reading," in *The Case for Books*, ch. 10; Beal, "Notions in Garrison"; and Schurink, "Manuscript Commonplace Books, Literature, and Reading."

17 Chipman, Commonplace Book, xii.

18 On the history and readership of the *Gentleman's Magazine*, with a crucial emphasis on the construction of gendered identities, see Williamson, *British Masculinity in the Gentleman's Magazine*, chs 2–3, and on the "benevolent affections" expressed in the magazine, see 124–7. See also Carlson, *The First Magazine*; and de Montluzin, *Daily Life in Georgian England*. For both the *Gentleman's* and *London* magazines, see Sullivan, ed., *British Literary Magazines*. To reverse the lens, see the portrayal of Chipman's colony in the *Gentleman's Magazine* in Currie, "Some Eighteenth-Century Observations on Nova Scotia."

19 McConville, *The King's Three Faces*, 83. On almanacs, see Capp, *English Almanacs*, esp. chs 3, 7, 8; and Tomlin, *A Divinity for All Persuasions*.

20 Allan, *Commonplace Books and Reading*, 233.

21 Chronologies as a historical form have their own long history, although eighteenth-century developments have not yet received much attention. For early modern chronologies and their renaissance and classical predecessors, see Grafton, "Joseph Scaliger and Historical Chronology" and *Joseph Scaliger*; Wilcox, *Measure of Times Past*; Knoespel, "Newton

in the School of Time"; Kidd, *British Identities before Nationalism*, 34–8; and Rosenberg, "Joseph Priestley and the Graphic Invention of Modern Time." I am grateful to Michael Hattem, an associate director of the Yale-New Haven Teachers Institute, for his observations on chronologies as a historical form, particularly in eighteenth-century America, and for his comments on one of Chipman's chronologies.

22 NSA Chipman, Commonplace Book, 5, 10–11, 11–17, 20, 21, 33, 135–6.

23 Colley, *Britons*, 22.

24 NSA Chipman, Commonplace Book, 11; *British Chronologist*, 3 vols. A copy of this work, perhaps the one that Chipman read, was included in a catalogue of a library in Cornwallis Township, for the use of the Congregational church. ECW Chipman Family Fonds, 1900.048–CHI/1, Handley Chipman, Ledger [No. 3] (1771–99), 300.

25 *Chronological Remembrancer.*

26 *British Chronologist*, I; emphasis in original.

27 Trusler, ed., *A Chronology; or, The Historian's Vade-Mecum*, title page.

28 McConville, *Three Faces of the King*, 49. The following discussion draws on his account of royalization in chapter 2. On "historical culture," see Woolf, *The Social Circulation of the Past* and "From Hystories to the Historical"; and Hattem, *Past and Prologue*.

29 On "internalizing," see McConville, *Three Faces of the King*, 200–1. On the use of the calendar for the cultivation of English national identity, see Cressy, *Bonfires and Bells*; and Wilson, *Sense of the People*, 21–4. For adaptation of the calendar in American identity-making, see Waldstreicher, *In the Midst of Perpetual Fetes.*

30 NSA Chipman, Commonplace Book, 10.

31 Ibid. On chronologies in almanacs, see Capp, *English Almanacs*, 215–24.

32 NSA Chipman, Commonplace Book, 20, 33.

33 Ibid., 5, 20, 21.

34 Anderson, *Imagined Communities*, 193. I am grateful to Elizabeth Mancke for making this point about Chipman's continuing commitment to a historically grounded identity.

35 See Calhoon, *Political Moderation*, 16, 298; and Stoermer, "The Success of Either Lies in the Womb of Time," 11–32.

36 NSA Chipman, Commonplace Book, 41. Quotation from Nathaniel Ames, *Almanac for 1762*, as reprinted in Briggs, ed., *Essays, Humor, and Poems of Nathaniel Ames*, 323.

37 Hurd, *Britons Behold the Best of Kings*, 1762. Engraving, hand-coloured. American Antiquarian Society, Worcester, MA.

38 NSA Chipman, Commonplace Book, 176–7. The address is selected from the *Gentleman's Magazine* (June 1765), 285.

39 Willis, "The Standing of New Subjects: Grenada and the Protestant Constitution after the Treaty of Paris (1763)."

40 Hattem, *Past and Prologue*, 50.

41 On petitions, see Bushman, *King and People in Provincial Massachusetts*, 46–54. On how emotional ties helped to structure the empire, see McConville, *King's Three Faces*, 106–12.

42 Paine, *Common Sense*, 69 and 76.

43 NSA Chipman, Commonplace Book, 99; quoting the *London Magazine* (October 1754), 506–7.

44 Mapp, "British Culture and the Changing Character of the Mid-Eighteenth-Century British Empire," 36–7.

45 NSA Chipman, Commonplace Book, 51–2; quoting Ames, *An astronomical diary, 1756*. On Braddock's defeat and the Seven Years' War, see Anderson, *Crucible of War*.

46 Bannister, *Masculinity, Militarism and Eighteenth-Century Culture*, 123–50. See also Williamson, *British Masculinity in the Gentleman's Magazine*; Capp, "'Jesus Wept' but Did the Englishman?" and Tosh, "The Old Adam and the New Man." On gendered and martial aspects of loyalty and patriotism in Upper Canada during the War of 1812, see Morgan, *Public Men and Virtuous Women*, 23–55.

47 NSA Chipman, Commonplace Book, 30; quoting *Bickerstaff's Boston Almanack, 1772*, front cover.

48 For influential treatments of the Whig tradition in England and America, see Pocock, *Machiavellian Moment*; Bailyn, *Ideological Origins of the American Revolution*; Colbourn, *Lamp of Experience*; and Wood, *Creation of the American Republic*. For the British and Whig roots of Loyalist thought, see Potter, *Liberty We Seek*, 84–106, 116–18. On conceptions of liberty in the Atlantic world, see Ducharme, *Idea of Liberty in Canada*, ch. 1.

49 McConville, *King's Three Faces*, 50, 76–80.

50 William Benton identified a category of colonial leaders whose Whig ideology led them to first agitate as Patriots during the imperial crisis, but who then, faced with the possibility of American independence, "switched sides" to become Loyalists; *Whig-Loyalism*. See also Launitz-Schürer, *Loyal Whigs and Revolutionaries*; Upton, *The Loyal Whig*; and Calhoon, *Political Moderation*, 80. Ruma Chopra has demonstrated how widespread Whig ideology was among New York colonists, including those

who later became Loyalists; see *Unnatural Rebellion*, ch. 1. Chipman seems to have held his Whig critique of arbitrary power *alongside* his loyal monarchism. It is, of course, difficult to know how he would have acted in a more polarized political environment.

51 NSA Chipman, Commonplace Book, 5; quoting *Bickerstaff's Boston Almanack, 1768*.

52 Ibid., 148; quoting from the *Gentleman's and London Magazine* (Dublin), (March 1764), 178–9.

53 Ibid., 147; quoting from the *Gentleman's and London Magazine* (Dublin), (March 1764), 178.

54 Ibid., 148. For the heading, see the *Gentleman's and London Magazine* (Dublin), (March 1764), 179.

55 Ibid., 149, quoting from an unidentified source, dated 1763.

56 Ibid., 1. See Wulf, "Bible, King, and Common Law."

57 On eighteenth-century views of the future of America *within* the British Empire, see Potter, *Liberty We Seek*, chs 6, 8.

58 NSA Chipman, Commonplace Book, 47; quoting Ames, *An astronomical diary, 1762.*

59 Benjamin Franklin, letter to Lord Kames, 3 Jan. 1760, in *The Papers of Benjamin Franklin*. See Potter, *Liberty We Seek*, 107–16, 156–72, for other Loyalists who saw no contradiction between British and American interests, including some comparisons with Franklin's early scheme.

60 In his important revisionist argument about the identity of Loyalists, Edward Larkin contends, "Understanding themselves as imperial subjects, loyalists saw no necessary contradiction between their local identity as Americans and their national identity as Britons"; Larkin, "What Is a Loyalist?" Jane Errington argues that for some this remained the case even *after* the American Revolution, as Loyalists and American settlers to Upper Canada maintained this kind of bi-focal political sensibility. Although such people "clearly had strong political and emotional ties to the empire, they saw no contradiction between this and their commitment to the New World and to their old homeland." Errington, *The Lion, the Eagle, and Upper Canada*, 7.

61 Colden, *History of the Five Indian Nations of Canada*. For this "affectionate" reading of the *History*, see Carter, "Anglicizing the League," 83–5. For a recent study of Colden, see Dixon, *Enlightenment of Cadwallader Colden*.

62 NSA Chipman, Commonplace Book, 191; quoting Colden, *History of the Five Indian Nations*, v–vi.

63 Ibid., 216–17.

64 Ibid., 241, 243.
65 Ibid., 216–17.
66 Ibid., 228.
67 Closer to home, Chipman's extant manuscripts are silent on Britain's ongoing violence against and displacement of the Mi'kmaq.
68 ECW Chipman Family Fonds, D1931.001.4.2. Handley Chipman, Diary (1794–96), 30 Aug. 1794. All the Chipman quotations in this section are from this long entry, unless otherwise noted.
69 NSA Chipman, Commonplace Book, 5.
70 Ibid., 244.
71 See Guyatt, *Providence and the Invention of the United States*; and McKim, *Boundless Dominion*.
72 ECW Chipman, Diary, 30 Aug. 1796.
73 Ibid.
74 On the changing meaning of British providentialism during the eighteenth century, see Guyatt, *Providence and the Invention of the United States*, ch. 2.
75 Claydon and McBride, "The Trials of the Chosen Peoples," 26–9.
76 NSA MG 1, vol. 183, items 218–19. Chipman Family Fonds. Handley Chipman, warrant against Timothy Newman, 2 Oct. 1781.
77 Mancke, *Fault Lines*, 81. See also Bumsted, *Understanding the Loyalists*, 48–9; Norton, *British-Americans*, 7; Errington, "Loyalists and Loyalism," 173; and Bannister, "Planter Studies and Atlantic Scholarship," 31–2.

CHAPTER TWO

1 ECW Chipman, Ledger, 302 [undated entry, ca 1792–93]; emphasis in original.
2 Ibid., 300; undated entry, ca 1790.
3 NSA MG 1, vol. 332B. Hugh Graham Fonds. 2 Sept. 1785, Graham to Parents. On Graham, see Candow, "Graham, Hugh." On various models of shared book collections in British North America, see Smith, "Community Libraries."
4 On the "steady sellers" of early modern devotional reading, see Hall, *Cultures of Print*. For more on the print and devotional culture of early modern Protestantism, including Puritan, dissenting, and evangelical traditions, see (among many others), Green, *Print and Protestantism*; Hambrick-Stowe, *Practice of Piety* and "The Spirit of the Old Writers"; Rivers, "Dissenting and Methodist Books of Practical Divinity" and *Reason, Grace, and Sentiment*; Brown, *Word in the World*; Whitehouse,

Textual Culture of English Protestant Dissent; and Yeager, *Jonathan Edwards and Transatlantic Print Culture.*

5 Baxter, *Saints Everlasting Rest*, especially chs 14 and 15. On Baxter's affectionate language, see Rivers, *Reason, Grace, and Sentiment*, vol. 1, ch. 3.

6 Vernage, *The Happy Life, or The Contented Man*; Henry, *Pleasantness of a Religious Life*. On changing conceptions of happiness, see McMahon, *The Pursuit of Happiness.*

7 Henry, *Pleasantness of a Religious Life*, 158; emphasis in original.

8 Henry, *Communicant's Companion*; Willison, *Sacramental Meditations and Advices.*

9 ECW Chipman, Diary, 17 June 1794.

10 On sacramental spirituality among early modern Protestants, including the use of devotional guides, see Schmidt, *Holy Fairs*, esp. chs 2–3; Coffey, "Between Puritanism and Evangelicalism"; Hunt, "Lord's Supper in Early Modern England"; Hambrick-Stowe, *Practice of Piety*, 206–18; and Winiarski, *Darkness Falls*, 41–9. Chipman expressed at length his thoughts on "family worship" – the setting in which he read Henry's *Communicant's Companion* – in a letter copied into his diary; ECW Chipman, Diary, 11 Nov. 1794.

11 Watts, *Discourses of the Love of God*. On Watts and the affections, see Rivers, *Reason, Grace, and Sentiment*; Beynon, *Isaac Watts*; and Whitehouse, *Textual Culture*. The Cornwallis library also included, among other volumes of Watts's work, *Humility, Represented in the Character of St. Paul.*

12 Watts, *Discourses of the Love of God*, 164.

13 Edwards, *History of the Work of Redemption* and *Some Thoughts Concerning the Present Revival*, 289–530; and Chauncy, *Seasonable Thoughts.*

14 Edwards, *Some Thoughts Concerning the Present Revival*, 298–9. His views on this theme were, of course, most clearly expressed in his *Treatise Concerning the Religious Affections*. See Taves, *Fits, Trances, and Visions*, 37–41.

15 Edwards is usually viewed by historians as a moderate revivalist who attempted to strike a course between the rationalism of Chauncy and the radicalism of evangelist James Davenport; see, for example, McClymond, "Jonathan Edwards," 404–17, esp. 407. However, Douglas Winiarski has lodged a significant dissenting perspective, documenting the more emotional, bodily ecstasies of the revival under Edwards's pastoral care; "Jonathan Edwards, Enthusiast?" and "Souls Filled with Ravishing Transport." Avihu Zakai emphasizes Edwards's opposition to, rather than

engagement with, Enlightenment thought and British moral philosophy,
such as Hutcheson on the moral sense; see his "Jonathan Edwards, the
Enlightenment."

16 On Chauncy, see Corrigan, *Hidden Balance*; and Taves, *Fits, Trances, and
Visions*, 21–37. On the theological and psychological premises that
Edwards and Chauncy shared, see Grasso, *A Speaking Aristocracy*, 92–3.

17 Smith, *Theory of Moral Sentiments*; Burstein, *Sentimental Democracy*, 10.

18 The phrase comes from Erik Seeman's description of another
eighteenth-century lay person who "constructed" his piety rather than
passively receiving it from clerical authorities; see Seeman, *Pious
Persuasions*, 15–43, quotation at 26.

19 ECW Chipman Family Fonds, 1931.005–CHI/3, Handley Chipman,
Scripture Commentaries (1789); 1931.005–CHI/3, Handley Chipman,
Scripture Commentaries (1797), vols. i and ii; 2007.004–CHI/1, Handley
Chipman, Essays (1793), part iii ("Some Short Sketches of Metaphors
[and] Parallels on Scriptural, Spiritual Matters").

20 ECW Chipman, Essays, iii.108–9.

21 Hambrick-Stowe, *Practice of Piety*, 157–8.

22 Green, *Print and Protestantism*; Hambrick-Stowe, *Practice of Piety*; Hall,
Cultures of Print; Rivers, "Dissenting and Methodist Books of Practical
Divinity" and *Reason, Grace, and Sentiment*; and Whitehouse, *Textual
Culture*.

23 Marchant, *An Exposition on the Books of the Old Testament*, cover page;
emphasis in original.

24 Colclough, "Recovering the Reader," 18–19.

25 Hall, *Cultures of Print*, 61–8; Hambrick-Stowe, *Practice of Piety*, 159–60.

26 ECW Chipman, Scripture Commentaries (1797), i.491.

27 Hambrick-Stowe, *Practice of Piety*, 161–75.

28 Brown, *Pilgrim and the Bee*, 15, 137–8; Hindmarsh, *Spirit of Early
Evangelicalism*, 69–101, esp. 73.

29 ECW Chipman, Scripture Commentaries (1789), 66, 74, 75.

30 ECW Chipman, Scripture Commentaries (1797), i and ii. George
Whitefield had a very similar devotional practice, writing similar prayers
at the bottom his diary after careful daily scripture reading. As it did for
Chipman, Matthew Henry's writing had a profound influence on
Whitefield's piety. See Hindmarsh, *Spirit of Early Evangelicalism*, 29–31.

31 ECW Chipman, Scripture Commentaries (1797), i.516.

32 Ibid., i.755.

33 Ibid., ii.1017.

34 Ibid., i.572.

35 Ibid., ii.817.

36 Ibid., ii.999.

37 ECW Chipman, Diary, 5 April 1794.

38 Ibid., 30 August 1794; emphasis added.

39 Ibid.

40 On the creation of these "wrote books" for others, as well as himself, see Chipman's comments at: ECW Chipman, Essays, iii.108–9; Scripture Commentaries (1797), ii.1083; Diary, 639; Family Memoir, 1796, 1931.005–CHI/4/1.25; and Will and Codicil.

41 For the phrase, "genealogy of piety," see ECW Chipman, Scripture Commentary (1797), on 1 Chronicles 3.

42 On the family acquaintance with the Mathers, see ECW Chipman, Family Memoir, 44–5.

43 On father John Chipman's association with the SPG, see Banks, *The History of Martha's Vineyard*, vol. 2, 40. For his family connection to Benjamin Colman, see ECW Chipman, Family Memoir, 37. Colman was a key figure in the transatlantic Protestant correspondence network that generally promoted the Great Awakening and facilitated many of its important publications. At Colman's Brattle Street Church, Jane Chipman would have been exposed to the "catholick piety" for which the congregation was known – attempting to integrate experiential orthodoxy with the Enlightenment moral philosophy of the affections. O'Brien, "A Transatlantic Community of Saints"; Corrigan, *Prism of Piety*; and Kidd, *Protestant Interest*, ch. 1. On Homes, see ECW Chipman, Family Memoir, 43–57; and Joseph Sewall and Thomas Prince, "Preface" to Homes, *The Good Government of Christian Families Recommended*, iii–x.

44 Although he migrated to Nova Scotia as a boy, Henry Alline was also from Newport, Rhode Island.

45 ECW Chipman, Family Memoir, 52.

46 Ibid., 54–6.

47 Homes, *Good Government of Christian Families*, 40, and *A Discourse Concerning Publick Reading*, 34.

48 ECW Chipman, Family Memoir, 55–6. On the structure of Puritan sermons, see Kimnach, "General Introduction to the Sermons of Jonathan Edwards."

49 Chipman noted on another occasion that his minister in Cornwallis had preached a sermon "with more Life and Vigour than usual." The difference, he said, was that "the word by [God's] Assistance went from the *heart* to me." ECW Chipman, Diary, 8 Sept. 1794.

50 ECW Chipman, Family Memoir, 57. See also, ECW Chipman, Essays, ii.117.
51 For Whitefield's Newport visit, see Whitefield, *A Continuation of the
    Reverend Mr. Whitefield's Journal*, 38–45. On Whitefield, see Stout, *Divine
    Dramatist*; Lambert, *Pedlar in Divinity*; Kidd, *George Whitefield*; Parr,
    Inventing George Whitefield; and Choi, *George Whitefield*. So important
    was Whitefield's influence upon the unfolding story of the religious
    awakenings in eighteenth-century New England that Winiarski refers to
    "New Lights" – including those in Nova Scotia – as "Whitefieldarians";
    see *Darkness Falls*, especially 15–17.
52 Whitefield, *Continuation of Whitefield's Journal*, 43.
53 Chipman was admitted to membership in the *Second* Congregational
    Church in Newport in 1736, when he was eighteen years old, and his first
    wife, Jane, was admitted to the church in 1740 after their marriage. By
    1744, they had transferred their membership to Newport's *First*
    Congregational Church, where latter-day Puritan Nathaniel Clap was the
    longstanding minister. On their membership, see Second Congregational
    Church Book, nos. 838 and 838B; First Congregational Church Book, nos
    832, 833, and 836D; Newport Historical Society, Newport, RI. I am
    grateful to Mr Bert Lippincott for research assistance. Also see Chipman,
    Family Memoir, 71–5.
54 Whitefield, *Continuation of Whitefield's Journal*, 42.
55 Stout, *Divine Dramatist*, 39–44, 93–5, 104–6; quotations at 39, 42.
    On Whitefield and emotions, especially in preaching, see also Cunha,
    "Whitefield and Literary Affect"; Anderson, *Imagining Methodism*;
    Barker-Benfield, *Culture of Sensibility*, 71–3; and Dixon, *Weeping
    Britannia*, 69–81.
56 Sarah Edwards, Letter to James Pierpont, 24 Oct. 1740, as quoted in
    Cunha, "Whitefield and Literary Affect," 194.
57 Brekus, *Sarah Osborn's World* and "Sarah Osborn's Enlightenment";
    and Brekus, ed., *Sarah Osborn's Collected Writings*. See also Hopkins,
    Memoirs of the Life of Mrs. Sarah Osborn; and *Familiar Letters, Written
    by Mrs. Sarah Osborn, and Miss Susanna Anthony*.
58 On Chipman's participation in this religious society, see Sarah Osborn,
    Diary, 13 April 1757 and 2 Jan. 1762; as cited in Brekus, *Sarah Osborn's
    World*, 198, 382. I am grateful to Catherine Brekus for our conversations
    about this Newport connection. See also Hopkins, *Memoirs of Sarah
    Osborn*, 70–4.
59 Osborn, *Nature, Certainty and Evidence of True Christianity*.
60 Ibid., 3; emphasis in original.
61 Brekus, *Sarah Osborn's World*, esp. 8–10, chs 4 and 6, and "Sarah

Osborn's Enlightenment"; Taves, *Fits, Trances, and Visions*, ch. 2; and Rivett, *Science of the Soul*, ch. 6.

62 Rivett, *Science of the Soul*, 274.

63 Revising a longstanding assumption that evangelicalism and Enlightenment were necessarily opposed, recent historiography has explored the extent to which evangelicalism was shaped by the Enlightenment. David Bebbington has offered the most sweeping and revisionist interpretation of evangelicalism as an Enlightenment religious movement, indeed arguing that "The Evangelical version of Protestantism was created by the Enlightenment"; *Evangelicalism in Modern Britain*, quotation at 74. Brekus's positioning of Sarah Osborn extends this argument. See also Yeager, *Enlightened Evangelicalism*. For studies that dispute that there was an "evangelical Enlightenment," see Zakai, *Jonathan Edwards's Philosophy of History*; Israel, *Enlightenment Contested*, esp. 38, and *Democratic Enlightenment*, esp. 43.

64 Osborn, *Nature, Certainty and Evidence*, 3–4; emphasis in original.

65 Ibid., 5, 7.

66 Brekus, *Sarah Osborn's World*, 19–25; Edwards, *Religious Affections*, "A Divine and Supernatural Light," and "Miscellany 782. Ideas. Sense of the Heart."

67 Osborn, *Nature, Certainty and Evidence*, 7.

68 Scheer, "Are Emotions a Kind of Practice," esp. 201. Considering emotions as "practices" maintains not only their internalization, but also their embodiment. The phrase "settled bent of the soul" was also used in the same way by itinerant Gilbert Tennant, a confidant of Osborn's; Tennant, *Sermons on Important Subjects*, 264.

69 Osborn, *Nature, Certainty and Evidence*, 14–15; emphasis in original.

70 Ibid., 10; emphasis in original.

71 ECW Chipman, Family Memoir, 64.

72 ECW 1900.048–CHI.2, transcription of Henry Alline's Journal [transcription attributed to Handley Chipman; ca 1785]. The journal was later published as *The Life and Journal of the Rev. Mr. Henry Alline* (Boston: Gilbert & Dean, 1806), and has been reprinted in a scholarly edition: *The Journal of Henry Alline*, ed. James Beverley and Barry Moody (Hantsport, NS: Lancelot Press, 1982). I am grateful to Barry Moody (Acadia University), David Bell (University of New Brunswick), and Patricia Townsend (Esther Clark Wright Archives) for conversations about the provenance of the shorthand, transcribed, and published versions of the journal.

73 For example, Rawlyk, *Canada Fire*, 5.

74 ECW Chipman, Essays, ii.117.

75 ECW Chipman Family Fonds, 1931.005–CHI/2. 30 June 1777, Handley Chipman to Daniel Cock and David Smith.

76 Harvey, ed., *The Diary of Simeon Perkins*, vol. 2, 4 Jan. 1782. On Perkins, see Harvey's "Introduction."

77 Ibid., 13 Feb. 1783; see also 3 Feb. 1782.

78 In his diary entry for 17 March 1784, Perkins mentioned a meeting about whether Liverpool New Lights could use the Meeting House, and expressed his disapproval. His reasons for this position? "That Mr. Alline had denied the Fundamental Articles of the Christian Religion." Ibid., 222. This comment stands out from Perkins's other positive remarks, and begs the question, what changed? One possibility is that the publication of Alline's *Two Mites* in 1784 may have aired some of his less orthodox theological positions – views that may not have been as clear in his preaching. It is interesting that Chipman, who was at least as orthodox as Perkins, did not register such a qualification, at least in his existing writings. See Rawlyk, *Wrapped Up in God*, 49–50.

79 ECW Chipman, Essays, 1793. Bound together: 1) "Some observations on the Sad Practice of Some of our New Light Preachers and Exhorters"; 2) "A Discourse concerning The Resurrection of the Body of Mankind ... also Sundry Matters about Errors in our Church here, called New Lights"; and 3) "Some Short Sketches of Metaphors [and] Parallels on Scriptural, Spiritual Matters." Only the first two essays touch on the contentions about emotions in the New Light church; the third, on scriptural metaphors, was discussed above as one of Chipman's self-made theological anthologies.

80 Cuthbertson, ed., *Journal of the Reverend John Payzant*, 44. For a discussion of this period in the New Light church, known as the New Dispensation, see Rawlyk, *Ravished by the Spirit*, 82–9, and *The Canada Fire*, 64–9; and Goodwin, *Into Deep Waters*, 102–4. For the New Dispensation movement beyond Cornwallis and to the end of the eighteenth century, see Bell, ed., *Newlight Baptist Journals*, 14–19.

81 ECW Horton-Cornwallis New Light Church Minutes (1778–95), D1900.075, Aug. 1791.

82 Cuthbertson, ed., *Journal of the Reverend John Payzant*, 53.

83 Ibid., 45.

84 Quoted in Armstrong, *Great Awakening in Nova Scotia*, 119.

85 ECW Horton-Cornwallis New Light Church Minutes, June 1792.

86 ECW Chipman, Essays, i.1.

87 Ibid.

88 Ibid., i.15.

89 Ibid., i.2, 3, 4.

90 Ibid., i.4.

91 Ibid., i.5, 10.

92 Ibid., i.6.

93 Ibid., i.7.

94 Inglis, *Steadfastness in Religion and Loyalty*, 22, 24, note. The attempt by moderate religious writers to explain enthusiasm in purely physical terms – in order to distance those behaviours or groups from what they considered true or rational religion – had the unintended consequence of undermining even orthodox supernatural claims. See Heyd, *"Be Sober and Reasonable"*; Taves, *Fits, Trances, and Visions*; and Laborie, *Enlightening Enthusiasm*.

95 ECW Chipman, Essays, i.3.

96 Ibid., i.8.

97 Ibid., i.6.

98 Ibid., i.8.

99 Ibid., i.10–11.

100 Ibid.; emphasis added.

101 Ibid., i.26.

102 Henry, *The Pleasantness of a Religious Life*, 28; emphasis added.

103 Scheer, "Are Emotions a Kind of Practice," 200. Also see Martín-Moruno and Pichel, eds, *Emotional Bodies*.

104 ECW Chipman, Essays, i.8.

105 The covenant and articles of the New Light church used the term "imbodied" (or "embodied") to describe the formation of a local ("visible") congregation of the "Church of Christ." ECW Horton-Cornwallis New Light Church, Articles of Faith and Church Covenant, 1778 [Copy, ca 1801].

106 ECW Chipman, Essays, i.15.

107 Ibid., i.17.

108 Ibid., i.25.

109 Ibid., ii.105–14, quotations at 108, 115, and 120. The largest part of this 150-page essay is "A Discourse concerning The Resurrection of the Body," in which Chipman examined historical heresies concerning the resurrection and then presented a systematic examination of biblical passages on the theme. He drew upon works by Matthew Henry and Benjamin Keach, among others, and wove together his own comments with paraphrases and quotations.

110 ECW Horton-Cornwallis New Light Church, "Articles on Church Order," no. 6 (also see no. 5). See Rivett, *Science of the Soul*, for the epistemological questions raised by seeking such "evidence."

111 ECW Chipman, Essays, ii.121. See also the brief notes in ECW Chipman, Ledger, 302 (discussed at the beginning of this chapter).

112 ECW Chipman, Essays, ii.121–2.

113 Ibid., ii.120.

114 Ibid., ii.139.

115 Ibid., ii.117.

116 Ibid.

117 Whitefield, "Marks of having received the Holy Ghost," in *The Works of the Reverend George Whitefield*, vol. 6, 170. See Alline, *A Sermon Preached on the 19ᵗʰ of Feb. 1783 at Port-Midway*, 33. Sarah Osborn similarly said she would rather see transformation in her affections than to hear a voice from heaven; Osborn, *Nature, Certainty and Evidence*, 10.

118 Cuthbertson, ed., *Journal of the Reverend John Payzant*, 45.

119 Ibid., 46, 52; ECW Horton-Cornwallis New Light Church Minutes, 6 Aug. 1792, and 1 April 1793.

120 ECW Chipman, Will and Codicil, 1799.

121 ECW Chipman, Family Memoir, 57.

CHAPTER THREE

1 LCOLL Jacob Bailey Papers, MG 1, 98–16 (Reel 8). Jacob Bailey, "The Humors of the Committee, or, Majesty of the Mob," undated stage script, 9–10, 12–13.

2 Records from Bailey's actual dealings with the Pownalborough Committee of Correspondence, Inspection, and Safety are found in Baxter, ed., *Documentary History of the State of Maine*, vol. 14, 349–54, 389–90, and 397–9, hereafter cited as DHSM. For a discussion of revolutionary committees that takes emotions into account and draws significantly on Bailey's appearance before the committee in Pownalborough, see Calhoon, "Committees of Safety and the Control of Disaffection," in *Loyalists in Revolutionary America*, ch. 26. On the experience of Bailey and other Loyalist Anglican clergy with the committees, see Bell, *War of Religion*, ch. 10.

3 The non-fictional committee similarly charged that Bailey "discover'd an undue Attachment to the Authority claimed by Great Britain over the united Colonies, and thereby has given great Reason to believe that he

does not wish Success to our Struggles for Freedom." DHSM, 14.349; emphasis added.

4 LCOLL Jacob Bailey, "Humors of the Committee," 27.

5 For his description of the Committee of Correspondence as an "unfeeling committee," see LCOLL Jacob Bailey Papers, MG 1, 91–21 (Reel 1). Letterbook. 24 Nov. 1778, Bailey to Mrs ___.

6 See especially Eustace, *Passion Is the Gale*. Bailey's description of the Committee of Safety provides a poignant illustration of what historian William Reddy has called an "emotional regime," highlighting how emotions are related to structures of power. Sociologists Ole Riis and Linda Woodhead observe that such structures are called "regimes" for a reason – "There are inducements to conform and sanctions for non-compliance." Reddy, *Navigation of Feeling*, 55, 61–2; and Riis and Woodhead, *Sociology of Religious Emotion*, 11.

7 For Bailey's biography, see Bartlet, *The Frontier Missionary*; Allen, *Rev. Jacob Bailey*; Ross, "Jacob Bailey, Loyalist"; Ross and Vincent, "Bailey, Jacob"; Thompson, *The Man Who Said No*; and Leamon, *Reverend Jacob Bailey*.

8 On Anglicanism in the colonies before the Revolution, see Calhoon and Chopra, "Religion and the Loyalists," 101–9; Bell, *Imperial Origins of the King's Church* and *A War of Religion*; Rhoden, *Revolutionary Anglicanism*, ch. 2; Woolverton, *Colonial Anglicanism in North America*; Calhoon, *Loyalists in Revolutionary America*, 208–17; Doll, *Revolution, Religion, and National Identity*; Walker, "The Church Militant"; and Frazer, *God against the Revolution*. For a discussion of how clergy navigated the political choices of the imperial crisis and Revolution, see McBride, *Pulpit and Nation*, ch. 4.

9 Shields, *Civil Tongues*, 209–62, quotations at 213 and 224. For a discussion of the affectionate aspect of polite Christianity, see Corrigan, *Prism of Piety*, and on the "moderate Enlightenment" of which polite Christianity was an expression, see May, *Enlightenment in America*, part 1. On politeness, see Langford, "The Uses of Eighteenth-Century Politeness"; Klein, *Shaftesbury and the Culture of Politeness*; and Bullock, *Tea Sets and Tyranny*.

10 On anglicization in relation to the growing numbers of American-born clergy in the colonial Church of England, see Bell, *Imperial Origins*, ch. 10. Thompson's description of Bailey's time in London is vivid and insightful; see *The Man Who Said No*, 87–161.

11 Bailey, as quoted in Thompson, *The Man Who Said No*, 124.

12 See Leamon, *Reverend Jacob Bailey*, ch. 4. On Gardiner's loyalism and settlement schemes, see Coolidge, *Colonial Entrepreneur*; Milford, *Gardiners of Massachusetts*; and Chopra, "Postwar Loyalist Hopes," 233–4.

13 On the "ordeal" of other Loyalists during the American Revolution, see especially: Bailyn, *Ordeal of Thomas Hutchinson*; Calhoon, *Loyalists in Revolutionary America*; Van Buskirk, *Generous Enemies*; Jasanoff, *Liberty's Exiles*; Rhoden, *Revolutionary Anglicanism*, chs 1, 3; and on Massachusetts in particular, see Brown, *The King's Friends*, 18–42. For background on Maine during the American Revolution, see Leamon, *Revolution Downeast*.

14 LCOLL Jacob Bailey Papers, MG 1, 91–20 (Reel 1). Letterbook. 26 Oct. 1774, Bailey to Mr and Mrs Bracket.

15 LCOLL Jacob Bailey Papers, MG 1, 95–16 (Reel 5). Bailey, Diary, 26 Sept. 1774.

16 LCOLL Jacob Bailey Papers, MG 1, 91–20 (Reel 1). Letterbook, 29 Dec. 1774, Bailey to an unnamed correspondent.

17 LCOLL Jacob Bailey Papers, MG 1, 91–20 (Reel 1). Letterbook. 10 Dec. 1778, Bailey to Mr ___. See Leamon, *Reverend Jacob Bailey*, ch. 5, 6.

18 LCOLL Jacob Bailey Papers, MG 1, 91–20 (Reel 1). Letterbook. 26 Aug. 1778, Bailey to Mr Domett.

19 LCOLL Jacob Bailey Papers, MG 1, 91–20 (Reel 1). Letterbook. 24 Nov. 1778, Bailey to Mrs ___. For a similar inventory of his ordeals, see MG 1, MG 1, 91–20 (Reel 1). Letterbook. 1 July 1779, Bailey to Rev. Mr Badger.

20 LCOLL Jacob Bailey Papers, MG 1, 92A–125 (Reel 2). Bailey, Petition to Council at Massachusetts Bay, 28 July 1778.

21 LCOLL Jacob Bailey Papers, MG 1, 91–21 (Reel 1). Letterbook. 27 Nov. 1778, Bailey to Mrs ___, and 28 Nov. 1778, Bailey to Rev. Weeks.

22 I have reconstructed Bailey's *Compendious History of the most important concerns in the history of New-England* (1774) as follows: LCOLL Jacob Bailey Papers, MG 1 (volume and item numbers in parentheses): 1638–56 (98–1; Reel 8), 1660–76 (98–2; Reel 8), 1670–1720s (98–3; Reel 8), 1727–40 (98–4; Reel 8), and 1740s – Great Awakening (99–8A; Reel 9); rough notes on 1746–55 are found at LCOLL Jacob Bailey Papers, MG 1, 91–20 (Reel 1), Letterbook (1774–17), 8–9. The extant volumes include approximately 230 quarto-sized pages. The first four chapters and probably some later ones are now missing, as are a few pages at the beginning or end of some notebooks. The numbering of the chapters is continuous in the first three notebooks (chapters v–xxii; items 98–1 to

98–3; Reel 8) but differs for subsequent notebooks. My references to the manuscript indicate numbered sections (§) within each chapter. There is one notebook that contains similar historical material and is numbered in the Bailey Papers as part of the series, but it actually appears to be part of a different history on the "Eastern Country" of Massachusetts (now Maine), about which more below; see notebook on 1650–1721, LCOLL Jacob Bailey Papers, MG 1, 98–5 (Reel 8).

23 On Loyalist histories, see Leder, *Loyalist Historians*. On Patriot histories, see Cohen, *Revolutionary Histories*. For a general overview of Revolutionary-era historical scholarship, see Kraus and Joyce, *The Writing of American History*, chs 2–5, and Hattem, *Past and Prologue*.

24 See Gould, *Writing the Rebellion*, ch. 5, for Loyalist accounts of the "radicalism" of Puritan New England as dangerous to the transatlantic Anglo-American community.

25 In an important essay, Edward Larkin demonstrates the cosmopolitan character of loyalism, a viable alternative to both American and British versions of nationalism; "Cosmopolitan Revolution," 52–76. For the argument that Britishness was not necessarily at odds with cosmopolitanism, see O'Brien, *Narratives of Enlightenment*. For cosmopolitanism as an aspect of polite Christianity, see Shields, *Civil Tongues*, 236.

26 LCOLL Jacob Bailey Papers, MG 1, 95–16 (Reel 5). Letterbook, 1 Nov. 1773, Bailey to Mr Russell. See also Bailey to Russell, 21 Jan. 1774 (in the same letterbook), in which he was optimistic that subscriptions could be procured if necessary.

27 LCOLL Jacob Bailey Papers, MG 1, 95–16 (Reel 5). Letterbook. 1 Nov. 1773, Bailey to Messrs Mills and Hicks. There are other brief descriptions of this project and its progress in letters to Mills and Hicks on 26 Nov. 1773 and 21 Jan. 1774 (in the same letterbook). For a partial draft of the natural history manuscript, see LCOLL Jacob Bailey Papers, MG 1, 98–6 (Reel 8). "A Description and Natural History of the new intended province between New Hampshire and Nova Scotia," [ca 1774].

28 LCOLL Jacob Bailey Papers, MG 1, 95–16 (Reel 5), Letterbook. 18 Dec. 1773, Bailey to Amos Bailey.

29 Bailey's extant papers do not include many letters from mid-1774 through 1778. On printers on both sides of the revolutionary conflict, see Davies, "New Brunswick Loyalist Printers"; and Adelman, *Revolutionary Networks*.

30 For examples, see LCOLL Jacob Bailey Papers, MG 1, 98–5 (Reel 8), Bailey, [History of Eastern Country] § 30; MG 1, 95–16 (Reel 5). Letterbook. 21 Jan. 1774, Bailey to Mssrs Mills and Hicks.

31 During the eighteenth century, various approaches to history writing competed and overlapped, from classical didacticism to Enlightenment-influenced "disinterest" to the documentary collecting of antiquarians. See Cheng, *Plain and Noble Garb of Truth* and "On the Margins"; Shapiro, *A Culture of Fact*, ch. 2; Phillips, *Society and Sentiment*; Levine, *Humanism and History*; and Woolf, "From Hystories to the Historical," 31–68.

32 On the role of sympathy in eighteenth-century histories as well as novels, see Phillips, *Society and Sentiment*, ch. 4.

33 LCOLL Jacob Bailey Papers, MG 1, 98–5 (Reel 8). Bailey, [History of Eastern Country], § 22.

34 Bailey intended to publish the book anonymously. In a letter to his brother in 1773, Bailey urged him to keep the book's publication in confidence, saying, "I design to keep my name as secret as possible." Similarly, he wrote to printer Ezekiel Russell, "I must repeat that I desire my name may be concealed." It is difficult to know how significant this decision was, given that anonymous publication was a common eighteenth-century practice, sometimes a form of intellectual humility. However, given the furor of the times, he may have thought that were "Jacob Bailey, A.M., SPG Missionary" to appear on the book's title page, potential readers would suspect it to be tinged with imperial and Anglican biases. The history, of course, does indeed express just those biases. LCOLL Jacob Bailey Papers, MG 1, 95–16 (Reel 5). Letterbook. 18 Dec. 1773, Bailey to Amos Bailey; and 21 Jan. 1774, Bailey to Ezekiel Russell. On anonymous publication, see Clark, "Early American Journalism," 350; and Hall, "Reader and Writers in Early New England," 558n109.

35 LCOLL Jacob Bailey Papers, MG 1, 98–3 (Reel 8). Bailey, *Compendious History*, ch. xiii, § 2.

36 Ibid., 98–1 (Reel 8), ch. vii, § 7.

37 Ibid., 98–1 (Reel 8), ch. ix, § 1, 2.

38 Ibid., 98–2 (Reel 8), ch. x, § 20.

39 Ibid., 98–1 (Reel 8), ch. viii, § 1; and 98–3 (Reel 8), ch. xiv, § 1.

40 Ibid., 98–1 (Reel 8), ch. viii, § 1.

41 Ibid., 98–1 (Reel 8), ch. viii, § 2.

42 Ibid., 98–1 (Reel 8), ch. viii, § 5.

43 Ibid., 98–2 (Reel 8), ch. xi, § 5.

44 Ibid., 98–3 (Reel 8), ch. xi, § 28.

45 Ibid., 98–3 (Reel 8), ch. xi, § 29; see also chs xx and xxii, and LCOLL Jacob Bailey Papers, MG 1, 98–5 (Reel 8), Bailey, [History of Eastern Country], § 14.

46 LCOLL Jacob Bailey Papers, MG 1, 98–5 (Reel 8). Bailey, [History of Eastern Country], § 15.

47 LCOLL Jacob Bailey Papers, MG 1, 98–2 (Reel 8). Bailey, *Compendious History*, ch. x, § 15.

48 Ibid., 98–3 (Reel 8), ch. xiii, § 3.

49 Ibid., 98–3 (Reel 8), ch. xiii, § 6–7.

50 Ibid., 98–3 (Reel 8), ch. xiii, § 7.

51 Ibid., 98–3 (Reel 8), ch. xiv, § 8.

52 LCOLL Jacob Bailey Papers, MG 1, 98–5 (Reel 8). Bailey, [History of Eastern Country], § 16.

53 LCOLL Jacob Bailey Papers, MG 1, 98–3 (Reel 8). Bailey, *Compendious History*, ch. xv, § 1.

54 Ibid., 98–3 (Reel 8), ch. xv, § 24.

55 Ibid., 98–3 (Reel 8), ch. xvii, § 2.

56 Ibid., 98–3 (Reel 8), ch. xvii, § 3.

57 Ibid., 98–3 (Reel 8), ch. xiv, § 8. See Baker and Reid, *New England Knight*.

58 LCOLL Jacob Bailey Papers, MG 1, 98–3 (Reel 8). Bailey, *Compendious History*, ch. xvii, § 4. For another discussion of Phips's career and virtues, see LCOLL Jacob Bailey Papers, MG 1, 98-5 (Reel 8). Bailey, [History of Eastern Country], § 20.

59 Bushman, *Refinement of America*.

60 LCOLL Jacob Bailey Papers, MG 1, 98–4 (Reel 8). Bailey, *Compendious History*, ch. 1, § 1.

61 Ibid.

62 LCOLL Jacob Bailey Papers, MG 1, 99–8A (Reel 9). Bailey, *Compendious History*, [no chapter indicated], § 1.

63 Ibid., § 2.

64 Ibid., § 1, 3.

65 Ibid., § 4.

66 On York as the "epicenter of the Great Awakening in northern New England," see Winiarski, "A Jornal of a Fue Days at York."

67 Bailey, *Compendious History*, [no chapter indicated], § 6.

68 Ibid., § 6, 9.

69 Ibid., § 12.

70 Annapolis Heritage Society, O'Dell Museum, Jacob Bailey Fonds, 2001–1139 T–13, sermon, 27 July 1784, page 3.

71 Annapolis Heritage Society, Bailey Fonds, 2001–1139 T-8, sermon, 24 Sept. 1782, pages 13–14.

72 LCOLL Jacob Bailey Papers, MG 1, 98–3 (Reel 8). Bailey, *Compendious History*, ch. xviii, § 5.
73 LCOLL Jacob Bailey Papers, MG 1, 95–16 (Reel 5). Letterbook. 16 April 1774, Bailey to Mr Weeks.
74 See Potter, *Liberty We Seek*, 12.
75 Eamon, *Imprinting Britain*, 19.
76 For an example of his writing on the Indigenous history of North America, see Bailey, "Observations and Conjectures on the Antiquities of America." For context, see Leamon, *Reverend Jacob Bailey*, 72–6. See Hattem, *Past and Prologue*, ch. 6, for how an Indigenous "deep past" was employed for purposes of nation building during the early republic.
77 LCOLL Jacob Bailey Papers, MG 1, 91–21 (Reel 1). Letterbook. 2 Dec. 1778, Bailey to Mrs Domett.
78 Knott, *Sensibility and the American Revolution*, ch. 5. For similar Loyalist critiques made during the early phases of the Revolution, see Potter, *Liberty We Seek*, 25–36; and Gould, *Writing the Rebellion*, 14–15.
79 Robert Calhoon remarks that the rhetoric and coercive methods revolutionaries employed had a variety of effects, one of which was the "breakdown of cohesion." See Calhoon, *Loyalists in Revolutionary America*, 326–39.
80 LCOLL Jacob Bailey Papers, MG 1, 91–21 (Reel 1). Letterbook. 24 Nov. 1778, Bailey to Mrs ___. For critiques of American rebelliousness found in the Loyalist press that echo Bailey's concerns, see Potter-MacKinnon and Calhoon, "Character and Coherence."
81 Knott, *Sensibility and the American Revolution*, 43.
82 LCOLL Jacob Bailey Papers, MG 1, 91–21 (Reel 1). Letterbook. 1 Dec. 1778, Bailey to unnamed correspondent.
83 LCOLL Jacob Bailey Papers, MG 1, 91–21 (Reel 1). Letterbook. 2 Dec. 1778, Bailey to Mrs Domett.
84 LCOLL Jacob Bailey Papers, MG 1, 91–21 (Reel 1). Letterbook. 1 Dec. 1778, Bailey to unnamed correspondent.
85 Ibid.
86 LCOLL Jacob Bailey Papers, MG 1, 91–21 (Reel 1). Letterbook. 24 Nov. 1778, Bailey to Mrs ___.
87 LCOLL Jacob Bailey Papers, MG 1, 91–21 (Reel 1). Letterbook. 26 Aug. 1778, Bailey to Mr Domett.
88 Ibid.
89 Ibid.

90 LCOLL Jacob Bailey Papers, MG 1, 98–10 (Reel 8). Bailey, *A Letter to a Friend on the Present Situation of our Publick Affairs*, [n.d.]. Internal evidence suggests that it was written after the outbreak of hostilities but before an American victory seemed possible, let alone inevitable. The final two pages of the extant version appear to be rough notes, not yet copied into a notebook in a neater hand.

91 Potter, *Liberty We Seek*, 45. On conspiracy theories as a common feature of Loyalist *and* Patriot explanations of their times, see Potter, *Liberty We Seek*, 17–25; Bailyn, *Ideological Origins*, 144–59; and Frazer, *God against the Revolution*, 144–53.

92 LCOLL Bailey, *Letter to a Friend*, 32.

93 Ibid., 3.

94 Ibid., 8, 7. Hancock and Bailey were at Harvard at the same time, graduating in 1754 and 1755, respectively, and Adams was in the same class as Bailey. Bailey viewed Franklin (the "phylosophical Hero") with particular vehemence. For Bailey's poetry on conspiracies involving some of these figures, see Leamon, *Reverend Jacob Bailey*, 180–2. Elsewhere Bailey wrote, "In my opinion … neither Adams nor Franklin were ever republican in principle … their ambition conducted them to lay the foundation of a mighty empire independent of Britain and to erect a monarchy in the new world … to manage according to their pleasure"; LCOLL Jacob Bailey Papers, MG 1, 94–8 (Reel 4). Letterbook. 21 Feb. 1781, Bailey to Mr Brown.

95 LCOLL Bailey, *Letter to a Friend*, 10–11.

96 Ibid., 25.

97 Ibid., 33.

98 Ibid., 4; emphasis added.

99 See Potter, *Liberty We Seek*, 45–6.

100 LCOLL Bailey, *Letter to a Friend*, 13.

101 Eustace, *Passion Is the Gale*, 387.

102 Ibid., 387.

103 LCOLL Bailey, *Letter to a Friend*, 15; emphasis added.

104 Ibid., 27–8.

105 Ibid., 19.

106 Ibid., 26–7.

CHAPTER FOUR

1 LCOLL Jacob Bailey Papers, MG 1, 94–19 (Reel 4). Letterbook. 10 May 1783, Bailey to Thomas Brown.

2 LCOLL Jacob Bailey Papers, MG 1, 98–16 (Reel 8). Bailey, "The Humors

of the Committee, or, Majesty of the Mob," undated stage script, 9; emphasis added.

3 See Gould, *Writing the Rebellion*, 8–10. On the view of Bailey as an "Augustan Tory," see Vincent, *Narrative Verse Satire in Maritime Canada*, xvii–xix.

4 See Gould, *Writing the Rebellion*, 19.

5 This chapter contributes an emotional element to a conversation about the place of Loyalist exiles in the British Empire. Considered "too British" in their American homes, they often became critics of British policy as they resettled. See Norton, *The British-Americans*; Bell, *Loyalist Rebellion*; Potter-MacKinnon and Calhoon, "The Character and Coherence of the Loyalist Press," in *Tory Insurgents*, 128; Tillman, *Stripped and Script*, 27–8.

6 LCOLL Jacob Bailey Papers, MG 1, 91–21 (Reel 1). Letterbook. 3 Dec. 1778, Bailey to Mr ___.

7 See the Carlisle Commission's *Manifesto and Proclamation*; Einhorn, "The Reception of the British Peace Offer"; and Gregory, "Formed for Empire."

8 LCOLL Jacob Bailey Papers, MG 1, 91–21 (Reel 1). Letterbook. 3 Dec. 1778, Bailey to Mr ___.

9 Ibid.

10 LCOLL Jacob Bailey Papers, MG 1, 95–21 (Reel 6). Bailey, Journal, 15 June 1779. See Leamon, *Reverend Jacob Bailey*, ch. 7.

11 On Loyalist experiences of exile, see especially Norton, *British-Americans*; Jasanoff, *Liberty's Exiles*; Schama, *Rough Crossings*; and Pybus, *Epic Journeys of Freedom*. On honour, grief, and anger in Loyalist ordeals and exile, see Compeau, "Dishonoured Americans." O'Brien, "Unknown and Unlamented," ch. 2, focuses on the emotional experience of homesick refugees.

12 LCOLL Jacob Bailey Papers, MG 1, 95–20 (Reel 6). Bailey, Journal, 7 June 1779.

13 Ibid., 95–22 (Reel 6). 19 June 1779.

14 Ibid., 95–23 (Reel 6). 21 June 1779.

15 Ibid., 95–20 (Reel 6). 8 June 1779.

16 Ibid., 95–23 (Reel 6). 21 June 1779.

17 Ibid.

18 For a comparison of two different groups of refugees in the Revolutionary Atlantic, see Jasanoff, "Revolutionary Exiles."

19 LCOLL Jacob Bailey Papers, MG 1, 95–21 (Reel 6). Bailey Journal, 15 June 1779.

20 Ibid., 95–27 (Reel 6). 14 Aug. 1779.

21 Ibid., 95–21 (Reel 6). 15 June 1779.

22 Ibid.

23 Ibid., 95–27 (Reel 6). 14 Aug. 1779.

24 For a study that often relies on Bailey's eyewitness accounts of refugee conditions, see MacKinnon, *This Unfriendly Soil*. Other studies of Loyalist experiences in British North America include: Blakeley and Grant, eds, *Eleven Exiles*; Bell, *Loyalist Rebellion in New Brunswick*; Condon, *Loyalist Dream for New Brunswick*; Whitfield, "Black Loyalists and Black Slaves in Maritime Canada" and *North to Bondage*; Potter-MacKinnon, *While the Women Only Wept*; Knowles, *Inventing the Loyalists*, ch. 1; and Jasanoff, *Liberty's Exiles*, ch. 5.

25 LCOLL Jacob Bailey Papers, MG 1, 91–26 (Reel 2). Letterbook. 8 Sept. 1780, Bailey to Mr Weeks.

26 Compare Bailey's rancour with the affection toward George III that many elite Loyalists in Upper Canada retained; Errington, *The Lion, the Eagle, and Upper Canada*, 23–7.

27 LCOLL Jacob Bailey Papers, MG 1, 91–27 (Reel 2). Letterbook. 6 Nov. 1780, Bailey to Mr Domett.

28 LCOLL Jacob Bailey Papers, MG 1, 95–27/27a (Reel 6). Letterbook. Bailey to an unnamed correspondent [undated].

29 Ibid.

30 Ibid.

31 LCOLL Jacob Bailey Papers, MG 1, 94–19 (Reel 4). Letterbook. 10 May 1783, Bailey to Mr Brown.

32 Gould, *Writing the Rebellion*, 5.

33 On Bailey in the context of a burgeoning regional literary culture, see Davies, "Literary Cultures in the Maritime Provinces."

34 For a modern scholarly edition, see Butler, *Hudibras*, edited by John Wilder. On *Hudibras*, see Terry, *Mock-Heroic from Butler to Cowper*, ch. 2; and Jack, *Augustan Satire*.

35 Butler, *Hudibras*, 1; emphasis in original.

36 Marshall, "Aims of Butler's Satire," 637–65, esp. 654.

37 Ibid., 660. The poem also asserts the importance of language and oaths in the maintenance of civil society; see Snider, "By Equivocation Swear."

38 Granger, "*Hudibras* in the American Revolution," statistics at 499. On the increasing popularity of Hudibrastic satire during the eighteenth century, see Terry, "*Hudibras* amongst the Augustans." "Mock-heroic is perhaps *the* exemplary genre of the English Augustan era"; Terry, *Mock-Heroic*, 3. Also see Gould, *Writing the Rebellion*, ch. 3.

39 Gould, *Writing the Rebellion*, 3.
40 On Odell, see Edelberg, *Jonathan Odell: Loyalist Poet*; Davies, *Studies in Maritime Literary History*, 30–3; Vincent, *Narrative Verse Satire*, 173–7; Gould, *Writing the Rebellion*, 3–5, 17–19; Parker, "Courting Local and International Markets"; and Sargent, *The Loyal Verses of Joseph Stansbury and Jonathan Odell*.
41 On Bailey's use of Hudibrastic satire, see Vincent, "Alline and Bailey," 128–31, *Narrative Verse Satire*, and "Keeping the Faith"; Davies, "Consolation to Distress: Loyalist Literary Activity in the Maritimes," in *Studies in Maritime Literary History*, 30–3; Granger, "The Hudibrastic Poetry of Jacob Bailey'" and *Political Satire in the American Revolution*.
42 LCOLL Jacob Bailey Papers, MG 1, 91–23 (Reel 1). Letterbook. 1779 (no specified date), Bailey to Mr Rogers.
43 LCOLL Jacob Bailey Papers, MG 1, 91–27 (Reel 2). Letterbook. 28 Nov. 1780, Bailey to Mr Clerk.
44 Bailey, *Jack Ramble*, 1.80–1, in Vincent, *Narrative Verse Satire*, 44. See Hill, *The World Turned Upside Down*. For this comparison in other Loyalist writers, see Potter, *Liberty We Seek*, 46.
45 Gould, *Writing the Rebellion*, 84. Joseph Addison argued, "Where the low Character is to be raised the Heroic is the proper Measure, but when an Hero is to be pulled down and degraded, it is done best in Doggerel"; *Spectator* 249, 15 December 1711, in the *Spectator*, 2:468; as quoted in Terry, *Mock-Heroic*, 8.
46 LCOLL Jacob Bailey Papers, MG 1, 91–27 (Reel 1). Letterbook. 8 Nov. 1780, Bailey to Mrs Domett. Elsewhere he wrote that with such poetry, "my design is to expose republican and leveling principles"; LCOLL Jacob Bailey Papers, MG 1, 91–27 (Reel 1). Letterbook. 4 Nov. 1780, Bailey to Mr Rogers.
47 LCOLL Jacob Bailey Papers, MG 1, 91–27 (Reel 2). Letterbook. 26 Nov. 1780, Bailey to Samuel Peters. Davies suggests, "For Bailey, writing poetry and prose was a form of consolation, a way of re-articulating his moral vision in the face of folly and insanity"; *Studies in Maritime Literary History*, 31.
48 Archives of the Episcopal Church, Austin, TX, Hawks Collection, Peters Papers, Vol. 1, no. 44, 4 May 1780, Bailey to Samuel Peters. I am grateful to Katherine Carté, Southern Methodist University, for sharing her research related to Jacob Bailey from this collection. The letterbook copy of this letter (without the enclosed poem) is found at LCOLL Jacob Bailey Papers, MG 1, 94–5 (Reel 4). Letterbook. 2 May 1780, Bailey to Samuel Peters.

49 See Leamon, *Reverend Jacob Bailey*, 174–5.

50 LCOLL Jacob Bailey Papers, MG 1, 91–23 (Reel 1). Letterbook. 1779 (no specific date), Bailey to Mr Rogers.

51 For the ambiguity in many Loyalists' perceptions of the people – sometimes rational, sometimes inflamed with passion (and therefore easily manipulated) – see Potter, *Liberty We Seek*, 45–6.

52 LCOLL Jacob Bailey Papers, MG 1, 91–27 (Reel 2). Letterbook. 26 Nov. 1780, Bailey to Samuel Peters.

53 Gould, *Writing the Rebellion*, 170.

54 On John Howe, see Beck, "Howe, John"; and Grant, "John Howe, Senior: Printer, Publisher, Postmaster, Spy." Howe was the father of publisher and politician Joseph Howe (1804–1873). For other Loyalist printers in British North America, see Davies, "New Brunswick Loyalist Printers," 128–61.

55 LCOLL Jacob Bailey Papers, MG 1, 94–6 (Reel 4). 31 Dec. 1780, Bailey to John How[e].

56 On Anthony Henry (1734–1800), see Lochhead, "Henry, Anthony.". Henry was the Nova Scotia publisher of some of Henry Alline's works. Young printer Isaiah Thomas agreed with Bailey's assessment of Henry's typographic abilities: "He might, with propriety, be called a very unskilful printer. To his want of knowledge or abilities in his profession, he added indolence." Thomas, *The History of Printing in America*, i.370.

57 LCOLL Jacob Bailey Papers, MG 1, 94–8 (Reel 4). Letterbook. 6 March 1781, Bailey to Thomas Brown.

58 Ibid.

59 LCOLL Jacob Bailey Papers, MG 1, 94–9 (Reel 4). Letterbook. 1 April 1781, Bailey to Thomas Brown.

60 LCOLL Jacob Bailey Papers, MG 1, 94–9 (Reel 4). Letterbook. 2 April 1781, Bailey to Mr Weeks.

61 Ibid.

62 LCOLL Jacob Bailey Papers, MG 1, 94–8 (Reel 4). Letterbook. 13 March 1781, Bailey to Mr Rogers. A slightly later version is reprinted as "Character of a Trimmer," in Vincent, ed., *Narrative Verse Satire*, 8–15.

63 Vincent, ed., *Narrative Verse Satire*, 1–7.

64 LCOLL Jacob Bailey Papers, MG 1, 94–12 (Reel 4). Letterbook. 1 Sept. 1781, Bailey to John How[e]; emphasis added.

65 Ibid.

66 Ibid.

67 LCOLL Jacob Bailey Papers, MG 1, 94–13 (Reel 4). Letterbook. 17 Dec. 1781, Bailey to John Howe.

68 Ibid.

69 The Paris Peace Treaty of 30 Sept. 1783.

70 LCOLL Jacob Bailey Papers, MG 1, 94–20 (Reel 4). Letterbook. 2 July 1783, Bailey to I. Jones.

71 LCOLL Jacob Bailey Papers, MG 1, 94–20 (Reel 4). Letterbook. 1 July 1783, Bailey to Mr Rogers.

72 Enclosed with LCOLL Jacob Bailey Papers, MG 1, 94–20 (Reel 4). Letterbook. 22 Aug. 1783, Bailey to Charles Inglis. See Vincent, ed., *Narrative Verse Satire*, 17–18; Mazoff, *Anxious Allegiances*, 50–1.

73 Calhoon, "Loyalist Perception," 10. A somewhat different reading is offered by Neil MacKinnon, who has suggested that for Nova Scotians like Bailey, loyalty became a virtue in itself, rather than emphasizing the object of that loyalty; "The Changing Attitudes of the Nova Scotian Loyalists," 52. On other poetic expressions of anger toward Britain and her Nova Scotian agents, see MacKinnon, "Bitter Verse," 111–21.

74 LCOLL Jacob Bailey Papers, MG 1, 98–7 (Reel 8). Bailey, Representation to the Nova Scotia Assembly about the 1785 election (1786). On the controversial election, see Moody, *A History of Annapolis Royal*, vol. 2, 94–6. This was not the only contested election in British North America in which Loyalists featured prominently; see Bell, *Loyalist Rebellion in New Brunswick*; and Condon, *Loyalist Dream for New Brunswick*, 152–72. For comparisons with Upper Canada, see Errington, *The Lion, the Eagle, and Upper Canada*, especially her comments on the challenges of translating British constitutional principles into a North American setting (esp. 191); and McNairn, *The Capacity to Judge*.

75 MacKinnon, "This Cursed Republican Spirit."

76 See Kernaghan, "Howe, Alexander"; and Tulloch, "Barclay, Thomas Henry."

77 LCOLL Jacob Bailey Papers, MG 1, 98–7 (Reel 8). Bailey, Representation to the Nova Scotia Assembly about the 1785 election (1786).

78 Though he does not mention it in the document, Bailey and Annapolis County Loyalists would have a further disappointment in the matter, when the Assembly also overturned the results and declared Howe duly elected.

79 Ibid.

80 Ibid.

81 Wahrman, "The English Problem of Identity" and *Making of the Modern Self*; and Mason, "The American Loyalist Problem," 42.

CHAPTER FIVE

1 Richey, *A Memoir of Rev. William Black*, 45. For introductions to Alline's life and influence, see Bumsted, "Alline, Henry," and *Henry Alline*; Rawlyk, *Ravished by the Spirit* and *Canada Fire*, 5–18; Rawlyk, ed., *Henry Alline: Selected Writings*; and Bell, *Henry Alline and Maritime Religion*.

2 Scott, *A Brief View*, 58. On Scott, see Stewart, "Scott, Jonathan"; and Trask and Trask, "The Reverend Jonathan Scott," 258–73. There are two published versions of Scott's journal, the most recent edition being more complete; *Journal of the Reverend Jonathan Scott*, ed. Henry Scott; and *Life of Jonathan Scott*, ed. Fergusson.

3 Scott, *Brief View*, 262; and *Journal of Henry Alline*, Beverley and Moody, eds, 216.

4 Scott, *Brief View*, 211; Scott to the Church and Society of Jebogue in Yarmouth, 15 March 1786, in Stewart, ed., *Documents*, 179.

5 Scott, *Brief View*, 168; emphasis in original. See *Brief View*, 204, where Scott makes a similar charge about the *Anti-Traditionist*.

6 *Journal of the Reverend Jonathan Scott*, ed. Scott, § 10, 16.

7 Rawlyk, "A Total Revolution," 148–9.

8 Foster, *Long Argument*.

9 Ibid., 9; emphasis added.

10 Bushman, *From Puritan to Yankee*; Balik, *Rally the Scattered Believers*; Jaffee, *People of the Wachusett*; Mancke, *Fault Lines of Empire*; Westfall, *Two Worlds*, 45–9; and Winiarski, *Darkness Falls*.

11 Nathan Hatch has influentially argued that late eighteenth- and early nineteenth-century populist religious movements such as Freewill Baptists, Methodists, and Mormons represented the "democratization of American Christianity." Hatch cites Henry Alline numerous times as an exemplar of this strain of individualistic religion; *Democratization of American Christianity*. Compare Den Hartog, *Patriotism and Piety*.

12 Bloch, "Religion, Literary Sentimentalism," 308–30. The relative importance of republican and liberal ideas in Revolutionary America and in the Early Republic was the subject of a long-running historiographical debate. See Rodgers, "Republicanism: The Career of a Concept." On how these issues coordinate with American Christianity, see Hatch, *Sacred Cause of Liberty* and *Democratization of American Christianity*; Bloch, *Visionary Republic*; Kloppenberg, "The Virtues of Liberalism"; and Noll, *America's God*.

13 Bloch, "Religion, Literary Sentimentalism," 328.

14 Ibid.," 323–4, 328. See Hindmarsh, *Evangelical Conversion*, 343–9.

15 Christie, "In These Times of Democratic Rage and Delusion."

16 Stewart and Rawlyk, *People Highly Favoured of God*, 80; and see Christie, "In These Times of Democratic Rage and Delusion," 34.

17 Cuthbertson, ed., *Journal of John Payzant*, 27. On Alline's humble origins and his self-conscious opposition to the established social order, see Christie, "In These Times of Democratic Rage and Delusion," 29.

18 Armstrong, *Great Awakening*, 82.

19 Discussions of Alline's thought and influences include Stewart and Rawlyk, *People Highly Favoured of God*, ch. 9; Beverley and Moody, eds, *Journal of Henry Alline*, 14–22; Rawlyk, ed., *Henry Alline: Selected Writings*, 19–29; and Faber, "My Stammering Tongue and Unpolished Pen."

20 Alline, *Two Mites*, 200; emphasis added.

21 Ibid., 128.

22 Alline, *Two Mites*, 2–3.

23 See especially Hatch, *Democratization of American Christianity*, 10, 13, 128; Marini, *Radical Sects of Revolutionary New England*, 41–3.

24 Alline, *Two Mites*, 106. On the democratization of public discourse in New England, see Grasso, *A Speaking Aristocracy*.

25 On the shades of Calvinism among early evangelicals, see Hindmarsh, *John Newton and the English Evangelical Tradition*, 119–25. On the moderation of Calvinism, in part due to the influence of the Enlightenment, see Bebbington, *Evangelicalism in Modern Britain*, 63–5. On Whitefield's Calvinism, see Jones, "George Whitefield and the Revival of Calvinism."

26 Alline, *Two Mites*, 46; see Alline, *A Sermon on a Day of Thanksgiving*, 8.

27 See Alline, *Two Mites*, 16.

28 Alline, *A Court for the Trial of an Anti-Traditionist*, 15; see Alline, *A Sermon on a Day of Thanksgiving*, 7.

29 Alline, *Two Mites*, 36.

30 Alline, *A Sermon Preached at Port-Midway*, 19.

31 Alline, *Two Mites*, 36.

32 Ibid., 4.

33 Ibid., 70–4, 81.

34 Ibid., 115.

35 Ibid., 115–20.

36 Ibid., 19.

37 Ibid., 89–90.

38 Ibid., 62–3.

39 Ibid., 109–11.
40 Ibid., 110.
41 On the centrality of conversion in evangelicalism, see Bebbingtion, *Evangelicalism in Modern Britain*, 5–10; and Hindmarsh, *Evangelical Conversion Narrative*.
42 Alline, *Two Mites*, 129–30.
43 Ibid., 121.
44 Ibid., 124; emphasis added.
45 Ibid., 125–6.
46 Ibid., 112–13.
47 Ibid., 110, 127–8.
48 Ibid., 131–2. See also, *A Court for the Trial of an Anti-Traditionist*, 42–3.
49 Mack, *Heart Religion*, 7.
50 Alline, *A Sermon Preached at Port-Midway*, 11.
51 Ibid., 13.
52 Alline, *Two Mites*, 182.
53 Ibid., 161.
54 Christie, "In These Times of Democratic Rage," 28. See Grasso, *A Speaking Aristocracy*.
55 Tennent, *Danger of an Unconverted Ministry* (1741).
56 Alline, *Two Mites*, 158.
57 Ibid., 185.
58 Ibid., 171.
59 E.g., Alline, *Two Mites*, 171–2; 256–57.
60 The literature on Puritan New England is vast, but helpful overviews and key works on the covenants of the New England Way include: Miller, *The New England Mind*, 365–462; Morgan, *Visible Saints*; Bremer, *The Puritan Experiment*; Grasso, *A Speaking Aristocracy*, 24–85; Hall, *A Reforming People*, 132–43, and *Puritans: A Transatlantic History*; and Winship, *Hot Protestants*.
61 On the Half-Way Covenant, see especially Bremer, *Puritan Experiment*, 143–7; Pope, *Half-Way Covenant*; Foster, *Long Argument*, 175–230; Noll, *America's God*, 31–50.
62 Alline, *Two Mites*, 237.
63 For "Paper Covenants," see Alline, *Two Mites*, 233, 237. Jonathan Edwards also rejected the Half-Way Covenant, insisting that true religion must involve the affections rather than merely outward morality. For a brief discussion, see Marsden, *Jonathan Edwards: A Life*, 353–6. It could be argued that both Alline and Edwards, in their different ways, still relied on the communal structures that they marginalized with their individualistic piety.

64 Noll, *America's God*, esp. 45.

65 Alline, *Two Mites*, ii–iii.

66 Ibid.; see also, 333.

67 Hall, *Contested Boundaries*, 133. See also Christie, "In These Times of Democratic Rage," 26.

68 For the religious history of the Yarmouth area, see Trask and Trask, eds, *Records of the Church of Jebogue*, 128–210; Stewart, ed., *Documents Relating to the Great Awakening in Nova Scotia*, 9–109; Stewart and Rawlyk, *People Highly Favoured of God*, ch. 6; Jaffee, *People of the Wachusett*, 191–9; and Goodwin, "From Disunity to Integration," 190–200.

69 On the argument and context of his *Brief View*, see Armstrong, "Jonathan Scott's 'Brief View.'"

70 Scott, *Brief View*, 167.

71 Ibid., 250; emphasis in original.

72 Ibid.

73 Ibid., 257.

74 Ibid., 262.

75 Ibid., 253.

76 Ibid., 250.

77 See Ibid., 1–14, on the centrality of scripture. On biblicism as a prominent feature of the early evangelical movement, see Bebbington, *Evangelicalism in Modern Britain*, 12–14; and Noll, *In the Beginning Was the Word*.

78 Scott, *Brief View*, 7; emphasis in original. Even if Alline himself did not espouse such a view, his focus on spiritual individualism could be bent in that direction without too much pressure.

79 Ibid., 258, 253.

80 Ibid., 251, 260–1; see 257.

81 Ibid., 260.

82 Ibid., 261.

83 See Alline, *Two Mites*, 110, 127–8.

84 Scott, *Brief View*, 255. Stewart and Rawlyk observe that despite Scott's avowed support of revivals, his preaching in Nova Scotia did not bring them about; *People Highly Favoured*, 106–8.

85 Scott, *Brief View*, 254.

86 Scott, *Brief View*, 265. Scott and his wife named one of their children Jonathan Edwards Scott: "Having his *Life*, and most of the Books that he Wrote, we had such a Regard to his memory and Books that we named our Child after him." Scott, ed., *Journal of Jonathan Scott*, § 66. For a discussion of some similarities between the writings of Alline and Edwards, see Rawlyk and Stewart, "Nova Scotia's Sense of Mission," 7–9.

87 Scott, *Brief View*, 263, quoting Edwards, *Treatise Concerning Religious Affections*.
88 Ibid., 138.
89 Ibid., 219.
90 Ibid., 144.
91 Ibid., 247. For the covenant signed by the members of Scott's own church at Jebogue, Yarmouth, Nova Scotia, see Stewart, ed., *Documents*, 42–3.
92 Jonathan Scott, Letter to the Church and Society of Jebogue in Yarmouth, in Stewart, ed., *Documents*, 179. On the controversy over itinerancy in the evangelical revivals, see Hall, *Contested Boundaries*; Lovegrove, *Established Church, Sectarian People*; and Balik, *Rally the Scattered Believers*.
93 Scott, *Brief View*, 238.
94 Mancke, *Fault Lines of Empire*, 109–37; Balik, *Rally the Scattered Believers*.
95 Scott, *Brief View*, 249.
96 Ibid., 242.
97 See Foster, *Long Argument*, 297.
98 Bumsted, *Henry Alline*, 88.

CHAPTER SIX

1 Alline, *Hymns and Spiritual Songs*, 70 (Hymn 1.92), verses 1–2. I am grateful to Kacy Dowd Tillman and Erica Johnson Edwards of the *Age of Revolutions* blog for incisive comments on an earlier draft of parts of this chapter.
2 The description of enthusiasts as "favourites of the divinity" was Joseph Priestly's (1772), as quoted in Goldstein, "Enthusiasm or Imagination?" 33.
3 Scott, *Brief View*, 211.
4 Inglis, *A Charge Delivered to the Clergy of Nova-Scotia in 1791*, 19. Excerpts reprinted in Rawlyk, ed., *New Light Letters and Spiritual Songs*, 304–9.
5 Armstrong, *Great Awakening in Nova Scotia*, 67.
6 Rawlyk, *Canada Fire*, 3.
7 Reddy, *Navigation of Feeling*, 55.
8 Rawlyk, *Ravished by the Spirit*, 77.
9 Mack, *Heart Religion*, 6.
10 Alline, *Journal of Henry Alline*, Beverley and Moody, "Introduction," 13.
11 See Hambrick-Stowe, *Practice of Piety*, 21.

12 Davis, *Patriarch of Western Nova Scotia*, 178. See Rawlyk, *Canada Fire*, 7. "Rapture," in this context, refers to a mystical spiritual experience, not the belief (popularized by nineteenth-century Dispensationalists) that Christians alive at the time of the Second Coming would be physically taken by God out of the world before a period of tribulation.

13 Alline, *Journal*, 63.

14 Rawlyk proposed that Alline's journal, which circulated in manuscript among New Lights before it was published, was embraced by ordinary Nova Scotians because they could relate to it: "If the Falmouth farmer-tanner could experience the intense spiritual ecstasy and also the certainty of the New Light – New Birth, then they could do so too"; *Canada Fire*, 6.

15 Alline's "journal" as published (including both the manuscript Handley Chipman transcription and the 1806 printed version) is a hybrid document. It begins with an autobiographical memoir of his early life, conversion in 1775, and first year of preaching. From September 1777 to December 1780, there are dated entries that summarize Alline's activities and reflections for various periods of time, from a few days to several months. On 1 January 1781, Alline wrote, "This year I intend, if God permit, to pen down the travels of my soul every day, which in the time past I have not done." Alline continued regular entries in that near-daily format until 17 November 1783, when he stopped because of sickness. An account of his last months and deathbed experience was added to the document by his host, Rev. David McClure of Newburyport, Massachusetts. Notwithstanding the stylistic differences between the memoir and journal portions, the entire document has been edited and intentionally narrated, some of it after considerable reflection. See Alline, *Journal of Henry Alline*, Beverley and Moody, "Introduction," 23–5; Bell, "All Things New," 78, and *Henry Alline and Maritime Religion*, 10; Saunders, *History of the Baptists*, plate opposite page 31. On reading Alline's *Life and Journal* as an autobiographical text, examining questions of form, history and fiction, and persona, see Davies, "Persona in Planter Journals," 210–17; and Scott, "Travels of My Soul."

16 Alline, *Journal*, 29–30.

17 Ibid., 31–59.

18 James, *Varieties of Religious Experience*, 134.

19 Alline, *Journal*, 34.

20 Ibid., 56.

21 Ibid., 60.

22 Ibid., 102; emphasis added.

23 Psalms 38 and 40; Alline, *Journal*, 61.

24 Alline, *Journal*, 61.

25 See Ibid., 90.

26 Ibid., 62.

27 Van Gent and Young, "Introduction: Emotions and Conversion," 463.

28 Alline, *Journal*, 63.

29 Ibid., 140.

30 Ibid., 147.

31 Ibid., 179.

32 Ibid., 135.

33 Ibid., 113; emphasis added.

34 Ibid., 148.

35 Ibid., 133, 158; see 118, 161.

36 Ibid., 152.

37 Ibid., 124.

38 Ibid., 112; emphasis in original.

39 Ibid., 136.

40 Ibid., 115.

41 Ibid., 116.

42 Ibid., 121.

43 Bebbington, *Evangelicalism in Modern Britain*, 42–50.

44 Alline, *Journal*, 29.

45 Ibid., 148.

46 Ibid., 149.

47 Ibid., 111.

48 Ibid., 189.

49 Ibid., 206.

50 Alline, *Two Mites*, 81; "happiness" appears as early as the first sentence of that book.

51 Alline, *Journal*, 192.

52 McMahon, *Pursuit of Happiness*, 13; emphasis in original, and see 204. For early modern definitions of happiness, see Ryrie, *Being Protestant*, 77–95; Roberts, *Puritanism and the Pursuit of Happiness*, 85–92; and Heimert, *Religion and the American Mind*, 42–9.

53 Alline, *Journal*, 148, 140.

54 Ibid., 113.

55 Mack, "Religion, Feminism, and the Problem of Agency," 156, and *Heart Religion*, 8–15. See Clement, *Reading Humility*, 16, 19–20, 129–32. Eustace suggests that early modern discourses about emotion moved away from self-negation, as first Protestantism and then moral philosophy emphasized individualism; *Passion Is the Gale*, 239.

56 Alline, *Journal*, 140.
57 Ibid., 102–3.
58 Ibid., 157; see 128.
59 Ibid., 140.
60 Alline first published a selection of twenty hymns in 1782 at Halifax,
    though no copies are known to be extant. This edition was reprinted as
    Hymns and Spiritual Songs (Windsor, VT: Alden Spooner, 1796). For a
    recent reprint of this edition, see Henry Alline, *Hymns and Spiritual Songs*,
    ed. J.M. Bumsted (Sackville, NB: Ralph Pickard Bell Library, 1987). The
    much longer volume with the same title (from which this study quotes)
    was published in four editions: Boston, 1786; Dover, NH, 1795 and 1797;
    Storington-Port, CT, 1802. For the bibliographic history, see Vincent,
    "Some Bibliographical Notes," 12–13. Many of the hymns are reprinted in
    Rawlyk, ed., *New Light Letters and Spiritual Songs*. On the widespread
    use of Alline's hymns, into the twentieth century among Freewill Baptists,
    see Burnett, "Henry Alline's Articles & Covenant," 18; and Bell, *Henry
    Alline and Maritime Religion*, 3. For examples of later eighteenth- and
    nineteenth-century use of Alline's hymns, see ECW Edward Manning
    Collection, 1846.001/3/1, Edward Manning, "Reminiscences," undated
    manuscript [pre-1846], page 8; and Knowles, *A Brief Sketch of the Life of
    Mrs. Ann Knowles*, 17. Also see Vincent, "Henry Alline: Problems of
    Approach," 201–10.
61 Vincent, "Alline and Bailey," 125, 132.
62 ECW Manning, "Reminiscences," 8.
63 On hymns in dissenting and evangelical Protestantism, see Coffey,
    "Between Puritanism and Evangelicalism," 29–49; Marini, "Hymnody
    as History" and *Radical Sects of Revolutionary New England*, ch. 9;
    Mouw and Noll, eds, *Wonderful Words of Life*; Blumhofer and Noll, eds,
    Singing the Lord's Song in a Strange Land; and Rivers and Wykes, eds,
    Dissenting Praise.
64 Alline, *Hymns and Spiritual Songs*, iii.
65 Ibid., iv.
66 Ibid.
67 Ibid., 57 (Hymn 1.72); emphasis added.
68 Ibid., Book 1, page 1.
69 For other examples, see Ibid., 14, 19, 28, 53. For this theme in early
    British Protestantism, see Ryrie, *Being Protestant*, 20–6.
70 Alline, *Hymns and Spiritual Songs*, 28 (Hymn 1.35).
71 Ibid., 36–7 (Hymn 1.46).
72 Ibid., 86 (Hymn 2.22).

73 On the theme of desire, see Ryrie, *Being Protestant*, ch. 4.

74 Alline, *Hymns and Spiritual Songs*, 147 (Hymn 2.87).

75 Ibid., 138 (Hymn 2.76).

76 Ibid., 191–2 (Hymn 3.45).

77 Ibid., 158–9 (Hymn 3.3); emphasis added.

78 Ibid., 284 (Hymn 4.71).

79 Ibid., 171–2 (Hymn 3.20).

80 Ibid., 20–1 (Hymn 1.26); emphasis added.

81 Ibid., 185–6 (Hymn 3.37); see also 234, 236–7, 238–9 (Hymns 4.1, 4.4, 4.7).

82 Ibid., 197–8 (Hymn 3.51); emphasis added.

83 Ibid., 318 (Hymn 5.14); emphasis added.

84 Ibid., Book 5, page 309.

85 Ibid., 202 (Hymn 3.55).

86 Ibid., 137 (Hymn 3.39).

87 Ibid., 181–2 (Hymn 3.33).

88 Ibid., 333 (Hymn 5.34) and 377 (Hymn 5.89).

89 Ibid., 320 (Hymn 5.16); emphasis added.

90 Charlotte Prescott to Sarah Brown, 23 May 1790, in Rawlyk, ed., *New Light Letters and Songs*, 100. See Rawlyk, *Canada Fire*, 84–5.

91 Bennett (d. 1800) was a schoolmaster in the Cornwallis area in the 1780s and early 1790s, and then in 1794 moved to Liverpool, where he was a merchant. He was a frequent correspondent and sometime itinerant preacher with the New Lights. Rawlyk, ed., *New Light Letters and Songs*, 56; and Cuthbertson, ed., *Journal of John Payzant*, 47. Reprinted in chronological order in Rawlyk, ed., *New Light Letters and Songs*, the manuscript volume is located at ECW Acadia University, Wolfville, NS, as the Thomas Bennett accession, "New Light letters and spiritual songs" [179?], 1900.471–BEN/1. Most of the letters appear to be handwritten copies. For provenance, see Rawlyk, ed., *New Light Letters and Songs*, 69–72.

92 See Rosenwein, *Emotional Communities*, 25.

93 Joseph Dimock to Thomas Bennett, 20 Aug. 1791, in Rawlyk, ed., *New Light Letters and Songs*, 129–31; and Joseph Bailey to Harris Harding, 11 July 1790, page 101.

94 On the agency and participation of women in Enlightenment-era debates, see Brekus, "Sarah Osborn's Enlightenment" and *Sarah Osborn's World*; Mack, *Heart Religion*; Hunt, ed., *Women and the Enlightenment*; Knott and Taylor, eds, *Women, Gender, and Enlightenment*; and Melton, *Rise of*

the Public in Enlightenment Europe, 197–225. On conversation among women, see Eger, "The Noblest Commerce of Mankind," 288–305.

95 On ordinary people, as well as elites, reflecting on their emotional experiences, see Mack, *Heart Religion*; Taves, *Fits, Trances, and Visions*, 4; Rawlyk, *Canada Fire*, 99–101; Hatch, *Democratization of American Christianity*; Christie and Gauvreau, *Christian Churches and Their Peoples*, 14; Seeman, *Pious Persuasions*; and Hall, *Worlds of Wonder*. For an insightful discussion of how Loyalist women in Nova Scotia forged an emotional community in their post-revolution refugee experience, see O'Brien, "Unknown and Unlamented," ch. 3.

96 See her letters to Thomas Bennett, 4 Aug. and 3 Nov. 1790, and n.d., in Rawlyk, ed., *New Light Letters and Songs*, 103, 115, 116. The Bennett collection also includes a letter to Betsy Lusby, perhaps a sister; Elizabeth Blair to Betsy Lusby, 17 Aug. 1790, in Rawlyk, ed., *New Light Letters and Songs*, 106–7.

97 Charlotte Lusby to Thomas Bennett, 3 Nov. 1790, in Rawlyk, ed., *New Light Letters and Songs*, 115.

98 Charlotte Lusby to Thomas Bennett, n.d. [1790 or 1791?], in Rawlyk, ed., *New Light Letters and Songs*, 116.

99 Ibid.; emphasis added.

100 Charlotte Lusby to Thomas Bennett, 4 Aug. 1790, in Rawlyk, ed., *New Light Letters and Songs*, 103.

101 Harris Harding to Marven Beckwith, 26 Aug. 1791, in Rawlyk, ed., *New Light Letters and Songs*, 144.

102 Elizabeth Blair to Betsy Lusby, 17 Aug. 1790, in Rawlyk, ed., *New Light Letters and Songs*, 106–7. Blair and Lusby had not met in person, though they shared an acquaintance with itinerant preacher Harris Harding. Blair draws on similar themes in a letter to Joseph Dimock, 20 Aug. 1790, in Rawlyk, ed., *New Light Letters and Songs*, 108–9. See Rawlyk, *Canada Fire*, 92–5.

103 See Blair's quotations from Song of Songs 1:15, 4:10, 4:19. Susan Juster briefly notes that Alline's rapturous writing (which Blair echoes in this letter) was "every bit as inflamed as the most *outré* medieval saint ... combin[ing] the erotics of mystical experience with the poetics of a venerable strand of visionary literature." Juster, *Doomsayers*, 93; see also Juster, "Eros and Desire in Early Modern Spirituality," 203–6, and *Disorderly Women*.

104 Astell, *Song of Songs in the Middle Ages*; Pardes, *Song of Songs: A Biography*.

105 Sarah Brown to Joseph Dimock, 20 Aug. 1790, and Elizabeth Prescott to Joseph Dimock, April 1790, in Rawlyk, ed, *New Light Letters and Songs*, 110, 99.

106 Blair to Lusby, 17 Aug. 1790, in Rawlyk, ed., *New Light Letters and Songs*, 106–7.

107 Harris Harding to Frederick Fitch, 1 Sept. 1791, in Rawlyk, ed., *New Light Letters and Songs*, 156. Harding arguably remained the most "enthusiastic" of the New Light itinerants, even after he adopted Baptist principles. See Bumsted, "Harding, Harris"; Davis, *The Patriarch of Western Nova Scotia*; Rawlyk, *Canada Fire*, 58–74, and Wrapped *Up in God*, 76–95; and Goodwin, *Into Deep Waters*, 42–74.

108 Harris Harding to Betsy Grimes and Nancy Smith, 20 Aug. 1791, in Rawlyk, ed., *New Light Letters and Songs*, 132; emphasis in original.

109 For biographical information on Lawrence, see Rawlyk, ed., *New Light Letters and Songs*, 351–4, and *Canada Fire*, 86–90.

110 Nancy Lawrence to Sally Bass, Aug. 1789, in Rawlyk, ed., *New Light Letters and Songs*, 276. Lawrence's letter was not in the Bennett collection, but she was active in the same New Light networks at the same time.

111 Ibid.

112 Charlotte Prescott to Sarah Brown, 23 May 1790, in Rawlyk, ed., *New Light Letters and Songs*, 100. For more on Prescott's life and spiritual experience, see Rawlyk, ed., *New Light Letters and Songs*, 332–3n202, and Goodwin, *Into Deep Waters*, 20–1, both of which draw upon Joseph Dimock's "Memoir of Mrs. Charlotte [Prescott] Boyle" in the *Baptist Missionary Magazine*.

113 Prescott to Brown, 23 May 1790, in Rawlyk, ed., *New Light Letters and Songs*, 100.

114 Rawlyk, ed., *New Light Letters and Songs*, 71.

CHAPTER SEVEN

1 ECW Edward Manning Collection, D1846.001. 31 Oct. 1796, Stephen Jones to Manning. For the context, see Mancke, *Fault Lines*, 116–18; and Bell, ed., *Newlight Baptist Journals*, 91–2.

2 ECW Manning Collection, D1846.001/3/7. 11 Nov. 1796, Manning to Jones.

3 On Manning's itinerancy, see Moody, "From Itinerant to Pastor." On evangelical itinerancy and its potentially disruptive consequences, see Hall, *Contested Boundaries*; Lovegrove, *Established Church, Sectarian People*; and Balik, *Rally the Scattered Believers*.

4 On Manning, see Moody, "Manning, Edward"; Rawlyk, *Ravished by the Spirit*, 80–103, and *Canada Fire*, 66–8, 77–84; and Goodwin, *Into Deep Waters*, 98–125. Julian Gwyn draws upon Manning's extensive diary for its portrayal of Manning's social environment in "The King's County World." The primary sources for studying Manning's life and thought are extensive, including a diary from 1807 to 1846 and approximately 800 letters from correspondents throughout the Maritime provinces and New England. They are located in the Edward Manning Collection of the Esther Clark Wright Archives, Acadia University, Wolfville, Nova Scotia, D1846.001. I am grateful to former university librarian Sara Lochhead and university archivist Patricia Townsend for permission to use a complete typed transcript of the Manning diary, created by Freeman Fenerty in consultation with Barry Moody.

5 Rawlyk, *Ravished by the Spirit*, 86.

6 Ibid., 83. Rawlyk goes further, asserting that for Manning and other former New Lights, their "abandonment of Allinite principles had created a certain emotional emptiness in their religious lives"; *Ravished by the Spirit*, 118. See Rawlyk, ed., *New Light Letters and Songs*, 64.

7 Goodwin, *Into Deep Waters*.

8 See especially Westfall, *Two Worlds*; Wolffe, *Expansion of Evangelicalism*; Webb, *Transatlantic Methodists*; and McLaren, *Pulpit, Press, and Politics* on the transformation of early nineteenth-century British North American evangelicalism in transatlantic context.

9 This account of Manning's conversion is based primarily on his undated manuscript, ECW Manning Collection, 1846.001/3/1, "Reminiscences." Quotations in this section are from the "Reminiscences" unless otherwise noted. See also the historical notes Manning sent to Rhode Island Baptist David Benedict: ECW Manning Collection, 1846.001/3/3, Manning, Notes on the History of the Baptist Denomination in Nova Scotia, New Brunswick, and Prince Edward Island [18??], and manuscript fragment of notes on New Lights and religion in Nova Scotia for David Benedict (D1846.001/3/7, "Other documents"). Also see Rawlyk, *Canada Fire*, 77–84.

10 Payzant was, in an ironic twist, the son-in-law of the man killed by Manning's father.

11 Cuthbertson, ed., *Journal of the Reverend John Payzant*, 47.

12 ECW Chipman, Essays, i.4. See Goodwin, *Into Deep Waters*, 102–4, on the experiences that led Manning to distance himself from the New Dispensation movement.

13 ECW Manning Diary, 4 April 1821.

14 Ibid., 5 June 1823.

15 Ibid., 10 July 1823.

16 Goodwin, *Into Deep Waters*, 106.

17 On the transformation of Manning and a cadre of ministerial colleagues from New Lights to Baptists, including their emotional moderation, see especially Bell, ed., *Newlight Baptist Journals*, 2–35; and Goodwin, *Into Deep Waters*.

18 ECW Manning Diary, 27 Nov. 1820.

19 Ibid., 28 Nov. 1820.

20 Moody, "From Itinerant to Pastor." On the persistence of the New Light/ Allinite tradition in the region, see Bell, "The Allinite Tradition" and "Yankee Preachers."

21 ECW Manning Diary, 28 Sept. 1817; see 27–30 Sept. 1817.

22 Ibid., 2 Sept. 1821.

23 Ibid., 4 Sept. 1821.

24 See Scheer, "Are Emotions a Kind of Practice." Manning's strong reaction to New Light passions may have had a gendered aspect. He particularly drew attention to the females in the Liverpool meeting, disturbed by their "screeching" and movement about the aisles of the meetinghouse. It may be that Manning felt that such prominent displays of one kind of female piety subverted the authority of the predominantly male ministers and deacons. Later the same day, while visiting with a Liverpool family, Manning was put off by the forthright conversation of the woman of the house: "I do not like to have an uninformed Woman take all the talk and so amaizing loquatious, and to be talking all the time when I am endeavouring to impart instruction. Told her so and she was more moderate." ECW Manning Diary, 2 Sept. 1821. See Rawlyk, *Canada Fire*, 129–30. For the role of women in public church life, see Lane, "Women and Public Prayer"; and Bell, "Allowed Irregularities."

25 ECW Manning Diary, 23 March 1821.

26 Buck, *A Treatise on Religious Experience*, in *The Works of the Rev. Charles Buck*, vol. 3, 84. See ECW Manning Diary, 3 and 16 March 1835. Manning also read Buck's *Theological Dictionary* regularly and with enjoyment. See, for example, ECW Manning Diary, 30 Dec. 1819; 17 April 1824; 11 May 1841; 20 Jan. 1845. Buck, *A Theological Dictionary*. For an assessment of that work in the context of North American evangelicalism, see Bowman and Brown, "Reverend Buck's Theological Dictionary."

27 For his reading of Owen, see ECW Manning Diary, 19–20 Jan. 1821 and 15 Feb. 1821, and for Flavel, see ECW Manning Diary, 20 April 1821 and

29 April 1843. Owen, *Phronema Tou Pneumatos*; Flavel, *A Treatise on Keeping the Heart*.

28 ECW Manning Diary, 27 Jan. 1821.

29 For his reading of Doddridge, see, for example, ECW Manning Diary, 29 July 1825; and for Watts, see ECW Manning Diary, 2 April 1821. Watts, *Discourses of the Love of God*.

30 ECW Manning Diary, 29 July 1825.

31 Ibid., 22 Oct. 1822.

32 For Edwards's writings on the affections and the "spiritual sense," see Edwards, *Religious Affections*, "A Divine and Supernatural Light," and "Miscellany 782. Ideas. Sense of the Heart." See Miller, "Jonathan Edwards on the Sense of the Heart"; and Fiering, *Jonathan Edwards's Moral Thought*.

33 ECW Manning Diary, 19 Apr. 1822; and 8 Apr. 1822.

34 Ibid., 8 Apr. 1822.

35 Ibid., 22 Oct. 1822.

36 On Fuller, see Morden, *Life and Thought of Andrew Fuller*; and Grant, *Andrew Fuller and the Evangelical Renewal of Pastoral Theology*, especially ch. 3.

37 Goodwin, *Into Deep Waters*, 13, 122–5.

38 Fuller, *Works*, vol. 1, 489. See Chun, *Legacy of Jonathan Edwards*.

39 Fuller, *Works*, vol. 1, 169.

40 ECW Manning Diary, 2 Sept. 1822.

41 Ibid., 11 Nov. 1845.

42 Ibid., 29 March 1823.

43 Ibid., 20 Jan. 1821.

44 Ibid., 16 Oct. 1814; 1 Feb. 1820.

45 Eustace, *1812: War and the Passions of Patriotism*, 220. For a discussion of historiographic themes around the War of 1812, including emotions, see Cleves et al., "Interchange: The War of 1812." For other elements of the cross-border conflict, see Taylor, *Civil War of 1812*; Hickey, *War of 1812*; Boileau, *Half-Hearted Enemies*; Morgan, *Public Men and Virtuous Women*, 23–55; and Errington, *The Lion, the Eagle, and Upper Canada*, ch. 4.

46 Murdoch, *A History of Nova-Scotia or Acadie*, as quoted in Boileau, *Half-Hearted Enemies*, 25.

47 Heath, "The Great Association Above," 1–22 (quotation at 4).

48 ECW Manning Diary, 9 Jan. 1813.

49 ECW Daniel Merrill to Manning, 2 June 1812. Despite his warmth for his British North American brethren, Merrill was less irenic toward the British

nation. Merrill, *Balaam Disappointed*, 27. See Watts, *The Republic Reborn*, 285. Gribbin, *The Churches Militant*, 87–8, suggests Merrill delivered his bellicose sermons "despite his friendship with ministers and churches of his faith in Nova Scotia and New Brunswick."

50 ECW David Benedict to Manning, 4 July 1812.
51 ECW Manning Diary, 24 May 1814.
52 Ibid.
53 Ibid., 27 May 1814.
54 Heath, "Great Association Above," 16n66.
55 For an insightful discussion of these twinned themes in British North American evangelicalism, see Gauvreau, "Protestantism Transformed."
56 ECW Manning Diary, 1 Feb. 1820.
57 On the turn to voluntary associations in Protestantism, see Foster, *An Errand of Mercy*; Roth, *Democratic Dilemma*; Johnson, *Redeeming America*, 115–54; Abzug, *Cosmos Crumbling*; Mintz, *Moralists and Modernizers*; Brackney, *Christian Voluntarism*; Sassi, *A Republic of Righteousness*; Wolffe, *Expansion of Evangelicalism*, 159–92; and Den Hartog, *Patriotism & Piety*. For voluntary societies among evangelical Anglicans and Methodists earlier in the eighteenth century, see Walsh, "Religious Societies" and Sirota, *Christian Monitors*.
58 For the role of voluntary associations in the public life of the period, see Sutherland, "Voluntary Societies"; Clark, *British Clubs and Societies*; McNairn, *Capacity to Judge*; Acheson, "Evangelicals and Public Life"; Ferry, *Uniting in Measures of Common Good*; Neem, *Creating a Nation of Joiners*; and Eamon, *Imprinting Britain*, ch. 5. For an influential perspective on how liberal individualism was related to state formation in Canada, see McKay, "The Liberal Order Framework"; and the responses in Ducharme and Constant, eds, *Liberalism and Hegemony*.
59 For an overview of Manning's benevolent activities, see Moody, "Manning, Edward."
60 ECW Manning Diary, 15 June 1821.
61 On the history of the British and Foreign Bible Society, see Barnard, "Religious Print Culture"; Howsam, *Cheap Bibles*; Fingard, "Grapes in the Wilderness"; Doull, *A History of the Bible Society in Nova Scotia*; and Friskney, "Christian Faith in Print." For the American context, see Noll, *In the Beginning Was the Word*; Fea, *The Bible Cause*; and Gutjahr, *An American Bible*.
62 ECW See John Burton to Manning, 18 Dec. 1813; and T.F. Addison to Manning, 31 March 1814; and Manning Diary, 5 Oct. 1814.
63 ECW Manning Diary, 16 Oct. 1814.

64 Manning, "Circular Letter (1814)," 5–10 (quotation at 6).

65 Ibid., 7.

66 Moody, "Burpee, Richard E."

67 ECW Manning Diary, 30 April 1818.

68 Ibid., 6 Aug. 1829. Beecher, *Six Sermons*; Kittredge, *An Address*; and Humphrey, *Parallel between Intemperance and the Slave Trade*. For the role of evangelical religion in the early phases of the temperance movement, see Noel, *Canada Dry*, chapter 2; Barry, "Shades of Vice and Moral Glory"; Tyrrell, *Sobering Up*; and Young, *Bearing Witness against Sin*.

69 For examples of his public reading, see ECW Manning Diary entries in 1829: 25 Feb., 12 March, 8 May, 28 July, 10 Dec. For the Temperance Society in Cornwallis, see 8 March 1834 and 6 July 1842.

70 Ibid., 5 Nov. 1841.

71 See Ibid., 9 and 11 Feb. 1820; and a document certifying that he was an agent for soliciting funds and books on behalf of the institution, ECW Manning Collection, D1846.001/3/7, Sept. 1819.

72 See ECW Manning Diary, 24–5 June 1828, entries for Jan.–Feb. 1829, 12–16 Nov. 1838; Nova Scotia Baptist Education Society, *Report* (Halifax), 1832–51. Moody, "Joseph Howe, the Baptists, and the College Question," "Breadth of Vision, Breadth of Mind," and "Maritime Baptists and Higher Education"; and Longley, *Acadia University*.

73 ECW Manning Diary, 15 Nov. 1838.

74 Bebbington, *Evangelicalism in Modern Britain*, 62, 81–6; Crawford, *Seasons of Grace*, 124–38; Westfall, *Two Worlds*, 159–90.

75 ECW Manning Diary, 24 May 1814.

76 Ibid., 29 April 1818.

77 See Goodwin, *Into Deep Waters*.

78 ECW Manning Diary, 2 Jan. 1821.

79 Ibid., 6 Nov. 1830.

80 Ibid., 26 March 1835.

81 For brief comments on his practice of diary-keeping, see ECW Manning Diary 8 Feb. 1827 ("Will any one ever read these lines! Perhaps not. Well I have had comfort in writing them. It is one way of recording the goodness of the Lord, and my own awful depravity. But each is done imperfectly"), and 26 July 1836.

82 Rosenwein, *Emotional Communities*, 193.

83 Tears have not been ignored by historians. See, for example, Vincent-Buffault, *The History of Tears*; Ellison, *Cato's Tears*; Dixon, "Weeping in Space" and *Weeping Britannia*; and Ebersole, "The Function of Ritual Weeping Revisited."

84 Capp, "Jesus Wept but Did the Englishman?" and Carter, "Tears and the Man."

85 As quoted in Carter, "Tears and the Man," 159, 165.

86 Brown, *The Word in the World*, 7–9, 88–95. See also Cayton, "Canonizing Harriet Newell"; Brumberg, *Mission for Life*, chapter 3. Nineteenth-century evangelical readers also continued to circulate many of the Protestant "steady sellers" of earlier generations; Hall, *Cultures of Print*, 61–8.

87 See, for examples, ECW Manning Diary, 5 Sept. 1833 (Judson); 26 March 1835 (Brainerd); 3 Jan. 1839 (Wilberforce); 17 Nov. 1821 and 7 Dec. 1821 (Fuller); and 22 Jan. 1822 and 23 Dec. 1826 (Pearce).

88 Casper, *Constructing American Lives*.

89 ECW Manning Diary, 25 March 1835.

90 Ibid., 20 April 1818.

91 Ibid., 6 Dec. 1821.

92 See Barker-Benfield, *Culture of Sensibility*; and Todd, *Sensibility*. Stokes, *Altar at Home*, and Van Engen, *Sympathetic Puritans*, assess literary scholarship on sentimental novels in relation to religious history. The canonical text for the sympathetic underpinnings of eighteenth-century moral philosophy is Smith's *The Theory of Moral Sentiments*, which begins by describing sympathy: "By the imagination we place ourselves in his situation, we conceive ourselves enduring all the same torments, we enter as it were into his body and become in some measure the same person with him" (13–14).

93 Barnes, *States of Sympathy*, 2. The same theme is also present in the period's hymnody, as in this verse from John Fawcett's "Blest Be the Tie That Binds" (1782): "We share our mutual woes, // our mutual burdens bear, // and often for each other flows // the sympathizing tear." I am grateful to Derek Murray for suggesting this connection at a conference in Manchester, England.

94 Van Engen, *Sympathetic Puritans*, 172.

95 William Hill Brown published *The Power of Sympathy* in 1789; for discussion, see Davidson, *Revolution and the Word*, chapter 5.

96 *Baptist Missionary Magazine of Nova Scotia and New Brunswick*, n.s. 1 (1834), 226, as quoted in Connors and MacDonald, *National Identity in Great Britain and British North America*, 81. For more general overlaps between evangelicalism and the culture of sensibility, see the discussion of Methodism in Barker-Benfield, *Culture of Sensibility*, 266–79; and Gibson, "Sarah Siddons, Sensibility and Enthusiastic Devotion."

97 ECW Manning Diary, 7 Dec. 1821.

98 Ibid., 30 March 1835. At other times Manning worried that his reading was not feelingly sensible *enough*: "I think there is nothing in any publications that interests my feelings"; Ibid., 15 Jan. 1825.

99 Darnton, "Readers Respond to Rousseau: The Fabrication of Romantic Sensitivity," in *Great Cat Massacre*, 243–4; Wittman, "Was There a Reading Revolution?"; and Melton, *Rise of the Public in Enlightenment Europe*, 110–19. For general worries about sentimental fiction, see Davidson, *Revolution and the Word*, 110–20. For specifically evangelical critiques of novels (even as others employed sentimental forms for religious ends), see Brown, *Word in the World*, 95–105; and Altick, *The English Common Reader*, 108–24.

100 ECW Manning Diary, 25 March 1835.

101 Ibid., 17 March 1835.

102 On deathbed piety and religious reading, see Schultz, "Holy Lives and Happy Deaths"; and on the agency afforded dying lay people, Seeman, "She Died Like Good Old Jacob."

103 ECW Manning Diary, 20 Nov. 1819.

104 Theophilus, "Importance of Actual Preparation for Death," 122.

105 Ibid., 121, 122.

106 ECW Manning Diary, 19 Nov. 1819.

107 Ibid., 22 Feb. 1820.

108 Reddy, *Navigation of Feeling*.

109 ECW Manning Diary, 27 Jan. 1820.

110 Ibid., 4 March 1820.

111 Ibid., 19 Feb. 1820. On the influence of this memoir, which Manning read often, see Cayton, "Canonizing Harriet Newell," and Moreshead, "Beyond All Ambitious Motives."

112 ECW Manning Diary, 25 Jan. 1820. Pearce's memoir was written by Andrew Fuller. Manning also found comfort and an emotional exemplar in the biography of Fuller himself.

113 For the phrase "imperial emotions," see Haggis and Allen, "Imperial Emotions."

114 ECW Manning Diary, 17 Jan. 1825.

115 Ibid., 3 Jan. 1828.

116 Thorne, "Religion and Empire at Home," 146.

117 Ibid., 154, 144. See also Thorne, "Congregational Missions and the Making of an English Middle Class"; and Elbourne, *Blood Ground*, 14. On the long history of reading missionary life-writing, see Friedrich, "On Reading Missionary Correspondence."

118 Anderson, *Imagined Communities*.

119   ECW Manning Diary, 20 Dec. 1826.
120   On sympathy and humanitarianism, see Smith, *Theory of Moral Sentiments*; Stevens, *Poor Indians*; Fiering, "Irresistible Compassion"; Ballantyne, *Entanglements of Empire*, chapter 6; Halttunen, "Humanitarianism and the Pornography of Pain." On the limits and contradictions of such sentiment in actually enacting humanitarianism, especially abolition, see Brown, *Moral Capital*, chapter 1.
121   Stevens, *Poor Indians*, especially 7–22. Also see Said, *Orientalism*; Haggis and Allen, "Imperial Emotions."
122   ECW Manning Diary, 10 Nov. 1838.
123   Stevens, *Poor Indians*, 7–8.
124   ECW Manning Diary, 3 Oct. 1834.
125   See Stevens, *Poor Indians*, 14. For the role of print to mediate a distinctive version of provincial British identity, see Eamon, *Imprinting Britain*; and Connors and MacDonald, *National Identity*. Also see Carey, *God's Empire*; and Christie, "Introduction: Theorizing a Colonial Past."
126   Darnton, "Readers Respond," 242. See also Vincent-Buffault, *History of Tears*, 10–14.

CONCLUSION

1   Boddice, *A History of Feelings*, 15. See Bourke, "Fear and Anxiety," 124.
2   See Heyd, *Be Sober and Reasonable*; Dixon, *From Passions to Emotions*; and Mee, *Romanticism, Enthusiasm, and Regulation*.
3   See Westfall, *Two Worlds*; Webb, *Transatlantic Methodists*; and Bebbington, *Dominance of Evangelicalism*, and *Victorian Religious Revivals*.
4   Most recently, Tillman, *Stripped and Script*.
5   On the "Long Age of Sensibility," see Gibson, "Sarah Siddons, Sensibility and Enthusiastic Devotion," 194 (and the scholarly literature referenced there).
6   For discussions of loyalism beyond the revolutionary period, see Errington, *The Lion, the Eagle, and Upper Canada*, and "Loyalists and Loyalism"; Knowles, *Inventing the Loyalists*; Morgan, *Public Men and Virtuous Women*, 23–55; O'Gorman, "English Loyalism Revisited"; Ducharme, *Idea of Liberty*; Malcom, "Loyal Orangemen and Republican Nativists"; Blackstock, "Papineau-O'Connell Instruments"; and the essays in Blackstock and O'Gorman, eds, *Loyalism and the Formation of the British World*.
7   Inglis, *Steadfastness in Religion and Loyalty*, 18.

8 Adamson, "God's Continent Divided."

9 Carté [Engel], "Connecting Protestants" and *Religion and the American Revolution*; and McKim, "Anxious Anglicans, Complicated Catholics, and Disruptive Dissenters." On the interaction between polity and evangelicalism, see the comparison of eighteenth-century New England and Nova Scotia in Mancke, *Fault Lines*, 109–38.

10 Carté, *Religion and the American Revolution*, including the perceptive reading of Inglis's rhetoric after the Revolution in provincial and imperial contexts, at 359–62.

11 Alline, sermon at Liverpool, NS, 21 Nov. 1782, in Rawlyk, ed., *Sermons*, 94–5. See Stewart and Rawlyk, *People Highly Favoured*; and McKim, "Anxious Anglicans, Complicated Catholics, and Disruptive Dissenters," 65.

Bibliography

MANUSCRIPT SOURCES

Annapolis Heritage Society, Annapolis Royal, NS
   Jacob Bailey Fonds
Archives of the Episcopal Church, Austin, TX
   Samuel Peters Papers, Hawks Collection
Esther Clark Wright Archives (ECW), Acadia University, Wolfville, NS
   Chipman Family Fonds
   Edward Manning Collection
   First Cornwallis Baptist Church (Upper Canard, Kings Co.), Records
   Horton-Cornwallis New Light Church Records
   Jacob Bailey Sermon notebook [n.d.]
   Thomas Bennett accession, "New Light letters and spiritual songs"
Loyalist Collection, University of New Brunswick, Fredericton, NB
   Jacob Bailey Collection (microfilm; originals held at the Nova Scotia
   Archives)
Newport Historical Society, Newport, RI
   First Congregational Church Book, nos 832, 833, and 836D
   Second Congregational Church Book, nos 838 and 838B
Nova Scotia Archives, Halifax, NS
   Chipman Family Fonds
   Hugh Graham Fonds

PRINT SOURCES

Abzug, Robert H. *Cosmos Crumbling: American Reform and the
   Religious Imagination.* Oxford: Oxford University Press, 1994.

Acheson, T.W. "Evangelicals and Public Life in Southern New Brunswick,
　1830–1880." In *Religion and Public Life in Canada: Historical and
　Contemporary Perspectives*, edited by Marguerite Van Die, 50–68.
　Toronto: University of Toronto Press, 2001.
Adams, John. *The Works of John Adams*. Edited by Charles Francis
　Adams. Vol. 10. New York: AMS Press, 1971.
Adamson, Christopher. "God's Continent Divided: Politics and Religion in
　Upper Canada and the Northern and Western United States, 1775 to
　1841." *Comparative Studies in Society and History* 36, no. 3 (1994):
　417–46.
Adelman, Joseph M. *Revolutionary Networks: The Business and Politics
　of Printing the News, 1763–1789*. Baltimore: Johns Hopkins University
　Press, 2019.
Ahmed, Sara. *The Cultural Politics of Emotion*. 2nd ed. Edinburgh:
　Edinburgh University Press, 2014.
Allan, David. *Commonplace Books and Reading in Georgian England*.
　Cambridge: Cambridge University Press, 2010.
Allen, Charles Edwin. *Rev. Jacob Bailey: His Character and Works*.
　Wiscasset, ME: Lincoln County Historical Society, 1895.
Alline, Henry. *A Court for the Trial of Anti-Traditionist*. Halifax, NS:
　A. Henry, [1783].
– *Hymns and Spiritual Songs*, 3rd ed. Dover, NH: Samuel Bragg, June, 1797.
– *Hymns and Spiritual Songs*. Edited by J.M. Bumstead. Sackville, NB:
　Ralph Pickard Bell Library, 1987.
– *The Journal of Henry Alline*. Edited by James Beverley and Barry
　Moody. Hantsport, NS: Lancelot Press, 1982.
– *The Life and Journal of the Rev. Mr. Henry Alline*. Boston: Gilbert &
　Dean, 1806.
– *A Sermon on a Day of Thanksgiving Preached at Liverpool: on the 21st,
　of November 1782*. Halifax, NS: Anthony Henry, 1782.
– *A Sermon Preached to, and at the Request of, a Religious Society of
　Young Men … in Liverpool on the 19th November 1782*. Halifax, NS:
　A. Henry, 1783.
– *A Sermon Preached on the 19th of Feb. 1783 at Port-Midway*. Halifax,
　NS: A. Henry, [1783].
–*Two Mites on Some of the Most Important and Much Disputed Points of
　Divinity*. Halifax, NS: A. Henry, 1781.
Altick, Richard D. *The English Common Reader: A Social History of the
　Mass Reading Public, 1800–1900*. Columbus: Ohio State University
　Press, 1998.

Ames, Nathaniel. *An astronomical diary: or, almanack for the year of our Lord Christ, 1756.* Portsmouth, NH: D. Fowle, 1755.

– *An astronomical diary: or, almanack for the year of our Lord Christ, 1762.* Portsmouth, NH: D. Fowle, 1761.

Amory, Hugh, and David D. Hall, eds. *The Colonial Book in the Atlantic World.* Vol. 1 of *A History of the Book in America.* Chapel Hill: University of North Carolina Press/The American Antiquarian Society, 2007.

Anderson, Benedict. *Imagined Communities: Reflections on the Origin and Spread of Nationalism.* Rev. ed. London: Verso, 2006.

Anderson, Fred. *Crucible of War: The Seven Years' War and the Fate of Empire in British North America, 1754–1766.* New York: Vintage Books, 2000.

Anderson, Misty G. *Imagining Methodism in Eighteenth-Century Britain: Enthusiasm, Belief, and the Borders of the Self.* Baltimore: Johns Hopkins University Press, 2012.

Andress, David. "Navigating Feelings in the French Revolution." *Age of Revolutions* blog. 1 Feb. 2016. https://ageofrevolutions. com/2016/02/01/navigating-feelings-in-the-french-revolution/

Andrews, Dee. *The Methodists and Revolutionary America, 1760–1800: The Shaping of an Evangelical Culture.* Princeton: Princeton University Press, 2000.

Appleby, Joyce. *Liberalism and Republicanism in the Historical Imagination.* Cambridge: Harvard University Press, 1992.

–"Republicanism and Ideology." *American Quarterly* 37, no. 4 (1985): 461–73.

Armitage, David. "Three Concepts of Atlantic History." In *The British Atlantic World, 1500–1800,* edited by Michael J. Braddick and David Armitage, 13–29. Houndmills, Hampshire, UK: Palgrave Macmillan, 2009.

Armitage, David, and Michael J. Braddick, eds. *The British Atlantic World, 1500–1800.* Houndmills, Hampshire, UK: Palgrave Macmillan, 2002.

Armstrong, Maurice W. *The Great Awakening in Nova Scotia, 1776–1809.* Hartford, CT: American Society of Church History, 1948.

– "Jonathan Scott's 'Brief View.'" *Harvard Theological Review* 40, no. 2 (1947): 121–36.

–"Neutrality and Religion in Revolutionary Nova Scotia." *New England Quarterly* 19, no. 1 (1946): 50–62.

Astell, Ann. *The Song of Songs in the Middle Ages.* Ithaca, NY: Cornell University Press, 1990.

Bailey, Jacob. "Observations and conjectures on the antiquities of
    America." Collections of the Massachusetts Historical Society, 1st series,
    4 (1795): 100–5.
Bailyn, Bernard. *The Ideological Origins of the American Revolution.* Rev.
    ed. Cambridge: Belknap Press, 1992.
–*The Ordeal of Thomas Hutchinson.* Cambridge: Belknap Press, 1974.
Baker, Emerson W., and John G. Reid. *The New England Knight: Sir
    William Phips, 1651–1695.* Toronto: University of Toronto Press, 1998.
Balik, Shelby M. *Rally the Scattered Believers: Northern New England's
    Religious Geography.* Bloomington: Indiana University Press, 2014.
Ballantyne, Tony. *Entanglements of Empire: Missionaries, Māori, and the
    Question of the Body.* Durham: Duke University Press, 2014.
Banks, Charles Edward. *The History of Martha's Vineyard, Dukes County,
    Massachusetts.* 3 vols. Boston: George H. Dean, 1911.
Bannister, Jerry. "Canada as Counter-Revolution: The Loyalist Order
    Framework in Canadian History, 1750–1840." In *Liberalism and
    Hegemony: Debating the Canadian Liberal Revolution,* edited by
    Michel Ducharme and Jean-François Constant, 98–146. Toronto:
    University of Toronto Press, 2009.
– "Liberty, Loyalty, and Sentiment in Canada's Founding Debates,
    1864–1873." In *Violence, Order, and Unrest: A History of British North
    America, 1749–1876,* edited by Elizabeth Mancke, Jerry Bannister,
    Denis McKim, and Scott See, 78–92. Toronto: University of Toronto
    Press, 2019.
– "Planter Studies and Atlantic Scholarship: The New History of
    18th-Century Nova Scotia." In *The Nova Scotia Planters in the Atlantic
    World,* edited by T. Stephen Henderson and Wendy G. Robicheau,
    21–35. Fredericton, NB: Acadiensis Press, 2012.
Bannister, Jerry, and Liam Riordan. "Loyalism and the British Atlantic,
    1660–1840." In Bannister and Riordan, *The Loyal Atlantic,* 3–36.
– eds. *The Loyal Atlantic: Remaking the British Atlantic in the
    Revolutionary Era.* Toronto: University of Toronto Press, 2012.
Bannister, Julia. *Masculinity, Militarism and Eighteenth-Century Culture,
    1689–1815.* Cambridge: Cambridge University Press, 2018.
Baptist Missionary Magazine of Nova Scotia and New Brunswick, 1834.
Barker-Benfield, G.J. *The Culture of Sensibility: Sex and Society in
    Eighteenth-Century Britain.* Chicago: University of Chicago Press, 1992.
Barnard, Stuart W. "Religious Print Culture and the British and Foreign
    Bible Society in Canada, 1820–1904." PhD diss., University of Calgary,
    2016.

Barnes, Elizabeth. *States of Sympathy: Seduction and Democracy in the American Novel*. New York: Columbia University Press, 1997.

Barry, Sandra Lynn. "'Shades of Vice and Moral Glory': The Temperance Movement in Nova Scotia, 1828–1848." MA Thesis, University of New Brunswick, 1987.

Bartlet, William S. *The Frontier Missionary: A Memoir of the Life of the Rev. Jacob Bailey*. Boston: Ide and Dutton, 1853.

Bartlett, John Russell, ed. *Records of the Colony of Rhode Island and Providence Plantations, in New England*. Vol. 6, 1757–1769. Providence, RI: Knowles, Anthony & Co., 1861.

Baxter, James Phinney, ed. *Documentary History of the State of Maine*. Vol. 14, *Collections of the Maine Historical Society*, Second Series. Portland: Lefavor-Tower/Maine Historical Society, 1910.

Baxter, Richard. *The Saints Everlasting Rest: Or, A Treatise of the Blessed State of the Saints in their Enjoyment of Heaven*. Abridged by Benjamin Fawcett. Salop, Shropshire, UK: J. Cotton and J. Eddowes, 1759.

Beal, Peter. "Notions in Garrison: The Seventeenth-Century Commonplace Book." In *New Ways of Looking at Old Texts: Papers of the Renaissance English Text Society, 1985–1991*, edited by W. Speed Hill, 131–47. Binghampton: Medieval and Renaissance Texts and Studies, 1993.

Bebbington, David W. *The Dominance of Evangelicalism: The Age of Spurgeon and Moody*. A History of Evangelicalism: People, Movements, and Ideas in the English-Speaking World. Downers Grove: InterVarsity Press, 2005.

–*Evangelicalism in Modern Britain: A History from the 1730s to the 1980s*. Grand Rapids, MI: Baker, 1992.

–*Victorian Religious Revivals: Culture and Piety in Local and Global Contexts*. Oxford: Oxford University Press, 2012.

Beck, J. Murray. "Howe, John," In *Dictionary of Canadian Biography*. Vol. 6. Toronto/Laval: University of Toronto/Université Laval, 2003–, accessed 16 March 2017, http://www.biographi.ca/en/bio/howe_john_6E.html.

Beecher, Lyman. *Six Sermons on the Nature, Occasions, Signs, Evils, and Remedy of Intemperance*. Boston: Crocker & Brewster, 1827.

Bell, David G. "The Allinite Tradition and the New Brunswick Free Christian Baptists, 1830–1875." In *An Abiding Conviction: Maritime Baptists and Their World*, edited by Robert S. Wilson, 55–82. Hantsport, NS: Lancelot Press, 1988.

–"All Things New: The Transformation of Maritime Baptist

Historiography." *Nova Scotia Historical Review* 4, no. 2 (1984): 69–81.
– "Allowed Irregularities: Women Preachers in the Early 19th-Century
   Maritimes." *Acadiensis* 30, no. 2 (2001): 3–39.
– "The Death of Henry Alline: Some Contemporary Reactions." *Nova
   Scotia Historical Review* 4, no. 2 (1984): 7–12.
– *Henry Alline and Maritime Religion.* Ottawa: Canadian Historical
   Association, 1993.
– *Loyalist Rebellion in New Brunswick: A Defining Conflict for Canada's
   Political Culture.* Halifax, NS: Formac, 2013.
– ed. *Newlight Baptist Journals of James Manning and James Innis.*
   Hantsport, NS: Lancelot Press, 1984.
– "Yankee Preachers and the Struggle for the New Brunswick Christian
   Conference, 1828–38." In *Revivals, Baptists, and George Rawlyk*,
   edited by Daniel C. Goodwin, 93–112. Wolfville, NS: Acadia Divinity
   College, 2000.
Bell, James B. *The Imperial Origins of the King's Church in Early
   America, 1607–1783.* New York: Palgrave Macmillan, 2004.
– *A War of Religion: Dissenters, Anglicans, and the American Revolution.*
   New York: Palgrave Macmillan, 2008.
Benedict, David. *A General History of the Baptist Denominations in
   America and Other Parts of the World.* 2 vols. Boston: Lincoln and
   Edmands, 1813.
Benton, William Allen. *Whig-Loyalism: An Aspect of Political Ideology in
   the American Revolutionary Era.* Madison, NJ: Farleigh Dickinson
   University Press, 1969.
Bercovitch, Sacvan. *The Puritan Origins of the American Self.* New
   Haven: Yale University Press, 1975.
Berland, Kevin, Jan Kirsten Gilliam, and Kenneth A. Lockridge, eds.
   The Commonplace Book of William Byrd II of Westover. Chapel Hill:
   University of North Carolina Press, 2001.
Beynon, Graham. *Isaac Watts: Reason, Passion, and the Revival of
   Religion.* London: T & T Clark, 2016.
Bickerstaff's Boston Almanack For the Year of our Lord, 1768. Boston:
   John Fleming, 1767.
Bickerstaff's Boston Almanack For the Year of our Lord, 1772. Boston:
   John Fleming, 1771.
Bill, I.E. *Fifty Years with the Baptist Ministers and Churches of the
   Maritime Provinces of Canada.* Saint John, NB: Barnes and Co., 1880.
Blackstock, Allan. "'Papineau-O'Connell Instruments': Irish Loyalism and
   the Transnational Dimensions of the 1837 Rebellions in Upper and

Lower Canada." In Bannister and Riordan, eds, *The Loyal Atlantic*,
    252–76.
Blackstock, Allan, and Frank O'Gorman, eds. *Loyalism and the Formation
    of the British World, 1775–1914*. Rochester, NY: Boydell Press, 2014.
Blakeley, Phyllis R., and John N. Grant, eds. *Eleven Exiles: Accounts of
    Loyalists of the American Revolution*. Toronto: Dundurn Press, 1982.
Blecki, Catherine L., and Karin A. Wulf, eds. *Milcah Martha Moore's
    Book: A Commonplace Book from Revolutionary America*. University
    Park: Pennsylvania State University Press, 1997.
Bloch, Ruth H. "Religion, Literary Sentimentalism, and Popular
    Revolutionary Ideology." In *Religion in a Revolutionary Age*, edited by
    Ronald Hoffman and Peter J. Albert, 308–30. Charlottesville: University
    Press of Virginia, 1994.
–*Visionary Republic: Millennial Themes in American Thought, 1756–
    1800*. Cambridge: Cambridge University Press, 1985.
Blumhofer, Edith, and Mark A. Noll, eds. *Singing the Lord's Song in a
    Strange Land: Hymnody in the History of North American
    Protestantism*. Tuscaloosa: University of Alabama Press, 2004.
Boddice, Rob. *A History of Feelings*. London: Reaktion Books, 2019.
Boileau, John. *Half-Hearted Enemies: Nova Scotia, New England and the
    War of 1812*. Halifax, NS: Formac, 2005.
Bonomi, Patricia U. *Under the Cope of Heaven: Religion, Society, and
    Politics in Colonial America*. Oxford: Oxford University Press, 1995.
Bourke, Joanna. "Fear and Anxiety: Writing about Emotion in Modern
    History." *History Workshop Journal*, no. 55 (2003): 111–33.
Bowman, Matthew, and Samuel Brown. "Reverend Buck's Theological
    Dictionary and the Struggle to Define American Evangelicalism,
    1802–1851." *Journal of the Early Republic* 29, no. 3 (2009): 441–73.
Brackney, William H. *Christian Voluntarism in Britain and North
    America: A Bibliography and Critical Assessment*. Westport, CT:
    Greenwood Press, 1995.
Brannon, Rebecca, and Joseph S. Moore, eds. *The Consequences of
    Loyalism: Essays in Honor of Robert M. Calhoon*. Columbia:
    University of South Carolina Press, 2019.
Brantley, Richard E. *Locke, Wesley, and the Method of English
    Romanticism*. Gainesville: University Presses of Florida, 1984.
Braude, Ann. *Sisters and Saints: Women and American Religion*. Oxford:
    Oxford University Press, 2000.
Brebner, J.B. *The Neutral Yankees of Nova Scotia*. 1937; reprint, Toronto:
    McClelland and Stewart, 1967.

–*New England's Outpost: Acadia before the Conquest of Canada*. New
  York: Columbia University Press, 1927.
– "Nova Scotia's Remedy for the American Revolution." *Canadian
  Historical Review* 15, no. 2 (1934): 171–80.
Breen, T.H. "An Empire of Goods: The Anglicization of Colonial America,
  1690–1776." *Journal of British Studies* 25, no. 4 (1986): 467–99.
– *The Marketplace of Revolution: How Consumer Politics Shaped
  American Independence*. Oxford: Oxford University Press, 2005.
Brekus, Catherine A. *The Religious History of American Women:
  Reimagining the Past*. Chapel Hill: University of North Carolina Press,
  2007.
– "Sarah Osborn's Enlightenment: Reimagining Eighteenth-Century
  Intellectual History." In *The Religious History of American Women:
  Reimagining the Past*, edited by Catherine A. Brekus, 108–41. Chapel
  Hill: University of North Carolina Press, 2007.
– *Sarah Osborn's World: The Rise of Evangelical Christianity in Early
  America*. New Haven: Yale University Press, 2013.
Bremer, Francis J. *The Puritan Experiment: New England Society from
  Bradford to Edwards*. Rev. ed. Hanover, NH: University Press of New
  England, 1995.
Briggs, Samuel, ed. *The Essays, Humor, and Poems of Nathaniel Ames,
  Father and Son: Of Dedham, Massachusetts, from their Almanacks,
  1726–1775*. Cleveland, OH: Short and Forman, 1891.
The British Chronologist. 3 vols. London: G. Kearsley, 1775.
Broomhall, Susan, ed. *Spaces for Feeling: Emotions and Sociabilities in
  Britain, 1650–1850*. New York: Routledge, 2015.
Brown, Candy Gunther. *The Word in the World: Evangelical Writing,
  Publishing, and Reading in America 1789–1880*. Chapel Hill: University
  of North Carolina Press, 2004.
Brown, Christopher L. *Moral Capital: Foundations of British
  Abolitionism*. Chapel Hill: University of North Carolina Press, 2006.
Brown, Matthew P. *The Pilgrim and the Bee: Reading Rituals and Book
  Culture in Early New England*. Philadelphia: University of Pennsylvania
  Press, 2007.
Brown, Richard D. "Microhistory and the Post-Modern Challenge."
  Journal of the Early Republic 23, no. 1 (2003): 1–20.
Brown, Wallace. *The King's Friends: The Composition and Motives of the
  American Loyalist Claimants*. Providence, RI: Brown University Press,
  1965.

Brumberg, Joan Jacobs. *Mission for Life: The Judson Family and American Evangelical Culture*. New York: New York University Press, 1984.

Buck, Charles. *A Theological Dictionary, Containing Definitions of All Religious Terms*. 2 vols. Philadelphia: W.W. Woodward, 1818.

– *A Treatise on Religious Experience*. In *The Works of the Rev. Charles Buck*, Vol. 3. Philadelphia: W.W. Woodward, 1822.

Bullock, Steven C. *Tea Sets and Tyranny: The Politics of Politeness in Early America*. Philadelphia: University of Pennsylvania Press, 2017.

Bumsted, J.M. "Alline, Henry," in *Dictionary of Canadian Biography*. Vol. 4. Toronto/Laval: University of Toronto/Université Laval, 2003–, accessed 19 May 2017, http://www.biographi.ca/en/bio/alline_henry_4E.html.

– "Emotion in Colonial America: Some Relations of Conversion Experience in Freetown, Massachusetts, 1749–1770." *New England Quarterly* 49, no. 1 (1976): 97–108.

– "Harding, Harris." In *Dictionary of Canadian Biography*. Vol. 8. Toronto/Laval: University of Toronto/Université Laval, 2003–, accessed 15 May 2017, http://www.biographi.ca/en/bio/harding_harris_8E.html.

–*Henry Alline*. Toronto: University of Toronto Press, 1971.

– *Understanding the Loyalists*. Sackville, NB: Centre for Canadian Studies, Mount Allison University, 1986.

Burke, Peter. *Popular Culture in Early Modern Europe*. 3rd ed. Farnham, Surrey, UK: Ashgate, 2009.

Burke, Victoria E. "Recent Studies in Commonplace Books." *English Literary Renaissance* 43 (2013): 153–77.

Burnett, Frederick C. "Henry Alline's 'Articles & Covenant of a Gospel Church.'" *Nova Scotia Historical Review* 4, no. 2 (1984): 13–24.

Burstein, Andrew. "The Political Character of Sympathy." *Journal of the Early Republic* 21, no. 4 (2001): 601–32.

–*Sentimental Democracy: The Evolution of America's Romantic Self-Image*. New York: Hill and Wang, 1999.

Bushman, Richard L. *From Puritan to Yankee: Character and the Social Order in Connecticut, 1690–1765*. New York: W.W. Norton & Company, 1970.

– *King and People in Provincial Massachusetts*. Chapel Hill: University of North Carolina Press, 1985.

– *The Refinement of America: Persons, Houses, Cities*. New York: Alfred A. Knopf, 1992.

Butler, Jon. *Becoming America: The Revolution before 1776*. Cambridge: Harvard University Press, 2000.

–"Enthusiasm Described and Decried: The Great Awakening as Interpretative Fiction." *Journal of American History* 69, no. 2 (1982): 305–25.

Butler, Samuel. *Hudibras*. Edited by John Wilders. Oxford: Oxford University Press, 1967.

Calhoon, Robert M. "The Loyalist Perception." In *Tory Insurgents: The Loyalist Perception and Other Essays*, Robert M. Calhoon, Timothy M. Barnes, and Robert S. Davis, 3–14. Rev. ed. Columbia: University of South Carolina Press, 2010.

–*The Loyalists in Revolutionary America, 1760–1781*. New York: Harcourt Brace Jovanovich, 1965.

– *Political Moderation in America's First Two Centuries*. Cambridge: Cambridge University Press, 2009.

Calhoon, Robert M., Timothy M. Barnes, and Robert S. Davis. *Tory Insurgents: The Loyalist Perception and Other Essays*. Rev. ed. Columbia: University of South Carolina Press, 2010.

Calhoon, Robert M., and Ruma Chopra. "Religion and the Loyalists." In *Faith and the Founders of the American Republic*, edited by Daniel Dreisbach and Mark David Hall, 161–19. Oxford: Oxford University Press, 2014.

Cambers, Andrew. "Reading, the Godly, and Self-Writing in England, Circa 1580–1720." *Journal of British Studies* 46, no. 4 (2007): 796–825.

Campbell, Carol, and James F. Smith. *Necessaries and Sufficiencies: Planter Society in Londonderry, Onslow and Truro Townships, 1761–1780*. Sydney, NS: Cape Breton University Press, 2011.

Candow, James E. "Graham, Hugh." In *Dictionary of Canadian Biography*. Vol. 6. Toronto/Laval: University of Toronto/Université Laval, 2003, accessed 6 May 2017, http://www.biographi.ca/en/bio/graham_hugh_1758_1829_6E.html.

Canny, Nicholas, and Anthony Pagden, eds. *Colonial Identity in the Atlantic World, 1500–1800*. Princeton: Princeton University Press, 1987.

Capp, Bernard. *English Almanacs, 1500–1800: Astrology and the Popular Press*. Ithaca, NY: Cornell University Press, 1979.

– "'Jesus Wept' but Did the Englishman? Masculinity and Emotion in Early Modern England." *Past and Present* 224, no. 1 (2014): 75–108.

Carey, Hilary M. *God's Empire: Religion and Colonialism in the British World, c.1801–1908*. Cambridge: Cambridge University Press, 2011.

[Carlisle Commission], *Manifesto and proclamation: To the members of the Congress, the members of the general assemblies or conventions of the several colonies ... and all others, free inhabitants of the said colonies*. New York: James Rivington, 1778.

Carlson, C. Lennart. *The First Magazine: A History of the Gentleman's Magazine*. Reprint. Westport, CT: Greenwood Press, 1974.

Carté, Katherine. *Religion and the American Revolution: An Imperial History*. Chapel Hill: Omohundro Institute of Early American History and Culture/University of North Carolina Press, 2021.

Carter, Philip. "Tears and the Man." In *Women, Gender and Enlightenment*, edited by Sarah Knott and Barbara Taylor, 156–73. Houndsmills, Basingstoke, Hampshire, UK: Palgrave Macmillan, 2005.

Carter, William Howard. "Anglicizing the League: The Writing of Cadwallader Colden's *History of the Five Indian Nations*." In *Anglicizing America: Empire, Revolution, Republic*, edited by Ignacio Gallup-Diaz, Andrew Shankman, and David J. Silverman, 83–108. Philadelphia: University of Pennsylvania Press, 2015.

Casper, Scott E. *Constructing American Lives: Biography and Culture in Nineteenth-Century America*. Chapel Hill: University of North Carolina Press, 1999.

Cayton, Mary Kupiec. "Canonizing Harriet Newell: Women, the Evangelical Press, and the Foreign Mission Movement in New England, 1800–1840." In *Competing Kingdoms: Women, Mission, Nation, and the American Protestant Empire, 1812–1960*, edited by Barbara Reeves-Ellington, Kathryn Kish Sklar, and Connie Anne Shemo, 69–93. Durham: Duke University Press, 2010.

— "The Expanding World of Jacob Norton: Reading, Revivalism, and the Construction of a 'Second Great Awakening' in New England, 1787–1804." *Journal of the Early Republic* 26, no. 2 (Summer 2006): 221–48.

Charlevoix, P. *An Account of the French Settlements in North America*. Boston: Rogers and Fowle, 1747.

Chauncy, Charles. *Seasonable Thoughts on the State of Religion in New-England*. Boston: Rogers and Fowle, 1743.

Cheng, Eileen. "On the Margins: The Mediating Function of Footnotes in Thomas Hutchinson's *History of Massachusetts-Bay*." *Early American Studies* 11, no. 1 (2013): 98–116.

– *Plain and Noble Garb of Truth: Nationalism and Impartiality in*

American Historical Writing, 1784–1860. Athens: University of Georgia Press, 2011.

Chipman, Bert Lee. *The Chipman Family: A Genealogy of the Chipmans in America, 1631–1920*. Winston-Salem, NC: Bert L. Chipman, 1920.

Chipman, J.H. *A Chipman Genealogy, ca. 1583–1969*. Boston: Blanchard Press, 1970.

Choi, Peter Y. *George Whitefield: Evangelist for God and Empire*. Grand Rapids, MI: Eerdmans, 2018.

Chopra, Ruma. "Enduring Patterns of Loyalist Study: Definitions and Contours." *History Compass* 11, no. 11 (2013): 983–93.

– "Postwar Loyalist Hopes: To Be 'Parts and Not Dependencies of the Empire.'" In *The Consequences of Loyalism: Essays in Honor of Robert M. Calhoon*, edited by Rebecca Brannon and Joseph S. Moore, 228–43. Columbia: University of South Carolina Press, 2019.

– *Unnatural Rebellion: Loyalists in New York City during the Revolution*. Charlottesville: University of Virginia Press, 2011.

Christie, Nancy. "'In These Times of Democratic Rage and Delusion': Popular Religion and the Challenge to the Established Order, 1760–1815." In *The Canadian Protestant Experience, 1760–1990*, edited by George A. Rawlyk, 9–47. Montreal & Kingston: McGill-Queen's University Press, 1990.

– ed. *Transatlantic Subjects: Ideas, Institutions, and Social Experience in Post-Revolutionary British North America*. Montreal & Kingston: McGill-Queen's University Press, 2008.

Christie, Nancy, and Michael Gauvreau. *Christian Churches and Their Peoples, 1840–1965: A Social History of Religion in Canada*. Toronto: University of Toronto Press, 2010.

The Chronological Remembrancer. Dublin: James Hoey, 1750.

Chun, Chris. *The Legacy of Jonathan Edwards in the Theology of Andrew Fuller*. Leiden: Brill, 2012.

Clark, Charles E. "Early American Journalism: News and Opinion in the Popular Press." In *The Colonial Book in the Atlantic World*, edited by Hugh Amory and David D. Hall, 347–65. A History of the Book in America 1. Chapel Hill: University of North Carolina Press & The American Antiquarian Society, 2007.

Clark, Charles E., James S. Leamon, and Karen Bowden, eds. *Maine in the Early Republic: From Revolution to Statehood*. Hanover, NH: University Press of New England, 1988.

Clarke, Ernest. *The Siege of Fort Cumberland, 1776: An Episode in the*

American Revolution. Montreal & Kingston: McGill-Queen's University Press, 1995.

Clark, Peter. *British Clubs and Societies, 1580–1800: The Origins of an Associational World*. Oxford: Clarendon Press, 2000.

Clark, S.D. *Church and Sect in Canada*. Toronto: University of Toronto Press, 1948.

Claydon, Tony, and Ian McBride. "The Trials of the Chosen Peoples: Recent Interpretations of Protestantism and National Identity in Britain and Ireland." In *Protestantism and National Identity: Britain and Ireland, c. 1650–c. 1850*, edited by Tony Claydon and Ian McBride, 3–31. Cambridge: Cambridge University Press, 1998.

Clement, Jennifer. *Reading Humility in Early Modern England*. Farnham, Surrey, UK: Ashgate, 2015.

Cleves, Rachel Hope, Nicole Eustace, and Paul Gilje. "Interchange: The War of 1812." *Journal of American History* 99, no. 2 (2012): 520–55.

Coffey, John. "Puritanism, Evangelicalism and the Evangelical Protestant Tradition." In *The Emergence of Evangelicalism: Exploring Historical Continuities*, edited by Michael A.G. Haykin and Kenneth J. Stewart, 252–77. Nottingham: Apollos, 2008.

– "Between Puritanism and Evangelicalism: 'Heart-Work' in Dissenting Communion Hymns, 1693–1709." In *Heart Religion: Evangelical Piety in England and Ireland, 1690–1850*, edited by John Coffey, 29–49. Oxford: Oxford University Press, 2016.

– ed. *Heart Religion: Evangelical Piety in England and Ireland, 1690–1850*. Oxford: Oxford University Press, 2016.

Cohen, Charles Lloyd. *God's Caress: The Psychology of Puritan Religious Experience*. New York: Oxford University Press, 1989.

Cohen, Lester H. *The Revolutionary Histories: Contemporary Narratives of the American Revolution*. Ithaca, NY: Cornell University Press, 1980.

Colbourn, H. Trevor. *The Lamp of Experience: Whig History and the Intellectual Origins of the American Revolution*. Chapel Hill: University of North Carolina Press, 1965.

Colclough, Stephen. "Recovering the Reader: Commonplace Books and Diaries as Sources of Reading Experience." *Publishing History* 44 (1998): 5–37.

Colden, Cadwallader. *The History of the Five Indian Nations of Canada, which are dependent on the Province of New-York in America, and are the barrier between the English and French in that part of the world*, 2nd ed. London: T. Osborne, 1747.

Colley, Linda. *Britons: Forging the Nation, 1707–1837.* 2nd ed. New
    Haven: Nota Bene/Yale University Press, 2005.
Compeau, Timothy J. "Dishonoured Americans: Loyalist Manhood and
    Political Death in Revolutionary America Revolutionary America." PhD
    diss. University of Western Ontario, 2015.
Condon, Ann Gorman. *The Loyalist Dream for New Brunswick: The
    Envy of the American States.* Fredericton, NB: New Ireland Press, 1984.
Connolly, William. "Critical Response I: The Complexity of Intention."
    Critical Inquiry 37, no. 4 (2011): 791–8.
Connors, Linda E., and Mary Lu MacDonald. *National Identity in Great
    Britain and British North America, 1815–1851: The Role of
    Nineteenth-Century Periodicals.* Farnham, Surrey, UK: Ashgate, 2011.
Conrad, Margaret, ed. *Intimate Relations: Family and Community in
    Planter Nova Scotia, 1759–1800.* Fredericton, NB: Acadiensis Press, 1995.
– ed. *Making Adjustments: Change and Continuity in Planter Nova Scotia,
    1759–1800.* Fredericton, NB: Acadiensis Press, 1991.
– ed. *They Planted Well: New England Planters in Maritime Canada.*
    Fredericton, NB: Acadiensis Press, 1988.
Conrad, Margaret, and Barry Moody, eds. *Planter Links: Community and
    Culture in Colonial Nova Scotia.* Fredericton, NB: Acadiensis Press,
    2001.
Coolidge, Olivia E. *Colonial Entrepreneur: Silvester Gardiner and the
    Settlement of the Kennebec River Valley.* Thomaston, ME: Tilbury
    House, 1999.
Coops, P.L., and D.J. Hessler. "George Alexander Rawlyk: A Bibliography,
    1962–1996." *Acadiensis* 25, no. 2 (1996): 159–73.
Corrigan, John. *Business of the Heart: Religion and Emotion in the
    Nineteenth Century.* Berkeley: University of California Press, 2002.
– *Emptiness: Feeling Christian in America.* Chicago: University of Chicago
    Press, 2015.
– "'Habits from the Heart': The American Enlightenment and Religious
    Ideas about Emotion and Habit." *Journal of Religion* 73, no. 2 (1993):
    183–99.
–*The Hidden Balance: Religion and the Social Theories of Charles
    Chauncy and Jonathan Mayhew.* Cambridge: Cambridge University
    Press, 1987.
– *The Prism of Piety: Catholick Congregational Clergy at the Beginning of
    the Enlightenment.* Oxford: Oxford University Press, 1991.
– ed. *The Oxford Handbook of Religion and Emotion.* Oxford: Oxford
    University Press, 2008.

– ed. *Religion and Emotion: Approaches and Interpretations*. Oxford: Oxford University Press, 2004.

Corrigan, John, Eric Crump, and John M. Kloos, eds. *Emotion and Religion: A Critical Assessment and Annotated Bibliography*. Westport, CT: Greenwood Press, 2000.

Crawford, Michael J. *Seasons of Grace: Colonial New England's Revival Tradition in Its British Context*. New York: Oxford University Press, 1991.

Cressy, David. *Bonfires and Bells: National Memory and the Protestant Calendar in Elizabethan and Stuart England*. London: Weidenfeld and Nicolson, 1989.

Cummings, Brian, and Freya Sierhuis, eds. *Passions and Subjectivity in Early Modern Culture*. Farnham, Surrey, UK: Ashgate, 2013.

Cunha, Emma Salgård. "Whitefield and Literary Affect." In *George Whitefield: Life, Context, and Legacy*, edited by Geordan Hammond and David Ceri Jones, 190–206. Oxford: Oxford University Press, 2016.

Currie, A.W. "Some Eighteenth-Century Observations on Nova Scotia." *Dalhousie Review* 47, no. 4 (Winter 1967): 567–76.

Cuthbertson, Brian C. *The First Bishop: A Biography of Charles Inglis*. Halifax, NS: Waegwoltic Press, 1987.

– ed. *The Journal of the Reverend John Payzant*. Hantsport, NS: Lancelot Press, 1981.

Dacome, Lucia. "Noting the Mind: Commonplace Books and the Pursuit of the Self in Eighteenth-Century Britain." *Journal of the History of Ideas* 65, no. 4 (2004): 603–25.

Darnton, Robert. *The Case for Books: Past, Present, and Future*. New York: Public Affairs, 2009.

– "Readers Respond to Rousseau: The Fabrication of Romantic Sensitivity." In *The Great Cat Massacre and Other Episodes in French Cultural History*, 215–56. New York: Basic Books, 1984.

Davidson, Cathy N. *Revolution and the Word: The Rise of the Novel in America*. 2nd ed. Oxford: Oxford University Press, 2004.

Davies, Gwendolyn. "Literary Cultures in the Maritime Provinces." In Fleming, Gallichan, and Lamonde, eds, *History of the Book in Canada*, vol. 1, 368–83.

– "New Brunswick Loyalist Printers in the Post-War Atlantic World: Cultural Transfer and Cultural Challenges." In Bannister and Riordan, *The Loyal Atlantic*, 128–61.

– "Persona in Planter Journals." In Conrad, *They Planted Well*, 211–17.

– *Studies in Maritime Literary History, 1760–1930*. Fredericton, NB: Acadiensis Press, 1991.

Davis, John. *The Patriarch of Western Nova Scotia: Life and Times of the Late Rev. Harris Harding, Yarmouth, N.S.* Charlottetown, PEI: W.H. Bremner, 1866.

Davison, James Doyle. *Handley Chipman: King's County Planter, 1717–1799*. Wolfville, NS: J. D. Davison, 1988.

Dawson, Taunya J. "Keeping the Loyalists Loyal in Post-Revolutionary Nova Scotia: The Preaching and Writing of Reverend Jacob Bailey." *Historical Papers: Canadian Society of Church History* (2014): 17–30.

de Montluzin, Emily Lorraine. *Daily Life in Georgian England as reported in the Gentleman's Magazine*. Lewiston, NY: Edwin Mellen Press, 2002.

Den Hartog, Jonathan J. *Patriotism and Piety: Federalist Politics and Religious Struggle in the New American Nation*. Charlottesville: University of Virginia Press, 2015.

Desserud, Donald. "Nova Scotia and the American Revolution: A Study of Neutrality and Moderation in the Eighteenth Century." In Conrad, *They Planted Well*, 89–112.

Dimock, Joseph. "Memoir of Mrs. Charlotte Boyle." *Baptist Missionary Magazine* (Jan. 1885): 1–8.

Dixon, John M. *The Enlightenment of Cadwallader Colden: Empire, Science, and Intellectual Culture in British New York*. Ithaca, NY: Cornell University Press, 2016.

Dixon, Thomas. *From Passions to Emotions: The Creation of a Secular Psychological Category*. Cambridge: Cambridge University Press, 2003.

– *Weeping Britannia: Portrait of a Nation in Tears*. Oxford: Oxford University Press, 2015.

– "Weeping in Space: Tears, Feelings, and Enthusiasm in Eighteenth-Century Britain." In *Spaces for Feeling: Emotions and Sociabilities in Britain, 1650–1850*, edited by Susan Broomhall, 137–58. New York: Routledge, 2015.

Doll, Peter M. *Revolution, Religion, and National Identity: Imperial Anglicanism in British North America, 1745–1795*. Madison, NJ: Fairleigh Dickinson University Press, 2000.

Doull, John. *A History of the Bible Society in Nova Scotia, 1813–1963*. Halifax, NS: Canadian Bible Society, 1963.

Dreyer, Frederick. "Faith and Experience in the Thought of John Wesley." *American Historical Review* 88, no. 1 (1983): 12–30.

Ducharme, Michel. *The Idea of Liberty in Canada during the Age of*

Atlantic Revolutions, 1776–1838. Translated by Peter Feldstein.
Montreal & Kingston: McGill-Queen's University Press, 2014.

Ducharme, Michel, and Jean-François Constant, eds. *Liberalism and Hegemony: Debating the Canadian Liberal Revolution.* Toronto: University of Toronto Press, 2009.

Eamon, Michael. *Imprinting Britain: Newspapers, Sociability, and the Shaping of British North America.* Montreal & Kingston: McGill-Queen's University Press, 2015.

Eaton, Arthur Wentworth Hamilton. *The History of Kings County.* 1910; reprint, Belleville, ON: Mika, 1972.

Ebersole, Gary L. "The Function of Ritual Weeping Revisited: Affective Expression and Moral Discourse." *History of Religions Journal* 39, no. 3 (2000): 211–46.

Edelberg, Cynthia Dubin. *Jonathan Odell: Loyalist Poet of the American Revolution.* Durham: Duke University Press, 1987.

Edwards, Jonathan. "A Divine and Supernatural Light." In *Sermons and Discourses, 1730–1733.* Edited by Mark Valeri, 405–26. Vol. 17 of *The Works of Jonathan Edwards.* New Haven: Yale University Press, 1999.

– *History of the Work of Redemption.* Edited by John F. Wilson. Vol. 9 of *The Works of Jonathan Edwards.* New Haven: Yale University Press, 1989.

– "Miscellany 782. Ideas. Sense of the Heart. Spiritual Knowledge or Conviction. Faith." In *The Miscellanies, 501–832.* Edited by Ava Chamberlain, 452–66. Vol. 18 of *The Works of Jonathan Edwards.* New Haven: Yale University Press, 2000.

– *Some Thoughts Concerning the Present Revival of Religion in New-England,* in *The Great Awakening.* Edited by C.C. Goen. Vol. 18 of *The Works of Jonathan Edwards.* New Haven: Yale University Press, 1972.

– *A Treatise Concerning Religious Affections.* Edited by John E. Smith. Vol. 2 of *The Works of Jonathan Edwards.* New Haven: Yale University Press, 1959.

Eger, Elizabeth. "'The Noblest Commerce of Mankind': Conversation and Community in the Bluestocking Circle." In *Women, Gender and Enlightenment,* edited by Sarah Knott and Barbara Taylor, 288–305. Houndsmills, Basingstoke, Hampshire, UK: Palgrave Macmillan, 2005.

Einhorn, Nathan R. "The Reception of the British Peace Offer of 1778." *Pennsylvania History* (1949): 190–214.

Elbourne, Elizabeth. *Blood Ground: Colonialism, Missions, and the Contest for Christianity in the Cape Colony and Britain, 1799–1853.* Montreal & Kingston: McGill-Queen's University Press, 2002.

– "A Complicated Pity: Emotion, Missions and the Conversion Narrative."
  In *Emotions and Christian Missions: Historical Perspectives*, edited by
  Claire McLisky, Daniel Midena, and Karen Vallgårda, 123–50. New
  York: Palgrave Macmillan, 2015.
Ellis, Markman. *The Politics of Sensibility: Race, Gender, and Commerce
  in the Sentimental Novel.* Cambridge: Cambridge University Press,
  1996.
Ellison, Julie. *Cato's Tears and the Making of Anglo-American Emotion.*
  Chicago: University of Chicago Press, 1999.
Engel, Katherine Carté. "Connecting Protestants in Britain's Eighteenth-
  Century Atlantic Empire." *William and Mary Quarterly* 75, no. 1
  (2018): 37–70.
–"Triangulating Religion and the American Revolution through Jedidiah
  Morse." *Common-Place: The Interactive Journal of Early American
  Life.* 15, no. 3 (2015). http://www.common-place-archives.org/vol-15/
  no-03/engel/#.WUsODxTdvNU/.
Errington, Jane. *Emigrant Worlds and Transatlantic Communities:
  Migration to Upper Canada in the First Half of the Nineteenth Century.*
  Montreal & Kingston: McGill-Queen's University Press, 2007.
– *The Lion, the Eagle, and Upper Canada: A Developing Colonial
  Ideology.* Rev. ed. Montreal & Kingston: McGill-Queen's University
  Press, 2012.
– "Loyalists and Loyalism in the American Revolution and Beyond."
  Acadiensis 41, no. 2 (2012): 164–73.
– "Webs of Affection and Obligation: Glimpse into Families and
  Nineteenth Century Transatlantic Communities." *Journal of the
  Canadian Historical Association* 19, no. 1 (2008): 1–26.
Eustace, Nicole. *1812: War and the Passions of Patriotism.* Philadelphia:
  University of Pennsylvania Press, 2012.
– "A Feeling for History." *Common-Place: The Interactive Journal of Early
  American Life* 10, no. 2 (2010). http://www.common-place-archives.
  org/vol-10/no-02/author/.
–*Passion Is the Gale: Emotion, Power, and the Coming of the American
  Revolution.* Chapel Hill: University of North Carolina Press, 2008.
– "The Theory of Civilized Sentiments: Emotion and the Creation of the
  United States." In *The World of the Revolutionary American Republic:
  Land, Labor, and the Conflict for a Continent*, edited by Andrew
  Shankman, 268–91. New York: Routledge, 2014.
Eustace, Nicole, Eugenia Lean, Julie Livingston, Jan Plamper, William M.
  Reddy, and Barbara H. Rosenwein. "AHR Conversation: The Historical

Study of Emotions." *American Historical Review* 117, no. 5 (2012): 1487–531.

Faber, Benne. "'My Stammering Tongue and Unpolished Pen': Henry Alline's Language and Literature." In *Revivals, Baptists, and George Rawlyk*, edited by Daniel C. Goodwin, 77–91. Wolfville, NS: Acadia Divinity College, 2000.

Familiar Letters, Written by Mrs. Sarah Osborn, and Miss Susanna Anthony, Late of Newport, Rhode-Island. Newport: Newport Mercury, 1807.

Fea, John. *The Bible Cause: A History of the American Bible Society*. New York: Oxford University Press, 2016.

Fergusson, C.B., ed. *The Life of Jonathan Scott*. Halifax, NS: Public Archives of Nova Scotia, 1960.

Ferry, Darren. *Uniting in Measures of Common Good: The Construction of Liberal Identities in Central Canada, 1830–1900*. Montreal & Kingston: McGill-Queen's University Press, 2008.

Fiering, Norman. "Irresistible Compassion: An Aspect of Eighteenth-Century Sympathy and Humanitarianism." *Journal of the History of Ideas* 37, no. 2 (1976): 195–218.

– *Jonathan Edwards's Moral Thought and Its British Context*. Chapel Hill: University of North Carolina Press, 1981.

– *Moral Philosophy at Seventeenth-Century Harvard: A Discipline in Transition*. Chapel Hill: University of North Carolina Press, 1981.

Fingard, Judith. *The Anglican Design in Loyalist Nova Scotia, 1783–1816*. London: SPCK, 1972.

– "'Grapes in the Wilderness': The Bible Society in British North America in the Early Nineteenth Century." *Histoire sociale/Social History* 5, no. 9 (1972): 5–31.

Flatt, Kevin. "Theological Innovation from Spiritual Experience: Henry Alline's Anti-Calvinism in Late Eighteenth-Century Nova Scotia and New England." *Journal of Religious History* 33, no. 3 (2009): 285–300.

Flavel, John. *A Treatise on Keeping the Heart*. New Brunswick, NJ: A. Blauvelt, 1801.

Fleming, James E., ed. *Passions and Emotions*, Nomos 53. New York: New York University Press, 2013.

Fleming, Patricia, Gilles Gallichan, and Yvan Lamonde, eds. *History of the Book in Canada*. Vol. 1: Beginnings to 1840. Toronto: University of Toronto Press, 2004.

Foster, Charles I. *An Errand of Mercy: The Evangelical Front, 1790–1837*. Chapel Hill: University of North Carolina Press, 1960.

Foster, Stephen. *The Long Argument: English Puritanism and the Shaping of New England Culture, 1570–1700*. Chapel Hill: University of North Carolina Press, 1991.

Franklin, Benjamin. *The Papers of Benjamin Franklin*. Vol. 9. Edited by Leonard W. Labaree, Helen C. Boatfield, Helene H. Fineman, and James H. Hutson. New Haven: Yale University Press, 1966. Online version: http://franklinpapers.yale.edu, accessed Jan. 19, 2017.

Frazer, Gregg L. *God against the Revolution: The Loyalist Clergy's Case against the American Revolution*. Lexington: University Press of Kentucky, 2018.

Frazer, Michael L. *The Enlightenment of Sympathy: Justice and Moral Sentiments in the Eighteenth Century and Today*. Oxford: Oxford University Press, 2010.

Freeman, Joanne B. *Affairs of Honor: National Politics in the New Republic*. New Haven: Yale University Press, 2002.

French, Goldwin. *Parsons and Politics: The Role of the Wesleyan Methodists in Upper Canada and the Maritimes from 1780–1855*. Toronto: Ryerson Press, 1962.

Frevert, Ute, ed. *Emotional Lexicons: Continuity and Change in the Vocabulary of Feeling, 1700–2000*. Oxford: Oxford University Press, 2014.

Friedrich, Markus. "On Reading Missionary Correspondence: Jesuit Theologians on the Spiritual Benefits of a New Genre." In *Cultures of Communication: Theologies of Media in Early Modern Europe and Beyond*, edited by Helmut Puff, Ulrike Strasser, and Christopher Wild, 186–208. Toronto: University of Toronto Press, 2017.

Friskney, "Christian Faith in Print." In Fleming, Gallichan, and Lamonde, eds, *History of the Book in Canada*, vol. 1, 138–44.

Fuller, Andrew. *The Complete Works of Rev. Andrew Fuller, with a Memoir of His Life by Andrew Gunton Fuller*. Edited by Joseph Belcher. 3 vols. Philadelphia: American Baptist Publications, 1845.

Gallup-Diaz, Ignacio. "Anglicization Reconsidered." In *Anglicizing America: Empire, Revolution, Republic*, edited by Ignacio Gallup-Diaz, Andrew Shankman and David J. Silverman, 239–48. Philadelphia: University of Pennsylvania Press, 2015.

Gallup-Diaz, Ignacio, Andrew Shankman, and David J. Silverman, eds. *Anglicizing America: Empire, Revolution, Republic*. Philadelphia: University of Pennsylvania Press, 2015.

Gauvreau, Michael. "Protestantism Transformed: Personal Piety and the Evangelical Social Vision, 1815–1867." In *The Canadian Protestant*

Experience, 1760–1990, edited by George A. Rawlyk, 48–97. Montreal & Kingston: McGill-Queen's University Press, 1990.

The Gentleman's and London Magazine (Dublin), 1764.

The Gentleman's and London Magazine (Dublin), 1765.

The Gentleman's Magazine (London), 1765.

Gerber, David A. *Authors of Their Lives: The Personal Correspondence of British Immigrants to North America in the Nineteenth Century*. New York: New York University Press, 2006.

Gibson, Megan E. "Fandom: Enthusiastic Devotion, Religious and Theatrical Celebrity." *Studies in Eighteenth-Century Culture* 48 (2019): 269–73.

– "Sarah Siddons, Sensibility and Enthusiastic Devotion in the British Enlightenment." *Journal for Eighteenth-Century Studies* 42, no. 2 (2019): 193–209.

Ginzburg, Carlo. *The Cheese and the Worms: The Cosmos of a Sixteenth-Century Miller*. Translated by John and Anne Tedeschi. Baltimore: Johns Hopkins University Press, 1980.

Goldstein, Jan. "Enthusiasm or Imagination? Eighteenth-Century Smear Words in Comparative National Context." In *Enthusiasm and Enlightenment in Europe, 1650–1850*, edited by Lawrence E. Klein and Anthony J. La Vopa, 29–49. San Marino, CA: Huntington Library Press, 1998.

Goodwin, Daniel C. "From Disunity to Integration: Evangelical Religion and Society in Yarmouth, Nova Scotia, 1761–1830." In Conrad, *They Planted Well*, 190–200.

– *Into Deep Waters: Evangelical Spirituality and Maritime Calvinistic Baptist Ministers, 1790–1855*. Montreal & Kingston: McGill-Queen's University Press, 2010.

– ed. *Revivals, Baptists, and George Rawlyk*. Wolfville, NS: Acadia Divinity College, 2000.

– "The Search for a Professional Ministry: Samuel Elder and 19th-Century Maritime Calvinistic Baptists." *Acadiensis* 32, no. 1 (2002): 69–83.

– "Silas Rand's Autobiography: Planter Religion in the Next Generation." In *The Nova Scotia Planters in the Atlantic World*, edited by T. Stephen Henderson and Wendy G. Robicheau, 269–84. Fredericton, NB: Acadiensis Press, 2012.

Gould, Philip. *Writing the Rebellion: Loyalists and the Literature of Politics in British America*. Oxford: Oxford University Press, 2013.

Grafton, Anthony T. *Joseph Scaliger: A Study in the History of Classical*

Scholarship. Vol. 2: *Historical Chronology*. Oxford: Clarendon Press, 1993.

–"Joseph Scaliger and Historical Chronology: The Rise and Fall of a Discipline." *History & Theory* 14, no. 2 (1975): 156–85.

Granger, Bruce. "*Hudibras* in the American Revolution." *American Literature* 27, no. 4 (1956): 499–508.

– "The Hudibrastic Poetry of Jacob Bailey." *Early American Literature* 17, no. 1 (1982): 54–64.

– *Political Satire in the American Revolution, 1763–1783*. 1960; reprint: New York: Russell & Russell, 1971.

Grant, John N. "John Howe, Senior: Printer, Publisher, Postmaster, Spy." In *Eleven Exiles: Accounts of Loyalists of the American Revolution*, edited by Phyllis R. Blakeley and John N. Grant, 25–57. Toronto: Dundurn Press, 1982.

Grant, Keith S. *Andrew Fuller and the Evangelical Renewal of Pastoral Theology*. Milton Keynes, Bucks, UK: Paternoster Press, 2013.

Grasso, Christopher. *A Speaking Aristocracy: Transforming Public Discourse in Eighteenth-Century Connecticut*. Chapel Hill: University of North Carolina Press, 1999.

Green, Ian M. *Print and Protestantism in Early Modern England*. Oxford: Oxford University Press, 2000.

Greenblatt, Stephen. *Renaissance Self-Fashioning from More to Shakespeare*. Chicago: University of Chicago Press, 1980.

Gregg, Melissa, and Gregory J. Seigworth, eds. *The Affect Theory Reader*. Durham: Duke University Press, 2010.

Gregory, Anthony. "'Formed for Empire': The Continental Congress Responds to the Carlisle Peace Commission." *Journal of the Early Republic* 38, no. 4 (Winter 2018): 643–72.

Gregory, Jenny, and Jill L. Grant. "The Role of Emotions in Protests against Modernist Urban Redevelopment in Perth and Halifax." *Urban History Review/Revue d'Histoire Urbaine* 42, no. 2 (2014): 44–58.

Greven, Philip J. *The Protestant Temperament: Patterns of Child-Rearing, Religious Experience, and the Self in Early America*. New York: Alfred A. Knopf, 1977.

Gribbin, William. *The Churches Militant: The War of 1812 and American Religion*. New Haven: Yale University Press, 1973.

Gross, Robert A., and Mary Kelley, eds. *An Extensive Republic: Print, Culture, and Society in the New Nation, 1790–1840*. Chapel Hill: University of North Carolina Press/American Antiquarian Society, 2010.

Gutjahr, Paul C. *An American Bible: A History of the Good Book in the United States, 1777–1880*. Stanford: Stanford University Press, 2001.

Guyatt, Nicholas. *Providence and the Invention of the United States, 1607–1876*. Cambridge: Cambridge University Press, 2007.

Gwyn, Julian. "The King's County World of the Reverend Edward Manning to 1846." *Journal of the Royal Nova Scotia Historical Society* 16 (2013): 1–18.

–*Planter Nova Scotia, 1760–1815: Cornwallis Township*. Wolfville, NS: Kings-Hants Historical Connection, 2010.

Habermas, Jürgen. *The Structural Transformation of the Public Sphere: An Inquiry into a Category of Bourgeois Society*. Translated by Thomas Burger. Cambridge: MIT Press, 1989.

Haggis, Jane, and Margaret Allen. "Imperial Emotions: Affective Communities of Mission in British Protestant Women's Missionary Publications c. 1880–1920." *Journal of Social History* 41, no. 3 (2008): 691–716.

Hall, Catherine. *Civilising Subjects: Colony and Metropole in the English Imagination, 1830–1867*. Chicago: University of Chicago Press, 2002.

Hall, Catherine, and Sonya O. Rose, eds. *At Home with the Empire: Metropolitan Culture and the Imperial World*. Cambridge: Cambridge University Press, 2006.

Hall, David D. *Cultures of Print: Essays in the History of the Book*. Amherst: University of Massachusetts Press, 1996.

– ed. *Lived Religion in America: Toward a History of Practice*. Princeton: Princeton University Press, 2001.

– *The Puritans: A Transatlantic History*. Princeton: Princeton University Press, 2019.

– *A Reforming People: Puritanism and the Transformation of Public Life in New England*. New York: Alfred A. Knopf, 2011.

– "What Is the Place of 'Experience' in Religious History?" *Religion and American Culture: A Journal of Interpretation* 13, no. 2 (2003): 241–50.

–*Worlds of Wonder, Days of Judgment: Popular Religious Belief in Early New England*. New York: Alfred A. Knopf, 1989.

Hall, Timothy D. *Contested Boundaries: Itinerancy and the Reshaping of the Colonial American Religious World*. Durham: Duke University Press, 1994.

Halttunen, Karen. "Humanitarianism and the Pornography of Pain in Anglo-American Culture." *American Historical Review* 100, no. 2 (1995): 303–34.

Hambrick-Stowe, Charles E. *The Practice of Piety: Puritan Devotional Disciplines in Seventeenth-Century New England*. Chapel Hill: University of North Carolina Press, 1986.

– "The Spirit of the Old Writers: The Great Awakening and the Persistence of Puritan Piety." In *Puritanism: Transatlantic Perspectives on a Seventeenth-Century Anglo-American Faith*, edited by Francis J. Bremer, 277–91. Boston: Massachusetts Historical Society, 1993.

Harvey, D.C., ed. *The Diary of Simeon Perkins*, vol. 2: 1780–1789. Toronto: The Champlain Society, 1958.

Hatch, Nathan O. *The Democratization of American Christianity*. New Haven: Yale University Press, 1989.

– *The Sacred Cause of Liberty: Republican Thought and the Millennium in Revolutionary New England*. New Haven: Yale University Press, 1977.

Hattem, Michael D. *Past and Prologue: Politics and Memory in the American Revolution*. New Haven: Yale University Press, 2020.

Heath, Gordon L. "'The Great Association Above': Maritime Baptists and the War of 1812." *Pacific Journal of Baptist Research* 7, no. 2 (2011): 1–22.

Hebb, Ross N. *Samuel Seabury and Charles Inglis: Two Bishops, Two Churches*. Madison, NJ: Fairleigh Dickinson University Press, 2010.

Heimert, Alan. *Religion and the American Mind: From the Great Awakening to the Revolution*. Cambridge: Harvard University Press, 1966.

Heimert, Alan, and Perry Miller, eds. *The Great Awakening: Documents Illustrating the Crisis and Its Consequences*. Indianapolis: Bobbs-Merrill, 1967.

Hempton, David. *The Church in the Long Eighteenth Century*. London: I.B. Tauris, 2011.

– *Methodism: Empire of the Spirit*. New Haven: Yale University Press, 2005.

Henderson, T. Stephen, and Wendy G. Robicheau, eds. *The Nova Scotia Planters in the Atlantic World*. Fredericton, NB: Acadiensis Press, 2012.

Henry, Matthew. *The Communicant's Companion: or, instructions and helps for the right receiving of the Lord's Supper*. 13th ed. London: R. Ware, 1746.

– *The Pleasantness of a Religious Life, Open'd and Prov'd; and Recommended to the Consideration of All, Particularly of Young People*. London: Eman. Matthews, 1714.

Heyd, Michael. *"Be Sober and Reasonable": The Critique of Enthusiasm in the Seventeenth and Early Eighteenth Centuries*. Leiden: E.J. Brill, 1995.

Hickey, Donald R. *The War of 1812: A Forgotten Conflict*. Rev. ed.
Chicago: University of Illinois Press, 2012.

Hill, Christopher. *The World Turned Upside Down: Radical Ideas during
the English Revolution*. London: Penguin Books, 1991.

Hindmarsh, D. Bruce. *The Evangelical Conversion Narrative: Spiritual
Autobiography in Early Modern England*. Oxford: Oxford University
Press, 2005.

–*John Newton and the English Evangelical Tradition*. Oxford: Clarendon
Press, 1996.

– "Reshaping Individualism: The Private Christian, Eighteenth-Century
Religion, and the Enlightenment." In *The Rise of the Laity in
Evangelical Protestantism*, edited by Deryck W. Lovegrove, 67–84.
New York: Routledge, 2002.

– *The Spirit of Early Evangelicalism: True Religion in a Modern World*.
Oxford: Oxford University Press, 2018.

Hirschman, Albert O. *The Passions and the Interests: Political Arguments
for Capitalism before Its Triumph*. Princeton: Princeton University
Press, 1977.

Hoffman, Ronald, Mechal Sobel, and Fredrika J. Teute, eds. *Through a
Glass Darkly: Reflections on Personal Identity in Early America*. Chapel
Hill: University of North Carolina Press, 1997.

Hollett, Calvin. *Shouting, Embracing, and Dancing with Ecstasy: The
Growth of Methodism in Newfoundland, 1774–1874*. Montreal &
Kingston: McGill-Queen's University Press, 2010.

Homes, William. *A Discourse Concerning the Publick Reading of the Holy
Scriptures by the Lords People, in Their Religious Assemblies*. Boston:
B. Green, 1720.

– *The Good Government of Christian Families Recommended: As That
Which Will Contribute Greatly to Their Peace and True Happiness. To
Which Is Added, a Discourse on Secret Prayer*. Boston: D. Henchman,
1747.

Hopkins, Samuel. *Memoirs of the Life of Mrs. Sarah Osborn*. Worcester,
MA: Leonard Worcester, 1799.

Howard, June. "What Is Sentimentality?" *American Literary History* 11,
no. 1 (1999): 63–81.

Howe, Daniel Walker. *Making the American Self: Jonathan Edwards to
Abraham Lincoln*. 1997; reprint, Oxford: Oxford University Press, 2009.

Howsam, Leslie. *Cheap Bibles: Nineteenth-Century Publishing and the
British and Foreign Bible Society*. Cambridge: Cambridge University
Press, 1991.

Hubbard, William. *A Narrative of the Troubles with the Indians in New-England*. Boston: John Foster, 1677.

Hull, N.E.H., Peter C. Hoffer, and Steven L. Allen. "Choosing Sides: A Quantitative Study of the Personality Determinants of Loyalist and Revolutionary Political Affiliation in New York." *Journal of American History* 65, no. 2 (1978): 344–66.

Hume, David. *A Treatise of Human Nature*. Edited by L. Selby-Bigge and P. Nidditch. Oxford: Clarendon Press, 1978.

Humphrey, Heman. *Parallel between Intemperance and the Slave Trade: An Address Delivered at Amherst College, July 4, 1828*. Amherst: J.S. and C. Adams, 1828.

Hunt, Arnold. "The Lord's Supper in Early Modern England." *Past & Present* 161, no. 1 (1998): 39–83.

Hunt, Margaret R., ed. *Women and the Enlightenment*. New York: Haworth Press, 1984.

Hurd, Nathaniel. *Britons Behold the Best of Kings*, 1762. Engraving, hand-coloured. American Antiquarian Society, Worcester, MA.

Huskins, Bonnie. "'Remarks and Rough Memorandums': Social Sets, Sociability, and Community in the Journal of William Booth, Shelburne, 1787 and 1789." *Journal of the Royal Nova Scotia Historical Society* 13 (2010): 103–32.

– "'Shelburnian Manners': Gentility and the Loyalists of Shelburne, Nova Scotia." *Early American Studies* 13, no. 1 (2015): 151–88.

Hutcheson, Francis. *An Essay on the Nature and Conduct of the Passions and Affections: With Illustrations on the Moral Sense*. Edited by Aaron Garrett. Indianapolis: Liberty Fund, 2002.

Hutchinson, Thomas. *The History of the Colony of Massachusets-Bay, from the first settlement thereof in 1628*. Boston: Thomas and John Fleet, 1764.

– *The History of the Province of Massachusets-Bay, from the charter of King William and Queen Mary, in 1691, until the year 1750*. Boston: Thomas and John Fleet, 1767.

Ingersoll, Thomas N. *The Loyalist Problem in Revolutionary New England*. Cambridge: Cambridge University Press, 2016.

Inglis, Charles. *A Charge Delivered to the Clergy of Nova-Scotia, at the Triennial Visitation Holden in the Town of Halifax, in the Month of June 1791*. Halifax, NS: Anthony Henry, 1812.

– *Steadfastness in Religion and Loyalty Recommended, in a Sermon Preached before the Legislature of His Majesty's Province of Nova-Scotia: In the Parish Church of St. Paul at Halifax, on Sunday, April 7, 1793*. Halifax, NS: John Howe, 1793.

–*The True Interest of America Impartially Stated, in Certain Strictures on a Pamphlet Intitled Common Sense*. 2nd ed. Philadelphia: James Humphreys, 1777.

Israel, Jonathan I. *Enlightenment Contested: Philosophy, Modernity, and the Emancipation of Man, 1670–1752*. Oxford: Oxford University Press, 2006.

– *Democratic Enlightenment: Philosophy, Revolution, and Human Rights, 1750–1790*. Oxford: Oxford University Press, 2011.

–*Radical Enlightenment: Philosophy and the Making of Modernity, 1650–1750*. Oxford: Oxford University Press, 2001.

Jack, Ian. *Augustan Satire: Intention and Idiom in English Poetry, 1660–1750*. Oxford: Clarendon Press, 1957.

Jaffee, David. *People of the Wachusett: Greater New England in History and Memory, 1630–1860*. Ithaca, NY: Cornell University Press, 1999.

James, Susan. *Passion and Action: The Emotions in Seventeenth-Century Philosophy*. Oxford: Clarendon Press, 1997.

James, William. *Varieties of Religious Experience*. 1902; reprint, New York: New American Library, 1958.

Jasanoff, Maya. *Liberty's Exiles: American Loyalists in the Revolutionary World*. New York: Alfred A. Knopf, 2011.

–"Revolutionary Exiles: The American Loyalist and French Émigré Disasporas." In *The Age of Revolutions in Global Context, c. 1760–1840*, edited by David Armitage and Sanjay Subrahmanyam, 37–58. New York: Palgrave Macmillan, 2010.

Johnson, Curtis D. *Redeeming America: Evangelicals and the Road to the Civil War*. Chicago: Ivan R. Dee, 1993.

Jones, C.B. *Radical Sensibility: Literature and Ideas in the 1790s*. London: Routledge, 1993.

Jones, Christopher C. "Methodism, Slavery, and Freedom in the Revolutionary Atlantic, 1770–1820." PhD diss., College of William and Mary, 2016.

Jones, David Ceri. "George Whitefield and the Revival of Calvinism in Eighteenth-Century Britain." *International Congregational Journal* 14, no. 1 (2015): 97–115.

Juster, Susan. *Disorderly Women: Sexual Politics and Evangelicalism in Revolutionary New England*. Ithaca, NY: Cornell University Press, 1994.

– *Doomsayers: Anglo-American Prophecy in the Age of Revolution*. Early American Studies. Philadelphia: University of Pennsylvania Press, 2003.

– "Eros and Desire in Early Modern Spirituality." *William and Mary Quarterly* 60, no. 1 (2003): 203–6.

Karant-Nunn, Susan C. *The Reformation of Feeling: Shaping the Religious Emotions in Early Modern Germany*. Oxford: Oxford University Press, 2010.

Kenny, Nicolas. *The Feel of the City: Experiences of Urban Transformation*. Toronto: University of Toronto Press, 2014.

Kernaghan, Lois K. "Howe, Alexander." In *Dictionary of Canadian Biography*. Vol. 5. Toronto/Laval: University of Toronto/Université Laval, 2003– accessed 9 March 2017, http://www.biographi.ca/en/bio/howe_alexander_5E.html.

Kidd, Colin. *British Identities before Nationalism: Ethnicity and Nationhood in the Atlantic World, 1600–1800*. Cambridge: Cambridge University Press, 1999.

Kidd, Thomas S. *George Whitefield: America's Spiritual Founding Father*. New Haven: Yale University Press, 2014.

– *God of Liberty: A Religious History of the American Revolution*. New York: Basic Books, 2010.

– *The Great Awakening: The Roots of Evangelical Christianity in Colonial America*. New Haven: Yale University Press, 2007.

– *The Protestant Interest: New England after Puritanism*. New Haven: Yale University Press, 2004.

Kimnach, Wilson H. "General Introduction to the Sermons: Jonathan Edwards' Art of Prophesying." In Jonathan Edwards, *Sermons and Discourses, 1720–1723*, edited by Wilson H. Kimnach, 1–258. Vol. 10 of *The Works of Jonathan Edwards*. New Haven: Yale University Press, 1992.

King, Joshua. *Imagined Spiritual Communities in Britain's Age of Print*. Columbus: Ohio State University Press, 2015.

Kittredge, Jonathan. *An Address Delivered before the Temperance Society of Bath, N.H. July 4, 1828. Also, an Address Delivered before the American Temperance Society at Its Second Annual Meeting, Held in Boston, Jan. 23, 1829*. Boston: Perkins & Marvin, 1829.

Klein, Lawrence E. *Shaftesbury and the Culture of Politeness: Moral Discourse and Cultural Politics in Early Eighteenth-Century England*. Cambridge: Cambridge University Press, 1994.

– "Sociability, Solitude, and Enthusiasm." In *Enthusiasm and Enlightenment in Europe, 1650–1850*, edited by Lawrence E. Klein and Anthony J. La Vopa, 153–177. San Marino, CA: Huntington Library Press, 1998.

Klein, Lawrence E., and Anthony J. La Vopa, eds. *Enthusiasm and Enlightenment in Europe, 1650–1850*. San Marino, CA: Huntington Library Press, 1998.

Kloppenberg, James T. "The Virtues of Liberalism: Christianity, Republicanism, and Ethics in Early American Political Discourse." *Journal of American History* 74, no. 1 (1987): 9–33.

Knoespel, Kenneth J. "Newton in the School of Time: The 'Chronology of Ancient Kingdoms Amended' and the Crisis of Seventeenth-Century Historiography." *The Eighteenth Century* 30, no. 3 (1989): 19–41.

Knott, Sarah. *Sensibility and the American Revolution.* Chapel Hill: University of North Carolina Press, 2009.

Knott, Sarah, and Barbara Taylor, eds. *Women, Gender and Enlightenment.* New York: Palgrave Macmillan, 2007.

Knowles, Charles. *A Brief Sketch of the Life of Mrs. Ann Knowles, Who Departed This Life August 13, 1845.* Boston: Howe's Sheet Anchor Press, 1846.

Knowles, Norman James. *Inventing the Loyalists: The Ontario Loyalist Tradition and the Creation of Usable Pasts.* Toronto: University of Toronto Press, 1997.

Knox, R.A. *Enthusiasm: A Chapter in the History of Religion.* Oxford: Oxford University Press, 1950.

Kraus, Michael, and Davis D. Joyce. *The Writing of American History.* Norman: University of Oklahoma Press, 1985.

Krysmanski, Bernd. "We See a Ghost: Hogarth's Satire on Methodists and Connoisseurs." *Art Bulletin* 80, no. 2 (1998): 292–310.

Laborie, Lionel L. *Enlightening Enthusiasm: Prophecy and Religious Experience in Early Eighteenth-Century England.* Manchester, UK: Manchester University Press, 2015.

Lambert, Frank. *Inventing the "Great Awakening."* Princeton: Princeton University Press, 1999.

–*Pedlar in Divinity: George Whitefield and the Transatlantic Revivals, 1737–1770.* Princeton: Princeton University Press, 1994.

Landsman, Ned C. *From Colonials to Provincials: American Thought and Culture, 1680–1760.* Ithaca, NY: Cornell University Press, 1997.

Lane, Hannah M. "Methodist Church Members, Lay Leaders, and Socio-Economic Position in Mid-Nineteenth Century St. Stephen, New Brunswick." PhD diss., University of New Brunswick, 2004.

– "Women and Public Prayer in the Mid-Nineteenth-Century 'Calvinistic' Baptist Press of New Brunswick and Nova Scotia." In *Canadian Baptist Women,* edited by Sharon M. Bowler, 3–19. Eugene, OR: Pickwick, 2016.

Langford, Paul. "The Uses of Eighteenth-Century Politeness." *Transactions of the Royal Historical Society* 12 (2002): 311–31.

Larkin, Edward. "The Cosmopolitan Revolution: Loyalism and the Fiction
     of an American Nation." NOVEL: A Forum on Fiction 40, no. 1/2 (2006):
     52–76.
– "Nation and Empire in the Early US." American Literary History 22,
     no. 3 (2010): 501–26.
– "What Is a Loyalist?" Common-place.org. 8.1 (October 2007). http://
     common-place.org/book/what-is-a-loyalist/.
Launitz-Schürer, Leopold S. Loyal Whigs and Revolutionaries: The
     Making of the Revolution in New York, 1765–1776. New York: New
     York University Press, 1980.
Leamon, James S. "Mr. Jacob Bailey and the Ladies." In In Our Own
     Words: New England Diaries, 1600 to the Present, edited by Peter
     Benes. Dublin Seminar for New England, Folklife. Boston: Boston
     University, 2009.
– "The Parson, the Parson's Wife, and the Coming of the Revolution to
     Pownalbororough, Maine." New England Quarterly 82, no. 3 (2009):
     514–28.
– The Reverend Jacob Bailey, Maine Loyalist: For God, King, Country,
     and for Self. Amherst: University of Massachusetts Press, 2012.
–Revolution Downeast: The War for American Independence in Maine.
     Amherst: University of Massachusetts Press, 1993.
Leder, Lawrence H. Loyalist Historians. New York: Harper & Row, 1971.
Lejeune, Philippe, On Diary. Edited by Jeremy D. Popkin and Julie Rak.
     Translated by Katherine Durnin. Honolulu: University of Hawai'i Press,
     2009.
Leverenz, David. The Language of Puritan Feeling: An Exploration in
     Literature, Psychology, and Social History. New Brunswick, NJ: Rutgers
     University Press, 1980.
Levine, Joseph M. Humanism and History: Origins of Modern English
     Historiography. Ithaca, NY: Cornell University Press, 1987.
Lewis, Jan. "'Those Scenes for Which Alone My Heart Was Made':
     Affection and Politics in the Age of Jefferson and Hamilton." In An
     Emotional History of the United States, edited by Peter N. Stearns and
     Jan Lewis, 52–65. New York: New York University Press, 1998.
Leys, Ruth. "Affect and Intention: A Reply to William E. Connolly."
     Critical Inquiry 37, no. 4 (2011): 799–805.
– "The Turn to Affect: A Critique." Critical Inquiry 37, no. 3 (2011):
     434–72.
Liliequist, Jonas, ed. A History of Emotions, 1200–1800. London:
     Pickering & Chatto 2012.

Little, J.I. "'A Brothers Feelings': Epistolary Emotions in a Time of Political Crisis, Georgeville, Lower Canada, 1838–1839." *Histoire Sociale/Social History* 53, no. 109 (2020): 651–61.

Lochhead, Douglas G. "Henry, Anthony." In *Dictionary of Canadian Biography*. Vol. 4. Toronto/Laval: University of Toronto/Université Laval, 2003–, accessed 16 March 2017, http://www.biographi.ca/en/bio/henry_anthony_4E.html.

The London Magazine (London), 1754.

Longley, R.S. *Acadia University, 1838–1938*. Wolfville, NS: 1939.

Lovegrove, Deryck W. *Established Church, Sectarian People: Itinerancy and the Transformation of English Dissent, 1780–1830*. Cambridge: Cambridge University Press, 2004.

Lovejoy, David S. *Religious Enthusiasm in the New World: Heresy to Revolution*. Cambridge: Harvard University Press, 1985.

Macdonald, Alastair. "Enthusiasm Resurgent." *Dalhousie Review* 42, no. 3 (1962): 352–63.

Mack, Phyllis. *Heart Religion in the British Enlightenment: Gender and Emotion in Early Methodism*. Cambridge: Cambridge University Press, 2008.

– "Religion, Feminism, and the Problem of Agency: Reflections on Eighteenth-Century Quakerism." *Signs: Journal of Women in Culture and Society* 29, no. 1 (2003): 149–77.

MacKinnon, Neil. "Bitter Verse: Poetry, Verse and Song of the American Loyalists in Nova Scotia." *Dalhousie Review* 65, no. 1 (1985): 111–21.

– "The Changing Attitudes of the Nova Scotian Loyalists towards the United States, 1783–1791." *Acadiensis* 2, no. 2 (1973): 43–54.

– "This Cursed Republican Spirit: The Loyalists and Nova Scotia's Sixth Assembly." *The Humanities Association Review (Kingston)* 27 (1976): 129–42.

– *This Unfriendly Soil: The Loyalist Experience in Nova Scotia, 1783–1791*. Kingston & Montreal: McGill-Queen's University Press, 1986.

Malcom, Allison O'Mahen. "Loyal Orangemen and Republican Nativists: Anti-Catholicism and Historical Memory in Canada and the United States, 1837–1867." In Bannister and Riordan, eds, *The Loyal Atlantic*, 211–51.

Mancke, Elizabeth. "Another British America: A Canadian Model for the Early Modern British Empire." *Journal of Imperial & Commonwealth History* 25, no. 1 (1997): 1–36.

– *The Fault Lines of Empire: Political Differentiation in Massachusetts and Nova Scotia, ca. 1760–1830*. New York: Routledge, 2005.

– "Idiosyncratic Localism, Provincial Moderation, Imperial Loyalty: Planter Studies and the History of Eighteenth-Century Nova Scotia." *Acadiensis* 42, no. 1 (2013): 169–81.

Mancke, Elizabeth, Jerry Bannister, Denis McKim, and Scott See, eds. *Violence, Order, and Unrest: A History of British North America, 1749–1876*. Toronto: University of Toronto Press, 2019.

Mancke, Elizabeth, and Carole Shammas, eds. *The Creation of the British Atlantic World*. Baltimore: Johns Hopkins University Press, 2005.

Manning, Edward. "Circular Letter, [From] the Ministers and Messengers composing the Nova-Scotia and New-Brunswick Association to the several Churches they represent." In *Minutes of the Nova-Scotia and New-Brunswick Association*, 5–10. Saint John, NB: Henry Chubb & Co., 1814.

Mapp, Paul W. "British Culture and the Changing Character of the Mid-Eighteenth-Century British Empire." In *Cultures in Conflict: The Seven Years' War in North America*, edited by Warren R. Hofstra, 23–59. Lanham, MD: Rowman & Littlefield, 2007.

Marchant, John. *An Exposition on the Books of the Old Testament*. London: R. Walker, 1745.

Marini, Stephen. "Hymnody as History: Early Evangelical Hymns and the Recovery of American Popular Religion." *Church History* 71, no. 2 (2002): 273–306.

– *Radical Sects of Revolutionary New England*. Cambridge: Harvard University Press, 1982.

– "Religious Revolution in the District of Maine, 1780–1820." In *Maine in the Early Republic: From Revolution to Statehood*, edited by Charles E. Clark, James S. Leamon, and Karen Bowden, 118–45. Hanover, NH: University Press of New England, 1988.

Marsden, George M. *Jonathan Edwards: A Life*. New Haven: Yale University Press, 2003.

Marshall, Ashley. "The Aims of Butler's Satire in *Hudibras*." *Modern Philology* 105, no. 4 (2008): 637–65.

Martín-Moruno, Dolores, and Beatriz Pichel, eds. *Emotional Bodies: The Historical Peformativity of Emotions*. Urbana: University of Illinois Press, 2019.

Mason, Keith. "The American Loyalist Diaspora and the Reconfiguration of the British Atlantic World." In *Empire and Nation: The American Revolution in the Atlantic World*, edited by Eliga H. Gould and Peter S. Onuf, 239–59. Baltimore: Johns Hopkins University Press, 2005.

– "The American Loyalist Problem of Identity in the Revolutionary

Atlantic World." In Bannister and Riordan, *The Loyal Atlantic*, 39–74.

– "Loyalism in British North America in the Age of Revolution, c. 1775–1812." In *Loyalism and the Formation of the British World, 1775–1914*, edited by Allan Blackstock and Frank O'Gorman, 163–79. Rochester, NY: Boydell Press, 2014.

Mather, Cotton. *Pietas in Patriam: The life of His Excellency Sir William Phips*. London: Samuel Bridge, 1697.

Matt, Susan J., and Peter N. Stearns, eds. *Doing Emotions History*. Urbana: University of Illinois Press, 2014.

May, Henry F. *The Enlightenment in America*. New York: Oxford University Press, 1976.

Mazoff, C.D. *Anxious Allegiances: Legitimizing Identity in the Early Canadian Long Poem*. Montreal & Kingston: McGill-Queen's University Press, 1998.

McBride, Spencer W. *Pulpit and Nation: Clergymen and the Politics of Revolutionary America*. Charlottesville: University of Virginia Press, 2016.

McClymond, Michael. "Jonathan Edwards." In *The Oxford Handbook of Religion and Emotion*, edited by John Corrigan, 404–17. Oxford: Oxford University Press, 2008.

McConville, Brendan. *The King's Three Faces: The Rise and Fall of Royal America, 1688–1776*. Chapel Hill: University of North Carolina Press, 2006.

McKay, Ian. "The Liberal Order Framework: A Prospectus for a Reconnaissance of Canadian History." *Canadian Historical Review* 81, no. 4 (2000): 617–45.

McKim, Denis. "Anxious Anglicans, Complicated Catholics, and Disruptive Dissenters: Christianity and the Search for Social Order in the Age of Revolution." In *Violence, Order, and Unrest: A History of British North America, 1749–1876*, edited by Elizabeth Mancke, Jerry Bannister, Denis McKim and Scott See, 53–77. Toronto: University of Toronto Press, 2019.

– *Boundless Dominion: Providence, Politics, and the Early Canadian Presbyterian Worldview*. Montreal & Kingston: McGill-Queen's University Press, 2017.

– "God & Government: Exploring the Religious Roots of Upper Canadian Political Culture." *Ontario History* 105, no. 1 (Spring 2013): 74–97.

– "Upper Canadian Thermidor: The Family Compact & the Counter-Revolutionary Atlantic." *Ontario History* 106, no. 2 (Fall 2014): 235–62.

McLaren, Scott. *Pulpit, Press, and Politics: Methodists and the Market for Books in Upper Canada.* Toronto: University of Toronto Press, 2019.

McLisky, Claire, Daniel Midena, and Karen Vallgårda, eds. *Emotions and Christian Missions: Historical Perspectives.* New York: Palgrave Macmillan, 2015.

McMahon, Darrin M. *The Pursuit of Happiness: A History from the Greeks to the Present.* London: Allen Lane, 2006.

McNairn, Jeffrey L. *The Capacity to Judge: Public Opinion and Deliberative Democracy in Upper Canada, 1791–1854.* Toronto: University of Toronto Press, 2000.

– "'The Common Sympathies of Our Nature': Moral Sentiments, Emotional Economies, and Imprisonment for Debt in Upper Canada." *Histoire sociale/Social History* 49, no. 98 (May 2016): 49–71.

Mee, Jon. *Romanticism, Enthusiasm, and Regulation: Poetics and the Policing of Culture in the Romantic Period.* Oxford: Oxford University Press, 2003.

Melton, James Van Horn. *The Rise of the Public in Enlightenment Europe.* Cambridge: Cambridge University Press, 2001.

Merrill, Daniel. *Balaam Disappointed: A Thanksgiving Sermon, delivered at Nottingham-West, April 13, 1815. A day recommended by the national government, in which to rehearse God's mighty acts, and praise his name.* Concord, NH: Isaac & W.R. Hill, 1815.

Milford, T.A. *The Gardiners of Massachusetts: Provincial Ambition and the British-American Career.* Durham: University of New Hampshire Press, 2005.

Miller, Carman. "Chipman, William Allen." In *Dictionary of Canadian Biography.* Vol. 7. Toronto/Laval: University of Toronto/Université Laval, 2003, http://www.biographi.ca/en/bio/chipman_william_allen_7E.html.

Miller, Perry. "Jonathan Edwards on the Sense of the Heart." *Harvard Theological Review* 41, no. 2 (1948): 121–45.

– *The New England Mind: The Seventeenth Century.* 1939; reprint, Cambridge: Belknap Press, 1982.

Mintz, Steven. *Moralists and Modernizers: America's Pre-Civil War Reformers.* Baltimore: Johns Hopkins University Press, 1995.

Moody, Barry. "Breadth of Vision, Breadth of Mind: The Baptists and Acadia College." In *Canadian Baptists and Christian Higher Education,* edited by George A. Rawlyk, 3–30. Montreal & Kingston: McGill-Queen's University Press, 1988.

– "Burpee, Richard E." In *Dictionary of Canadian Biography.* Vol. 8.

Toronto/Laval: University of Toronto/Université Laval, 2003–, accessed 18 May 2017, http://www.biographi.ca/en/bio/burpee_richard_e_8E.html.

– "From Itinerant to Pastor: The Case of Edward Manning (1767–1851)," *Historical Papers: Canadian Society of Church History* (1981): 1–25.

– "George Rawlyk's Henry Alline." In *Revivals, Baptists, and George Rawlyk*, edited by Daniel C. Goodwin, 53–75. Wolfville, NS: Acadia Divinity College, 2000.

– *A History of Annapolis Royal*. Vol. 2. Halifax, NS: Nimbus, 2014.

– "Joseph Howe, the Baptists, and the College Question." In *The Proceedings of the Joseph Howe Symposium, Mount Allison University*, edited by Wayne A. Hunt, 53–70. Sackville, NB: Mount Allison University, Centre for Canadian Studies, 1984.

– "Manning, Edward." In *Dictionary of Canadian*. Vol. 8. Toronto/Laval: University of Toronto/Université Laval, 2003–, accessed 17 May 2017, http://www.biographi.ca/en/bio/manning_edward_8E.html.

"The Maritime Baptists and Higher Education in the Early Nineteenth Century." In *Repent and Believe: The Baptist Experience in Maritime Canada*, edited by Barry M. Moody, 88–102. Hantsport, NS: Lancelot Press, 1980.

– ed. *Repent and Believe: The Baptist Experience in Maritime Canada*. Hantsport, NS: Lancelot Press, 1980.

Morden, Peter J. *The Life and Thought of Andrew Fuller (1754–1815)*. Milton Keynes, Bucks, UK: Paternoster, 2015.

Moreshead, Ashley E. "'Beyond All Ambitious Motives': Missionary Memoirs and the Cultivation of Early American Evangelical Heroines." *Journal of the Early Republic* 38, no. 1 (2018): 37–60.

Morgan, Cecilia. *Public Men and Virtuous Women: The Gendered Languages of Religion and Politics in Upper Canada, 1791–1850*. Toronto: University of Toronto Press, 1996.

– *Travellers through Empire: Indigenous Voyages from Early Canada*. Toronto: University of Toronto Press, 2017.

Morgan, Edmund S. *Visible Saints: The History of a Puritan Idea*. New York: New York University Press, 1963.

Mouw, Richard J., and Mark A. Noll, eds. *Wonderful Words of Life: Hymns in American Protestant History and Theology*. Grand Rapids, MI: Eerdmans, 2004.

Mullan, John. *Sentiment and Sociability: The Language of Feeling in the Eighteenth Century*. Oxford: Oxford University Press, 1988.

Murdoch, Beamish. *A History of Nova-Scotia or Acadie*. Halifax, NS: James Barnes, 1867.

Murrin, John M. "England and Colonial America: A Novel Theory of the American Revolution." Reprinted in *Anglicizing America: Empire, Revolution, Republic*, edited by Ignacio Gallup-Diaz, Andrew Shankman, and David J. Silverman, 9–19. Philadelphia: University of Pennsylvania Press, 2015.

Neem, Johann N. *Creating a Nation of Joiners: Democracy and Civil Society in Early National Massachusetts*. Cambridge: Harvard University Press, 2008.

Nelson, Eric. *The Royalist Revolution: Monarchy and the American Founding*. Cambridge: Harvard University Press, 2014.

Noel, Janet. *Canada Dry: Temperance Crusades before Confederation*. Toronto: University of Toronto Press, 1995.

Noll, Mark A. "The American Revolution and Protestant Evangelicalism." *Journal of Interdisciplinary History* 23, no. 3 (1993): 615–38.

– *America's God: From Jonathan Edwards to Abraham Lincoln*. New York: Oxford University Press, 2002.

– *In the Beginning Was the Word: The Bible in American Public Life, 1492–1783*. Oxford: Oxford University Press, 2016.

– ed. *Religion and American Politics: From the Colonial Period to the 1980s*. Oxford: Oxford University Press, 1990.

– *The Rise of Evangelicalism: The Age of Edwards, Whitefield and the Wesleys*. Downers Grove, IL: InterVarsity Press, 2003.

Norton, Mary Beth. *The British-Americans: The Loyalist Exiles in England, 1774–1789*. Boston: Little, Brown and Company, 1972.

O'Brien, G. Patrick. "'Unknown and Unlamented': Loyalist Women in Nova Scotia from Exile to Repatriation, 1775–1800." PhD diss., University of South Carolina, 2019.

O'Brien, Karen. *Narratives of Enlightenment: Cosmopolitan History from Voltaire to Gibbon*. Cambridge: Cambridge University Press, 1997.

O'Brien, Susan. "A Transatlantic Community of Saints: The Great Awakening and the First Evangelical Network, 1735–1755." *American Historical Review* 91, no. 4 (1986): 811–32.

O'Gorman, Frank. "English Loyalism Revisited." In *Politics and Political Culture in Britain and Ireland, 1750–1850: Essays in Tribute to Peter Jupp*, edited by Allan Blackstock and Eoin Magennis, 223–41. Belfast: Ulster Historical Association, 2007.

Olney, James, ed. *Autobiography: Essays Theoretical and Critical*. Princeton: Princeton University Press, 1980.

Orsi, Robert A. *Between Heaven and Earth: The Religious Worlds People*

Make and the Scholars Who Study Them. Princeton: Princeton University Press, 2005.

Osborn, Sarah. *The Nature, Certainty and Evidence of True Christianity. In a Letter from a Gentlewoman in New-England, to Another Her Dear Friend, in Great Darkness, Doubt and Concern of a Religious Nature*. Boston: S. Kneeland, 1755.

Owen, John. *Phronema Tou Pneumatos; or, the Grace and Duty of Being Spiritually Minded: Declared and Practically Improved*. London: J. Murgatroyd, 1798.

Paine, Thomas. *Common Sense*. Edited by Isaac Kramnick. New York: Penguin, 1976.

Palmer, R.R. *The Age of the Democratic Revolution: A Political History of Europe and America, 1760–1800*. Princeton: Princeton University Press, 2014.

Pardes, Ilana. *The Song of Songs: A Biography*. Lives of Great Religious Books. Princeton: Princeton University Press, 2019.

Parker, George L. *The Beginnings of the Book Trade in Canada*. Toronto: University of Toronto Press, 1985.

– "Courting Local and International Markets." In Fleming, Gallichan, and Lamonde, eds, *History of the Book in Canada*, vol. 1, 329–51.

Parr, Jessica M. *Inventing George Whitefield: Race, Revivalism, and the Making of a Religious Icon*. Jackson: University Press of Mississippi, 2015.

Paster, Gail Kern, Katherine Rowe, and Mary Floyd-Wilson, eds. *Reading the Early Modern Passions: Essays in the Cultural History of Emotion*. Philadelphia: University of Pennsylvania Press, 2004.

Pearsall, Sarah M.S. *Atlantic Families: Lives and Letters in the Later Eighteenth Century*. Oxford: Oxford University Press, 2008.

– "'The Power of Feeling'? Emotion, Sensibility, and the American Revolution." *Modern Intellectual History* 8, no. 3 (2011): 659–72.

Phillips, Mark Salber. *Society and Sentiment: Genres of Historical Writing in Britain, 1740–1820*. Princeton: Princeton University Press, 2000.

Plamper, Jan. *The History of Emotions: An Introduction*. Translated by Keith Tribe. Oxford: Oxford University Press, 2015.

Pocock, J.G.A. "British History: A Plea for a New Subject." *Journal of Modern History* 47, no. 4 (1975): 601–21.

– "Enthusiasm: The Antiself of Enlightenment." *Huntington Library Quarterly* 60, no. 1/2 (1997): 7–28.

– *The Machiavellian Moment: Florentine Political Thought and the Atlantic Republican Tradition*. Princeton: Princeton University Press, 1975.

Pope, Robert G. *The Half-Way Covenant: Church Membership in Puritan New England*. Princeton: Princeton University Press, 1984.

Potter, Janice. *The Liberty We Seek: Loyalist Ideology in Colonial New York and Massachusetts*. Cambridge: Harvard University Press, 1983.

Potter-MacKinnon, Janice. *While the Women Only Wept: Loyalist Refugee Women in Eastern Ontario*. Montreal & Kingston: McGill-Queen's University Press, 1993.

Potter-MacKinnon, Janice, and Robert M. Calhoon. "The Character and Coherence of the Loyalist Press." In *Tory Insurgents: The Loyalist Perception and Other Essays*, edited by Robert M. Calhoon, Timothy M. Barnes, and Robert S. Davis. Rev. ed., 125–59. Columbia: University of South Carolina Press, 2010.

Putnam, Lara. "To Study the Fragments/Whole: Microhistory and the Atlantic World." *Journal of Social History* 39, no. 3 (2006): 615–30.

Pybus, Cassandra. *Epic Journeys of Freedom: Runaway Slaves of the American Revolution and Their Global Quest for Liberty*. Ypsilanti, MI: Beacon Press, 2006.

Rawlyk, George A., ed. *The Canada Fire: Radical Evangelicalism in British North America, 1775–1812*. Montreal & Kingston: McGill-Queen's University Press, 1994.

– ed. *The Canadian Protestant Experience, 1760–1990*. Montreal & Kingston: McGill-Queen's University Press, 1990.

– "Henry Alline (1748–1784): The Shaping of the Conversion Paradigm." In *The Canada Fire: Radical Evangelicalism in British North America, 1775-1812*, edited by George A. Rawlyk, 5–18. Montreal & Kingston: McGill-Queen's University Press, 1994.

– ed. *Henry Alline: Selected Writings*. New York: Paulist Press, 1987.

– ed. *The New Light Letters and Spiritual Songs, 1778–1793*. Hantsport, NS: Lancelot Press, 1983.

– *Nova Scotia's Massachusetts: A Study of Massachusetts-Nova Scotia Relations, 1630–1784*. Montreal & Kingston: McGill-Queen's University Press, 1976.

– *Ravished by the Spirit: Religious Revivals, Baptists, and Henry Alline*. Montreal & Kingston: McGill-Queen's University Press, 1984.

– ed. *Revolution Rejected, 1775–1776*. Scarborough, ON: Prentice-Hall, 1968.

– ed. *The Sermons of Henry Alline*. Hantsport, NS: Lancelot Press, 1986.

– "'A Total Revolution in Religious and Civil Government': The Maritimes, New England, and the Evolving Evangelical Ethos, 1776–1812." In *Evangelicalism: Comparative Studies of Popular*

Protestantism in North America, the British Isles, and Beyond, 1700–
1990, edited by Mark A. Noll, David W. Bebbington, and George A.
Rawlyk, 137–55. Oxford: Oxford University Press, 1994.
– *Wrapped Up in God: A Study of Several Canadian Revivals and*
Revivalists. Burlington, ON: Welch Publishing Company, 1988.
Rawlyk, George A., and Gordon T. Stewart. "Nova Scotia's Sense of
Mission." *Histoire Sociale/Social History*, no. 2 (Nov. 1968): 5–17.
Reddy, William. "Historical Research on the Self and Emotions." *Emotion*
Review 1, no. 4 (2009): 302–15.
– *The Navigation of Feeling: A Framework for the History of Emotions*.
Cambridge: Cambridge University Press, 2001.
– "Sentimentalism and Its Erasure: The Role of Emotions in the Era of the
French Revolution." *Journal of Modern History* 72, no. 1 (2000): 109–52.
Reiter, Eric H. *Wounded Feelings: Litigating Emotions in Quebec, 1870–*
1950. Toronto: Osgoode Society for Canadian Legal History/University
of Toronto Press, 2019.
Rhoden, Nancy L. *Revolutionary Anglicanism: The Colonial Church of*
England Clergy during the American Revolution. New York: New York
University Press, 1999.
Richey, Matthew. *A Memoir of the Late Rev. William Black*. Halifax, NS:
William Cunnabell, 1839.
Riis, Ole, and Linda Woodhead. *A Sociology of Religious Emotion*.
Oxford: Oxford University Press, 2010.
Rivers, Isabel. "Dissenting and Methodist Books of Practical Divinity."
In *Books and Their Readers in Eighteenth-Century England*, edited by
Isabel Rivers, 127–64. Leicester: Leicester University Press, 1982.
– *Reason, Grace, and Sentiment: A Study of the Language of Religion and*
Ethics in England, 1660–1780. 2 vols. Cambridge: Cambridge
University Press, 1991, 2000.
– "Shaftesburian Enthusiasm and the Evangelical Revival." In *Revival and*
Religion since 1700: Essays for John Walsh, edited by H.C.G. Matthew
and Jane Garnett, 21–39. London: Hambledon Press, 1993.
Rivers, Isabel, and David L. Wykes, eds. *Dissenting Praise: Religious*
Dissent and the Hymn in England and Wales. Oxford: Oxford
University Press, 2011.
Rivett, Sarah. *The Science of the Soul in Colonial New England*. Chapel
Hill: University of North Carolina Press, 2011.
Roberts, Stephen Bryn. *Puritanism and the Pursuit of Happiness: The*
Ministry and Theology of Ralph Venning, c.1621–1674. Woodbridge,
Suffolk, UK: Boydell Press, 2015.

Robertson, Allen B. "Methodism among Nova Scotia's Yankee Planters." In Conrad, *They Planted Well*, 178–89.

Rodgers, Daniel T. "Republicanism: The Career of a Concept." *Journal of American History* 79, no. 1 (1992): 11–38.

Rorty, Amélie Oksenberg. "From Passions to Emotions and Sentiments." *Philosophy* 57, no. 220 (1982): 159–72.

Rosenberg, Daniel. "Joseph Priestley and the Graphic Invention of Modern Time." *Studies in Eighteenth-Century Culture* 36 (2007): 55–103.

Rosenberg, J. "'Accumulate! Accumulate! That is Moses and the Prophets!': Secularism, Historicism, and the Critique of Enthusiasm." *Eighteenth Century* 51, no. 4 (2010): 471–90.

Rosenfeld, Sophia. "Thinking About Feeling, 1789–1799." *French Historical Studies* 32, no. 4 (Fall 2009): 697–706.

Rosenwein, Barbara H. *Emotional Communities in the Early Middle Ages*. Ithaca, NY: Cornell University Press, 2006.

– *Generations of Feeling: A History of Emotions, 600–1700*. Cambridge: Cambridge University Press, 2016.

–"Worrying About Emotions in History." *American Historical Review* 107, no. 3 (2002): 821–45.

Ross, Julie Martha. "Jacob Bailey, Loyalist: Anglican Clergyman in New England and Nova Scotia." MA thesis, University of New Brunswick, 1975.

Ross, Julie, and Thomas B. Vincent. "Bailey, Jacob." In *Dictionary of Canadian Biography*. Vol. 5. Toronto/Laval: University of Toronto/ Université Laval, 2003–, accessed 3 July 2017, http://www.biographi.ca/ en/bio/bailey_jacob_5E.html.

Roth, Randolph A. *The Democratic Dilemma: Religion, Reform, and the Social Order in the Connecticut River Valley of Vermont, 1791–1850*. Cambridge: Cambridge University Press, 1987.

Rothschild, Emma. *The Inner Life of Empires: An Eighteenth-Century History*. Princeton: Princeton University Press, 2011.

Rowlandson, Mary. *A Narrative of the Captivity, Sufferings and Removes of Mrs. Mary Rowlandson*, 1682.

Ryrie, Alec. *Being Protestant in Reformation Britain*. Oxford: Oxford University Press, 2015.

– *Unbelievers: An Emotional History of Doubt*. Cambridge, MA: Belknap Press, 2019.

Ryrie, Alec, and Tom Schwanda, eds. *Puritanism and Emotion in the Early Modern World*. Houndmills, Hampshire, UK: Palgrave Macmillan, 2016.

Said, Edward. *Orientalism*. London: Penguin, 1977.

Sargent, Winthrop. *The Loyalist Poetry of the Revolution*. Philadelphia, 1857.

– *The Loyal Verses of Joseph Stansbury and Doctor Jonathan Odell Relating to the American Revolution*. Albany: J. Munsell, 1860.

Sassi, Jonathan D. *A Republic of Righteousness: The Public Christianity of the Post-Revolutionary New England Clergy*. Oxford: Oxford University Press, 2001.

Saunders, Edward Manning. *History of the Baptists of the Maritime Provinces*. Halifax, NS: John Burgoyne, 1902.

Schama, Simon. *Rough Crossings: Britain, the Slaves, and the American Revolution*. New York: Ecco, 2006.

Scheer, Monique. "Are Emotions a Kind of Practice (and Is That What Makes Them Have a History)? A Bourdieuian Approach to Understanding Emotion." *History and Theory* 51 (2012): 193–220.

Schlereth, Thomas J. *The Cosmopolitan Ideal in Enlightenment Thought*. Notre Dame: University of Notre Dame Press, 1977.

Schmidt, Leigh Eric. *Holy Fairs: Scottish Communions and American Revivals in the Early Modern Period*. Princeton: Princeton University Press, 1989.

Schultz, Cathleen McDonnell. "Holy Lives and Happy Deaths: Popular Religious Reading in the Early Republic." PhD diss., New York University, 1996.

Schurink, Fred. "Manuscript Commonplace Books, Literature, and Reading in Early Modern England." *Huntington Library Quarterly* 73, no. 3 (2010): 453–69.

Scobie, Charles H.H., and John Webster Grant, eds. *The Contribution of Methodism to Atlantic Canada*. Montreal & Kingston: McGill-Queen's University Press, 1992.

Scott, Henry E., ed. *The Journal of the Reverend Jonathan Scott*. Boston: New England Historic Genealogical Society, 1980.

Scott, Jamie S. "'Travels of My Soul': Henry Alline's Autobiography." *Journal of Canadian Studies* 18, no. 2 (1983): 70–90.

Scott, Jonathan. *A Brief View of the Religious Tenets and Sentiments lately published and spread in the province of Nova-Scotia: which are contained in a book entitled 'Two mites on some of the most important and much disputed points of divinity, &c.' and in a sermon preached at Liverpool, November 19, 1782, and in a pamphlet entitled 'The Antitraditionist,' all being publications of Mr. Henry Alline ... together with a discourse on external order*. Halifax, NS: John Howe, 1784.

Scribner, Robert W. *Religion and Culture in Germany (1400–1800)*.
    Leiden: Brill, 2001.
Seeman, Erik R. *Pious Persuasions: Laity and Clergy in Eighteenth-Century
    New England*. Baltimore: Johns Hopkins University Press, 1999.
–"'She Died Like Good Old Jacob': Deathbed Scenes and Inversions of
    Power in New England,
1675–1775." *Proceedings of the American Antiquarian Society* 104, no. 2
    (1994): 285–314.
Semple, Neil. *The Lord's Dominion: The History of Canadian Methodism*.
    Montreal & Kingston: McGill-Queen's University Press, 1996.
Shaftesbury, Lord. *Characteristics of Men, Manners, Opinions, Times*.
    Edited by Lawrence E. Klein, Karl Ameriks, and Desmond M. Clarke.
    Cambridge: Cambridge University Press, 2000.
Shapiro, Barbara. *A Culture of Fact: England, 1550–1720*. Ithaca, NY:
    Cornell University Press, 2003.
Shea, Daniel B. *Spiritual Autobiography in Early America*. Princeton:
    Princeton University Press, 1968.
Shields, David S. *Civil Tongues and Polite Letters in British America*.
    Chapel Hill: University of North Carolina Press, 1997.
Sirota, Brent S. *The Christian Monitors: The Church of England and the Age
    of Benevolence, 1680–1730*. New Haven: Yale University Press, 2014.
Smith, Adam. *The Theory of Moral Sentiments*. Edited by Ryan Patrick
    Hanley. New York: Penguin, 2009.
Smith, Craig Bruce. *American Honor: The Creation of the Nation's Ideals
    during the Revolutionary Era*. Chapel Hill: University of North
    Carolina Press, 2018.
Smith, Karen. "Community Libraries." In Fleming, Gallichan, and
    Lamonde, eds, *History of the Book in Canada*, vol. 1, 144–51.
Smith, Peter J. "Civic Humanism Versus Liberalism: Fitting the Loyalists
    In." In *Canada's Origins: Liberal, Tory, or Republican?* edited by Janet
    Ajzenstat and Peter J. Smith, 25–43. Ottawa: Carleton University Press,
    . 1997.
Smith, T. Watson. *History of the Methodist Church within the Territories
    Embraced in the Late Conference of Eastern British America, Including
    Nova Scotia, New Brunswick, Newfoundland, Prince Edward Island
    and Bermuda*. 2 vols. Halifax, NS: Methodist Book Room, 1877.
Snider, Alvin. "By Equivocation Swear: *Hudibras* and the Politics of
    Interpretation." *The Seventeenth Century* 5, no. 2 (1990): 157–72.
Stearns, Peter N., and Jan Lewis, eds. *An Emotional History of the United
    States*. New York: New York University Press, 1998.

Stearns, Peter N., and Carol Z. Stearns. "Emotionology: Clarifying the
    History of Emotions and Emotional Standards." *American Historical
    Review* 90, no. 4 (1985): 813–36.

Stevens, Laura M. *The Poor Indians: British Missionaries, Native
    Americans, and Colonial Sensibility*. Philadelphia: University of
    Pennsylvania Press, 2006.

Stewart, Gordon T., ed. *Documents Relating to the Great Awakening
    in Nova Scotia, 1760–1791*. Toronto: The Champlain Society,
    1982.

–"Scott, Jonathan (1744–1819)." In *Dictionary of Canadian Biography*.
    Vol. 5. Toronto/Laval: University of Toronto/Université Laval,
    2003–, accessed 19 May 2017, http://www.biographi.ca/en/bio/scott_
    jonathan_1744_1819_5E.html.

Stewart, Gordon T., and George A. Rawlyk. *A People Highly Favoured of
    God: The Nova Scotia Yankees and the American Revolution*. Toronto:
    Macmillan, 1972.

Stoermer, Taylor. "'The Success of Either Lies in the Womb of Time': The
    Politics of Loyalty in the Revolutionary Chesapeake." In *The
    Consequences of Loyalism: Essays in Honor of Robert M. Calhoon*,
    edited by Rebecca Brannon and Joseph S Moore, 11–32. Columbia:
    University of South Carolina Press, 2019.

Stokes, Claudia. *The Altar at Home: Sentimental Literature and
    Nineteenth-Century American Religion*. Philadelphia: University of
    Pennsylvania Press, 2014.

Stout, Harry S. *The Divine Dramatist: George Whitefield and the Rise of
    Modern Evangelicalism*. Grand Rapids, MI: Eerdmans, 1991.

Sullivan, Alvin, ed. *British Literary Magazines*. 4 vols. Westport, CT:
    Greenwood Press, 1983.

Sutherland, David A. "Voluntary Societies and the Process of Middle-Class
    Formation in Early-Victorian Halifax, Nova Scotia." *Journal of the
    Canadian Historical Association* 5 (1994): 237–63.

Taves, Ann. *Fits, Trances, and Visions: Experiencing Religion and
    Explaining Experience from Wesley to James*. Princeton: Princeton
    University Press, 1999.

Taylor, Alan. *The Civil War of 1812: American Citizens, British Subjects,
    Irish Rebels, and Indian Allies*. New York: Vintage, 2010.

Taylor, Charles. *Sources of the Self: The Making of the Modern Identity*.
    Cambridge: Harvard University Press, 1989.

Tennant, Gilbert. *The Danger of an Unconverted Ministry*. Philadelphia:
    Benjamin Franklin, 1740.

–*Sermons on Important Subjects, adapted to the perilous state of the British Nation*. Philadelphia: James Chattin, 1758.

Terry, Richard. "*Hudibras* amongst the Augustans." *Studies in Philology* 90, no. 4 (1993): 426–41.

– *Mock-Heroic from Butler to Cowper: An English Genre and Discourse*. Farnham, Surrey, UK: Ashgate, 2005.

Theophilus, "Importance of Actual Preparation for Death [Part 2]," *American Baptist Magazine and Missionary Intelligencer*, New Series 22.4 (July 1819): 121–4.

Thomas, Isaiah. *The History of Printing in America: With a Biography of Printers, and an Account of Newspapers: To Which Is Prefixed a Concise View of the Discovery and Progress of the Art in Other Parts of the World*. 2 vols. Worcester, MA: Isaiah Thomas, June, 1810.

Thompson, Kent. *The Man Who Said No: Reading Jacob Bailey, Loyalist*. Kentville, NS: Gaspereau Press, 2008.

Thorne, Susan. *Congregational Missions and the Making of an Imperial Culture in Nineteenth-Century England*. Stanford: Stanford University Press, 1999.

– "Religion and Empire at Home." In *At Home with the Empire: Metropolitan Culture and the Imperial World*, edited by Catherine Hall and Sonya O. Rose, 143–65. Cambridge: Cambridge University Press, 2006.

Tillman, Kacy Dowd. *Stripped and Script: Loyalist Women Writers of the American Revolution*. Amherst: University of Massachusetts Press, 2019.

Todd, Janet. *Sensibility: An Introduction*. London: Methuen, 1986.

Tomlin, T.J. *A Divinity for All Persuasions: Almanacs and Early American Religious Life*. Oxford: Oxford University Press, 2014.

Tosh, John. "The Old Adam and the New Man: Emerging Themes in the History of English Masculinities, 1750–1850." In *English Masculinities, 1660–1800*, edited by Tim Hitchcock and Michèle Cohen, 217–38. London: Longman, 1999.

Trask, Gwen Guiou and F. Stuart Trask. "The Reverend Jonathan Scott, Planter, Preacher, Patriarch." In *Intimate Relations: Family and Community in Planter Nova Scotia, 1759-1800*, edited by Margaret Conrad. Fredericton, NB: Acadiensis Press, 1995.

Trask, Stuart, and Gwen Trask, eds. *The Records of the Church of Jebogue in Yarmouth, Nova Scotia, 1766–1851*. Yarmouth, NS: Stoneycroft, 1992.

Trusler, John, ed. *A Chronology; or, The Historian's Vade-Mecum*. 5th ed. London, 1772.

Tucker, Susie I. *Enthusiasm: A Study in Semantic Change*. Cambridge: Cambridge University Press, 1972.

Tulloch, Judith. "Barclay, Thomas Henry." In *Dictionary of Canadian Biography*. Vol. 6. Toronto/Laval: University of Toronto/Université Laval, 2003–, accessed 9 March 2017, http://www.biographi.ca/en/bio/barclay_thomas_henry_6E.html.

Tyrrell, Ian R. *Sobering Up: From Temperance to Prohibition in Antebellum America, 1800–1860*. Westport, CT: Greenwood Press, 1979.

Upton, L.F.S. *The Loyal Whig: William Smith of New York and Quebec*. Toronto: University of Toronto Press, 1969.

Van Buskirk, Judith L. *Generous Enemies: Patriots and Loyalists in Revolutionary New York*. Philadelphia: University of Pennsylvania Press, 2002.

Van Engen, Abram C. *Sympathetic Puritans: Calvinist Fellow Feeling in Early New England*. Oxford: Oxford University Press, 2015.

Van Gent, Jacqueline. "Sarah and Her Sisters: Letters, Emotions, and Colonial Identities in the Early Modern Atlantic World." *Journal of Religious History* 38, no. 1 (2014): 71–90.

Van Gent, Jacqueline, and Spencer E. Young. "Introduction: Emotions and Conversion." *Journal of Religious History* 39, no. 4 (2015): 461–7.

Van Sant, Ann Jessie. *Eighteenth-Century Sensibility and the Novel: The Senses in Social Context*. Cambridge: Cambridge University Press, 1993.

Vernage, Étienne François. *The Happy Life, or The Contented Man*. London: R. Main, 1767.

Vincent, Thomas B. "Alline and Bailey." *Canadian Literature* 68–69 (1976): 124–33.

– "Henry Alline: Problems of Approach and Reading the *Hymns* as Poetry." In Conrad, *They Planted Well*, 201–10.

– "Keeping the Faith: The Poetic Development of Jacob Bailey, Loyalist." *Early American Literature* 14, no. 1 (1979): 3–14.

– ed. *Narrative Verse Satire in Maritime Canada, 1779–1814*. Ottawa: Tecumseh Press, 1978.

– "Some Bibliographical Notes on Henry Alline's *Hymns and Spiritual Songs*." *Canadian Notes and Queries* 12 (Nov. 1973).

– "Some Examples of Narrative Verse Satire in the Early Literature of Nova Scotia and New Brunswick." *Humanities Association Review* 27 (1976): 161–75.

Vincent-Buffault, Anne. *The History of Tears: Sensibility and Sentimentality in France*. New York: St Martin's Press, 1991.

Wahrman, Dror. "The English Problem of Identity in the American
   Revolution." *American Historical Review* 106, no. 4 (2001): 1236–62.
– *The Making of the Modern Self: Identity and Culture in Eighteenth-
   Century England.* New Haven: Yale University Press, 2004.
Waldstreicher, David. *In the Midst of Perpetual Fetes: The Making of
   American Nationalism, 1776–1820.* Chapel Hill: University of North
   Carolina Press, 1997.
Walker, Peter W. "The Church Militant: The American Loyalist Clergy and
   the Making of the British Counterrevolution, 1701–92." PhD diss.,
   Columbia University, 2016.
Walsh, John. "Religious Societies: Methodist and Evangelical 1738–1800."
   In *Voluntary Religion*, edited by W.J. Sheils and Diana Wood. Studies in
   Church History, 279–302. Oxford: Basil Blackwell, 1986.
Walton, Brad. *Jonathan Edwards, Religious Affections, and the Puritan
   Analysis of True Piety, Spiritual Sensation, and Heart Religion.*
   Lewiston, NY: Edwin Mellen Press, 2002.
Ward, W.R. *Early Evangelicalism: A Global Intellectual History, 1670–
   1789.* Cambridge: Cambridge University Press, 2006.
– *The Protestant Evangelical Awakening.* Cambridge: Cambridge
   University Press, 1992.
–"The Relations of Enlightenment and Religious Revival in Central
   Europe and in the English-Speaking World." In *Reform and
   Reformation: England and the Continent, 1500–1750*, edited by Derek
   Baker. Studies in Church History Subsidia. Oxford: Blackwell, 1979.
Watts, Isaac. *Discourses of the Love of God and the Use and Abuse of the
   Passions in Religion ... To Which Is Prefix'd, a Plain and Particular
   Account of the Natural Passions, with Rules for the Government of
   Them.* London: J. Clark and R. Hett, 1729.
– *Humility, Represented in the Character of St. Paul: The chief Springs of
   it opened, And its various Advantages display'd.* London: R. Ford & R.
   Hett, 1737.
Watts, Steven. *The Republic Reborn: War and the Making of Liberal
   America, 1790–1820.* Baltimore: Johns Hopkins University Press, 1987.
Webb, Todd. *Transatlantic Methodists: British Wesleyanism and the
   Formation of an Evangelical Culture in Nineteenth-Century Ontario
   and Quebec.* Montreal & Kingston: McGill-Queen's University Press,
   2013.
Westerkamp, Marilyn J. *Women and Religion in Early America, 1600–
   1800: The Puritan and Evangelical Traditions.* New York: Routledge,
   1999.

Westfall, William. *Two Worlds: The Protestant Culture of Nineteenth-Century Ontario.* Montreal & Kingston: McGill-Queen's University Press, 1989.

White, Eugene Edmond. *Puritan Rhetoric: The Issue of Emotion in Religion.* 1972; reprint, Carbondale: Southern Illinois University Press, 2009.

Whitefield, George. *A Continuation of the Reverend Mr. Whitefield's Journal from Savannah, June 25, 1740, to his arrival at Rhode-Island, his travels in the other governments of New-England, to his departure from Stanford for New-York.* Boston: S. Kneeland and T. Green, 1741.

– *The Works of the Reverend George Whitefield.* 6 vols. London: Edward and Clark Dilly, 1771–1772.

Whitehouse, Tessa. *The Textual Culture of English Protestant Dissent, 1720–1800.* Oxford: Oxford University Press, 2015.

–"'Upon Reading over the Whole of This Letter I Am Sensibly Struck': Affectionate Networks and Schemes for Dissenting Academies." *Lives and Letters* 3, no. 1 (2011): 1–17.

Whitfield, Harvey Amani. "Black Loyalists and Black Slaves in Maritime Canada." *History Compass* 5, no. 6 (2007): 1980–97.

– *North to Bondage: Loyalist Slavery in the Maritimes.* Vancouver: University of British Columbia Press, 2016.

Wickberg, Daniel. "What Is the History of Sensibilities? On Cultural Histories, Old and New." *American Historical Review* 112, no. 3 (2007): 661–84.

Wigger, John H. *Taking Heaven by Storm: Methodism and the Rise of Popular Christianity in America.* Oxford: Oxford University Press, 1998.

Wigginton, Caroline, and Abram Van Engen, eds. *Feeling Godly: Religious Affections and Christian Contact in Early America.* Amherst: University of Massachusetts Press, 2021.

Wilcox, Donald J. *The Measure of Times Past: Pre-Newtonian Chronologies and the Rhetoric of Relative Time.* Chicago: University of Chicago Press, 1987.

Williamson, Gillian. *British Masculinity in the Gentleman's Magazine, 1731–1815.* Houndmills, Hampshire, UK: Palgrave Macmillan, 2016.

Willis, Aaron. "The Standing of New Subjects: Grenada and the Protestant Constitution after the Treaty of Paris (1763)." *Journal of Imperial & Commonwealth History* 42, no. 1 (March 2014): 1–21.

Willison, John. *Sacramental Meditations and Advices, Grounded upon Scripture-Texts, Proper for Communicants to Prepare their Hearts,*

Excite their Affections, Quicken their Graces, and Enliven their Devotions on Sacramental Occasions. Edinburgh: Thomas Lumisden, 1747.

Wills, Garry. *Inventing America: Jefferson's Declaration of Independence*. Garden City, NY: Doubleday, 1978.

Wilson, Kathleen. *The Sense of the People: Politics, Culture and Imperialism in England, 1715–1785*. Cambridge: Cambridge University Press, 1995.

Winiarski, Douglas L. *Darkness Falls on the Land of Light: Experiencing Religious Awakenings in Eighteenth-Century New England*. Chapel Hill: University of North Carolina Press, 2017.

– "Jonathan Edwards, Enthusiast? Radical Revivalism and the Great Awakening in the Connecticut Valley." *Church History* 74, no. 4 (2005): 683–739.

– "'A Jornal of a Fue Days at York': The Great Awakening on the Northern New England Frontier." *Maine History* 42, no. 1 (2004): 46–85.

– "Souls Filled with Ravishing Transport: Heavenly Visions and the Radical Awakening in New England." *William and Mary Quarterly* 61, no. 1 (2004): 3–46.

Winship, Michael. *Hot Protestants: A History of Puritanism in England and America*. New Haven: Yale University Press, 2019.

Wise, S.F. *God's Peculiar Peoples: Essays on Political Culture in Nineteenth-Century Canada*. Edited by A.B. McKillop and Paul Romney. Ottawa: Carleton University Press, 1993.

Wittman, Reinhard. "Was There a Reading Revolution at the End of the Eighteenth Century?" In *A History of Reading in the West*, edited by Guglielmo Cavallo, Roger Chartier, and Lydia G. Cochrane, 284–312. Amherst: University of Massachusetts Press, 1999.

Wolffe, John. *The Expansion of Evangelicalism: The Age of Wilberforce, More, Chalmers and Finney*. Downers Grove, IL: InterVarsity Press, 2007.

Wood, Gordon S. *The Creation of the American Republic, 1776–1787*. Reprint. Chapel Hill: University of North Carolina Press, 1998.

Woolf, Daniel. "From Hystories to the Historical: Five Transitions in Thinking About the Past, 1500–1700." In *The Uses of History in Early Modern England*, edited by Paulina Kewes, 31–68. San Marino, CA: Huntington Library, 2006.

–*Reading History in Early Modern England*. Cambridge: Cambridge University Press, 2000.

– *The Social Circulation of the Past: English Historical Culture, 1500–1730*. Oxford: Oxford University Press, 2003.

Woolverton, John Frederick. *Colonial Anglicanism in North America.* Detroit: Wayne State University Press, 1984.

Worthen, Molly. *Apostles of Reason: The Crisis of Authority in American Evangelicalism.* Oxford: Oxford University Press, 2014.

Wulf, Karin. "Bible, King, and Common Law." *Early American Studies, An Interdisciplinary Journal* 10, no. 3 (Fall 2012): 467–502.

Yeager, Jonathan M. *Enlightened Evangelicalism: The Life and Thought of John Erskine.* Oxford: Oxford University Press, 2011.

– *Jonathan Edwards and Transatlantic Print Culture.* Oxford: Oxford University Press, 2016.

Young, Jeremy C. "Transformation in the Tabernacle: Billy Sunday's Converts and Emotional Experience in the Progressive Era." *Journal of the Gilded Age and Progressive Era* 14, no. 3 (2015): 367–85.

Young, Michael P. *Bearing Witness against Sin: The Evangelical Birth of the American Social Movement.* Chicago: University of Chicago Press, 2006.

Zakai, Avihu. "Jonathan Edwards, the Enlightenment, and the Formation of Protestant Tradition in America." In *The Creation of the British Atlantic World*, edited by Elizabeth Mancke and Carole Shammas, 182–208. Baltimore: Johns Hopkins University Press, 2005.

– *Jonathan Edwards's Philosophy of History: The Reenchantment of the World in the Age of Enlightenment.* Princeton: Princeton University Press, 2003.

Index

Acadia University (known as Acadia College until 1891), 183, 194
Acadians, 16
Adams, John (poet), 80
Adams, John (president), 9, 94, 98
affect: definition of, 214n19; as synonym for embodied emotions, 8, 134
affections, definition of, 8. *See* emotions
African Americans, 9
agency, 12, 46–7, 135–6, 152, 158–9. *See* Calvinism; self-fashioning
Ahmed, Sara, 219n70
Allan, David, 28
Alline, Henry: assurance, 73–4; biography, 19, 130; on Calvinism, 135–7; and church schisms, 146–7; comparison with Jonathan Scott, 130–4, 148–9; conversion, 138–40, 152–6; on covenants, 140–2; ecstasy, 156–7; education, 134; and Edward Manning, 160, 179–81, 183; emotions in journal, 152–9;

and George Whitefield, 62, 65; and Handley Chipman, 64; happiness, 157–8; hymns, 160–7; individualism, 133, 141–2, 147; itinerant, 130–1, 147, 156; Jonathan Scott's critique of, 142–7; journal, 64–9, 159; and republicanism, 188, 211; on social order, 140–2; themes in theology, 134
almanacs, 28, 35–6
American Revolution, changes to religious communities, 211; comparison with English Civil War, 113–18; conspiracy theories, 97–101; contrary to Enlightenment cosmopolitanism, 94–5; Handley Chipman's commentary, 23–5, 42–4; Jacob Bailey's commentary, 94–101; Nova Scotia in, 17, 23–4, 46; print culture, 94–5; role of emotions in, 6, 25, 79, 99–100, 210; tragedy for Britain, 43; turning point in history of emotions, 9–11. *See* Loyalists/loyalism; Patriot emotions

Ames, Nathaniel, poetry of, 34,
37–8
Anderson, Benedict, 8–9, 31, 202,
215n25
Andros, Edmund, 88–9
Anglicans. *See* Church of England
anglicization, 26–7, 80–1
Annapolis Royal, 104, 126–8,
245n74
Arminianism, 137
Armstrong, Maurice, 151
assurance of salvation, 62–4,
72–4, 157, 168–70; in hymnody,
164–6

Bailey, Charley, 107
Bailey, Jacob: affection for
American locale, 94; biography
of, 18; conspiracy theory,
97–101, 124; conversion to
Church of England, 80–1; and
Charles Inglis, 124–5; and civic
society, 207–8; correspondence
with John Howe, 118–24; and
cosmopolitanism, 210; disaffection with Britain, 103–4, 210;
disaffection with king, 109–10;
and Handley Chipman, 92–3,
211; history of New England,
84–94; loyalist ordeal in
Massachusetts, 82–4; loyalty
despite disaffection, 105–6;
"Majesty of the Mob" drama,
77–9; oaths of allegiance, 96–7;
petition to Massachusetts
assembly, 83–4; petition to Nova
Scotia assembly, 126–8; before
the Pownalborough Committee
of Correspondence and Safety,
77–9; refugee to Nova Scotia,
104, 106–8; satirical poetry,
109–10, 112–18
Baily, Joseph, 168
Bannister, Jerry, 10–11, 219n65
Bannister, Julia, 35
Baptists, 20, 178, 187, 193–4,
258n17; as British subjects,
192–3; as cross-border emotional
community, 188–91; and New
Lights, 183–4; and voluntary
societies, 192–3
Barnes, Elizabeth, 198
Baxter, Richard, 51
beatific vision, 170
Bebbington, David, 217n44,
230n63
Beecher, Lyman, 193
Benedict, David, 189
benevolence, 33, 108, 112, 192–3;
of God, 136
Bennett, Thomas, 167–8
Bernard of Clairvaux, 171
Bible societies, 192–3
biblicism, 145, 249n77
Blair, Elizabeth, 170–2
Blair, Hugh, 196
Bloch, Ruth, 132–3
Bourdieu, Pierre, 63
Bowman, Jonathan, 82
Braddock, Edward, 34–5
Brainerd, David, 195, 197, 199
Brekus, Catherine, 230n63
British constitution, 5–6, 35, 126–9
British Empire, 17–8, 27, 201–3,
211; and benevolence, 112; and
Indigenous people, 38–40; mili-
tary, 23, 30, 33–5, 40–3; place of
North America within, 28, 30–1,
37–8, 47, 79, 85, 93, 102; and
religious pluralism, 192, 211

British identity, 26–7, 215n26; before the American Revolution, 26; and cosmopolitanism, 84–5, 93, 210; emotions in construction of, 8–9; and historical culture, 28–31; and print culture, 27; and Protestantism, 29–30; and providence, 44–6

Brown, John, 54

Brown, Sarah, 167, 171–2, 174–5

Brown, Thomas, 103, 119–20

Buck, Charles, 185

Bumsted, J.M., 148

Bunyan, John, 154

Burpee, Richard, 193

Butler, Samuel, 113–18

Byles, Mather, 80

Calhoon, Robert, 10, 126

Calvinism, 135–7, 186–7, 247n25

Carey, William, 187

Carlisle Commission, 105–6

Carté, Katherine, 211

Casper, Scott, 197

Charlevoix, Pierre François Xavier de, 85

Chauncy, Charles, 53, 146, 186

children, 49–50, 73

Chipman, Handley: accused of being a rebel, 46; affection for king, 43–4; biography, 18, 25–6; chronologies, 23, 28–31, 207; church membership, 61, 74; commonplace book, 31–8; and Edward Manning, 68, 182; English family, 37; and Jacob Bailey, 46, 92–3, 211; library, 74–5; manuscript devotional books, 54–9, New England family, 37; Protestantism, 48; on providence in history, 44–6; religious moderation, 50–1; sacramental piety, 52; support for Henry Alline, 64–6; wars of his lifetime, 40–3; Whig political sensibility, 35–7, 42–3; will, 74–6; writing on religious emotions, 66–74

Chipman, Jane, 62–3

Christie, Nancy, 140, 220n10

chronologies, 23, 28–31

Church of England, 80–3, 93, 133, 234n8; and polite Christianity, 80–1

civility, 94–5

Civil War (England), 13, 113–18, 208–9

Claydon, Tony, 45

clergy: critique of, 19, 92, 135, 140

Colby College, 183, 194

Colden, Cadwallader, 38–40

Colman, Benjamin, 59, 80

Committees of Correspondence and Safety, 77–9, 82, 100, 210

commonplace books, 27–8, 46–7

Congregational churches, 49, 64–5, 72–3, 86, 115. *See* Cornwallis New Light Congregational Church; Puritans/puritanism

conspiracy theories, 97–101, 124

Continental Congress, 105

conversion, 179–82; despair and, 154–6; and emotions, 138–40, 155–6, 172–4; in hymnody, 161–3

Cornwallis New Light Congregational Church, 49–50, 65, 67, 68, 72–3, 182

Cornwallis Township, NS: Bible society in, 192; celebration of

victory over Napoleon, 190–1;
culture of reading, 51; history
of ,15–17; republicanism in,
114–15; in transatlantic
networks, 21, 206
Corrigan, John, 216n41
cosmopolitanism, 80, 84–5, 93,
111–12, 210
covenants, 72–3, 140–2, 147
Crawford, Michael, 12
Cushing, Charles, 82

Darnton, Robert, 199, 203
de Vernage, Étienne François, 51
deathbed piety, 199–201
Declaration of Independence,
31, 158
diaries, 27, 159, 167–8, 185, 196
Dimock, Joseph, 68, 168
disaffection, 78–9, 103–6, 210
disestablishment, 204
Doddridge, Philip, 56
Dudley, Joseph, 89

Eamon, Michael, 27, 93
ecstasy/ecstatic experience, 13, 51,
138, 145, 151–4, 172; desiring
God, 162–3; in Edward
Manning's piety, 185–8; as
elusive, 156–7
Edwards, Jonathan, 134, 146,
173–4, 186–7, 195; on agency,
137; Calvinism, 186; emphasis
on affections, 7; moderate view
of affections, 53; sense of the
heart, 63; use by Jonathan
Scott, 146
Edwards, Sarah, 61
embodiment, 68–72, 157, 184

emotional communities: and British
Empire, 201–3; definition of, 10,
21; and Great Awakening, 133;
Loyalists as, 112, 210; and missionary expansion, 12, 195–7;
New Lights as, 19, 67, 150–2,
167–8, 174; and print culture,
12, 207–8; Puritanism as, 132;
and sympathy, 12, 195, 178–9,
197–201; as textual communities, 167–8, 207–8; transcending
nationalism, 188–91
emotions: and American
Revolution, 9–11; and British
identity, 8–9; changing meaning
of, 7–8, 209; contested meaning
of, 50–1; conventions, 20, 196;
desire, 162–3; as domain of
effort, 21, 150–2, 200; and
embodiment, 68–72, 157, 184;
and gender, 152, 170–1; and
loyalism, 32–3; and military culture, 40–3, 123–4; and nationalism, 8–9, 26–7, 47; and print
culture, 207–8; public history of,
6, 8; and reading, 195–203;
self-fashioning, 12; social order,
72, 92; terminology, 7–8
emotives, 20
empiricism, 7, 12, 62–4, 73
Enlightenment, 179; benevolence,
94, 108, 192–3; cosmopolitanism, 94; epistemology, 49, 59–64;
and evangelicalism, 62–4, 73,
173, 186, 208; happiness in, 158;
participation of ordinary people,
15, 148; preoccupation with
emotions, 7, 11–12, 208–9; and
religion, 11–12; self-fashioning,

12, 152, 158; women in, 62, 168.
See empiricism
enthusiasm: of the American
Revolution, 117–18; and conspiracy, 97–101; as contagion,
99; contrasted with empiricism,
64; definition of, 4–5, 13, 208–9;
and elusive feelings, 150–2; and
English Civil War, 13, 209; and
loyalism, 5–6, 17; and madness,
70; political, 3–4; and populism,
115–17; and rationalism, 187;
and social order, 210–12; and
subjectivity, 208; as unsocial,
5–6, 13, 72, 92, 132–3, 208–9.
See emotions
epistemology, 62–4, 161–2,
233n110
erotic imagery, 170–1
Errington, Jane, 224n60
Eustace, Nicole, 9, 100, 215n25
evangelicals/evangelicalism, 11–12,
19–20, 132–3, 151–2, 217n44;
as emotional community, 197–
203; and Enlightenment, 62–4,
73, 173, 186, 208–9; and enthusiasm, 187, 208–9; heart-felt
preaching, 59–64; more than
revival, 209; women in, 62. *See*
Great Awakening; New Lights;
Protestant devotional culture

Falmouth, NS, 181
feelings: as sensory experience, 8.
See emotions
Fiering, Norman, 12
Flavel, John, 56, 177, 185
Fordyce, James, 196
Fort Cumberland: siege of, 17

Foster, Stephen, 132
Franklin, Benjamin, 38, 98
French Empire in North America,
33–4, 38–40
French Revolution, 3–4, 43, 191,
213n3, 215n30
Fuller, Andrew, 187, 197, 201, 203,
263n112

Gardiner, Sylvester, 82
gender, 34–5, 170–1, 196, 216n40,
254n94, 258n24; and New Light
emotions, 152; and political
rhetoric, 95–6. *See* masculinity
George III, 5–6, 31, 43–4, 109–110,
124–5
Glorious Revolution, 23, 30, 88–9
Goodwin, Daniel, 178, 183, 187
Gorton, Samuel, 86
Gould, Philip, 112, 118
Graham, Hugh, 50–1, 67
Great Awakening, 53, 66, 91–3,
132–3, 157, 186; anticlericalism
of, 140; assurance, 157; comparison with Allinite revivals, 65–6;
contesting emotions in, 50–1, 53,
132–3, 144; emotions in, 11–12,
excessive emotionalism of, 186;
Handley Chipman and, 50,
59–64, 92–3; Jacob Bailey and,
91–3. *See* evangelicals/
evangelicalism; New Lights
Grenada, 32–3
Gunpowder Plot, 23, 30

Habermas, Jürgen, 215n25
habits, 63
Halifax, NS, 3–5, 70, 106–7, 115,
118–24, 188

Hancock, John, 98, 116
happiness, 157–8; in Enlightenment, 51; and heaven, 166–7; and politics, 32, 127–8; and self-surrender, 172
Harding, Harris, 169, 172
Hatch, Nathan, 246n11
Hattem, Michael, 32
Haudenosaunee, 38–40
Heath, Gordon, 189, 191
Henry, Anthony, 118–19
Henry, Matthew, 51–2, 54, 56–7, 71
historical culture, 28–31, 46–7
Hogarth, William, 13
Hollett, Calvin, 12
Homes, William, 59–60
Howe, Alexander, 126–7
Howe, John, 118–24
Hubbard, William, 85
human nature, 5, 89, 134–7, 174; and capacity for feeling, 95; and sensibility, 162
Hume, David, 7, 134
humility, 158–9
Humphrey, Heman, 193
Hurd, Nathaniel, 31
Hutcheson, Francis, 7, 162, 186
Hutchinson, Thomas, 85
hymns, 160–7

incarnation of Jesus Christ, 137–8
Indigenous people, 9, 12, 34, 38–40, 202–3, 239n76; history of, 94; violence of colonization, 87–9. See Haudenosaunee; Mi'kmaq; Wampanoag
individualism, 132–3, 140–1, 147
Inglis, Charles, 17, 124–5; on enthusiasm and social order, 3–6, 191; loyalty and enthusiasm in conflict, 210–12; and New Lights, 4–5, 133, 151, 188
itinerants/itinerancy, 68, 92, 146–7, 177–8, 250n92, 256n3; Edward Manning, 182

James, William, 154
Johnson, Samuel, 13
Jones, Stephen, 176–8
Judson, Ann, 197
Juster, Susan, 255n103

Keach, Benjmain, 54
Kennebec, MA (now ME), 82, 90, 94
King Philip's War, 87
Kittredge, Jonathan, 193
Knott, Sarah, 10

laity, 132, 174
Larkin, Edward, 224n60
Lawrence, Charles, 16
Lawrence, Nancy, 172–4
Lessing, Gotthold, 199
letters, 10, 167–75
liberalism, 132–3
liberty, 35–7, 223n48; in Patriot rhetoric, 95–7
liberty pole, 82
libraries, 50–4. See print culture, reading
Liverpool, NS, 65–6, 184, 231n78, 254n91, 258n24
Locke, John, 27, 62, 186
Lord's Supper, 52
Louisbourg, Cape Breton Island, 30, 41, 45
Loyalists/loyalism: before the American Revolution, 10–11, 25, 46, 209–10; contested meaning

of, 210; and cosmopolitanism, 84–5, 93–4, 210; critique of British policies, 36–7, 45–6; and culture of sentiment, 10; definition of, 209–10; and disaffection, 103–6, 210; as emotional community, 112, 210; and enthusiasm, 5–6, 17; and Federalists, 210; histories by, 84; and historiography, 10–11; literary culture, 112–18, 118–24; in post-revolutionary period, 179; as refugees, 106–8, 109–12; respectability, 211; and social order, 5–6; and zeal, 120–4

Lusby, Charlotte, 168–70
Lusby, Elizabeth, 170–2

Mack, Phyllis, 12, 20, 139, 151–2, 159
MacKinnon, Neil, 245n73
madness, 4–5, 70
Madockawando, 89
magazines, gentlemen's, 26, 28, 35–6, 221n18
Magna Carta, 36
Maine, 82–3, 91–2, 176–8, 182
Mancke, Elizabeth, 46, 218n61, 222n34
Manning, Edward: and Andrew Fuller, 187, 197; balance of affections and reason, 187; as Baptist, 183; biography, 19–20; British loyalism, 179, 188; charged with enthusiasm, 176–9, 182; conversion, 179–82; and culture of sentiment, 209; at daughter's deathbed, 199–201, 207; education, 177; emotional transformation, 178–9; excesses of

early preaching, 68; execution of father, 179, 196; and expanding British empire, 201–3; George Rawlyk on, 178; and Handley Chipman, 68, 182; and Henry Alline, 160, 179–81, 183, 204; and higher education, 183, 194; as itinerant, 176–7, 182, 194; and John Payzant, 183–4; and Jonathan Edwards, 186–7; and Jonathan Scott, 183; in Maine, 176–9, 183; and memoirs, 196–7; moderate Calvinism, 186–7 203–4; on Napoleonic Wars, 190–1; and New Dispensation movement, 182; preaching, 182; as reader, 195–203; reading of Puritans, 185–6; restrained nationalism, 190–1; and social order, 188; and social reform, 142, 204; and temperance, 193; theological change, 183; voluntary associations, 142, 191–5, 211; and War of 1812, 188–91; and women, 18
Manning, James, 68, 176–8, 182
Manning, Nancy, 199–201
Manning, Peter, 179
masculinity, 8, 35, 152, 221n18; and sympathy, 96. See gender
Mason, Keith, 128
Mather, Cotton, 59, 85
Mather, Increase, 59
McBride, Ian, 45
McConville, Brendan, 35
McKim, Denis, 211
McNairn, Jeffrey, 215n26
meditation, 54–9
memoirs, 197–201
Merrill, Daniel, 189

Metacom, 87
Methodists/Methodism, 4, 12, 70,
    139, 246n11
Mi'kmaq, 16, 225n67
millennialism, 189, 194–5
Mills and Hicks, printers, 85
ministry, British government, 40–3,
    98, 124
missions/missionaries, 12, 187,
    192–4, 201–4
moderation, 10, 31, 50, 53, 120–4
monarchy, 29–33, 43, 109, 113;
    colonial devotion to, 35–6. See
    George III
Monongahela, Battle of, 34
Murdoch, Beamish, 188
Murphy, James, 176–8

Napoleonic wars, 43, 190–1, 194
nationalism, 8, 188–91. See British
    identity
New Brunswick, 4–5, 110–11, 130,
    182, 193
new dispensation movement,
    66–74, 182
Newel, Harriett, 200
New England: history, 84–94
New England Planters in Nova
    Scotia, 16–17, 114–15, 218n61
Newfoundland, 12
New Lights: balance between expe-
    rience and order, 132; contesting
    emotions, 49–51, 142–7;
    difficulty of cultivating emotions,
    150–2; as emotional community,
    64–5, 66–74, 150–2, 167–8; and
    gendered emotions, 152; itiner-
    ancy, 146–7, 176–8; leadership
    of Henry Alline, 64–6, 130–4;
    membership and religious

experience, 72–3; satire about,
    114; women, 167–75. See
    Cornwallis New Light
    Congregational Church;
    evangelicalism; Great Awakening
Newman, Timothy, 46
newspapers, 27, 118–24
Nova Scotia/Nova Scotians: in
    American Revolution, 17, 23–4,
    46; election of 1785, 126–8; as
    less polarized than Thirteen
    Colonies, 46, 211; literary
    culture, 118–24, 207–8; partici-
    pating in transatlantic debates,
    15, 21–2, 50, 66, 75, 134, 148–9,
    206, 208–9; plight of Loyalist
    refugees in, 108–12; republican-
    ism in, 114–15, 119
novels, sentimental, 7, 198–9,
    262n92, 263n99

oaths, 96–7, 114
Odell, Jonathan, 113
Osborn, Sarah, 59–60, 62–4
Owen, John, 185

Paine, Thomas, 3, 33
passions: contrasted with
    affections, 145; definition of, 7;
    and interests, 93. See emotions
Patriot emotions, 9–10, 25,
    100, 210
Payzant, John, 67, 74, 134, 181,
    182, 183–4
Pearce, Samuel, 197, 201
Pearsall, Sarah, 10
Perkins, Simeon, 65–6
Peters, Samuel, 115
petitions, 32–3, 126–8
Phips, William, 90

Pitt, William, 31, 35
polite Christianity, 80
political polarization, 25, 37, 46, 78–9; 120–2, 211
populism, 97, 115–17, 178, 182
Potter, Janice, 10
Pownalborough, MA (now ME), 77–8, 82–3
prayer, 57–9
preaching, 60–2, 68–72
Prescott, Charlotte, 167, 174–5
Prescott, Elizabeth, 172
press, freedom of, 36–7
print culture, 54–9, 94–5, 118–24, 197–201, 207–8; and British identity, 27; and imperial expansion, 201–3; and nationalism, 46–7. *See* reading
privateering, 25–6
Protestant devotional culture, 54–9, 75, 185–6, 225n4, 262n86
Protestantism and British identity, 19, 23, 29–30, 45, 48, 211
providence, 44–5, 190
Puritans/puritanism, 11, 59, 60–1, 117; congregationalism, 141; Edward Manning's reading of, 185–6; heart religion in, 51; and religious intolerance, 86–7; Half-Way Covenant, 140–2; tension between purity and order, 132. *See* Congregational churches; covenants

Quakers, 86

Randall, Lydia, 67
Rawlyk, George, 133, 151, 175, 178

reading, 27, 51–4, 54–9, 74–5; and tears, 195–203. *See* libraries; print culture
Reddy, William, 20, 21, 151, 200
refugees: Loyalists as, 106–8, 109–112
republicanism, 19, 114–15, 132–3, 188, 191, 211, 246n12
Revolutions, Age of: emotions in, 7–8
Rhode Island, 25–6, 61–2, 154
Richardson, Samuel, 199
Riordan, Liam 10–11
Rivers, Isabel, 12
Rivett, Sarah, 12, 62
Rogers, Jeremiah Dummer, 113–14, 121
Romanticism, 179, 209
Rosenwein, Barbara, 20, 21, 196
Rothschild, Emma, 15
Rousseau, Jean Jacques, 199, 203
Rowe, Elizbeth Singer, 80
Russell, Ezekiel, 85

Saint John, NB, 110–11
Salem witch trials, 89–90
satire, 112–18
Scheer, Monique, 71
Scott, Jonathan: biography, 130; comparison with Henry Alline, 130–4, 148–9; critique of Henry Alline, 142–7; and Edward Manning, 183; influence of Jonathan Edwards, 146; as revivalist, 146
Seabury, David, 126–7
self-fashioning, 12, 27–8, 46–8, 163, 167–75, 199–201; in contrast to self-surrender, 158–9; and daily emotional regulation,

152–4; and journals, 185; of ordinary people, 206; and religious print, 196–7

sensibility, 9–11, 94–7, 137, 197–201, 215n30; and civility, 94–5; definition of, 8; difficulty attaining, 168–9; and human nature, 162; long age of, 210; restored by grace, 137

sentiment: culture of (sometimes culture of sensibility), 9–11, 84, 94–7, 111–12, 179; importance of Adam Smith's *Theory of Moral Sentiments* to, 53; and loyalism, 101–2; and military masculinity, 35; and polite Christianity, 80; and reading, 197–201

sentiments: definition of, 8

Seven Years' War, 33–5, 41–2

Shaftesbury, Lord (Anthony Ashley Cooper), 80, 134, 162, 186

Shields, David, 80

Smith, Adam, 7, 53, 262n92

Society for the Propagation of the Gospel (SPG), 59, 80–2

Song of Songs, 152, 170–1

Squando, 89

Stamp Act, 42

state of nature, 5

Stevens, Laura, 202

Stewart, Gordon, 133

Strachan, John, 133

sympathy: definition of, 8; and reading, 195–203

Taves, Ann, 12, 15, 217n46

taxation, 36, 42

tea: destruction of, 98

Tea Act, 42

tears, 195–203

temperance, 192–3

Tennent, Gilbert, 62, 140

Teresa of Avila, 171

Thorne, Susan, 201

Treaty of Paris (1783), 124–6

Van Engen, Abram, 11

Vincent, Thomas, 122

violence, 10, 82–3, 88, 102, 114

voluntary associations, 191–5

Wahrman, Dror, 128

Wampanoag, 87–8

War of 1812, 188–91

Watts, Isaac, 52–3, 56, 80, 185, 200

Wesley, John, 134, 136

Westminster Confession of Faith, 177

Westminster Shorter Catechism, 173

Whitefield, George, 65, 91–3, 136, 227n30, 229n51; assurance, 73–4; as enthusiast, 13; and Henry Alline, 62, 65; preaching, 59–62, 91–3; use by Edward Manning, 177

Wilberforce, William, 197

Willis, Aaron, 32

Willison, John, 52

Winiarski, Douglas, 226n15, 229n51

Wolfe, James, 31

Yarmouth, NS, 131, 142, 147, 250n91

Young, Edward, 136

Zakai, Avihu, 226n15

zeal, 118–24, 187